Transp   nd
Economic Regul

Transportation Policy and Economic Regulation

Essays in Honor of Theodore Keeler

Edited by

John D. Bitzan
James H. Peoples

Elsevier
Radarweg 29, PO Box 211, 1000 AE Amsterdam, Netherlands
The Boulevard, Langford Lane, Kidlington, Oxford OX5 1GB, United Kingdom
50 Hampshire Street, 5th Floor, Cambridge, MA 02139, United States

Notices
Knowledge and best practice in this field are constantly changing. As new research and experience broaden our understanding, changes in research methods, professional practices, or medical treatment may become necessary.

Practitioners and researchers must always rely on their own experience and knowledge in evaluating and using any information, methods, compounds, or experiments described herein. In using such information or methods they should be mindful of their own safety and the safety of others, including parties for whom they have a professional responsibility.

To the fullest extent of the law, neither the Publisher nor the authors, contributors, or editors, assume any liability for any injury and/or damage to persons or property as a matter of products liability, negligence or otherwise, or from any use or operation of any methods, products, instructions, or ideas contained in the material herein.

Library of Congress Cataloging-in-Publication Data
A catalog record for this book is available from the Library of Congress

British Library Cataloguing-in-Publication Data
A catalogue record for this book is available from the British Library

ISBN: 978-0-12-812620-2

For information on all Elsevier publications visit our website at
https://www.elsevier.com/books-and-journals

Working together
to grow libraries in
developing countries

www.elsevier.com • www.bookaid.org

Publisher: Joe Hayton
Acquisition Editor: Tom Stover
Editorial Project Manager: Andrae Akeh
Production Project Manager: Priya Kumaraguruparan
Designer: Mark Rogers

Typeset by Thomson Digital

Contents

Contents   **vii**

List of Contributors

John D. Bitzan   North Dakota State University, Fargo, ND, United States

Kenneth Button   George Mason University, Fairfax, VA, USA

Thomas M. Corsi   University of Maryland, College Park, MD, United States

Rolf Färe   Oregon State University, Corvallis, OR, United States

Richard Fowles   University of Utah, Salt Lake City, UT, USA

David Gillen   University of British Columbia, Vancouver, BC, Canada

Curtis M. Grimm   University of Maryland, College Park, MD, United States

Ashish Lall   National University of Singapore, Singapore

Peter D. Loeb   Rutgers University, Newark, NJ, USA

Taylor K. McKenzie   University of Oregon, Eugene, OR, United States

Eric T. Micheels   University of Saskatchewan, Saskatoon, Saskatchewan, Canada

James F. Nolan   University of Saskatchewan, Saskatoon, Saskatchewan, Canada

James H. Peoples   University of Wisconsin-Milwaukee, Milwaukee, WI, United States

Russell Pittman   U.S. Department of Justice, Washington, DC, United States

Randall Pozdena   QuantEcon, Incorporated, ECONorthwest, Incorporated

Lindsay A. Pollard   University of Saskatchewan, Saskatoon, Saskatchewan, Canada

Kenneth A. Small   University of California at Irvine, CA, USA

B. Starr McMullen   Oregon State University, Corvallis, OR, United States

Wayne K. Talley   Old Dominion University, Norfolk, VA, USA

Philip A. Viton   The Ohio State University, Columbus, OH, USA

Wesley W. Wilson   University of Oregon, Eugene, OR, United States

Wenfeng Yan   Symantec, Mountain View, CA, United States

Theodore Keeler's impact on transportation economics and policy

John D. Bitzan*, James H. Peoples**
*North Dakota State University, Fargo, ND, United States;
**University of Wisconsin-Milwaukee, Milwaukee, WI, United States

Chapter Outline

Dedication

John Bitzan: My first job after getting a master's degree in economics in 1990 was at a transportation research center, doing economic research in transportation. The area that interested me the most was the area of railroad freight transportation, and the author I admired the most was Ted Keeler. His 1983 book introduced me to the history of railroad regulation, the problems that existed in the industry, and the likely impacts of the regulatory changes that took place in the late 1970s and 1980. This is a book that I still read today, and one that I think any student of transportation should read. Moreover, his 1974 article on excess capacity in the railroad industry was another one that I marveled at—his elegant and useful application of economic theory to an important problem.

In 1993, when I went back to graduate school to pursue my Ph.D., I was fortunate to have one of Ted's students, James Peoples as my professor for Industrial Organization. In James' class, I learned a lot more about transportation economics and applied economic analysis. Clearly, the approach used by Professor Peoples was influenced heavily by his training from Ted Keeler. Moreover, I have been able to work with James for a number of years, and he possesses many of the same characteristics that I admire in Ted.

After completing my dissertation on railroad costs in 1997, James shared my work with Ted Keeler. Much to my surprise, I received an email from Ted noting his interest in my results and asking if

Transportation Policy and Economic Regulation. http://dx.doi.org/10.1016/B978-0-12-812620-2.00001-8

I was interested in doing further work with him. This was an opportunity that I could not believe—an opportunity to actually work with Ted Keeler! Subsequently, we published four papers together.

I cannot express enough how grateful I am for having had the opportunity to work with Ted. In working with Ted, I learned a lot about performing economic research and about regulation and railroads. Moreover, although Ted's knowledge in these areas dwarfed mine, he never made me feel that way. He always valued my input and made me feel like an equal partner in research, insisting that my name go first on the publications.

In addition to a research partnership, I have also developed a friendship with Ted. He is always interested in my family and about how things are going outside of research. Not only am I grateful for being able to work with Ted, but I am even more grateful for getting the opportunity to know Ted. He is a great researcher and a great person, and this book is one small way to express the great impact he has had on the field of transportation economics and the people he has come in contact with.

James Peoples: In the early to mid-1980s, I had the pleasure to serve as Professor Keeler's teaching assistant for intermediate microeconomics and the opportunity to benefit from his guidance as my dissertation advisor. Professor Keeler also agreed to serve as my mentor during a one year leave of absence from my initial employment in the professoriate in the late 1980s. The time that Professor Keeler graciously invested in me over the years was critical to my professional development. Some of the gifts I received from this association include the recognition of how important it is as a researcher to understand the institutional history of the subject under observation. He also stressed the importance of clearly communicating an idea no matter how complicated the subject matter. While I highly value these insights, it is Professor Keeler's long lasting professional and personal support that stands out in my experience with him. This support has not been limited to our one-on-one relationship, as he has introduced me to many of his former students and current colleagues as sources of assistance and guidance. Indeed, many of the contributors to this volume were his former students and/or research collaborators, and they did not hesitate to support this project when asked to contribute a chapter.

While I can provide many more examples of how Professor Keeler has positively influenced my career, for the purpose of brevity I can say unequivocally that without my association with Professor Keeler I would not have the opportunity to enjoy the benefits this profession has to offer. I thank him for his kindness, understanding, and especially his patience.

1   Introduction

As the title of this book (Transportation Policy and Economic Regulation: Essays in Honor of Theodore Keeler) suggests, Theodore Keeler has had a tremendous impact on the field of transportation economics, in assessing the impacts and appropriateness of various policies and in helping to shape regulatory policies concerning the transportation industries. Moreover, in addition to his own work, he has trained many of the most prominent economists in the field of transportation economics. This book is a tribute to Professor Keeler, and the impact he has had and continues to have on transportation policy.

Professor Keeler's research in transportation economics resulted in publications for more than 40 years, starting in 1970. The timeframe for his research career is significant, as it spans the years prior to and after major regulatory changes occurring in the airline, railroad, and motor carrier industries. This allowed him to not only help to illuminate the problems occurring in these industries as a result of regulation, but also to examine the changes that regulatory reform created in these industries and compare these changes to predictions. Remarkably, many of the predictions made by Professor Keeler regarding the impacts of regulatory change turned out to be very accurate. His ability to use economic theory and available data to make such predictions, and later his ability to measure the accuracy of such predictions empirically, are major contributions. As will be highlighted later, in addition to the obvious direct impact of these predictions in shaping policy, the methods used to develop these predictions created a template for future researchers to make similar predictions.

Theodore Keeler's research in transportation economics was truly multimodal. He performed research in the areas of rail, airlines, airports, motor carriers, automobiles, and highway investment and pricing. His research on these various modes examined a variety of issues with policy implications, issues such as pricing, market structure, productivity, costs, investment, and safety.

A distinguishing feature of the work of Professor Keeler is that his research has always had policy implications. While many economic researchers are fascinated with theory, Keeler showed that theory and empirical evidence can be combined to obtain important predictions on the impacts of alternative policies.

In fact, Professor Keeler's use of counterfactual analysis to make predictions is one of his important contributions. Keeler extensively used simulations to make an assessment of how economic results (e.g., pricing, costs, and efficiency) would be different under a different scenario (e.g., if the railroad industry was regulated, as opposed to the current situation when it is not regulated). Not only were his predictions accurate, but his use of the counterfactual provided a roadmap for future researchers in making predictions.

Professor Keeler has also always had a knack for thinking about important aspects of a problem that are outside the conventional view. An example is in the area of economies of scale. Most analyses of economies of scale in any industry exclusively consider the cost savings that might be realized from producing more output. However, in evaluating the potential benefits of scale in various transportation industries (e.g., rail, trucking, and airlines), Professor Keeler noted the importance that scale might play in service quality. These important insights have played an important role in facilitating a better understanding of these industries. Moreover, they are important considerations for current researchers.

In multiple contexts, he also showed the importance of having a detailed understanding of history and how it can aid in understanding the implications of potential policy change. An example is in his examination of the history of airline regulation, how routes were assigned, and how it led to the misperception that regulation was needed to prevent destructive competition (by those who did not know the full history of regulation). Another example, is in his examination of the history of railroad regulation, where he showed that regulations conferring benefits to "disadvantaged" shippers, low-density areas, and weak railroads were all consistent with a model of regulation that maximized political support rather than maximizing social welfare.

In the following sections of this chapter, we provide more details on the research Professor Keeler has performed in the various transportation industries, his important insights, and his contributions to policy change and subsequent research. After that, we highlight the remaining chapters of this volume.

2 Airlines

An important justification for removing tight federal regulations on carrier entry and pricing into the US Airline Industry in 1978 was the belief that airfares could come down and improve airline efficiency. Prior to the work of Keeler in 1972, however, little reliable information on how regulatory change might affect fares and efficiency existed. As Keeler noted, some authors used the observation of a normal rate of return in the airline industry as evidence that airlines were not charging supra-normal fares. Other authors compared the relatively unregulated intrastate airfares to similar distance interstate airfares to suggest that fares would come down substantially. However, outside of such speculation, no information existed on what long-haul fares would be if the industry were deregulated.

Keeler (1972) estimated a cost function for interstate regulated carriers, and adjusted it for the efficient operating practices of the relatively unregulated California carriers to predict unregulated fares on the 30 highest density airline routes in the United States. This simulation approach, which predicted California intrastate fares very accurately, served as a counterfactual for the regulated interstate airline industry, that is, what would fares be if the industry were deregulated. The study found that regulated fares were 20%–95% higher than they would have been if unregulated in 1968 and 48%–84% higher in 1972.

Not only did the study reveal the substantial consumer benefits that could be realized with deregulation, but also the problems associated with inferring that market performance is good because of a lack of above normal profits. Keeler (1972) argued that the cartel-level rates (as illustrated by his simulations) did not result in cartel-level profits for at least two reasons: (1) unable to compete in fares because of tight regulatory control, airlines competed through excess capacity, eliminating profits, and (2) high coach fares cross subsidized first class fares. Thus the normal profits earned by the major airlines were the result of inefficiencies, rather than the result of competitive fares. This study, as well as testimony before the US Senate that updated these results in 1975, played an important role in leading to deregulation of the industry (Keeler, 1975).

Once the airline industry became deregulated, Keeler performed a series of studies to assess the impacts of the regulatory change, examining the accuracy of predictions made by proponents and opponents of regulatory change on a variety of issues, and examining appropriate future policies regarding the industry.

In 1981, Keeler and Abrahams examined the likely long-run structure of the airline industry under deregulation, and the appropriate policies in achieving that long-run structure. Interestingly, the authors predicted approximately six major carriers with an integrated nationwide route network in the long run. In making this prediction, the authors admitted the speculative nature of such a prediction, and given the difficulty in making such predictions (especially predicting almost 40 years into the future), the prediction is remarkably close to the current four to six major, integrated airlines in the United States (American, Delta, Southwest, United, and possibly Alaska and JetBlue).

Aside from the prediction on the number of carriers, another very insightful aspect of the study by Keeler and Abrahams was their identification of a different type of economies of integration in the airline industry. When examining likely market structure of an industry, an important consideration is the extent of economies of scale. In the transportation industries, economies of scale are advantages related to increasing traffic over existing routes (economies of density) or advantages related to increasing traffic by expanding the number of routes (economies of size). Most often, such economies are thought to be revealed in the form of cost savings. However, Keeler and Abrahams showed that they also may occur in the form of better service. In the airline industry, density economies might occur from an airline's ability to offer more frequent flights and consequently less waiting time with more passengers, while size economies might occur from a reduced need for passengers to switch planes and/or carriers when connecting from one route segment to another when the carrier serves more routes. While this is an important insight for the airline industry, it is also a very important consideration in other industries, and one that many researchers still do not consider.

Keeler's 1981 study for a book entitled Case Studies in Regulation showed that the early effects of airline deregulation were to encourage entry of carriers into new markets and to encourage price competition on high-density routes, without causing deterioration of service on low-density routes (Keeler, 1981). A noteworthy aspect of this study, and one that shows up throughout the work of Professor Keeler, was his careful review of regulation history.

Keeler showed the importance of an accurate understanding of history in making predictions and in interpreting existing data. For example, Professor Keeler noted that the Airmail Act of 1934 allowed airlines to bid for airmail contracts on various routes, with the ability to raise rates in the following year without another bid. This created an incentive for airlines to submit very low bids to get the contracts, and the Interstate Commerce Commission (ICC) did not allow the rate increases as quickly as those bidders anticipated. The resulting financial harm realized by those carriers was presented as evidence later (during the era of regulation) that regulation was needed to prevent destructive competition. In detailing the history, and explaining the incentive system that was created, Professor Keeler showed how such an interpretation was a clear misunderstanding or uniformed view of this history.

A further review of history from the same study (Keeler, 1981) also shed light on the expected impacts of deregulating the industry. In reviewing the expected impacts of deregulation, Professor Keeler looked at the Civil Aeronautics Board's (CAB) motivation for regulating the industry in the first place. He noted the desire to try to ensure service to most communities, but with few government subsidies. This was to be achieved by cross-subsidizing low-density and short-haul service through more profitable high-density and long-haul service. However, Professor Keeler noted that this did not work because the carriers were not required to serve the low-density and short-haul markets, and they did have incentives to compete in other more lucrative long-haul and high-density markets. This only resulted in profits on the long-haul and high-density routes being competed away by excess capacity, and the federal government subsidizing different carriers on low-density and short-haul routes. Professor Keeler noted that this suggested the concern deregulation opponents had that service to low-density, short-haul routes would suffer from deregulation was unlikely to be realized.

In assessing the impacts of deregulation in the airline industry, as in other industries, Professor Keeler was careful to recognize the importance of understanding market structure and behavior. Call and Keeler (1985) showed the importance of understanding market behavior in assessing the impacts of airline deregulation. A popular theory used in predicting the likely impacts of airline deregulation in the early 1980s was the theory of perfect contestability—the idea that the amount of actual competition in an airline market does not matter, as firms will be constrained to charge competitive fares by the mere threat of competition. If the airline market were perfectly contestable, the effects of deregulation on fares would be felt immediately. While Bailey and Baumol (1984) argued that the concept is not likely to apply in the short run due to the time needed for the low-cost carriers (LCCs) to build up capacity and reputation to make them realistic threats, Call and Keeler provided evidence that it might not apply in the long run either—finding that entry of established carriers into new routes had a negative impact on fares.

Call and Keeler's empirical evidence supported a model of behavior where incumbent firms matched new entry fares on a capacity-controlled basis. However, they also found evidence that fares were falling on an unrestricted basis as low-cost airlines expanded to new markets. They predicted that as LCCs continue to gain acceptance, major carriers would be forced to compete with them, and a more competitive market would emerge. Moreover, they predicted a greater role for potential competition in determining future airfares. These predictions have turned out to be remarkably accurate, as full service carriers (the former trunk carriers) and LCCs are increasingly serving the same routes (Henrickson and Wilson, 2016), the fare premiums charged by full-service carriers over LCCs have eroded (Borenstein, 2011; Huschelrath and Muller, 2012), full service carrier/LCC business models are converging (Leick and Wensveen, 2014), and so are their costs (Bitzan and Peoples, 2016).

As in his research with regulatory change for other modes, Professor Keeler had the insight that lessons from regulatory change in one country may give important insights for regulatory change in other countries. Professor Keeler's 1991 study examined the available evidence on the experience with airline deregulation in the United States, and the implications for deregulating European airline markets (Keeler, 1991). In reviewing previous studies and in providing some new evidence, he found overall success from deregulating US airline markets. He highlighted large benefits in fare reductions, improvements in service, acceleration of productivity, returns on investment consistent with competitive levels, and no deterioration in safety. However, he also highlighted some policy problems, suggesting that while deregulation would also be beneficial in Europe, several considerations would be prudent. These included caution in approving mergers, airport capacity planning, separation of reservation systems from the airlines, more research on appropriate policies toward predatory practices, expanded safety inspections for new airlines, a policy for opening slot-controlled airports to new entrants, and peak load pricing policies to allocate capacity.

As highlighted by Professor Keeler in many studies, the overall effects of airline deregulation were very positive for the United States. However, one of the downsides of deregulation predicted by some was that there would be a deterioration in safety. Although even in the deregulated environment, the Federal Aviation Administration still required rigorous safety standards for new entrants, skeptics of deregulation believed that the restrictions on entry imposed by the CAB served as an additional check on safety. They believed that new firms might try to save money on maintenance, pilot training, etc., resulting in a deleterious impact on safety. Professor Keeler performed a series of studies with Adib Kanafani to investigate the impacts that deregulation had on safety.

Noting the major concern some observers had that deregulation would harm safety because of new entrants, Kanafani and Keeler (1989) examined whether there was a difference in the safety performance between established carriers and those that entered after deregulation. They noted that theoretically, arguments could be made for new entrants being less safe or more safe than established firms. On the one hand, it might be argued that they would be less safe due to less experience and financial resources, while on the other it might be argued that they would be more safe due to the need for new carriers to develop a reputation for safety. Because of a lack of data regarding large fatal accidents, the authors used indirect data such as maintenance expenditures, inspections data, near midair collisions data, and accidents not involving fatalities to assess safety. They found no difference in the safety performance of new and established carriers, suggesting that if safety changed after deregulation the cause was not new entry.

Despite the 1989 study by Kanafani and Keeler, the controversy over the impact of deregulation on safety remained. Skeptics noted that most studies of safety impacts focused either on jet or commuter service, and that safety may have deteriorated do to substituting commuter service for jet service. Moreover, the data on fatalities was limited, making an evaluation of safety difficult using annual fatality data. Kanafani and Keeler (1990) used monthly data on fatalities for all carriers (jet and commuter) to examine the impacts of deregulation on safety. Using a time-trend shifter and using a counterfactual simulation (as if deregulation had not occurred), they found improving safety over time and no effect on safety from deregulation.

Kanafani et al. (1993) added to the evidence of the impacts of deregulation on safety by examining airline safety posture. They noted difficulties in performing analyses of safety with rare fatality data, using data from service difficulty reports as indicators of safety posture. Their results provided further evidence that airline deregulation did not harm safety, finding that new entrants did not have worse safety posture than incumbents. They also found better safety posture for larger carriers and worse safety for longer stage lengths (more exposure).

As highlighted in this section, the work of Professor Keeler was instrumental in convincing policymakers of the benefits of removing entry and pricing regulations in the airline industry. Moreover, his predictions about the long-run equilibrium in the industry and the effects of deregulation have been remarkably accurate. His work in this area has also provided many insights and techniques that have been used by other researchers, and will continue to be used by other researchers in assessing policy change. Examples include his use of counterfactual analysis to assess policy change, his revelation that understanding history is important in assessing the impacts of policy change, his insights on the importance of understanding market structure in assessing policy change, and his use of policy change experiences to reveal lessons for similar policy changes elsewhere.

3 Airports

While most of Professor Keeler's aviation economics research was in the area of airlines, he performed one of the first cost studies for the airport industry (Keeler, 1970). At the time of his study, there was discussion of an "airport problem"—a high demand for local airport services, but a lack of profitability to attract investment, resulting in unmet needs, airport congestion, and the need for federal funding.

As in his research in other areas of transportation, Professor Keeler looked to the economic evidence for a solution to the problem. He noted that the problem of high demand and lack of profitability to attract more investment seemed to have a simple solution—increase user charges for using airport services to long-run marginal costs. However, he also recognized that such a solution would not work if the industry faced increasing returns to scale, that is, long-run marginal costs below long-run average costs.

Thus he estimated a statistical cost function for US airports. To our knowledge, this was the first estimation of its kind. He found evidence consistent with constant returns to scale for airports, suggesting that marginal cost pricing would be feasible and would solve the airport financing problem. As he noted, this also suggested the possibility that airports could be privatized. Interestingly, the issue of scale economies in the airport industry has still not been resolved (Bottasso and Conti, 2017). On the issue of privatization, 450 airports throughout the world have been at least partially privatized (GAO, 2014).

Another important issue addressed by Professor Keeler in this study was the allocation of costs among commercial aircraft and general aviation aircraft. He found that the marginal cost of general aviation events was very similar to commercial aircraft. He noted that this surprising result was due to a lack of separate runway facilities, and the tying up of facilities by general aviation that were meant for larger planes. He noted a solution of building separate, shorter runways for general aviation aircraft, and charging all aircraft the marginal costs of the services they use.

4 Railroads

As in the case of the airline industry, an understanding of the likely effects of deregulating the railroad industry in 1976 and 1980 required an understanding of the economics of the industry, the history of regulation in the industry, and the empirical evidence related to the impacts of various elements of regulation. Professor Keeler's 1983 book, entitled "Railroads, Freight, and Public Policy," contains an excellent and comprehensive examination of a variety of relevant issues, including the financial viability of the industry under regulation, a detailed history of regulation and regulatory reform—examining the impacts of regulation and the motivations for regulation and regulatory change, an examination of the theoretical and empirical evidence regarding the market structure likely to prevail in a deregulated environment, an assessment of the likely impacts of deregulation based on theoretical and past empirical evidence, an assessment of the early impacts of deregulation, and an examination of other policy changes that may impact the future of railroads.

Although this book came out in 1983 (after the Staggers Act was passed), it is important to recognize that there was still some uncertainty as to how regulatory change would be implemented by the ICC at that time. As Professor Keeler pointed out in his book, the most important policy change in The Staggers Act of 1980 was removing the common carrier obligation that forced railroads to provide service where it was not profitable. However, as he also pointed out, there was room for interpretation in The Staggers Act that could have thwarted this. Moreover, there was also a lot of uncertainty regarding the impacts that would occur with deregulation, since its implementation had just started. Professor Keeler's detailed analysis of the industry, his analysis of the problems created by regulation, and his assessment of the improvements that were likely to occur with regulatory change provided an encouragement for supporters of regulatory reform and served as an important roadmap for how regulatory change should be implemented by the ICC.

As in other contexts, Professor Keeler made a number predictions in his 1983 book. Some of his predictions on the impacts of deregulating the railroad industry included increasing railroad profitability, large benefits from abandoning unprofitable service (and attracting more profitable service) and the resulting realization of the benefits of economies of density, large benefits from changing work rules in the deregulated environment, large productivity gains from rate and service freedom, and efficiency/ service improvements from mergers. Professor Keeler's work in the 2000s and work of other researchers has shown that these predictions have been remarkably accurate.

Perhaps the boldest prediction made in the book, given the state of the industry at the time, was that "relief from these obligations in both rates and services could in some cases generate improved profits for railroads and lower prices for consumers" (Keeler, 1983, p. 96). In fact, this is exactly what has happened. The consensus of economic studies done since deregulation has been that removing regulations has resulted in large price decreases to consumers and major improvements in railroad profitability.[1]

However, the value of Professor Keeler's 1983 book goes well beyond the predictions and understanding the impacts of deregulating the US railroad industry in 1980. Important insights regarding the economics of the industry, the historical perspective

---

[1] Real revenue per ton-mile decreased by more than 40 percent between 1980 and 2014 (BTS, National Transportation Statistics and BEA GDP Implicit Price Deflator). Moreover, 4 out of the 7 Class I railroads were deemed revenue adequate in 2015 by the Surface Transportation Board (STB).

on regulatory change—including motivations of regulators and impacts of regulatory change, and discussion of other policy issues potentially impacting railroads make this an essential read for anyone who wants to understand or research the industry. Researchers who want to examine current policy issues in the railroad industry need to understand the issues discussed in this book. No other book that we are aware of, contains the depth, perspective, and economic insights available in this book for understanding the railroad industry.

As one example, consider current discussions taking place in the Surface Transportation Board (STB) regarding the revision of maximum rate guidelines for small shippers. A full understanding of the current discussion requires an understanding of a number of issues discussed in this book, including things like the history of railroad financial problems and causes, the historical common carrier obligations of railroads and how they have changed, the extent of economies of scale in the industry and the need for differential pricing, and the motives of regulators. Unfortunately, current research in this area sometimes loses sight of these important issues—issues that are as relevant today as they were in 1983.

A further illustration of the relevance of Professor Keeler's insights from this book to current policy debates is seen in the area of a proposed "open access" framework. In an "open access" framework, competition would occur in operations over infrastructure owned by other railroads (or possibly by government). Advocates of such a policy routinely highlight the procompetitive effects without mentioning the potentially negative impacts on the use of resources. In neglecting to mention negative resource effects, they often assume that any cost savings that railroads realize from increased traffic over a particular route (economies of density) are realized due to spreading out of "fixed" way and structures costs among more traffic. Thus they reason that an open access framework would not change this. However, while "open access" advocates often frame this as a new idea, it was one that was discussed by Keeler in 1983. He noted the misperception that economies of density are realized primarily in way and structures costs. Professor Keeler discussed this extensively in his 1983 book, noting that a large portion of the economies of density realized by railroads occurs in operations, resulting from better utilization of labor and equipment. Despite Keeler pointing this misperception out in 1983, it is one that still exists among many observers.

Moreover, current researchers can also benefit from understanding the detailed history of regulatory change and regulatory motives discussed in this book. The book presents compelling evidence that regulators aimed to maximize political support, rather than social welfare. Extending the models of Stigler (1971) and Peltzman (1976), and tying them to empirical evidence on the history of regulation in the railroad industry was an important contribution of Professor Keeler. This insight suggests that even if introducing some economic regulation may seem to be beneficial from a public interest perspective, it is important to keep in mind the potential for regulators to pursue a different goal. This point was also made in Keeler (1984), where he showed that an extension of the Peltzman model could explain economic regulation and the move to deregulation in several industries, and that the support maximizing behavior of the extended Peltzman model could sometimes improve economic welfare.

In addition to the important influence of Professor Keeler's 1983 book, he performed a variety of other important research studies of the railroad industry. As highlighted in his 1983 book, the US railroad industry suffered from severe financial problems in the 1970s and the future viability of the industry was very much in doubt. It was speculated by some, in the 1970s, that the industry might be helped toward viability by allowing more liberalized abandonment of railroad lines. However, little was known about the extent of excess capacity in the industry.

Keeler's 1974 study examined railroad returns to scale and excess capacity. He noted several problems with previous railroad cost studies, with most either assuming a long-run cost function or assuming factor proportions between track and other inputs are fixed. At the time when regulations prevented railroads from abandoning many miles of track, there was good reason to doubt that railroads were optimally adjusting track miles to traffic levels (as would be the case if railroads were minimizing long run costs). Further, as Professor Keeler pointed out, the fixed factor proportions assumption made much less sense than assuming that marginal maintenance and operating costs would increase as railroad plant is used more intensively. He formulated a model that did not require the unrealistic assumptions of long-run cost minimization or of fixed factor proportions.

An important innovation made by Professor Keeler in this study was to estimate railroad costs using a model consistent with economic theory. He estimated a short-run cost function, assuming the amount of track was fixed. He then obtained the optimal amount for track by minimizing short-run costs with respect to the amount of track. Finally, he plugged the optimal amount of track into the short-run cost equation to get the long-run cost function. Though this method was straight from economic theory, it was one that was not used by other researchers in estimating costs, and it was an extremely important advancement in econometric estimation of cost functions. This method allowed Professor Keeler to estimate the amount of excess capacity in the industry, and the cost savings that would result from abandoning excess capacity. He estimated that more than 200,000 miles of excess track capacity existed, and that $2.5 billion could be saved annually from reducing track miles to optimal levels.

The study was also very important in that it distinguished two different types of scale economies in the rail industry—economies of density and economies of size. Economies of density are reductions in costs that result from handling more traffic over a fixed network, while economies of size are reductions in cost resulting from serving a larger network. These concepts, and the ability to distinguish them, play extremely important roles in many policy debates regarding the railroad industry.

As highlighted in Professor Keeler's 1983 book, one of the well-known problems in the US rail industry with regulatory underpinnings was the loss of railroad traffic to competing modes. The "value of service" pricing structure, where more valuable commodities paid higher transportation rates worked to the advantage of railroads during the era where trucks and barges were not viable options for transportation. However, with the development of highway and waterway networks, the structure meant lost traffic when the ICC used it to deny rate reductions by railroads.

While the distortion was recognized by most transportation economists in the 1960s and 1970s, there was disagreement about whether railroad rate reductions on manufactured products would actually allow railroads to recapture such traffic. Keeler (1977) examined modal shares in Australia, where long-haul transportation was deregulated much earlier, to assess the likelihood and extent that US railroads would successfully capture manufactured product traffic with deregulation. As with other debates at the time, Professor Keeler provided empirical evidence that gave insights unavailable from other existing evidence.

After evaluating differences and similarities between the United States and Australia in regulatory policies, geography, traffic characteristics, taxation and subsidies, technology, relative rail/truck costs, and market shares, Keeler (1977) found evidence to suggest that US railroads would be unlikely to gain much market share in manufactured products from truck as a result of deregulation. He noted the low cross-price elasticity between rail and truck due to the inferior service of rail in manufactured products; he also noted that truck rates would fall with trucking deregulation. While railroads have been able to recapture some market share in long-haul markets, the technological change allowing double-stack container service could not have been anticipated in the 1970s (Gallamore, 1999).

Professor Keeler's 1977 study was also interesting in pointing out the similarity in US regulatory policy and Australian regulatory policy before reform. He noted that both were meant to keep rail rates high so that cross-subsidies could support a larger network than would be supported by market forces. Because US railroads did not have enough monopoly power on captive routes to support this larger than optimal system, it led to losses and deterioration of plant and equipment. Professor Keeler noted that restoring railroad viability would require allowing abandonment of unprofitable service or subsidies, just like what was required in Australia once regulations preventing trucking from competing with rail were eliminated.

In the late 1970s and early 1980s, the "railroad problem" was well known, with several bankruptcies, poorly maintained trackage, poor service, and lost traffic to competing modes. Harris and Keeler (1981) highlighted that at the root of all of these problems was a lack of profitability. Their study examined three institutional factors that made it difficult for the industry to adapt to a changing economic and competitive environment: (1) excess capacity—regulation not allowing abandonment of unprofitable service, (2) balkanization—an unintegrated rail system with frequent interlining, and (3) obsolete work rules and high wages.

An extremely insightful aspect of this paper, and an observation made by Professor Keeler in other contexts, was the recognition that economies of integration could be realized in the form of better service in addition to the more obvious cost savings. Harris and Keeler (1981) noted that their study, by examining carrier profits instead of costs, had the ability to capture these benefits of integration. They found that poor profitability was related to several things, such as excess capacity, balkanization, deferred maintenance, and obsolete work rules. They suggested that policies allowing system rationalization through abandonments or parallel mergers, and those that modernize work rules would help to restore profitability.

As in the airline industry, Professor Keeler performed a number of studies in the railroad industry to assess the impacts of the reform he advocated. In the 2000s, he performed a variety of studies to test his earlier predictions: (1) examining productivity change and changes in work rules, (2) examining economies of density and the benefits of increased traffic densities realized as a result of rationalization and pricing freedom, (3) benefits of pricing freedom and railroads' abilities to change their traffic composition, and (4) the impacts of pricing freedom on the markups on various commodities.

Professor Keeler's early work in railroad economics consistently highlighted the adverse effects of restrictive work rules on the industry (Harris and Keeler, 1981; Keeler, 1977, 1983). In 2003, he performed a retrospective study on the impacts of these work rules. Bitzan and Keeler (2003) estimated productivity growth in the railroad industry between 1983 and 1997, isolating the impact of the elimination of the caboose and related crew members. As Professor Keeler highlighted in his 1983 book, "forced use of 5-man crews and 100-mile days on freight trains, combined with the fact that wages of everyone in the industry, from secretaries to mechanics, tend to be higher than elsewhere, would seem to exact a high price in both economic efficiency and level of industry viability" (Keeler, 1983, p. 128). Using the fraction of train-miles operating with cabooses to capture the changes in work rules that occurred in the 1980s, this study found annual cost savings ranging between $2 billion to $3.3 billion for Class I railroads from such changes. Moreover, the counterfactual estimation of what railroad costs would have been with 1983 technology showed that costs would have been 32%–43% higher than they actually were in 1997 due to other changes. This study provided strong support for the accuracy of Professor Keeler's earlier predictions of accelerated productivity from deregulation and productivity benefits from work rule changes.

As highlighted previously, one of the major benefits of deregulation highlighted by Professor Keeler (1974, 1983) was the ability of railroads to reduce excess capacity. Using a counterfactual simulation of what railroad density and costs would have been had regulation continued, Bitzan and Keeler (2007) estimated railroad freight traffic density that is 34% higher in 2001 than it would have been under regulation and cost savings of $7–$10 billion resulting from the increased freight traffic density. These results of cost savings were somewhat higher than those predicted by Professor Keeler and others in the late 1970s and early 1980s. However, the cost savings from reduced route mileage only were very close to the predictions of Professor Keeler and others, as the large increase in railroad freight traffic handled from deregulation was not anticipated.

In another study highlighting benefits of deregulating the railroad industry, Bitzan and Keeler (2011) showed important environmental benefits from intermodal rail traffic growth that resulted from deregulating the rail, trucking, and energy industries. As highlighted by Gallamore (1999), growth in railroad intermodal traffic was facilitated by various elements of railroad and motor carrier deregulation, such as allowing railroad contract rates, eased motor carrier restrictions allowing filling empty backhauls, and improved railroad profitability allowing investments in new technologies. Moreover, market based energy prices have facilitated the shift of traffic toward more energy efficient modes. The authors showed substantial reductions in carbon emissions and fuel used as a result of the growth in intermodal rail traffic.

One of the themes of Professor Keeler's early work in the area of railroads was his realization that restoring the industry to viability would require more market based pricing. In a study that examined changes in price-cost margins for various commodities between 1986 and 2008, Bitzan and Keeler (2014) found no single trend in revenue-cost margins—some increased while others rose. Interestingly, for commodities where Professor Keeler found a significant cost advantage for rail in his 1983 book (coal and chemicals), they found no large increase in revenue-cost ratios, while finding larger increases for some commodities considered to be "noncaptive." The authors conclude that the market-based pricing enabled by deregulation has benefited railroads and shippers alike.

Like his work in the airline industry, Professor Keeler's work in railroads has had a major impact on the industry and on subsequent research in the industry. His work in the rail industry served as an encouragement to regulators to aggressively pursue regulatory reform. Moreover, it provided a basis for understanding the industry, with insights that are as relevant today as they were at the time when he shared them. As in his work in other areas of transportation, his predictions on the future of the railroad industry have turned out to be remarkably accurate, and his methods of prediction and measurement provide a template for use by future researchers.

5 Trucking

At the same time that the airline and railroad industries were experiencing regulatory reform, so was the trucking industry with the passage of the Motor Carrier Act of 1980. Like the reforms in the other industries, the Motor Carrier Act gave trucking firms much more freedom in setting rates and in the markets they could serve. Professor Keeler performed a series of studies examining the impacts of motor carrier deregulation and motor carrier performance in the deregulated environment.

Professor Keeler's initial study in this area (Keeler, 1986) examined three important policy changes likely to affect trucking productivity: (1) major investments in highway infrastructure, including the interstate system, (2) the introduction of the 55 mile per hour speed limit in the mid-1970s, and (3) trucking deregulation. Using a conventional cost function approach with a sample of large firms from 1966 through 1983, he found that trucking costs fell as a result of the 55 MPH speed limit, that infrastructure investment had no impact on trucking costs, and that costs rose with deregulation (after controlling for factor prices—which fell from deregulation).

While Professor Keeler noted that the results were only suggestive due to the limited amount of data available at the time, his results and analysis provided some very important insights. For example, he noted that one reason for the lack of significance of investment and the positive impact of deregulation was likely due to the fact that service quality impacts do not show up in a cost estimation. That is, infrastructure investment may have improved service of trucking firms instead of reducing their costs. Moreover, savings in costs from lower factor prices (e.g., labor) from deregulation may be used to provide better service—showing up as an increase in costs after factor prices are controlled for. He also noted other reasons for these unexpected findings, including the fact that many highway investments were aimed at automobiles, rather than trucks, the fact that most of the postderegulation data available was during a recession, and the possibility of a transition period where firms were still adjusting to deregulation.

Professor Keeler was able to build upon this work by obtaining regional data for all Class I motor carrier firms from 1950 through 1973. Keeler and Ying (1988) estimated a long-run cost function for motor carrier firms to quantify the benefits of investment in the US Federal-Aid Highway System. The authors noted that using data through 1973 was preferable to using later data, as the amount of system investment did not change much after 1973.

The authors found large cost savings to trucking firms resulting from the growth in highway investment that occurred between 1950 and 1973. Using a counterfactual analysis (where the counterfactual was trucking costs that would have occurred in later years if investment stayed at 1950 levels), the authors found cost savings for US Trucking Firms ranging between $5.97 billion and $8.79 billion in 1973, accounting for between 1/3 and 1/2 of the costs of the investment in the system. The authors noted that this was significant, as it did not account for all the other benefits of the system. Moreover, the study highlighted the importance of actually measuring the benefits of public investment projects, rather than just speculating on what they might be before the investment is made.

Professor Keeler examined the extent of economies of scale in the trucking industry using a new approach (Keeler, 1989). His important insight that he also made in other contexts (e.g., airlines and railroads) was that economies of scale can be realized through service improvement, in addition to cost savings. He pointed out the potential benefits to shippers from dealing with one trucking company that can provide an array of services to various locations and the potential for the carrier to provide more frequent service over a denser network.

His approach for measuring economies of scale was to employ a statistical estimation of the survival principle (Keeler, 1989). The idea was to estimate the probability of various sizes of trucking firms maintaining or gaining market share over time as a function of size and other explanatory variables.

Interestingly, in contrast to studies of scale economies done using prederegulation data, Keeler found increasing returns to scale in trucking. He hypothesized that these results occurred for two reasons: (1) there are scale economies in trucking that are due to service quality and cannot be measured with cost analysis, and (2) the technology of the industry changed with deregulation as companies were given more pricing and service flexibility to operate on a more fully loaded basis, resulting in scale economies.

Professor Keeler pointed out that these results were not evidence that the trucking industry should be reregulated. He pointed out that the extent of economies of scale identified were not large enough to prevent competition, the important role played by potential entry in trucking, and the successful experiences with deregulation of trucking in Australia and with agricultural goods in the United States. This study of scale economies in trucking showed the importance of recognizing the potential impacts of integration beyond the impact on costs, and that there are creative ways to test economic hypotheses.

The final study Professor Keeler performed in the trucking industry examined the dynamic impacts of deregulation on rates. Ying and Keeler (1991) noted the problems leading to high trucking rates under regulation, where motor carriers realized monopoly power due to restrictions on which firms could serve various routes and who could enter the industry, rates set by rate bureaus, and value of service pricing, where firms were inefficient for the same reasons, and where labor extracted monopoly rents from trucking firms.

Using a cost equation to estimate marginal costs and a rate equation with rates as a function of marginal cost using firm level data from 1975 through 1985, they found a fall in rates from regulatory reform that grew over time. They estimated rate savings of 15%–25% by 1983 and rate savings of 25%–35% by 1985 as a result of regulatory reform. As with other work performed by Professor Keeler, this study performed a counterfactual analysis to assess the impacts that deregulation had on the industry and whether those impacts were in line with previous predictions. The study showed results in line with those predicted by the advocates of deregulation.

As with his work in other areas, Professor Keeler's work in trucking offered important insights in terms of policy and policy change, and presented new ways of thinking about and measuring relevant economic variables. In particular, although many industry cost analyses have been performed in recent years, Professor Keeler's important insight that scale economies might be realized in service improvement is one that should be revisited with more recent data and for other industries.

6 Automobile regulation

In the 1960s and 1970s various events heightened concerns over negative effects of automobiles in the US. Professor Keeler took interest in the ways the US federal government tried to reduce problems with automobile safety, emissions, and fuel use. In a series of studies, he examined the effectiveness of regulations regarding these concerns with the automobile.

In the first study, Crandall et al. (1982) estimated the full costs of owning and operating an automobile as a function of regulatory variables to obtain preliminary estimates of the consumer costs from safety and emissions regulations. After estimating a long-run cost function to identify the determinants of the costs of owning and operating an automobile, the authors compared a counterfactual estimate of what these costs would be with 1967 regulatory standards with the estimated costs in 1980. They found that the costs of owning and operating an automobile were 18% higher than they would have been with the 1967 standards in place.

Interestingly, they also found that most of the cost increase was due to tighter emissions standards, rather than due to increased safety regulation. The authors stated that automobile manufacturers were able to make safety improvements at a relatively low cost. This initial study set the stage for more detailed work in a book on the subject by Crandall et al. (1986).

Crandall et al. (1986) performed a detailed study of the costs and benefits of government regulation of the automobile in the United States in the 1960s and 1970s.

Their study examined the problems in the US automobile industry in the 1970s, the costs and benefits of regulating safety, emissions, and fuel economy, conflicts between various regulations, and lessons for the future. The authors reported several interesting findings in this study, including benefits from safety regulation well above the costs, costs of emissions standards well exceeding the benefits, and an ill-conceived CAFE standards program whose goals could be better achieved through fuel taxes.

As with the other works of Professor Keeler, this study is very careful in measuring the impacts of such regulations, and it includes many important insights. In measuring impacts of automobile regulations, the econometric estimation of safety regulations is particularly interesting, showing large positive impacts of safety regulations on passengers that are partially (though not nearly completely) eliminated by negative impacts on non passengers. In measuring separate impacts of safety regulation on passengers and nonpassengers, they showed that the arguments of Peltzman (1975) that drivers may not drive as carefully with safer cars have merit, but that this "offsetting" effect is not big enough to eliminate the benefits of safety regulations. Other important insights in this study include a discussion of how various regulations can conflict with each other, for example, safer vehicles tend to be heavier, reducing fuel efficiency, how regulations that increase automobile costs may delay the use of safer, cleaner, and more efficient cars by consumers, and how the way regulations are enacted can influence their effectiveness. These insights have important policy implications.

Adding to this work, Crandall and Keeler (1987) examined the potential for policies of diverting people from automobiles to other modes to address safety, emissions, and energy concerns, in addition to the direct regulations discussed in the previous study. In exploring the evidence, they found that the benefits of alternative modes over the automobile in these areas were not very large. Moreover, they noted that the success of policies aimed at moving people to other modes was likely to be limited, due to various other modes of travel (e.g., buses or rail) being poor substitutes for automobiles in cases outside of urban work trips.

An interesting insight made by Crandall and Keeler (1987) in this study was that airline deregulation likely had a positive impact on safety and the environment for an unexpected reason. As air travel became less expensive for travelers due to lower fares, they substituted air travel for auto travel for some long distance trips. This, in turn, led to increased safety and lower emissions.

Finally, in a paper dealing with the determinants of highway safety, Keeler (1994) made several improvements upon previous studies. Some of the important innovations made in this study included: (1) using a panel of data on US counties, resulting in many more observations than previous studies and allowing for correcting an omitted variable bias that may have been present in previous cross-sectional studies, (2) examining determinants of highway safety not previously considered, such as education, and (3) allowing for differences in the influence of independent variables on safety in rural and urban areas.

In this study, Keeler (1994) found several interesting things, including a lack of effectiveness of safety device regulation, effectiveness of speed limits in enhancing safety only in urban areas, a significant impact of education in improving safety, and more frequent license renewal testing improving safety. One of the more interesting findings of this study (and one that has policy implications) was the finding that lower rural speed limits did not reduce fatalities. Professor Keeler speculated that this may suggest that offsetting behavior or evasion is taking place in rural areas, where it is easier to do so. He also speculated that it might be speed variance rather than speed limit that matters. His results suggested that increasing the speed limit to 65 MPH on rural expressways would not harm safety.

Professor Keeler's work in automobile regulation was very much in line with his work in other areas. He explored areas empirically that others were only able to specu-late about, he thought about aspects of regulation that were not thought about by others, and he performed work that had important policy implications. Insights from his work in this area that stand out in particular are his observations with coauthors on the im-portance of viewing regulations in an appropriate context. The work done in conjunc-tion with Crandall, Gruenspecht, and Lave showed that automobile regulations dealing with safety, emissions, and fuel consumption will have different effects together than if implemented separately, that regulations may have effects opposite their intention due to raising the prices of automobiles and delaying implementation, and that the flexibil-ity in the way regulations are administered can have a major impact on their success.

7   Highway pricing and investment and resource allocation in urban transportation

An important policy problem facing government agencies has been the amount to in-vest in highway capacity, and the related problem of how to price such capacity. Kee-ler and Small (1977) developed a theoretical model to determine the optimal amount of lane capacity and the optimal congestion tolls, and used data consisting of 57 road segments in the 9 San Francisco Bay area counties.

Their theoretical model maximized the net benefit of all automobile trips on the road segment for its life, showing that a maximum was obtained where the marginal cost of user savings from the investment was equal to the marginal cost of extra capac-ity. In empirical implementation of their model, they showed how highway construc-tion costs varied with the degree of urbanization and that there were constant returns to scale in terms of width in highway construction (suggesting that optimal user charg-es would just recover total costs of construction). Moreover, they used an estimated relationship between speed and volume-capacity-ratio, estimates of the value of travel time, peaking characteristics on typical Bay area roads, and the capacity costs, in con-junction with their theoretical model to estimate optimal capacity utilization, speed, and toll during different periods.

Keeler and Small (1977) showed that roads were well underpriced in the Bay area, with optimal peak tolls of 2–7 cents per car mile, 2–9 cents per car mile, and 6–35 cents per car mile on rural, suburban, and central city highways, respectively. How-ever, they also noted that this did not suggest an overuse of highways during peak hours. They pointed to the fact that the higher tolls would lead to higher service qual-ity, which could actually increase demand during this time period.

As with the other works of Professor Keeler, this study was important for several reasons. First, it showed that the economic theory of highway investment can be applied in a meaningful way with actual data. It also provided many useful insights regarding the relationships between optimal tolls at various times and for various degrees of urbanization. Finally, it provided important policy implications regarding highway pricing.

The work with Kenneth Small on urban highway pricing and investment was part of a larger project on costs and optimal service levels for all modes of urban transportation, called "The Comparative Costs of Bay Area Transportation Modes," funded by the National Science Foundation, for which Keeler was Principal Investigator. This project, completed in 1975, included other investigators, Leonard Merewitz, Peter Fisher, and (early on) Douglas Lee. In addition, it included graduate research assistants, including Randall Pozdena, Kenneth Small, and Philip Viton, with further contributions by George Cluff and Jeffrey Finke. Finally it included (then) undergraduate research assistants who also played important roles, including Bruce Horowitz, Eileen Kadish, Clifford Winston, and others.

From Keeler's view as project leader, the overall thrust of the study was inspired by the work of Meyer et al. (1965). Meyer and associates compared the costs of auto, fixed rail, and bus transportation in a pioneering work. Keeler wanted to take things a step further, by including travelers' time costs in such a comparison, and by including more complete expenses, such as environmental costs. But inclusion of travelers' time costs also suggested that services for each mode should be optimized to minimize the combination of time and operating costs, so that the minimum, optimally priced costs of each mode would be the basis for comparison.

Consistent with Meyer and associates, cost analysis was done under widely varying assumptions on passenger flows per unit of time, for buses, fixed rail, and private autos, with some additional analysis of the costs of light rail. Optimal frequencies were estimated for bus and fixed rail, and optimal volume-capacity ratios and prices were estimated for auto and highway transport.

The results showed that optimally planned and scheduled buses dominated other modes under a wide range of circumstances, with costs of time and highway right-of-way included. But, for this to work, it was necessary to have bus frequencies and speeds optimized in a way not often seen in practice in urban transportation, at least when the study was done. At lower densities and high time values, the private auto dominated all other modes, again including environmental and right-of-way costs. Only at the very highest densities was it found that fixed rail (with feeder bus service) might be cost efficient.

The full analysis and results of this study were published in a relatively obscure place, as three monographs of the Institute of Urban and Regional Development at the University of California, Berkeley, entitled overall *The Full Costs of Urban Transportation*. Keeler was responsible for Volume III, entitled *Automobile Costs and Final Intermodal Cost Comparisons*. The results were summarized in the piece by Crandall and Keeler (1987), cited earlier. Nevertheless, Keeler has said that one of his big professional regrets was that he did not submit the full analysis and results of this project (with the exception of the part on autos and highways) for publication in a more widely circulated journal or book. Meanwhile, Small, Winston, and others have expanded this path of research, started by Meyer and associates, well beyond what the 1975 study did; they have included, among many other things, demand analysis, which is largely excluded from the 1975 study discussed here.

The remainder of this chapter highlights the individual contributions in this book. This book contains 12 more chapters that examine the transportation policy issues examined by Professor Keeler, utilizing the tools and ideas that he developed. It is our hope that this book provides a fitting tribute to Theodore Keeler—a man who has had an important and lasting impact on the field of transportation economics.

8   Remaining chapters

The following chapter of this book by Kenneth Button examines Theodore Keeler's views, analyses, and early predictions regarding regulation and regulatory reform of airlines, railroads, and motor carriers. The chapter highlights the importance of the applied (as opposed to theoretical) approach of Professor Keeler, his contributions to theory of regulation and regulatory change, and the general accuracy of his short-term and long-term predictions of the impacts of regulatory change in these industries. The chapter offers rich insights regarding the work of Professor Keeler by placing his work in the context of the prevailing thinking and events occurring at the time of regulatory change.

Button examines the contrasting views on the role of regulation at the time when Keeler started studying the transportation industries. He notes the role that Keeler played in more fully integrating the political support view of regulation with consumer and production theory, and his more nuanced approach to explaining regulation that considered the characteristics of specific industries.

Subsequently, he goes on to briefly describe the problems in aviation and surface freight transportation during the regulatory era, the tone of regulatory change in those industries, Keeler's early assessments of deregulation, and developments in those industries since those early assessments. While noting the surprises that have occurred in these industries, Button also notes that for the most part, Keeler's short- and long-term predictions regarding the impacts of regulatory change have held up. He concludes by noting that many other observers did not have such a positive view of the regulatory reforms that were taking place at the time.

As highlighted previously, Professor Keeler performed extensive research on airlines and the changes occurring after deregulation. He predicted an increasingly competitive environment between LCCs and legacy carriers, and an increasing role for potential competition. Chapter 3, by David Gillen and Ashish Lall examines recent changes in the nature of competition and in business models in the airline industry in the United States.

In an extensive review of recent literature on airline pricing and airline business models, Gillen and Lall find a significant transformation in the industry since 2000, with LCCs expanding market shares and increasingly competing with legacies, with legacies reducing network sizes and cutting capacities, and with a new form of carrier—the ultra-low-cost carrier (ULCC) emerging to meet underserved markets of price sensitive consumers.

Gillen and Lall highlight the recent research findings that show the important role of LCCs and ULCCs in reducing fares on the routes that they enter, on routes that are adjacent or substitute routes, and on routes where presence at one of the endpoints suggests they may become a competitor in the future (potential competition). Moreover, they show that recent research suggests the role of legacy entry in promoting competition has diminished over time. They suggest that the US airline market has become commoditized to a certain extent, preventing legacies from maintaining their traditional advantages for brand loyal customers.

They also show the large number of changes that have occurred in airline business models over recent years, with LCC and legacy strategies converging to a certain extent. For example, LCCs are increasingly using larger airports, providing connecting services, and using a variety of aircraft, while legacies are unbundling traditionally bundled services and increasingly relying on ancillary revenues. Moreover, they highlight the large variation in business models among airlines in the same general class (e.g., LCCs), and the enduring features of business strategy that have made some airlines successful (e.g., Southwest)—even in difficult times. In summary, Gillen and Lall's chapter provides a number of insights into the long-term changes in the airline industry that have occurred with deregulation, the evolution of business models, and the likely changes in airline business models in the future.

Rolf Fare, Taylor McKenzie, Wesley Wilson, and Wenfeng Yan (Chapter 4) examine productivity gains in the US railroad industry between 1983 and 2008, with a specific focus on the role of mergers in enhancing productivity. Using a nonparametric approach, the authors apply two different types of Data Envelopment Analysis (DEA) models to assess efficiency and productivity gains in the industry—a single technology frontier model and a dynamic technology model.

In applying the single technology model, Fare, et al. obtain several interesting findings, including: (1) marked improvement of technical efficiency over time, with relative stability in the efficiency rankings of firms, (2) little change in scale efficiency over time, with firm sizes remaining stable, and (3) no effects of mergers on overall industry technical efficiency or scale efficiency, although some significant effects occur for individual mergers. The authors interpret these results to support the idea that US railroad mergers have not had large cost savings effects, although they acknowledge that the scale results may reflect data construction that combines unmerged firms into one observation prior to a merger.

The authors' dynamic Attribute-Incorporated Malmquist Productivity Index (AMPI) also shows large productivity gains for the industry, overall, with an annual growth rate in AMPI of 3.6%. In breaking this down, they find large gains from improvements in technology (2.1% per year) and large gains from changes in network attributes (average length of haul, percent of shipments in unit trains, and route miles—average of 1.4% per year). The authors conclude that large efficiency gains have occurred in the US railroad industry since deregulation, but that mergers were not a major cause of such gains. The chapter also shows how an enhanced understanding of productivity, efficiency, and their causes in the transportation industries might be obtained from nonparametric methods.

The next chapter, by Curtis Grimm and Russell Pittman, takes into consideration Keeler's prediction suggesting significant merger activity among Class 1 carriers in the US following regulatory reform in the railroad industry. Indeed, these authors reveal the potential for noncompetitive rate setting due to postregulatory reform mergers resulting in two major Class 1 rail carriers providing service in the Western US (BNSF and the Union Pacific) and two major Class 1 rail carriers providing service for the Eastern US [Norfolk Southern (NS) and CSX]. Their analysis of the post-Staggers US railroad industry focuses on competition policy: evaluating potential reductions in competition from merger activity and potential policies to increase competition through competitive access. Grimm and Pittman also expand their analysis to examine rail competitive issues in North America more broadly and globally, particularly the EU and Russia.

Grimm and Pittman focus the analysis of US railroad competition and merger policy by examining the application of traditional antitrust analysis to the railroad industry. This is a complex issue, one which Keeler urged his student Grimm to study in his doctoral dissertation. They argue that rather than focusing on the number of carriers serving a particular route, merger analysis should often identify the number of independent alternatives between origin and destination business economic areas (BEAs) as a more accurate definition of the market. They argue that using this broader market definition is often a better way to assess whether a given merger is likely to result in competitive harm to shippers. When expanding the North American regulatory reform railroad analysis to include Mexico and Canada, the two major US trading partners in North America, Grimm and Pittman identify the potential for vertical foreclosure as a possible competitive harm from end-to-end mergers. The authors provide a critique of approaches, such as dividing revenue between integrated and unintegrated carriers, to address welfare shortcomings associated with vertical foreclosure. Their critique reveals the shortcomings associated with these approaches, and the authors provide suggestions to address these shortcomings.

Grimm and Pittman's examination of competition policy issues outside of North America is in keeping with Keeler's earlier observation that rail competition associated with changing economic policy was a global issue (See for example Keeler's work on railroad policy in Australia (Keeler, 1977)). In the spirit of this acknowledgment of the global shift in policy, the authors examine the movement from state-owned rail monopolies to vertically separated privatized providers of rail transport service (both passenger and freight) in Europe and Russia. The analysis focuses on third party access, and its benefits and shortcomings. Overall, Grimm and Pittman's global analysis of competition policy in the rail industry reveals that while a more market oriented approach toward railroad operations has contributed to a more efficient and profitable industry, care should be taken by policymakers when implementing competition policy in this industry.

While Grimm and Pittman identify a number of competitive concerns associated with post-Staggers merger activity in the United States, James Nolan, Eric Micheels, and Lindsay Pollard (Chapter 6) note that a lot of insight about various concerns associated with rail mergers might be obtained by examining submissions in STB merger proceedings. Using a unique dataset of submissions in a historical

US railroad merger proceeding, they identify common themes and explore whether such themes still persist.

As highlighted by Nolan, et al., no US railroad merger has occurred since Conrail was acquired by NS and CSX in 1999. The authors explore the rejected cross-border merger of 1999 between Canadian National (CN) and BNSF, performing a qualitative analysis of the most frequent issues mentioned in all submissions by interested parties to the STB. This merger proposal is significant, as it spurred a moratorium on mergers by the STB, and no merger has occurred since.

After identifying common railroad and merger terms, the authors find three frequently mentioned issues in the submissions to the STB regarding the proposed CNBN merger. These include the issues of "captive shipper", "improved service," and "trackage rights." While noting that their qualitative analysis does not identify context, the authors surmise that the frequency of these terms suggests concern over increased captivity and the need for competitive access remedies to ensure adequate competition and service levels. Interestingly, in examining various statements made and provisions regarding a more recently proposed cross-border merger between Canadian Pacific (CP) and NS, they find that the merger proposal contained regulated access provisions to mitigate concerns over increased captivity and concerns over service quality. The authors suggest that these were made to increase the likelihood that such a merger would be approved. Nolan, Micheels, and Pollard's chapter shows how qualitative analysis might be used to gain insight into future merger policy and concerns, and suggests that future proposed rail mergers in North America are likely to yield similar concerns.

Chapter 7 written by Wayne Talley examines the influence of technology, government investment, and international trade policies on the growth and development of ocean container shipping—the ocean transportation of cargo in a standardized container. An examination of the economics of this industry contributes to a better understanding of how ocean container shipping carriers and ports have met consumer demand in a globalized society. Talley's presentation of technological advancements in this transport sector includes an explanation of the significance of the shift from shipping products on pallets to using standard-size containers (starting in 1955). He reveals that the use of containers substantially lowered the costs of ocean transportation by reducing the labor content in transferring cargo between ships and land (truck and rail) vehicles. His analysis shows significant improvements in the quality of ocean container shipping, attributable to government funding for such projects as the Suez, Panama, and Nicaragua canals, the opening of the Northeast Passage, and China's one belt-one road initiative. The decline in the transportation costs incurred in transporting containerized cargo due to such investments also reduced cargo inventory costs of shippers. Government policy promoting international trade underscores the significance of shippers meeting customer demands for imports. Indeed, Talley observes that international trade policies that include the General Agreement on Tariffs and Trade (GATT), the North America Free Trade Agreement (NAFTA), and the Central America Free Trade Agreement (CAFTA) promoted growth in ocean container shipping by lowering barriers to trade. He follows this multinational analysis of ocean container shipping by focusing on the economic activity of this transport sector in the US.

Highlighting this country allows for an examination of national liberalization policies that influence rate setting and the industry's labor market. The author concludes his analysis of the United States by noting that despite US liberalization policies, limitations still remain due to the prohibition of cabotage that protects US flagged container ships from foreign competition in the United States.

In the following chapter, B. Starr McMullen discusses the shift in the focus of policymakers, and thus some transportation economists, from questions about the impacts of economic regulation to those regarding the financing of transportation infrastructure and the allocation of scarce public resources between modes. Improved fuel efficiency of cars due, partly to the enforcement of corporate average fuel economy (CAFE) requirements, has resulted in more vehicle miles traveled (VMT) using less fuel. Hence, roads and bridges experience increased wear and tear as drivers travel more; but highway funding, reliant on per gallon gas tax receipts, is lower compared to potential receipts from a less fuel efficient fleet of cars, all else equal.

Recognizing the shortcomings associated with depending on revenues from a fuel tax, McMullen provides a review of work on the VMT tax as an alternative to the fuel tax. Her nuanced analysis argues that the VMT tax, by taxing usage, provides a disincentive to driving (thus producing less VMT and road damage), while helping to reduce emissions compared to a fuel tax. McMullen shows that while the impact of a VMT is slightly more regressive than a fuel tax, the impact is relatively minor (less than $10/year). Concerns that households in rural areas would be harmed appear to be unfounded as, for the most part, they pay slightly less under a VMT than a fuel tax whereas urban areas pay slightly more, due in part to the fact that rural households usually have a fleet of vehicles with lower fuel efficiency than urban areas. However, McMullen cautions that these impacts can vary considerably between different urban areas and different rural areas.

A more serious problem with a fuel tax is due to the fact that road damage increases exponentially for vehicle weights over 26,000 pounds whereas fuel consumption increases at a more proportional rate, resulting in heavy trucks underpaying for the damage they do to the road under a fuel tax. For heavy vehicles there is the more refined VMT tax option of using an equivalent single axle load (ESAL) tax that allows drivers the option to lower the price per mile they are taxed by presenting the opportunity to employ truck configurations with lower ESALs that cause less damage to the road.

McMullen's analysis of resource allocation for transportation infrastructure concludes with an examination of the multimodal decision policymakers face when deciding how many resources to devote to roads maintenance and repair, and to the funding of public transit. She observes that current estimation methodologies grossly overestimate the benefits of highway alternative investment due to the overestimation of passenger/drivers shifting modes of transportation. In sum, this chapter highlights the benefits of using the tools of economic theory to assess policies intended to employ cost-effective methods to finance transportation infrastructure.

In Chapter 9, Philip Viton notes the increase in policies aimed at introducing private sector competition in traditionally public-sector industries (e.g., mail service, education, transit, and roads), due to tight public budgets and a reluctance by taxpayers to fund budget deficits. In light of these policies, an important policy question is: How should the public provider respond to the entry of private firms?

To answer this, Viton develops a theoretical model of a public urban transit provider that aims to maximize community welfare along a transportation corridor in response to the entry of a profit-maximizing private provider. The situation is modeled as a Cournot-Nash game, where each player (i.e., the public and private providers) takes the other's actions as given at each stage. After parameterizing the model to reflect the conditions that prevail in large urban areas during peak periods, the author simulates the impact of private entry and public response for a variety of possible actions by the public transit provider.

Several interesting findings are obtained by Viton, including that entry always results in a social welfare improvement—regardless of the response taken by the public provider. In assessing the responses that should be taken by the public provider, he finds that the optimal response to entry in terms of social welfare is to drastically reduce fares. As a result, traffic congestion is reduced substantially, but at the cost of a substantial increase in public deficits.

Because of this, he explores various alternatives to the social welfare maximizing response, including the public provider exiting the market (privatization), the public provider maintaining the status quo in terms of its previous service, and the public provider maximizing social welfare conditional on various budget constraints. He finds that while the only policy that would eliminate public sector deficits completely would be public provider exit (privatization), the status quo, and especially attempting to maximize social welfare conditional on a budget constraint, are preferred on social welfare grounds.

Finally, he notes that a large portion of the welfare benefits of entry and response are achieved from entry alone, suggesting the possibility that a public provider could try to provide the benefits that would occur with entry by providing its own differentiated service alongside its existing service. However, he also notes that this might require the public provider act to deter entry by the private sector, which would be extremely costly. Viton concludes that the public and private providers can work together to provide product differentiation to maximize social welfare.

Randy Pozdena (Chapter 10) makes the case for a dramatic change in the role of government in transportation. In examining the appropriate level of authority over transportation systems (i.e., local, state, or national), the link between costs imposed by transportation users and the prices they pay, and the desirability for public or private provision of transportation facilities and services, he makes a strong argument for reducing the level of involvement in transportation by the federal government, for pricing transportation facilities based on costs imposed, and for privatizing transportation services.

Pozdena highlights transportation funding patterns, showing that half of all government transportation spending uses revenues that are not obtained from transportation activities, that most revenues obtained from transportation use are not based on costs imposed, and that significant modal cross-subsidies exist (particularly from highways to public transit). In examining the question of the appropriate level of authority, the author uses data from the National Household Travel Survey and the US Commodity Flow survey, to show that most passenger trips and freight trips are for short distances (with some exceptions—e.g., air travel, freight rail, pipeline, and water). He uses this, along with evidence (or lack thereof) of the likelihood of spillover effects, network effects, and economies of scale to argue that the large amount of federal oversight of transportation that exists is unwarranted. This is particularly true for transit, where it is obvious that the beneficiaries are local residents, and for highways, where short-distance travel dominates.

The author also notes problems in the way transportation services are priced. Transportation facilities (particularly highways) are priced in a way that is unrelated (or remotely related) to the costs imposed by the users of those facilities. Pozdena highlights how this leads to over-used, worn-out facilities in some cases, and overbuilt facilities in others. Pricing facilities based on time of day, wear imposed, etc. would enable more appropriate decisions by users and allow improved investment decisions. The author also argues that the inefficiencies and lack of responsiveness of transportation systems to the needs of users is made worse by the prevention of private alternatives. Highlighting how technological advances are enabling private provision of transportation services (e.g., GPS technology for collecting tolls and internet technology for shared ride services), Pozdena argues that more privatization of transportation services is warranted.

Pozdena makes compelling arguments for reducing the role of the federal government, and for government in general, in the provision of transportation services. In examining the way that transportation pricing and finance has developed in the United States, the chapter also provides an example of how current transportation pricing and investment has been shaped by history.

Kenneth Small (Chapter 11) notes that economists have not reached a consensus on the key impacts of CAFE standards. Economists disagree on the extent that CAFE standards reduce fossil fuel consumption and carbon emissions, the impacts they have on vehicle manufacturing costs and vehicle fuel costs, and the impacts they have on the adoption of and investment in various vehicle technologies. As Small explains, there are a number of uncertainties that complicate the evaluation of the impacts of CAFE standards, including (1) the extent to which consumers consider the full value of fuel savings associated with various vehicles in their purchasing decisions, (2) the way that consumers form expectations about future fuel prices, (3) the extent to which consumers drive more miles in reaction to savings in fuel economy, (4) the way that used car markets change in reaction to CAFE standards, (5) the actions that vehicle manufacturers take to meet higher fuel economy standards, and (6) the overall level of fuel prices in the future.

To address some of these uncertainties and the role they play in influencing the measured impacts of CAFE standards, he performs a number of simulations with various modifications to the National Energy Modeling System (NEMS). Small shows that accounting for manufacturers' pricing responses to higher CAFE standards is an extremely important consideration. He shows that if manufacturers did not adjust vehicle prices in response to higher CAFE standards, average fuel efficiency would be lower and manufacturers would invest in more expensive technologies. The author notes that some studies evaluating CAFE impacts do not account for manufacturer pricing responses, suggesting an obvious avenue for improving such studies.

In addition, he shows that consumer valuation of fuel cost savings and the overall level of fuel prices have important impacts on the net costs of higher CAFE standards. He finds that the impacts of increasing CAFE standards on vehicle manufacturing costs and fuel costs depend heavily on the proportion of actual fuel savings considered by consumers in their automobile purchasing decisions. When consumers severely undervalue these savings, CAFE standards have a much bigger policy impact than when consumers take the full value of fuel savings into account in their decisions. Interestingly, in examining how policy impacts depend on overall fuel prices, he finds that an increase in CAFE standards has a much bigger net cost (vehicle manufacturing cost increases less fuel cost savings) when oil prices are lower than expected (although environmental benefits are largest in this case).

In exploring the impacts of other factors in evaluating CAFE standards, Small finds that consumer price expectations, the way the CAFE standard varies with vehicle size, and the magnitude of the fines seem to have little impact. The study contributes to our understanding of how the impacts of CAFE (and policy in general) can vary depending on a number of uncertainties and assumptions. Moreover, the study aids in intelligent policy formulation by showing how the impacts of CAFE depend on a number of factors.

While the policy trend toward less stringent economic regulation prevailed in the US during the latter part of the 20th century, greater emphasis has been placed on stronger safety regulation. Keeler recognized the importance of such regulation in his work examining the efficacy of highway safety regulation. Further analysis of surface transportation safety policy is addressed in Chapters 12 and 13. In Chapter 12 Thomas Corsi reveals declining large truck fatality and crash rates following regulatory reform in the trucking industry until 2009, and an increasing crash rate thereafter. Corsi reports the cost to society and to trucking companies due to truck crashes and highlights the federal government's recognition of the importance of highway safety in the motor carrier industry. An example of government emphasis on highway safety is the establishment of the Federal Motor Carrier Safety Administration (FMCSA) in 1999. As Corsi observes, the mission of this administration is to reduce crashes, injuries, and fatalities involving large trucks and buses. The collection and dissemination of accurate safety performance data (including results of compliance reviews, safety audits, roadside inspections, crashes, and other safety indicators) is a key activity of the FMCSA that contributes to it meeting the goals of this mission. Access to this data provides vital information to the shippers as well as to brokers and third party logistic providers (3PLs) to use when contracting with trucking carriers. Corsi argues that these noncarrier entities have a monetary incentive to employ carriers with strong safety records. His chapter provides support for this argument by initially presenting an in depth analysis on the quality of large truck crash data available to shippers and broker/3PLs. He then follows that analysis by exploring the "chain of responsibility" in truck crash liability cases by focusing on the responsibility of shippers and of broker/third party logistics providers in selecting motor carriers to transport freight in interstate commerce. He concludes by noting that the best hope for improving large truck crashes is for broker/third party logistics providers and for shippers to be vigilant in their efforts to insure that the motor carrier they contract out to operates in a safe and efficient manner. The liability costs associated with truck crashes presents an incentive for these entities to seek carriers with strong driver safety records. The availability of trucking safety performance records presents shippers and broker/third party logistics providers the ability to make informed choices.

Surface transportation safety concerns are not limited to large trucks as these vehicles share the road with passenger vehicles. In addition, these smaller motor vehicles are also involved in a nontrivial number of crash fatalities. In the succeeding chapter, Richard Fowles and Peter Loeb examine several determinants of motor vehicle fatalities with emphasis on the influence of new motor vehicle technology. Such an analysis is timely given automakers shift toward building cars with new and improved safety devices such as driverless technology. Due to insufficient data available to directly examine the safety performance of driverless cars compared to the performance of conventional cars, these authors specify fatality models that account for a car fleet's model year. The empirical approach used in this chapter is novel in that it considers the determinants of motor vehicle fatality rates using classical econometric methods and a new Bayesian technique developed by Edward Leamer to address the ambiguity and uncertainty associated with empirical models which are not addressed using classical methods. This approach requires estimation of millions of fatality crash models, which enhances confidence in the empirical findings as well as enhancing confidence in policy measures suggested to reduce motor vehicle fatality crashes. The key results derived from this thorough empirical approach are supportive of fleet modernization as a contributor to improved vehicle safety performance.

References

Bailey, E.E., Baumol, W.J., 1984. Deregulation and the theory of contestable markets. Yale J. Reg. 1, 111–137.

Bitzan, J.D., Keeler, T.E., 2003. Productivity growth and some of its determinants in the deregulated U.S. railroad industry. South. Econ. J. 70 (2), 232–253.

Bitzan, J.D., Keeler, T.E., 2007. Economies of density and regulatory change in the U.S. railroad freight industry. J. Law Econ. 50, 157–179.

Bitzan, J.D., Keeler, T.E., 2011. Intermodal traffic, regulatory change and carbon energy conservation in US freight transport. Appl. Econ. 43, 3945–3963.

Bitzan, J.D., Keeler, T.E., 2014. The evolution of U.S. rail freight pricing in the post-deregulation era: revenues versus marginal costs for five commodity types. Transportation 41, 305–324.

Bitzan, J.D., Peoples, J.H., 2016. A comparative analysis of cost change for low-cost, full-service, and other carriers in the US airline industry. Res. Transp. Econ. 56, 25–41.

Borenstein, S., 2011. Moving beyond deregulation: why can't US airlines make money? Am. Econ. Rev. Papers Proc. 101 (3), 233–237.

Bottasso, A., Conti, M., 2017. The cost structure of the airport industry: methodological issues and empirical evidence. In: Bitzan, J.D., Peoples, J.H. (Eds.), Advances in Airline Economics, Volume 6: Airport Economics. Emerald Group Publishing Limited, Bingley, UK.

Call, G.D., Keeler, T.E., 1985. Airline deregulation, fares, and market behavior: some empirical evidence. In: Daughety (Ed.), Analytical Studies in Transport Economics. Cambridge University Press, Cambridge, UK, pp. 221–247.

Crandall, R.W., Gruenspecht, H.K., Keeler, T.E., Lave, L.B., 1986. Regulating the Automobile. The Brookings Institution, Washington.

Crandall, R.W., Keeler, T.E., 1987. Public policy and the private auto. In: Gordon, R., Jacoby, H., Zimmerman, M. (Eds.), Essays in Honor of Morris A. Adelman. Massachusetts Institute of Technology Press, Cambridge, pp. 137–160.

Crandall, R.W., Keeler, T.E., Lave, L.B., 1982. The cost of automobile safety and emissions regulations to the consumer: some preliminary results. Am. Econ. Rev. 72 (2), 324–327, Papers and Proceedings of the Ninety-Fourth Annual Meeting of the American Economic Association.

Gallamore, R.E., 1999. Regulation and innovation: lessons from the American railroad industry. In: Gomez-Ibanez, J., Tye, W.B., Winston, C. (Eds.), Essays in Transportation Economics and Policy: A Handbook in Honor of John R. Meyer. The Brookings Institution, Washington, DC, pp. 493–530.

Harris, R.G., Keeler, T.E., 1981. Determinants of railroad profitability: an econometric study. In: Boyer, K., Shepherd, W. (Eds.), Economic Regulation: Essays in Honor of James R. Nelson. Michigan State University Press, East Lansing, pp. 37–53.

Henrickson, K.E., Wilson, W.W., 2016. Convergence of low-cost and legacy airline operations. In: Bitzan, J.D., Peoples, J.H., Wilson, W.W. (Eds.), Advances in Airline Economics, Volume 5: Airline Efficiency. Emerald Group Publishing Limited, Bingley, UK.

Huschelrath, K., Muller, K., 2012. Low cost carriers and the evolution of the domestic U.S. airline industry. Compet. Regul. Network Ind. 13 (2), 133–159.

Kanafani, A., Keeler, T.E., 1989. New entrants and safety: some statistical evidence on the effects of airline deregulation. In: Moses, L., Savage, I. (Eds.), Transportation Safety in an Age of Deregulation. Oxford University Press, Oxford, UK, pp. 115–128.

Kanafani, A., Keeler, T.E., 1990. Air deregulation and safety: some econometric evidence from time series. Logist. Transp. Rev. 26 (3), 203–210.

Kanafani, A., Keeler, T.E., Sathisan, S.K., 1993. Airline safety posture: evidence from service-difficulty reports. J. Transp. Eng. 119 (4), 655–664.

Keeler, T.E., 1970. Airport costs and congestion. Am. Econ. 14, 47–53.

Keeler, T.E., 1972. Airline regulation and market performance. Bell J. Econ. Manage. Sci. 3 (2), 399–424.

Keeler, T.E., 1974. Railroad costs, returns to scale, and excess capacity. Rev. Econ. Stat. 56 (2), 201–208.

Keeler, T.E., 1975. Regulation and trunk air fares. U.S. Senate Subcomittee on Administrative Practices and Procedures, Oversight of Civil Aeronautics Board Practices and Procedures, 2, pp. 1296–1305.

Keeler, T.E., 1977. Regulation and modal market shares in long-haul freight transport: a statistical comparison of Australia and the United States. In: Nelson, J.R., Whitten, H.O. (Eds.), Foreign Regulatory Experiments: Implications for the U.S.: An Analysis and Evaluation of Foreign Transportation Regulatory Experience. U.S. Department of Transportation, Federal Railroad Administration, Washington.

Keeler, T.E., 1981. The revolution in airline regulation. In: Weiss, L., Klass, M. (Eds.), Case Studies in Regulation: Revolution and Reform. Little Brown & Co., Boston, pp. 53–85.

Keeler, T.E., 1983. Railroads, Freight, and Public Policy. The Brookings Institution, Washington.

Keeler, T.E., 1984. Theories of regulation and the deregulation movement. Public Choice 44, 103–145.

Keeler, T.E., 1986. Public policy and productivity in the trucking industry: some evidence on the effects of highway investments, deregulation, and the 55 MPH speed limit. Am. Econ.

Rev. 76 (2), 153–158, Papers and Proceedings of the Ninety-Eighth Annual Meeting of the American Economic Association.

Keeler, T.E., 1989. Deregulation and scale economies in the U.S. trucking industry: econometric extension of the survivor principle. J. Law Econ. 32 (2), 229–253.

Keeler, T.E., 1991. Airline deregulation and market performance: the economic basis for regulatory reform and lessons from the US experience. In: Banister, D., Button, K. (Eds.), Transport in a Free Market Economy. Macmillan, London, pp. 121–170.

Keeler, T.E., 1994. Highway safety, economic behavior, and driving environment. Am. Econ. Rev. 84 (3), 684–693.

Keeler, T.E., Abrahams, M., 1981. Market structure, pricing, and service quality in the airline industry under deregulation. In: Sichel, W., Gies, T. (Eds.), Applications of Economic Principles in Public Utility Industries. Michigan Business Studies, Ann Arbor, pp. 103–120.

Keeler, T.E., Small, K.A., 1977. Optimal peak-load pricing, investment, and service levels on urban expressways. J. Political Econ. 85 (1), 1–25.

Keeler, T.E., Ying, J.S., 1988. Measuring the benefits of a large public investment: the case of the U.S. federal-aid highway system. J. Public Econ. 36, 68–85.

Leick, R., Wensveen, J., 2014. The airline business. In: Prokop, D. (Ed.), The Business of Transportation. Praeger Publishing, Santa Barbara, pp. 65–99.

Meyer, J.R., Kain, J.F., Wohl, M., 1965. The Urban Transportation Problem. Harvard University Press, Cambridge.

Peltzman, S., 1975. The effect of automobile regulation. J. Political Econ. 83 (4), 677–725.

Peltzman, S., 1976. Toward a more general theory of regulation. J. Law. Econ. 19, 211–240.

Stigler, G.J., 1971. The theory of economic regulation. Bell J. Econ. 2, 1–21.

U.S. Government Accountability Office, 2014. Airport privatization: limited interest despite FAA's pilot program. GAO Highlights, GAO-15-42.

Ying, J.S., Keeler, T.E., 1991. Pricing in a deregulated environment: the motor carrier experience. Rand J. Econ. 22 (2), 264–273.

Theodore Keeler's analysis of the early effects of deregulation of US transportation industries

Kenneth Button

George Mason University, Fairfax, VA, USA

Chapter Outline

Dedication

In the late 1970s, I began working on the implications of what Americans, often exaggeratedly, call "economic deregulation", a process that had began in the United Kingdom in 1968 when the Transport Act of that year removed market restrictions on the trucking industry. As part of a wider geographical interest in the topic, I spent a large part of 1982 at the Universities of British Columbia and of California, Berkeley, on leave of absence from my position at Loughborough University. After all, in 1977, with the Air Cargo Deregulation Act, the United States had belated realized that trying to regulate prices and market entry was a rather ineffectual way of furthering human welfare. I was interested in seeing what was happening in North America as the all-too-frequent transtlantic reinventing of the wheel, in this case market liberalization, occurred there.

At UBC, I spent time with Steve Morrison, who later went on to have a distinguished career at Northeastern University and had been one of Ted Keeler's PhD students at Berkeley. At the time, I was more familiar with Keeler's work on urban transportation than with that on aviation and railroads—both of which functioned in very different institutional environments in the United Kingdom to the United States. Morrison, however, with his near addiction to aviation and Garland Chow, with his equal enthrallment with intercity freight transportation, widened my interest into areas Keeler was then actively engaged in. When I moved south from UBC to Berkeley for the second part of my North America visit, I sought out Keeler. We had a few discussions on matters regarding regulation, but my stay was short. It struck me that his approach to the relevant issues was more in line with those of UK economists of the time with a background in Oxford, such as Arthur Brown who had taught me. Keeler was more interested in applying economics to real-life issues than in the development of abstract theory that, while intellectually stimulating, often does little to solve the immediate problems confronting society.

Resulting from this rather modest encounter, Keeler and I produced a short paper for the *Economic Journal* regarding general issues in transportation regulation, and later, Keeler contributed a paper on US airline regulatory reform to a volume on *Transport in a Free Market Economy* that I edited with David Banister.

2.1   Introduction

For anyone studying economics in the late 1960s and early 1970s, the dominant theme of virtually all courses in regulation was the role of the benign regulator in ensuring the public interest is served. While the Anglo-Saxon idea was that markets would deliver the maximum social welfare if perfect and pure competition prevailed, there was always the real danger that market imperfections would creep in. In this light, the job of regulatory agencies was to diagnose such imperfections and initiate and enforce laws and practices to eliminate them, or at least mitigate their effects. This was, for example, a period of regulatory bodies seeking Marshall-Lerner and Ramsey pricing to initially restrain monopoly and subsequently, if the latter were not practical, to ensure somehow that at least second-best conditions prevailed in these markets. Outside of the United States, in economies like France, conversely the Continental philosophy on regulation ruled. Here, while markets were not entirely eschewed as in Soviet style states, the onus of proof was that markets produce superior results to the planning and extensive oversight and regulations espoused by graduates of the Grande Écoles.

The idea that some forms of economic regulation are necessary in some markets is not novel, and the on-going debate is a matter of its degree and nature. Economic regulation certainly dates to the days of the mercantilists. Even with the Enlightenment, ideas that markets need the occasional tweak to handle malfunctions were prevalent in Smith's *Wealth of Nations*, which foresaw a need for government to, at least, invest in public infrastructure because of failures in private finance markets. The onset of the Industrial Revolution brought to the fore questions about handling the inevitable rents that accompanied the emergence of economies of scale in production, and later problems of empty cores when competition was accompanied by significant fixed costs. The institutional outcome in some countries was to initiate economic regulations seeking to counter distorted markets, whereas in others, and notably continental Europe, state ownership was commonplace (Kahn, 1970, 1971).

It was this sort of economic environment that Ted Keeler would have encountered as a student at Reed, and more so later at MIT. But he also studied economics at a time when thinking about the role of economic regulation was going through something of a transformation. Experience had shown that in many cases, regulation did not produce desired results, and theoretically it was also discovered that by changing a few assumptions about motivation, the idea that regulators always served the public interest is neither useful nor realistic. But the realignment of this thinking took time, and changes in policy took even longer. One problem was that if traditional economic regulations were removed, what was to replace them? Monopolies still existed, yet many public goods were still socially desirable, as Smith observed. This problem was addressed, in part, by new ideas, or at least the reassessment of some old ones, concerning market structure and the way firms behave, with the development of more efficient ways of regulating when regulation is still believed to be necessary (Button and Keeler, 1993; Keeler and Foreman, 1998).

A general shift in policy occurred in the late 1970s and 1980s in the United States toward what is often misleadingly called deregulation. It was in fact a liberalization of economic regulatory structures, with many regulations remaining, with some only modified, and with matters of safety and environmental regulation tightened. This policy era has been extensively studied from an academic perspective, and Keeler was on the vanguard of such analysis. The transportation sector, possibly because of more available and better data, coupled with the pioneering nature of its reforms, and because transportation experienced fewer autonomous dynamic technology shifts compared to other sectors such as telecommunications, has arguably been the most closely examined of the US liberalized industries.[1]

Ted Keeler made important contributions to the economic regulation of literature, much of it relating to transportation. This chapter does not strictly offer a critique of Keeler's work on transportation regulation, although this tone is not absent, but rather we set the outcomes against his applied analysis as conducted through the 1980s; thereafter for a period, he shifted most of his research focus to health economics. Here, we focus on economic regulation of transportation in the United States—including the regulation of fares/rates, quantities, and market entry restrictions—although there is some limited overlap with social regulation, most notably involving environmental concerns. Our focus is even narrower than this in that Keeler's work on the automobile sector and on matters not pertaining to traditional notions of economic efficiency, for example, those of safety and pollution externalities, are not directly included in this work.

This chapter, in rather a broad way, may be viewed in the same vein as the exercise conducted in the later 1980s by the former Chair of the Civil Aeronautics Board (CAB), Alfred Kahn (1988), as presented to the annual conference of the American Economic Association. Kahn looked exclusively at the surprises brought about by airline deregulation a decade after the enactment of the Airline Deregulation Act. Here we are mainly taking the output of Keeler's early work on deregulation up until the mid-1980s and evaluating if the trends and patterns he found at that time have endured into the present. In other words, was Keeler just observing short-term disruptions or instead was he able to identify genuine structural shifts in transportation markets? This is not intended in any way to imply that Keeler did not contribute to the transportation regulation literature after 1986 (our cut-off point). While much of his engagement for a period immediately after 1986 shifted elsewhere, mainly into health economics,

---

[1] This is not to say the United States led the way in deregulation. The UK 1968 Transport Act that freed trucking from market entry controls other than for safety reasons, set the trend. UK trucking never had its rates regulated, on the very elementary economic grounds that if you regulate Q, then the market establishes P (Button and Chow, 1982).

his subsequent return to transportation matters from the late 1980s was as broad as before, looking at trucking (Keeler, 1989; Ying and Keeler, 1991), air transportation (Keeler, 1991), and railroads (Bitzan and Keeler, 2003, 2007, 2014). It is often of a more reflective nature taking a long-term perspective, and whilst touched upon here, is not the core of the discussion.

While the underlying approach we take is like that adopted by Kahn, there are significant differences. The timeframe between the expectations of Keeler and outcomes exceeds that examined by Kahn, and the modes covered here are more extensive since modes of surface transportation are examined in addition to aviation. Perhaps more importantly, Kahn was in part assessing his own, not always public, views of his success as a regulator in his retrospective paper of 1989. After all he was the man who deregulated the US air passenger airlines and must have made use of the findings of his staff (Button, 2015). By contrast, Keeler was a *de facto* observer and commentator and thus his views and calculations are more fully public. But in line with Kahn's historical piece, this overview will focus almost completely on the United States and on the economic regulation or liberalization of transportation industry.

In doing this, we accept that all sensible economists appreciate that trying to predict in any detail what will happen when market forces are given more play is inevitably a fool's game, except on occasions for the "lucky" few. However, they, nonetheless, often offer general guidance to assist in policy formulation.

2.2   Applied economic analysis

Before moving to the core of the chapter, a few words are necessary regarding Keeler's (1984) approach to regulatory analysis and to economics, in general. His economic research on transportation, accepting Backhouse and Biddle (2000) Backhouse and Biddle's (2000) highlighting of the flexibility of such a moniker, has been very much that of a traditional applied economist. By this, I mean someone who applies both qualitative and quantitative techniques to examine an economic issue. His analyses have not only often been innovative in terms of theory, but much more so in that he often applied state-of-the-art methodology, coupled with available empirical information, often setting his work within a dynamic institutional setting to explore how markets respond to new stimuli.

Ironically, the role of applied economics has often been downplayed in the profession, despite the insistence of Alfred Marshall and others of its importance. As Backhouse and Biddle put it (Backhouse and Biddle, 2000, p. 5), "… at least by the turn of the century [1900], and probably earlier, it had become common for economists to talk and think in terms of applying applied political economy/economics." The recent mainstream seems to have been drifting away from this and as Noble Laureate, Ronald Coase (2006) states, the profession is now strong on theory but weak on facts and this has led economics into error.[2] Having said this, the microeconomic

---

[2] Of specific relevance to regulatory economics, this has recently been a position supported by Littlechild (2008), as both an academic and a regulator. Littlechild is the person who developed the concept of price–cap regulation.

regulatory reforms of the 1970s and 1980s in the United States that Keeler researched was considerably influenced by economics.

The standard intellectual and technical groundwork for the modern study of economic deregulation was laid out in a succession of empirically motivated theoretical papers from the early 1970s. Key contributions by Stigler (1971), Posner (1971), as well as Peltzman (1976) and the overall consistency of their conclusions in spite of differences in their detailed focus pointed to the almost inevitable failure of the public interest concept when looking at regulatory regimes from the early 1970s. Rather than focusing on the welfare of the broader population, it turned out that the system of regulation that had evolved was often in place to serve the private interests of various, powerful industry stakeholders.

While some researchers highlighted this new "regulatory capture" concept within economic regulation, the 1970s and 1980s saw the emergence of other novel ideas, or more strictly the rediscovery of older ideas stemming from English economists such as Chadwick and Coase, of how markets will function under various institutional structures. Alternative approaches emerged to replace regulations originally designed in the 19th and early 20th centuries that, while initially intended to control excessive rent seeking by monopoly suppliers or powerful vested interests, had transmogrified into instruments that protected such rents. These ideas, for example, included the concept of contestable markets whereby it was asserted that the economic power of market incumbents was largely limited by the credible threat of entry by other firms outside that market (Baumol et al., 1982). As for the need to regulate or publicly own transportation infrastructure, Demsetz (1968) had shown that competition for the market could be enacted with regular auctioning of concessions to operate in the market. Added to this, empirical work by the likes of Levine (1965) on airlines showed that when economic regulations were relaxed, considerable user benefits typically emerged. In other words, arguments were coalescing that deregulation could well be in the public interest.

But even while accepting the power of these ideas and findings, a rational economic outcome often does not emerge in imperfect political markets. There are transactions costs in making changes, and rather than enacting drastic reforms, tinkering with an existing regulatory system is often preferred. This was what was done in practice with a series of acts affecting the largely bankrupt US railroad industry from 1970 until the final and major deregulatory actions contained in the Staggers Act of 1980. Even at this period with major intellectual shifts taking place regarding regulations, certain academics still supported gradual modification of regulations rather than major changes, with an example in the airline context being the work of Douglas and Miller (1974).[3]

---

[3] One reason for this seems to be that Douglas and Miller found airline costs to be inherently higher than other studies and thus there would be little reduction in X-inefficiency if the market were substituted for regulation of fares. Keeler (1981, p. 153) also questions whether higher costs found for inter-state routes over intra-state could justify significantly higher fares, "… it is difficult to see what quality difference Douglas and Miller might be talking about between the Los-Angeles–San Francisco run and equivalent interstate runs elsewhere."

2.3   Keeler's views on the forces for regulatory reform

There are numerous accounts of the nature of the regulatory regime that constrained US transportation markets until the late 1970s, and another detailed account does not seem very productive in our context. Suffice it to say that by 1975, we find Edward Kennedy, whom most would not consider the most right-wing politician of his day, saying the following: "Regulation has gone astray … Either because they have become captives of regulated industries or captains of outmoded administrative agencies, regulators all too often encourage or approve unreasonably high prices, inadequate service, and anticompetitive behavior. The cost of this regulation is always passed on to the consumer. And that cost is astronomical."[4] The age of regulatory reform in the United States had, at least in rhetoric, begun.

Reforms were slow to come about, however. For example, the dire financial position of the railroads resulted in the removal of some regulatory controls under the Railroad Revitalization and Regulatory Reform Act of 1976. In the following year, air cargo was deregulated, a change leading to the rapid growth of express carriers such as FedEx, UPS, and others. Domestic passenger airline deregulation in 1978 also led the way for liberalization of trucking under the Motor Carrier Act of 1980, while intercity buses were deregulated under the Bus Deregulation Act of 1982. More complete deregulation of the railroad industry came with the passing of the Staggers Act in 1980. None of these measures entirely abandoned regulation, but they did significantly reduce it, in effect leaving market forces as the main economic allocative mechanism.

As Williamson (2000) pointed out, sea-changes in governance, and even more so for government, are rare. So why was there a surge in regulatory reform at that time and why did it take the form it did? The changes took place at a time of stagflation with very little economic growth and high inflation coupled with high unemployment. This combination defied accepted notions of the Phillips Curve-based Keynesian approach to unemployment and the monetarists approach to inflation. The Carter administration moved, in anticipation of the subsequent Reagan supply-side economics, to reduce production costs both as a stimulus for growth and a damper on inflationary costs. Less economic regulation, as Kennedy had earlier implied, was now in vogue as a macroeconomic tool.

While the larger picture as well as the timing of these reforms was largely dictated by macroeconomic necessity, there were pressures at the micro- and meso-levels to be considered. The argument that the driving force for change was a recognition that the extant regulatory structure did not serve the public interest because it had been captured by rent seekers, and that a more liberalized structure did, was not completely accepted by Keeler. In his study of rail freight transportation, Keeler (1983), for example, certainly highlighted the importance of Peltzman's (1976) ideas but more completely integrated them with consumer and production theory in a network context in explaining the reforms of the 1970s and the subsequent Staggers Act. In effect, US

---

[4] Senator Edward Kennedy, *Opening remarks to the Subcommittee on Administrative Practice and Procedure*, 6 February 1975.

railroads were not earning enough profits to sustain cross-subsidies for unprofitable services, suggesting that regulators had lost the political leverage of those favoring such support.[5] It was thus in the regulator's interests to change the regime.

Similar arguments were used regarding the liberalization of air transportation markets. Here, Keeler (1984), having examined in detail the history and performance of scheduled airlines from as early as 1972, provided some insights by considering the power of various coalitions of shareholders in the US airline industry. Fares were found to be well above competitive levels, affording high returns to investors and wages to machinists and pilots, with low-density routes being cross-subsidized (Caves, 1962). The trucking industry was slightly different, as there were few cross-subsidies under the 1935 Motor Carrier Act, but it appeared that significant economic rents were being retained by suppliers and labor. There were, however, possibilities for private carriage haulers to develop their own fleets, and this was a growing problem for many truckers who felt more flexible rates would allow them to compete. Reform here also may have been a knock-on from the new rate setting freedoms enjoyed by railroads that could also otherwise enjoy a competitive advantage.

More specifically, looking across transportation industries as whole, Keeler and Foreman (1988) set this within the wider picture of the forces that can lead to regulation/deregulation cycles in many sectors. They also summed up in broad terms the main winners from the regulation of the various transportation industries: "railroad investors (initially), as well as organized labor, low-density shippers, and passengers benefited from rail regulation. Truck investors and labor benefited from trucking regulation. In airlines, there were benefits for low-density users, first-class passenger, labor, and perhaps investors" (p. 219). There were histories of strong coalitions for the *status quo* in each transportation industry, but circumstances and the effects of regulation itself had changed things over the years, and airlines had pursued their own patterns.

Why the composition of such coalitions fluctuated, or the motivations of coalitions changed, and the role of the regulator in these process, is, rightly, treated as something that is not fully understood and may well have varied by sector and was affected by domino type effects after the earliest reforms. Keeler's work on these topics came at a time when the public interest theory of economic regulation was being challenged through the emergence of the works of Posner, Stigler, and Peltzman, but Keeler saw features of individual industries as requiring the nuancing of the application of more general arguments. While not strictly part of our retrospective analysis of Keeler's findings regarding the effects of regulatory reform, these ideas provide some additional insights into the way he saw the processes of regulatory change.

---

[5] As Keeler put it later (Keeler and Foreman, 1998, p. 220), "By the 1980s competition had eliminated most rents from regulation. Railroads operated at substantial losses and sought greater rate flexibility in order to gain lost volume. Based on the losses, many railroads had been granted abandonments of service and the economic and political interests of groups receiving cross-subsidies had been weakened. Thus, there were few 'interests' to oppose deregulation. Economic theory would predict the deregulation that occurred."

2.4   Aviation

Keeler (1981, p. 149) summarized the situation regarding academic thinking about the aviation industry in the early 1980s:

> *Economists do not often agree among themselves on policy issues ... but on one most important issue, there is no disagreements to reconcile: many academic economists with widely differing political views and research methodologies have analyzed the economic effects of CAB regulation over the past 15 years and have all come to a common basic conclusion that the trunk airline industry would function far more efficiently (with lower fares) than it currently does with less regulation and more competition.*

Keeler's engagement in the US airline economic regulation debate started in the early 1970s at a time when airline fares and market entry were strictly controlled under the 1938 Civil Aeronautics Act by the CAB. Fares were regulated on a rate-of-return basis, set according to an estimation of costs of providing a service, plus a margin to reflect what was deemed to be a normal profit. Routes, with few exceptions, were effectively licensed to carriers on a monopoly basis, with the onus on any potential entrants to demonstrate a need for additional seat capacity. His work up to 1986 focused on the initial effects of the 1978 Airline Deregulation Act. This was a transition period, and one that was later affected by further changes in legislation, technology, and managerial practices.[6] But even before this time, Keeler (1972) had conducted analysis on how regulatory structure in the airline industry was working.

His early approach to analysis was, in many ways, a hybrid of the subsequent analysis of Caves (1962) and Douglas and Miller (1974), on the one hand, and that of the work of Levine (1965) and Jordan (1970), on the other hand. Keeler basically constructed a simulated minimum cost model to compare against actual airline costs—the Caves/Douglas and Miller approach—and then validated it against fares on the relatively deregulated California intrastate routes—the Levine/Jordan methodology. His modeling followed that of his earlier work on railroads discussed below—see also, Keeler (1974). Basically, it entailed deriving a series of short-run cost curves, and from these he estimated the long-run cost curve.

His findings were largely in line with what others found at the time, excepting the somewhat earlier and oft cited study of Caves (1962, p. 428) that had found, "On the whole, the airlines' record is not bad if compared with unregulated industries of similar seller concentration in the American economy; and it is definitely good by comparison with many consumer goods industries." Specifically, Keeler, as with Levine, Jordan, and others, found that fares were excessive: "The results of our study indicate that as of 1968, the markup was as low as 20% on short-haul regulated routes and 95% on long-haul regulated routes. For 1972 on the other hand, the results are much closer to those of Jordan for the mid-1960s—a markup of 45%–84%" (Keeler, 1972, p. 421).

---

[6] For an account of some of the challenges of the various market transitions in the 1980s that followed regulatory reform, see Meyer and Tye (1985).

In terms of the nature of the market, he argued that cartel competition within the extant regulatory structure had led to the interstate air carriers competing away profits by offering excessive levels of costly capacity, as compared to intrastate airlines operating between 1956 and 1965.[7] There was some agreement between Caves's and Keeler's findings that there was a degree of cross-subsidization from long- to short-haul routes, with even Caves arguing the former could benefit from some deregulation.

These findings, and the methodology upon which they are based, are consistent with the notion of static X-inefficiency, with the airlines effectively capturing the regulatory process through their ability to pass on excessive costs through the extant rate-of-return fare-setting mechanism. There was limited incentive before the 1978 Act for management to minimize operating costs, especially if this involved conflicts with labor unions or harder commercial bargaining with airports, and with airframe and engine suppliers.

Ted Keeler's subsequent work after the enactment of US airline deregulation in 1978 provided confirmation of the benefits to users of the legislation, but at the same time provided several cautions as to the possible economic distortions that might emerge in the new institutional situation. Empirically, Keeler (1981) pointed to the almost immediate entry of new carriers into inter-state air markets and significant reductions in the ratio of the lowest unrestricted daytime fare to the standard formula CAB fares in 1980, as compared to those in 1975 on the 90 highest density inter-state routes, although by 1980 the reforms had only partially been completed.[8] He nuanced these findings by looking in more detail at a number of regional markets and the actions of specific carriers, including both legacy airlines and those intra-state carriers that moved into inter-state markets. The overall downward pattern of fares immediately after deregulation as seen in Fig. 2.1 is a clear indication that market liberalization in these markets reduced consumer costs of flying.[9]

The US airline industry has undergone significant restructuring and consolidation over the last 30 or so years since Keeler's early assessments of deregulation, although some of the trends he only foresaw in general terms. In his 1981 paper, Keeler highlighted three "potential problems", emphasizing that at the time it was likely too early to draw anything like conclusions. These problems were: (i) possible loss of services to smaller communities; (ii) the need for mergers to "better suit" the new liberalized

---

[7] These results were confirmed by Keeler (1981) in a later retrospective study that examined the period 1975–1980 and compared fares for intrastate services in Texas and California with those inter-state regulated fares on comparable length routes. He concludes, "Evidence from the intrastate markets ... strongly support the contention that interstate trunk fares are being set 'artificially' high by the civil Aeronautics Board and that the potential excess profits from these high fares are being competed away through service-quality and flight-frequency competition" (p. 64).

[8] The 1978 Act phased in liberalization over a 5-year period, and by 1980 fare flexibility was permitting fares of up to 50% below the industrial standard fare and up to 130% above it. Existing carriers could gradually enter inter-state routes, with some very limited powers to block automatic entry by others on routes they already served. In cases where an airline was certified to serve a route but had not done so for 6 months, others could enter it on a first-come first-serve basis.

[9] Fares could, of course, have fallen anyway under the rate-of-return regulatory system if costs fallen. This point was dealt with by Morison and Winston (1986), who found lower fares after deregulation using a counterfactual approach consisting of the CAB formula with updated costs as the point of reference.

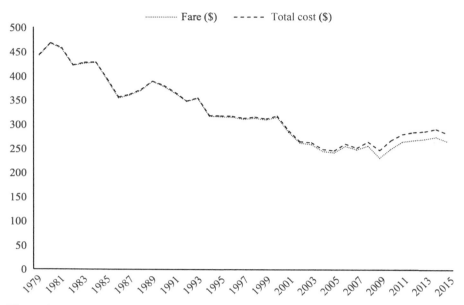

Figure 2.1 Average fares and total passenger costs including supplementary fees for a round flight 1979–2015 (2000 prices). *Note*: The average fare is per domestic round-trip journey based on average yield and average total fare is the amount paid by domestic passengers, including the fare and any reservation change fees or baggage fees. No allowance is made for frequent flyer flights nor for changes in the average flight length over the period.

economic market; and (iii) the possibility of reduced safety levels. Here, we focus on the first two problems because there is no evidence that trends in safety were made worse by deregulation, and the subject itself falls outside of the main theme of the paper.[10]

The 1978 Act recognized the potential problems associated with thin routes, and subsequent measures were enacted to provide some support for air service to small communities. The Essential Air Services (EAS) program, which replaced the earlier Local Service Airlines' subsidy, provides direct subsidies to airlines for serving rural communities that the Department of Transportation deems would otherwise not receive any scheduled air service. As of November 1, 2013, the program subsidized 160 communities, of which 43 were in Alaska, with funding in 2014 amounting to $241 million. To this end, there is also the Small Community Air Service Development Program initiated in 2000, that awards 40 service grants each year costing an estimated $5.5 million as of 2015. Unlike the EAS, the latter program is relatively flexible, with eligibility criteria being broader and providing a grant applicant the opportunity to self-identify its air service deficiencies and propose an appropriate solution.

---

[10] Kanafani and Keeler (1990) was a contribution to this debate, with them finding that aviation safety had continually improved for the 50 years up to their time of publishing, there was no disruption to the trend after deregulation.

The immediate impact of deregulation was often beneficial for smaller communities in that services increased with smaller, more efficient planes gradually being adopted, while fares often fell as competition emerged. In turn, many thinner routes were subsumed within growing hub-and-spoke air networks. In the 20 years from 1978, airline competition brought enhanced services to many markets, primarily aboard small, more economical turbo-prop aircraft. One General Accounting Office (1996) study looking at 87 small- to mid-sized markets found, for example, that 65 of the markets enjoyed a combination of lower fares and better service under deregulation.

Over time, airline costs have fallen more dramatically on higher-traffic, longer-distance routes than on shorter ones. The Regional Airline Association found that between 2013 and 2016, 309 US airports experienced scheduling reductions of at least 10%, whereas 208 airports lost at least 20%, while 52 lost all passenger service. In 2015, the latest year of available data, all US airlines, using planes of all sizes, carried a record 798 million passengers, an 11% rise from 2010 levels, but enplanements on regional carriers were down by 4%. Another indicator of more recent airline trends has been the increase in average length of flights since 1978, which have gradually risen from 1947 miles in 1979 to 2384 miles in 2015.[11] This growth can, in part, be explained by the lower unit costs of longer-distance trips, combined with the growth of hub-and-spoke operations, but the trend also reflects, at least in recent years, a withdrawal of services from some thinner, shorter routes.

Second, regarding those mergers and consolidation that Keeler felt would be needed to capture economies of scale and density, Keeler and Abrahams (1981, pp. 116–117) offered that "… the domestic airline industry will very likely be reconstructed into a group of approximately six or seven integrated nationwide carriers."[12] By the end of 1994, the top three airlines were American Airlines (17% of the market), United Airlines (16%), and Delta Airlines (13%), with a combined 46% of industry revenue. The next three airlines at that time—US Air, Continental, and Northwest—have all subsequently been merged into the first three. Southwest, with a 3% passenger share in 1994 and ranked 7th with respect to operating revenues moved to second in terms of passengers carried and 4th in terms of revenue by 2014. By that time, the big four of American, United, Delta, and Southwest generated over two-thirds of the industry's revenues, not the "six or seven" airlines as foreseen by Keeler. Two regional airlines, Alaska and Hawaiian, were the only other airlines that broadly operated in their current form back in 1994 but have survived to enjoy more than $1 billion in revenues. In fact, the period from 1990 to 2011 saw 189 bankruptcies in the airline

---

[11] This pattern at least partly came about because under the CAB, long-haul routes had fares well above costs, whereas those for short-haul routes fares were held below costs. Thus, while the short-term effects of greater flexibility allowed costs to fall on short-routes pulling down fares, these were inadequate in all cases to close the implicit fare subsidies of the CAB.

[12] In the same paper (p. 117), it was also argued "There will also be numerous corridor carriers who build their service around origin–destination traffic of various lengths and hence little need for feed. There will be both short-haul intra-state and long-haul international carriers such as World and Laker." While low-cost carriers initially avoided online services, this has changed and most offer inter-state services and transfers. Unfortunately, both World and Laker did not survive deregulation, and in 2015 over 60% of air passenger miles were done by carriers from the main strategic alliances, Star, Oneworld, and SkyTeam.

industry, with most new entrants either dissolving or being acquired by one of their larger competitors.

In addition to this, four new airlines that either did not exist in 1994 or were trivial in size managed to attract enough capital and grow their operations to achieve more than $1 billion in revenue as of 2014. In an industry where competitors bear significant fixed costs, have logistical difficulties in making rapid capacity changes, face volatile demand due to economic changes, are further buffeted by changing oil prices, and face challenging labor relations, survival has proved difficult for both established firms and entrants. But Allegiant, Virgin America, JetBlue, and Spirit have all staked out a viable position in the modern US airline industry. Analyzing the strategies utilized by these latter airlines and identifying similarities across the firms provide considerable insights into successful entrepreneurial strategies in highly competitive industries.

Although preregulation fears existed that consolidation of the airlines would lead to the Harberger and X-inefficiency costs associated with monopolized industry, the introduction of free market entry, and with it the forces of contestability, was seen by many, at least in the long term, as a counterbalance (Bailey and Baumol, 1984). Keeler (1978) certainly felt before the passing of the Airline Deregulation Act that potential market entry would temper the behavior of incumbent airlines at a route level, and later in Call and Keeler (1985, p. 246), he continued, with some refinements and caveats to argue, "if the 'competitive' long-run scenario for the airline industry is correct, it is likely that potential entry … will play a more important role on setting fares than it does now."

The outcome found in subsequent empirical analysis offers some support for this latter position. Keeler himself found little evidence for effective short-term contestability effects, but subsequent studies by Moore (1986a), Morison and Winston (1987), Hurdle et al. (1989), and Morison (2001) provide partial backing for Keeler's longer-term argument. Their collective evidence endorses the idea of "weak contestability", alluded to initially by Alfred Kahn, and in line with the caveats voiced by Call and Keeler. Morrison found, for example, that actual competition from Southwest Airlines produced aggregate fare savings of $12.9 million in 1998, whereas potential and adjacent competition produced savings of only $9.5 million. Even some of the ardent initial supporters of strong contestability, along the lines of Keeler, have subsequently questioned the limits of its usefulness in explaining the modern airline market. To wit, "We now believe that transportation by truck, barges, and even buses may be more contestable than passenger air transportation" (Baumol and Willig, 1986).

There is one further development that has affected domestic air carrier revenues from 1990 to the present, an effect that was not really considered in the 1980s. This has been the ability of airlines to generate supplementary revenues from additional fees and sales on their aircraft. Domestic air fares fell by 18.2% between the final quarter of 1995 and that of 2015, but fares have gradually accounted for a smaller percentage of operating revenues. For example, in the 1990s, domestic US air carriers received just under 90% of their revenues from passenger fares. Through the 2000s, however, that percentage declined from 88.8% in 2000 to 73.7 in 2009 and has remained around 74% in subsequent years. Airlines began gradually increasing baggage fees and reservation change fees as of 2008. By 2015, passenger airlines collected $3.8 billion from baggage fees and $3.0 billion from reservation change fees, and these fees accounted for 2.3 and 1.8% of operating revenue, respectively. Fig. 2.1 provides more detail.

In most of the early assessments of deregulation in aviation, including those of Keeler and Kahn, the policy focus was on static efficiency, namely the degree to which airlines moved out to the existing production frontier—a reduction of static X-efficiency improvements being one way of thinking about this. This focus was somewhat different from the approach at the time in the United Kingdom where the impetus, possibly explained by extensive privatization there, was more on dynamic efficiency—the adoption of price-cap regulation on monopoly transportation undertakings including major airports epitomizing this philosophy. The time frame of the US academic studies and the inevitable challenges for the airlines in handling stranded costs associated with moving to a more market-oriented industrial structure also largely explains this. There was, nevertheless, a lack of appreciation in the United States of the business flexibility of the existing industry that rapidly introduced dynamic price discrimination ("yield management"), code sharing, and loyalty programs in due course. Of equal importance was the introduction of alternative business models into the air transportation industry and the proliferation of low-cost airlines.[13] The latter changed the focus of competition away from product differentiation to that of fares, and with it had the knock-on effect of forcing legacy airlines to modify their business model (Morison, 2001).

2.5   Long-haul freight transportation

Surface freight modes were regulated from as far back as 1887 by the Interstate Commerce Commission (ICC). The ICC existed until 1996 when the Surface Transportation Board was set up to replace it. Through its existence, the ICC ultimately held broad economic regulatory oversight of railroads, including rates, service, construction, acquisition, and abandonment of rail lines, railroad mergers, and the interchange of traffic among carriers. Although its remit changed over time, the ICC's purpose included regulating freight railroads and trucking to ensure "fair rates", to eliminate rate discrimination, and to regulate other aspects of surface common carriers. The ultimate outcome of regulation, however, was that railroads, because of rate controls, growing labor restrictions, an inability to shed unprofitable capacity, and the reluctance of the ICC to permit mergers that would reduce balkanization, only averaged a 2.42% rate of return on investment between 1962 and 1978. In practical terms, these factors contributed to the railroads' share of inter-city ton-miles falling from about 75% in the 1920s to 35% by 1980.

The deregulation of US freight railroads was incremental in nature. Passenger rail operations had been separated from freight railways in 1970 under the Rail Passenger Service Act. The Regional Rail Revitalization Act of 1973 had begun to allow bankrupt

---

[13] Low-cost airlines were already operating in some liberalized intra-state markets (e.g. Pacific Southwest Airlines and Air California in California and Southwest Airlines in Texas) but not on any major inter-state route.

railroads to abandon unprofitable lines and helped develop consolidation plans for establishing Conrail, a new northeastern railroad comprising elements of multiple bankrupt carriers in that region. This was followed by the Railroad Revitalization and Regulatory Reform Act (4R Act) of 1976 that reduced federal regulation of railroads, essentially giving them more rate-setting independence, and more freedom regarding market entry and exit. The latter also authorized implementation details for the creation of Conrail. Finally, the Staggers Rail Act was passed in 1980. This allowed for several new freedoms, including the freedom to set rates unless there was no effective rail competition, rail shippers and carriers were free to establish contracts without review unless the contract service interfered with the rail carrier's ability to provide common carrier service, and, with some minor exceptions, the Act also permitted an across the board dismantling of the collective rate-making machinery. The imposition of time limits on abandonment and merger proceedings allowed railroads to more easily get out of common carrier obligations (Bitzan and Keeler, 2003).

The economic regulations under which railroads operate, and the effects of reform cannot, however, be treated in isolation (Keeler, 1983). Regulatory controls imposed on the competing trucking industry had also led to high rates but for different reasons than those applying to railroads (Moore, 1986b). Legislation such as the Motor Carrier Act 1935, which forced truckers seeking market enter to prove a demand for their services, and for all truckers to file their rates 30 days before they became effective, had led to the generation of monopoly rents and rate rigidity. Congress's repeal of the Reed-Bulwinkle Act in 1948 exempting motor carriers from the antitrust laws allowed truckers to fix rates in concert. The ICC, as a result, then encourage the formation of rate bureaus that facilitated various cartel arrangements. The system also limited backhaul operations, thus increasing the average cost of a haul, a situation that was then fed through to the value of service price structure. Secondary capture came about with the Teamsters Union manipulating the regulatory system to push up labor costs.[14]

Unlike the reforms to the railroads that involved a series of actions, the Motor Carrier Regulatory Reform and Modernization Act (the Motor Carriers Act) 1980 adopted a "Big Bang" style approach: there were no major regulatory changes affecting trucking that preceded it.[15] The Act, by amongst other things, making it easier for truckers to secure a certificate of public convenience and necessity and allowing them to set rates within a zone of reasonableness, led to more flexible pricing and service arrangements disciplined by competition rather than fiat.

This legislation clearly had implications regarding the terms of competition of trucking with the freight railroads. Overall, it, together with the Staggers Act, puts the

---

[14] The differing situations regarding railroads and trucking were largely due to the ways the industries were viewed when initially regulated. Using modern terminology, the railroads were treated as traditional monopolies that would under supply and over price, and operate with considerable X-inefficiency. The trucking industry was intuitively considered, because of relatively low entry costs but fixed costs for each service, as potentially unstable because of the lack of a "core", an argument developed from the work of Edgeworth (1881).

[15] For a discussion of the economics differences between the gradualist and big bang approaches, see Button and Johnson (1998).

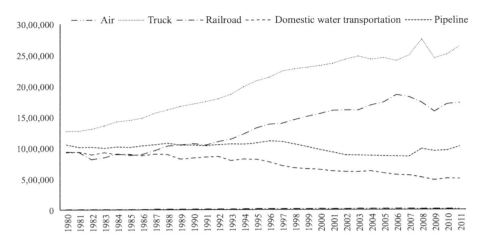

Figure 2.2 Ton-miles of freight by mode (millions). *Source*: U.S. Bureau of Transportation Statistics.

two modes of surface freight transportation on a more even competitive footing, both operating in much more open market conditions (Keeler, 1989).

In his Brookings Institution study of the railroads, Keeler (1983, p. 147) concluded that the outcome of this, "Freed of its medieval shackles of common carrier service obligations, the railroad industry should continue to play an important and profitable role in the US economy for many years to come." This was based on very short-term analysis of both the problems encountered by the railroads prior to the Staggers Act and a limited period after its enactment. Regarding the latter, while he found that rates and services had become more flexible by 1982, that line abandonments had increased, and the need to cross-subsidize common carrier obligations had been reduced, the most important change observed was an increase in the profitability of freight railroads. In addition, while their returns were over 4% for the first time in more than a quarter century, this had been achieved without reductions in maintenance or investment, and in fact the opposite occurred. And this happened in the face of mounting rate wars.

But what of Keeler's optimism regarding the dynamics of the railroad industry? Turning to longer-term trends, it is apparent from Fig. 2.2 that railroads both increased the ton-miles they have provided since the enactment of the Staggers Act, as well as their relative share in the surface freight market.

Fig. 2.3 provides a time series changes in labor productivity for the main US transportation industries from 1990 to 2015. Relevant to the previous section, air transportation, which had been the least productive back in 1990, became the second most productive mode by 2015 with an increase of 158%. Railroads had the second least productive labor force in 1990, but became the most productive mode by 2015 with productivity increase by 129% over that period. By way of comparison, the labor force in long-distance freight trucking and the US Postal Service had smaller productivity

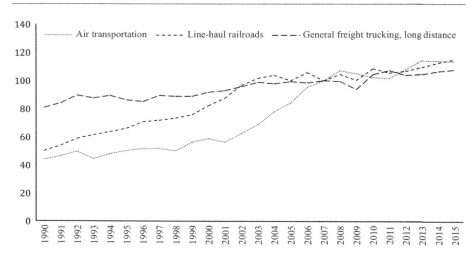

Figure 2.3 Labor productivity indices for transportation industries, 1990–2015. *Note*: index based on 2009. *Source*: U.S. Department of Labor, Bureau of Labor Statistics.

increases of 33% and 15%, with Postal Service labor productivity falling from the highest in 1990 to the lowest by 2015. With respect to revenues, if we consider Producer Price Index data that measures changes in the sales price received by these transportation service providers, domestic air carriers experienced the largest increase in revenue per ton-mile—143% per ton-mile between 1990 and 2012—with Class I railroads experiencing an increase of 48% over the same period.

Between 1990 and 2012, nominal freight revenue per ton-mile increased for all modes. Class I railroads and line-haul freight railroads with annual operating revenues of $475.75 million or more in 2014 enjoyed an increase in revenue per ton-mile of 48% over this time. Oil pipelines experienced an increase of 44% from 1990 to 2009, whereas trucks experienced an increase of 28% from 1990 to 2007. In addition, the value per ton of freight shipments rose by 17.5% between 1997 and 2013, from $763 to $896 per ton in 2007 dollars. But at the same time, we find that the producer price index increased by 63%, thus real freight revenue per ton-mile increased only for domestic air carriers during this period.

Added to these general patterns in the postderegulation era, there have been numerous, more specific technical academic studies of US railroads supporting Keeler's (1982) longer-term optimism. In what follows, we remain narrow in our assessment and focus attention just on Keeler's own more recent analyses.[16]

In several papers with John Bitzan, Keeler explored the implications of the Staggers Act on metrics like traffic density, pricing, and productivity. As with most other studies, these analyses provide support for the positive economic benefits that have flowed

---

[16] Other works on various aspects of the subject include Bitzan (2003), Davis and Wilson (1999, 2003), Interstate Commerce Commission (1997), Ivaldi and McCullough (2001), Wilson (1997), Bitzan and Wilson (2007), Chapin and Schmidt (1999), and Winston et al. (2011).

from freight railroad deregulation. For example, using trans-logarithmic cost functions in looking at the productivity of the Class I railroads, they find that productivity rose not only between 1983 and 1997, but it did so at a slightly accelerating rate and, as a specific factor associated with the deregulated rail operating environment, the elimination of the caboose reduced costs by between 5% and 8% (Bitzan and Keeler, 2003).

Looking at claims that captive rail traffic has been subject to excessive pricing, Bitzan and Keeler (2014) found that between 1986 and 2008, there was no statistical evidence of the revenue–cost ratio for rail increasing for the most captive commodity groups, but rather there was something of a widening of this gap for those less captive commodity groups. In sum, they concluded that, "Over the period since regulatory reform in the railroad industry, rail rates have been responsive to market forces, to a degree which would seem never to have happened before.... Ironically, proposed changes in the railroad regulations to protect the captive shipper are likely to limit the ability of the industry to respond to market forces, having harmful impacts on the railroads and shippers themselves" (p. 322).[17] Finally, Bitzan and Keeler (2007) found that the significant cost savings associated with the greater density of traffic carried by the freight railroads after the enactment of the Staggers Act, coupled with the resultant abandonments and consolidations had, by 2001, produced combined net annual benefits of between $7 and $10 billion for shippers and carriers.

As a reminder, the focus in this chapter was on Keeler's analysis of the economic regulation of surface freight and air modes of transportation. The chapter explicitly does not consider either passenger railroads or passenger cars, although Keeler has published work on passenger railways as well as automobile policy issues.[18]

2.6 Conclusions

As with any attempt to take a longer view of institutional change, there are inevitable on-going autonomous trends that must be considered, together with trend-breaks and new trends. In the case of long-standing transportation regulations in the United States, there were effectively "pent-up" technologies and managerial models that had been kept from that marketplace that would prove important as more business flexibility was allowed. And there was also significant technical development surely stimulated by institutional reforms. Added to this, there is significant complementarity and substitutability between the various transportation modes that makes foreseeing the effects of near simultaneous regulatory regime changes especially challenging.

[17] In the work on the trucking industry, Ying and Keeler (1991) find that trucking rates also fell after the passing of the Motor Carrier Regulatory Reform and Modernization Act of 1980. This was much more expected because there was a feeling that the industry was highly competitive and that consumer interest could be protected by market forces. This was not the case for the railroads where monopoly was taken as inevitable given the extensive economies of scale thought to exist.

[18] For example, Keeler (1971) on passenger railroads and Keeler and Small (1977), Crandall et al. (1982), Keeler and Crandall (1982), and Keeler and Ying (1988) on various aspects of automobile policy.

But, in general, we find that Keeler's early assessments regarding the short-term effects of US transportation regulatory reform, at least as far as the airline and freight rail modes are concerned, have held up. His more speculative commentaries about the longer-term implications of the reforms have also often transpired to be broadly correct. In retrospect, of course, these outcomes may seem to be obvious, but in the late 1970s and early 1980s, this was not the case and there were plenty of sceptics who thought deregulation would have serious adverse economic welfare implications, including reducing the economic efficiency of transportation industry.

References

Backhouse, R.E., Biddle, J., 2000. The concept of applied economics: a history of ambiguity and multiple meanings. History of Political Economy 32, 1–24.

Bailey, E.E., Baumol, W.J., 1984. Deregulation and the theory of contestable markets. Yale Journal on Regulation 1, 111–137.

Baumol, W.J., Willig, R.D., 1986. Contestability: developments since the book. Oxford Economic Papers 38, 9–36.

Baumol, W.J., Panzar, J.C., Willig, R.D., 1982. Contestable Markets and the Theory of Industry Structure. Harcourt Brace Jovanovich, New York.

Bitzan, J.D., 2003. Railroad costs and competition: the implications of introducing competition to railroad networks. Journal of Transport Economics and Policy 37, 201–225.

Bitzan, J.D., Keeler, T.E., 2003. Productivity growth and some of its determinants in the deregulated U.S. railroad industry. Southern Economic Journal 70, 232–253.

Bitzan, J.D., Keeler, T.E., 2007. Economies of density and regulatory change in the U.S. railroad freight industry. Journal of Law and Economics 50, 157–180.

Bitzan, J.D., Keeler, T.E., 2014. The evolution of U.S. rail freight pricing in the post-deregulation era: revenues versus marginal costs for five commodity types. Transportation 41, 305–324.

Bitzan, J.D., Wilson, W.W., 2007. Industry costs and consolidation: efficiency gains and mergers in the U.S. railroad industry. Review of Industrial Organization 30, 81–105.

Button, K.J., 2015. A book, the application and the outcomes: how right was Alfred Kahn in *The Economics of Regulation* about the effects of the deregulation of the U.S. domestic airline market? History of Political Economy 47, 1–39.

Button, K.J., Chow, G., 1982. The economic regulation of road haulage in Canada and the United Kingdom. Journal of the Transportation Research Forum 22, 642–652.

Button, K.J., Johnson, K., 1998. Incremental versus trend-break change in airline regulation. Transportation Journal 37, 25–34.

Button, K.J., Keeler, T.E., 1993. The regulation of transport markets. Economic Journal 103, 1017–1027.

Call, G., Keeler, T.E., 1985. Air deregulation, fares, and market behavior: some empirical evidence. In: Daughety, A.F. (Ed.), Analytical Studies in Transport Economics. Cambridge University Press, Cambridge, pp. 241–247.

Caves, R.E., 1962. Air Transport and its Regulators. Harvard University Press, Cambridge, MA.

Chapin, A., Schmidt, S., 1999. Do mergers improve efficiency? Evidence from deregulated rail freight. Journal of Transport Economics and Policy 33, 147–162.

Crandall, R., Keeler, T.E., Lave, L., 1982. The costs of automobile safety and emissions regulation to the consumer. American Economic Review 72, 324–327.

Davis, D.E., Wilson, W.W., 1999. Deregulation, mergers, and employment in the railroad industry. Journal of Regulatory Economics 15, 5–22.

Davis, D.E., Wilson, W.W., 2003. Wages in rail markets: deregulation, mergers, and changing network characteristics. Southern Economic Journal 69, 865–885.

Demsetz, H., 1968. Why regulate utilities? Journal of Law and Economics 11, 55–65.

Douglas, G.W., Miller, J.C., 1974. Economic Regulation of Domestic Air Transport: Theory and Policy. Brookings Institution, Washington, DC.

Edgeworth, F.Y., 1881. Mathematical Physics. Kegan Paul, London.

General Accounting Office, 1996. Airline Deregulation: Changes in Airfares, Service, and Safety at Small, Medium-sized, and Large Communities. GAO, Washington, DC, GAO/RCED-96-79.

Hurdle, G.J., Johnson, R.L., Joskow, A.S., Werden, G.J., Williams, M.A., 1989. Concentration, potential entry, and performance in the airline industry. Journal of Industrial Economics 38, 119–139.

Interstate Commerce Commission, 1997. Railroad cost recovery procedures and productivity adjustments. Decision STB Ex Parte 290 (Sub-No. 4). Interstate Commerce Commission, Washington, DC.

Ivaldi, M., McCullough, G.J., 2001. Density and integration effects on Class I U.S. freight railroads. Journal of Regulatory Economics 19, 161–182.

Jordan, W.A., 1970. Airline Regulation in America: Effects and Imperfections. Johns Hopkin University Press, Baltimore.

Kahn, A.E., 1970. The Economics of Regulation: Principles and Institutions, Vol. I. Economic Principles. John Wiley and Sons, New York.

Kahn, A.E., 1971. The Economics of Regulation: Principles and Institutions, Volume II Institutional Issues. John Wiley and Sons, New York.

Kahn, A.E., 1988. Surprises of airline deregulation. American Economic Review, Papers and Proceedings 78, 316–322.

Kanafani, A., Keeler, T.E., 1990. Airline deregulation and safety: some econometric evidence from times series. Logistics and Transportation Review 26, 203–210.

Keeler, T.E., 1971. The economics of passenger trains. Journal of Business 44, 148–174.

Keeler, T.E., 1972. Airline regulation and market performance. Bell Journal of Economics and Management Science, 399–424.

Keeler, T.E., 1974. Railroad costs, returns to scale, and excess capacity. Review of Economics and Statistics 56, 201–208.

Keeler, T.E., 1978. Domestic airline regulation: an economic evaluation. In: Weiss, L., Klass, M. (Eds.), Study on Federal Regulation, U.S. Senate, Committee on Governmental Affairs, VII, U.S. Government Printing Office, Washington, DC, pp. 77–160.

Keeler, T.E., 1981. The revolution in airline regulation. In: Weiss, L., Klass, M. (Eds.), Case Studies in Regulation: Revolution and Reform. Little Brown & Co., Boston, MA, pp. 53–85.

Keeler, T.E., 1983. Railroads, Freight, and Public Policy. The Brookings Institution, Washington, DC.

Keeler, T.E., 1984. Theories of regulation and the deregulation movement. Public Choice 44, 103–145.

Keeler, T.E., 1989. Deregulation and scale economies in U.S. trucking: an econometric extension of the survivor principle. Journal of Law and Economics 32, 229–254.

Keeler, T.E., 1991. Airline deregulation and market performance: the economic basis for regulatory reform and lessons from the U.S. experience. In: Banister, D., Button, K.J. (Eds.), Transport in a Free Market Economy. Macmillan, London, pp. 121–169.

Keeler, T.E., Abrahams, M., 1981. Market structure, pricing, and service quality in the airline industry under deregulation. In: Sichel, W., Gies, T. (Eds.), Applications of Economic Principles in Public Utility Industries, 2, Michigan Business Studies, Ann Arbor, MI, pp. 103–120.

Keeler, T.E., Foreman, S.E., 1998. Regulation and deregulation. In: Newman, P. (Ed.), New Palgrave Dictionary of Economics and the Law, 3, Macmillan, London, pp. 213–222.

Keeler, T.E., Small, K.A., 1977. Optimal peak-load pricing, investment, and service levels on urban expressways. Journal of Political Economy 85, 1–26.

Keeler, T.E., Ying, J.S., 1988. Measuring the benefits of a large public investment: the case of the U.S. Federal-Aid Highway System. Journal of Public Economics 36, 69–85.

Levine, M.E., 1965. Is regulation necessary? California air transportation and national regulatory policy. Yale Law Journal 74, 1422–1423.

Littlechild, S., 2008. UK chairs of applied economics and economic theory. Paper was originally presented at a Conference in Honour of the 65th birthday of professor David M.G. Newbery, Cambridge.

Meyer, J.R., Tye, W.B., 1985. The regulatory transition. American Economic Review, Papers and Proceedings 75, 46–51.

Moore, T.G., 1986a. U.S. airline deregulation: its effects on passengers, capital, and labor. Journal of Law and Economics 29, 1–28.

Moore, T.G., 1986b. Rail and trucking deregulation. In: Weiss, L.W., Klass, M.W. (Eds.), Regulatory Reform: What Actually Happened. Little Brown, and Co., Boston.

Morison, S.A., 2001. Actual, adjacent, and potential competition: estimating the full effects of Southwest airlines. Journal of Transport Economics and Policy 35, 239–256.

Morison, S.A., Winston, C., 1987. Empirical implications and tests of the contestability hypothesis. Journal of Law and Economics 30, 53–66.

Peltzman, S., 1976. Toward a more general theory of regulation. Journal of Law and Economics 19, 211–240.

Posner, R.A., 1971. Taxation by regulation. Bell Journal of Economics and Management Science 2, 22–50.

Stigler, G.J., 1971. The theory of economic regulation. Bell Journal of Economics and Management Science 2, 3–19.

Williamson, O.E., 2000. The new institutional economics: taking stock, looking ahead. Journal of Economic Literature 38, 595–613.

Wilson, W.W., 1997. Cost savings and productivity gains in the railroad industry. Journal of Regulatory Economics 11, 21–41.

Winston, C., Maheshri, V., Dennis, S.M., 2011. Long run effects of mergers: the case of U.S. western railroads. Journal of Law and Economics 54, 275–304.

Ying, J.S., Keeler, T.E., 1991. Pricing in a deregulated environment: the motor carrier experience. Rand Journal of Economics 22, 264–273.

Further Reading

Crandall, R., Keeler, T.E., 1987. Public policy and the private auto. In: Gordon, R., Jacoby, H., Zimmerman, M. (Eds.), Essays in Honor of Morris A. Adelman. Massachusetts Institute of Technology Press, Cambridge, MA, pp. 137–160.

Harris, R.G., Keeler, T.E., 1981. Determinants of railroad profitability. In: Boyer, K., Shepherd, W. (Eds.), Economic Regulation: Essays in Honor of James R. Nelson. Michigan State University Institute of Public, Lancing, MI, pp. 37–54.

Keeler, T.E., 1975. Regulation and Trunk Air Fares, in U.S. Senate Subcommittee on Administrative Practices and Procedures, Oversight of Civil Aeronautics Board Practices and Procedures Volume II. U.S. Government Printing Office, Washington, DC, pp. 1296-1305.

Keeler, T.E., 1977. Regulation and modal market shares in long-haul freight transportation: a statistical comparison of Australia and the United States. In: Nelson, J.R., Whitten, H.O. (Eds.), Foreign Regulatory Experiments: Implications for the U.S. U.S. Department of Transportation Contract Report FRA-OPPD-77-24, Washington, DC, Chapter IX.

Keeler, T.E., 1986. Public policy and productivity in the trucking industry: some evidence on the effects of highway investments deregulation, and the 55-mile-per-hour speed limit. American Economic Review 76, 153–158.

Commoditization and segmentation of aviation markets

David Gillen*, Ashish Lall**
*University of British Columbia, Vancouver, BC, Canada;
**National University of Singapore, Singapore

Chapter Outline

Ted Keeler Influence on our Research and Careers

David Gillen: It was good fortune that I was starting my PhD program in 1971 when Ted Keeler was beginning to make the first of numerous contributions to the Industrial Organization (IO) and Public Policy literature. In my IO and Transportation Economics courses, his name appeared frequently on the reading lists. The most influential articles for me is his *Review of Economics and Statistics* paper on railway cost functions (*Review of Economics and Statistics*, May 1974). In this piece, he showed how the long-run cost function could be derived from the estimated short-run function, a wonderful application of empirics and simple economic theory and remarkably drawn from his undergraduate honors economics thesis. His second railway article with his then student Robert Harris (*Bell Journal of Economics*, Autumn 1977) developed the idea of economies of density, a concept that I, and many others, subsequently used in my aviation research 10 years later. The third article was his famous article on what would be the outcome if the airline industry were deregulated (*Bell Journal of Economics*, Autumn 1972). Here was a piece a young graduate student could only marvel at, a combination of empirical IO, coupled with simulation that could inform public policy. His work was a catalyst that democratized the airline business. Ted Keeler had a significant impact on my desire to pursue research in applied IO and primarily Transportation Economics and to use empirically based models to inform public policy.

Ashish Lall: Ted Keeler's work in Transportation Economics and empirical IO had a very significant influence on my graduate studies as well as on my early career in the public and private sectors. My decision to work on costs and productivity in Canadian railways for my PhD dissertation was based, in no small part, on his work on US railways. Subsequently, when I worked in the research division of the Canadian Royal Commission on National Passenger Transportation as

Transportation Policy and Economic Regulation. http://dx.doi.org/10.1016/B978-0-12-812620-2.00003-1
Copyright © 2018 Elsevier Inc. All rights reserved.

an analyst, his work on other modes of transportation provided a fertile background for my own research. Later, when I joined Abt Associates of Canada, I worked on a project relating to the taxation of tobacco and fortunately Ted Keeler had just written the first of his many pieces on this theme. Ted Keeler's work is a remarkable illustration of how simple yet well thought-out empirical economics can inform the important policy challenges of our times. I continue to be influenced by his "way of proceeding".

"There are no bad industries, only bad firms"
Michael E. Porter

3.1 Introduction

Deregulation of the domestic airline market in the United States in 1978 opened opportunities for incumbent and potential entrant carriers to introduce new business models and new ways of delivering airline services. The development of the hub-and-spoke network model, the growth of the low-cost carrier (LCC) model, and the development of revenue management by American Airlines to counter the LCC threat are well documented (Williams, 1994).[1] The United States with the largest aviation market in the world provided a fertile field for carriers to try to adjust to the new reality of freedom to set fares, routes, schedules, and services and for new entrants to define a new way of thinking about airline strategies, networks, pricing, and products. This institutional change coupled with the economic growth of the US economy provided opportunity for fundamental change in the airline business in the United States and subsequently worldwide.

In the next two decades, significant change was introduced to every part of the airline value chain from airframe and engine manufacturers through infrastructure providers (airports, air traffic control, and air navigation systems) to distribution systems to airlines. It was the fundamental changes in airline markets that stimulated change upstream. Deregulation and the Internet revolution democratized air travel and allowed more people to fly to more places. The growth in air travel continued unabated, and numerous airlines of every ilk came and went as the market sorted out sustainable business strategies (Doganis, 2006). The number of carriers and their affiliations continued to grow but a number of events, the Tech sector bust in 2000, the tragic events of September 11, 2001, and the continued rise in aviation fuel prices were to underlay another airline industry transformation. The price of jet fuel peaked in 2008 and although it dropped dramatically in 2009, it remained high from about 2011–2014. However, new aircraft have integrated the reality of high fuel prices into their design and engine efficiency with the result that narrow body aircraft can now

---

[1] van Ryzin and Talluri (2005) provide the history of the development of revenue management after deregulation. Robert Crandall of American Airlines developed this system to counter the threat from PeopleExpress. Crandall introduced purchase restrictions as well as capacity-controlled fares where a fixed number of seats on every flight were sold at low fares. Later, American Airlines developed a computerized system known as Dynamic Inventory Allocation and Maintenance Optimizer (DINAMO). Yield or revenue management contributed to the demise of PeopleExpress.

serve some traditional long-haul (widebody) routes. After deregulation in 1978, a substantial number of carriers emerged with the LCC service revolution really occurring in the 1990s and continuing unabated.

The aviation sector in the United States has undergone a significant transformation since the early 2000. Every major legacy carrier has filed for bankruptcy and there have been numerous mergers and acquisitions. Hüschelrath and Müller (2012) document the evolution of the LCC service sector from 1997 to 2009. It increased its share of the US domestic passenger market from 13% in 1997 to 28% in 2009, and to over 34% in 2016. While both LCCs and legacy carriers behaved similarly in terms of market entry, each entering approximately 1200 markets; the LCCs sustained their positions with only about 400 market exits compared to over 2200 by legacy carriers. From 2010, legacy carriers realized that maximizing market share was a profit-reducing outcome and they altered capacity growth. In this process of rationalization, carriers cut costs, reduced the size of their network, and practiced "capacity discipline" (Gillen and Gados, 2008; Wittman and Swelbar, 2013).

Meanwhile, LCCs have expanded their networks and services, both in the United States and in Europe. They no longer operate from fringe airfields, providing only point-to-point service from secondary airports on short-haul routes. They are providing services from large and medium hubs, and the average length of the haul has increased. In addition, American LCCs are offering international services to Central and South America and the Caribbean. Although there have been some mergers and acquisitions, much of the long-term LCC growth has been organic. As a result, Southwest has become the largest (by passenger count) domestic carrier in the United States, and Ryanair has become the largest European carrier. As well, a new category of "ultra-low-cost carriers" (ULCCs) has emerged; examples in the United States include Spirit and Allegiant. Long-haul LCC service has also begun to emerge, with carriers such as Air Asia X, Norwegian, and Scoot and this has been assisted by new, more fuel-efficient aircraft such as the B787 and the increased fuel efficiency and range of the Boeing 737 and Airbus 320 families of aircraft.

The literature on "business models" suggests that there has been a convergence in the business models of network carriers and LCCs on both the demand and cost side (Daft and Albers, 2013). Network carriers are using value appropriation tactics by removing services earlier included in the ticket price, such as assigned seating, checked-in baggage, and meals. These services are then added back at a price, providing new revenue streams for network carriers. Empirical evidence on the introduction of bag fees suggests that while leisure ticket prices fell when legacy carriers in the United States introduced bag fees in 2008, the full trip price (including a paid checked bag) increased by at least 50% of the bag fee and possibly as much as 80%–90% of the bag fee (Brueckner et al., 2015; Scotti and Dresner, 2015). At the same time, the legacy carriers have become more cost-efficient and brought their costs down relatively closer to those of LCCs. LCCs, on the other hand, are diversifying fleets, providing connects, entering into code-sharing agreements, and providing early boarding and seat assignment in a bid to attract business travelers (Lohmann and Koo, 2013). LCCs have added value to the demand side which in turn has eroded some of the significant cost advantages they have held over legacy carriers.

This chapter reviews some of the changes that have taken place in the industry over the last decade and a half. In particular, it focuses on the competitive impacts of these developments as well as the changes in strategic responses and the evolution of business models. The first issue we examine is the price response by incumbents when LCCs enter as a competitor. The price response is both an initial reaction and the move to a long-term equilibrium. The second issue is the evolution of airline business models, in particular, the LCC model.

3.2   Impact of entry by LCCs

Entry by LCCs in new markets lead to numerous savings for passengers. LCCs expand the market by making air travel more affordable. Passengers from other modes of transportation such as road or rail may switch to the air mode. Existing air passengers may also switch from incumbent carriers to LCCs. Fares between Dallas and Houston declined from $25 to $18.52, when Southwest entered that market in 1971 (Keeler, 1972, p. 421). Fares on the Baltimore–Cleveland route declined by 66% and traffic increased by between three and four times, when Southwest began service from Baltimore airport (BWI) in 1993 (Dresner et al., 1996, p. 315).

Incumbents may drop their prices in response to entry by LCCs, resulting in more savings for consumers. Studies which focus on average prices on a route combine these two sources of savings. This is the "in-market" response to entry. LCC entry may also impact adjacent and potential competition (Dresner et al., 1996; Morrison, 2001). Adjacent competition is the impact of LCC entry on carriers operating at proximate airports (or on a route, which is a reasonable substitute). For example, Southwest's entry on the Baltimore–Cleveland route could affect Cleveland-bound flights from Dulles (IAD) and Washington National (DCA) airports, as they are both proximate to Baltimore. Potential competition is the impact of LCC entry on carriers at the same airport, but serving other (noncompeting) routes. After starting the Baltimore–Cleveland service, Southwest could serve other destinations from BWI. Incumbents at BWI may drop prices on noncompeting destinations to dissuade potential entry by Southwest, or by other LCCs that may be considering commencing service from BWI. Dresner et al. (1996, p. 317) suggest that the effects of adjacent competition from Southwest's entry at BWI were small, but those of potential competition were large. They found that fares from BWI to destinations (other than Ohio) within a 500-mile radius of the Washington area declined by about 35%–40% within a year of Southwest's entry.

Dresner et al. (1996) also used an econometric model (for the top 200 domestic routes, 1990–1994) to estimate the in-market and adjacent competition (competitive routes) effects of Southwest's entry and by LCCs, in general. They found that the presence of Southwest on a route led to a 53% reduction in yields, and, on average, the presence of an LCC reduced yields by 38%. Prices also declined if Southwest operated on a competitive route. The magnitude was determined by the number of competitive routes on which Southwest operated. The fare reduction was 8% if Southwest operated on one competitive route and 27%, 45%, and 38% for two, three, or four and five or more, respectively. The presence of LCCs on one competitive route did not have a statistically significant impact on fares, but presence on two, three, or four and five or more reduced fares by 31%, 35%, and 41%, respectively.

Morrison (2001) provided dollar estimates of the "Southwest effect". Morrison (2001) found that in 1998 Southwest was in a position to influence fares on routes accounting for 94% of domestic passenger miles. Passengers saved $12.9 billion, with $3.4 billion coming from Southwest's lower fares and the reminder $9.5 billion from the reaction of incumbents to actual, adjacent, and potential competition. These savings amounted to 20% of the airline industry's domestic scheduled passenger revenue at the time, and about half the fare reductions accredited to airline deregulation. Morrison (2001, p. 239) found it "troubling" that one carrier could have such a large effect. Recent studies find that this large effect persists, as do the findings of Dresner et al. (1996) that the "Southwest effect" is in general larger than that of other LCCs.

Goolsbee and Syverson (2008) examined the price impacts of the threat of entry by Southwest. During their sample period (1993–2004), Southwest added service at 22 airports and tripled its passenger miles (18.8–54.3 billion) and revenues ($2.3–$6.5 billion). They examined situations where Southwest served various destinations from two endpoints (A and B) but did not have a service between A and B. There was a high probability (70% higher than commencing service on other routes from A or B) that it would start a service between A and B. How did incumbents react to this potential threat of entry? Goolsbee and Syverson (2008) found preemptive price drops on those routes (17%) and higher volumes. If Southwest did enter a route, prices were lower by another 12%. They did not find any evidence of capacity preemption and concluded that incumbents accommodated entry. Call and Keeler (1985, p. 246) predicted that potential entry would be an important determinant of fares over the long-term. They also observed that "models of oligopoly may give way to models of competition … in explaining airfares and service." They also suggested that as LCCs expanded market shares and gained acceptance among the wider traveling public, incumbents would lose their "discretionary power over fares" and passengers would have many low frill options, at least on high-density routes. The business model convergence literature which we discuss later also points to this type of phenomenon.

More recent research adds detail to prior work at many levels. It provides a more nuanced, and, in some instances, more comprehensive analysis. For example, considering nonstop and one-stop markets; distinguishing the impact of legacy competition from LCC competition; examining price levels and price dispersion (Tan, 2016); examining how pricing varies with Southwest's market share (Kwoka et al., 2016); and separating LCCs from ULCCs (Bachwich and Wittman, 2017). Nonetheless, many of the broad conclusions of earlier work remain valid.

Brueckner et al. (2013) studied the period 2007–2008 and estimated a variety of models. While magnitudes may differ across models, their work suggests that Southwest continues to exert a large competitive effect on fares, larger than other LCCs. In contrast, competition from legacy carriers is slight or muted and much lower in 2007–2008 than it was in 2000. In-market nonstop competition from

Southwest reduces fares as much as 33%, whereas other LCCs have a smaller effect of about 21% or less.[2] Adjacent nonstop competition from Southwest reduces fares by 19% and that from other LCCs by 5%. Potential competition from Southwest reduces fares by 8%, whereas that from LCCs has no impact. Connecting competition from all LCCs including Southwest has a small impact of around 4%. In contrast, adding a second legacy nonstop carrier reduces fares by at most 5% and a third legacy carrier has no impact. The size of these effects depends on the LCC share in the market. The impact is lower (3%) if the LCC share is 10% or more. Adjacent nonstop competition from a legacy carrier reduces prices by 2.7% and a connecting legacy competitor has no impact. Legacy competition has a small impact throughout the fare distribution.

Comparing some of these results with the year 2000, Brueckner et al. (2013) found that the competitive effect of legacy carriers had declined over the years. In the year 2000, adding a second legacy nonstop carrier reduced fares by 11.4% although a third legacy carrier had no impact. Adjacent nonstop competition from a legacy carrier reduced prices by 4.6% and a connecting legacy competitor reduced fares by 6.2%. They offered three potential explanations for the declining competitive impact of legacy carriers. First, LCCs had increased their market share through growth as well as new entry into the low-cost segment. This led to a commoditization of domestic air service which allowed the low-cost provider to set fares. Second, an attempt by the corporate sector to reduce travel budgets; and lastly, price transparency resulting from the proliferation of the Internet travel sites. Using 2004 data from a computer reservation system, Sengupta and Wiggins (2014) found that after controlling for ticket characteristics, tickets purchased on the Internet were cheaper by 11%, relative to those purchased through travel agents.

Tan (2016) studied the impact of entry by LCCs on top 150 most-traveled routes in the United States. Between 1993 and 2009, there were more than 2000 instances of entry on these routes. The study examined the effect of entry on average prices as well as on price dispersion. Tan (2016) measured price dispersion using the standard deviation of airfares, the Gini coefficient, and by comparing the effects on the most expensive fares (90th percentile) and the lowest fares (10th percentile). The intent was to distinguish competitive effects from displacement effects (Hollander, 1987). LCCs target price-sensitive customers, or appeal to a segment of the market that makes decisions based on prices rather than on brand loyalty. If the price difference is substantial, brand loyal customers may also switch to LCCs. Incumbents could respond in one of the two ways. They may reduce prices for both segments, resulting in lower average prices as well as lower price dispersion. Or, they could reduce prices for price-sensitive customers and exploit switching costs to increase prices for brand-loyal customers. In this case, the displacement

[2] Hüschelrath and Müller (2014) estimate the price and welfare effects of entry by JetBlue using data for the period 1995–2009. They find that average nonstop prices decline by 15%. The drops are high in long-haul (27%) than in short-haul (19%) markets and there is no statistically significant impact in medium-haul markets. Long-haul entry increased consumer welfare (compensating variation) by $661 million in the first year after entry.

effect may dominate, leading to higher price dispersion and possibly to higher average prices as well. The earlier literature on the "Southwest effect" (Dresner et al., 1996; Morrison, 2001) suggests that the competitive effect dominates the displacement effect. This is confirmed by Tan (2016) although the impacts differ by the entrants. For example, one quarter after entry by Southwest, legacy incumbents dropped their average fares by 14.7%. In comparison, the reduction was 9.5% and 6.5% in response to entry by JetBlue and Spirit, respectively. Incumbents also dropped both their 10th and 90th percentile prices, indicating lower price dispersion. Entry by Southwest led to a 10.8% reduction in average 10th percentile prices and a 17.4% reduction in average 90th percentile prices. Entry by other LCCs had a similar but smaller impact.

Kwoka et al. (2016) used data for four quarters in 2009–2010 and their results are very similar to those of previous studies. For example, like Brueckner et al. (2013) they found that legacy competition had a limited impact. The presence of a second legacy carrier may reduce fares by about 3%, but that of a third was less important and may even increase fares. But bringing a single LCC into a market reduced fares by about 22% and adding a second and a third continued to drive down prices charged by other carriers. What distinguishes Kwoka et al. (2016) from previous studies is their finding that the competitive impact of LCCs on fares is nonlinear, or that it tapers off after a 75% LCC share. Southwest's own pricing behavior is also influenced by its market share. They indicate that the data cannot be pooled and estimated separate models for legacy carriers, for LCCs, and for Southwest. They found that markets were segmented; competition between legacy carriers was limited and had no impact on LCC pricing.[3] On the other hand, LCCs competed among themselves and provided competition to legacy carriers. The impact of LCCs on legacy carriers and intra-LCC competition was carrier-specific.

The legacy carrier regression results show that Southwest had the largest impact on average prices charged by legacy carriers, leading to declines of 31%, followed by AirTran (23%), JetBlue (18%), and other LCCs (14%). The share of Southwest also affected prices charged by legacy carriers. If Southwest's share was less than 25%, legacy carrier prices were 23% lower; a share of between 25% and 50% led to a further price decline of 9.3%; between 50% and 75%, the incremental impact was slightly smaller and there was no impact beyond 75%. This could be because as Southwest increased its market share, legacy carriers became fringe players and focused on business travelers, or, Southwest changed its pricing on routes that it dominated.

The LCC regressions show that if Southwest's share was less than 25%, LCC prices were 11.9% lower; a share of between 25% and 50% led to a further price decline of 5.4%; between 50% and 75% there was no impact; and there was a partial reversal (increase of 5.1%) beyond 75%. These results also showed that AirTran had the largest impact on mean LCC prices (14%) followed closely by Southwest (13.5%). The impact of JetBlue was considerably smaller.

---

[3] Boeing (2017) indicates that the fragmentation in the aviation market is mirrored at large hubs, since growth has come from more destinations and frequency, while seats per flight were constant between 2000 and 2016.

Their investigation of Southwest's prices shows that while these were independent of prices charged by legacy carriers, Southwest was constrained, by a second and a third LCC in the market, with prices falling by about 17% in each case. AirTran (subsequently merged with Southwest in 2014) had the largest effect, reducing Southwest's prices by about 21%, followed by other LCCs (16.8%) and JetBlue (12%). Southwest's market share affected its pricing as well, with its prices rising by 4.7% if its share was between 50% and 75% and 6.8% if its share was in excess of 75%.[4]

In a similar vein, Bachwich and Wittman (2017) suggest that ULCCs should be studied as a separate category, primarily because they have different characteristics than LCCs. In recent years, the US airline industry has seen many changes. LCCs have expanded shares and dominate roughly a third of all nonstop routes, collectively accounting for about a quarter of passengers as well as revenue passenger miles (Kwoka et al., 2016). Legacy carriers have reduced capacity, whereas LCCs have added available seat miles. The business models of LCCs and network carriers have converged to some extent. For example, many LCCs no longer restrict themselves to secondary airports and also have interline agreements.[5] Many LCCs, including Southwest and JetBlue, and ULCCs, such as Spirit, are no longer domestic carriers and serve Mexican, Caribbean, and Central American destinations. LCC costs have increased, and legacy carriers have tried to bring theirs down through consolidation and filing for bankruptcy reorganization. ULCCs have emerged to fill the gap and have done so profitably. They (Frontier, Spirit, and Allegiant) have low labor costs and charge low base fares, primarily for transportation; like Ryanair, everything else has to be paid for. These three carriers meet the following criteria: they have lower costs than LCCs, and they rely heavily on ancillary revenues (at least 33% of total passenger revenue). But their total system unit revenue is about 10% lower than that of LCCs and 19% lower than legacy carriers (Bachwich and Wittman, 2017, pp. 156–158).[6]

Bachwich and Wittman (2017) treat ULCCs as a separate category in their fare regressions and hypothesize that ULCCs will exert more downward pressure on fares than LCCs. They also examine the effects of entry and exit on fares. Their results show that on average ULCCs exert more downward pressure on fares. Relative to routes where neither LCCs or ULCCs were present, the presence of both reduced average one-way market fares by between 11.3% to 19.8% over the period 2010–2015. The presence of LCCs alone reduced fares by 4.9%–8.6% and ULCCs alone by 7.7%–20.5%. The gap between ULCC and LCC presence was not statistically significant in 2010. This suggests that their business models have diverged in recent years. Over the years, the additive effect (ULCCS and LCCs relative to LCCs or ULCCs alone) had

---

[4] Bin Salam and McMullen (2013) also observed a dampening of the "Southwest effect" and fare hikes in markets where Southwest faced less competition from other LCCs or ULCCs. Wittman and Swelbar (2013) and Wittman (2014) suggest that some of the fare increases were due to capacity discipline by network carriers.

[5] In southeast Asia, LCCs operate primarily from key hubs (Bowen, 2016).

[6] LCCs include Southwest, JetBlue, Alaska, and Virgin America. The latter two have recently merged. Network or legacy carriers include American, Delta, and United.

declined and almost disappeared by 2015. In 2015, they found that markets served by ULCCs alone saw the same price reduction as markets served by both ULCCs and LCCs, suggesting that LCCs have become more like network carriers.

The differential downward pressure on fares from ULCC and LCC competition disappears in the model which incorporates entry and exit; after entry, both types of carriers exert the same downward pressure on prices of approximately 8%. They attribute this to small-scale entry and low frequency of ULCCs. ULCCs have a higher likelihood of leaving newly entered markets. LCCs abandoned only 3% of markets within a year of commencing service and 8% within 2 years. Legacy carriers and ULCCs abandoned about 6%–7% within 1 year, whereas after 2 years, legacy carriers abandoned 16% of routes and ULCCs abandoned 26%.

Southwest Airlines carries more (scheduled) passengers than any other US carrier, although on the basis of revenue passenger miles, it is a close second to American Airlines.[7] Similarly, Ryanair carried 117 million passengers in 2016, overtaking Lufthansa to become the largest European carrier (Bryan, 2017). LCCs no longer operate on the fringe. In the United States, network or legacy carriers have become the fringe; they impose little pricing discipline on each other and LCCs and ULCCs set their prices independently (Kwoka et al., 2016).[8] Wittman (2014) found that over the period 2007–2012, legacy carriers reduced flights at large airports in the United States by 8.8% and by 21.7% at smaller airports.[9] As a result of this capacity discipline, fares increased at some airports; the largest increases (11.9% over the period 2007–2012) being at the medium-sized airports. In addition to reducing capacity, legacy carriers have become more profit-focused and have reduced costs through bankruptcy reorganization. The cost advantage of LCCs such as Southwest (over legacy carriers) has either remained the same or declined over the years, whereas that of ULCCs has increased.[10] In addition, as a tactical response to competition, they have imitated the activities of ULCCs and are charging for ancillaries, previously included in the ticket price. In other words, they are attempting to increase their profits by appropriating value from consumers and like ULCCs, ancillary revenue is becoming an important

[7] BTS data show that for the year ending May 2017, Southwest carried 150.7 million passengers or about a fifth of all passengers. Its share of revenue passenger miles was 18.4%, whereas that of American Airlines was 18.7%. See https://www.transtats.bts.gov/carriers.asp?pn=1 (accessed 24.08.17).

[8] The impact of LCCs is likely even higher in South and Southeast Asia where the LCC share of total seats was 46% and 53%, respectively, in February 2017. The share in Europe and North America was 37% and 31%, respectively (Boeing, 2017). Asia will remain at the center of short- and medium-haul LCC growth since traffic flows in domestic PRC, domestic India, and domestic emerging Asia are expected to increase by 3.6 times, 5.4 times, and 3.7 times, respectively, between 2017 and 2036 (Airbus, 2017).

[9] Lieshout et al. (2016) indicate that the remote and previously underserved regions of the United Kingdom, Spain, and Italy benefitted the most from liberalization and LCC growth in Europe. This was at the expense of major alliances such as One World and Star Alliance. Competition among airports also increased in the United Kingdom, Benelux countries, Switzerland, and some parts of Germany and Italy due to proximate large- and medium-sized airports offering similar options and products to many destinations.

[10] See MIT Airline Data Project. http://web.mit.edu/airlinedata/www/default.html (accessed 24.08.17). A comparison of 2007 and 2016 (cents per equivalent seat mile, excluding fuel and transport) shows a gap of 3.04 cents in 2007 and 3.22 cents in 2016 between network carriers and LCCs. The gap between network carriers and ULCCs was 1.28 cents in 2007 and 3.8 cents in 2016.

income stream for legacy carriers.[11] Ghemawat (2009) indicates that imitating competitors is not uncommon. However, as product offerings become more similar and competition becomes more intense, the profit spread between firms decline, converging around the mean. ULCCs have stepped in to fill in some of the service gaps left by legacy carriers, particularly at smaller airports in the United States. Keeler (1972) was confident that small communities could be served profitably. While addressing the issue of cross-subsidy in the deregulation debate, Keeler (1972) observed that some smaller communities were being served on a profitable basis by commuter or air-taxi services.[12]

3.3   Airline business models

The literature on business models points to convergence between legacy carriers and LCCs/ULCCs (Daft and Albers, 2015), although it acknowledges, through the use of spider diagrams, that there is no generic LCC model and there are differences between LCCs (Mason and Morrison, 2008; Lohmann and Koo, 2013; Fageda et al., 2015). Since company strategies are not known and often stated in broad terms, this literature attempts to infer strategy from the activities of a firm.[13] Many LCCs started by providing point-to-point service and now offer connects; they served secondary airports and have now moved to major airports (Ryanair, easyjet); similarly, many started with a single type of aircraft and have now added variety to their fleets (JetBlue). Legacy carriers included meals, checked-in-bags, and seat selection in the fare, but now charge for basic transportation like ULCCs and have explicit charges for ancillary services. These are all simple examples of convergence. Nonetheless, important differences remain, all of which may not be evident from the business model literature.

---

[11] Cutting services and costs is not just an American phenomenon. British Airways has recently started charging for meals on its short-haul routes in Europe. Some legacy carriers are also adding more seats and reducing legroom in the "economy cabin". Many LCCs as well as legacy carriers have been charging markups for online credit card payments, over and above the interchange charged by card companies to airlines. Australian airlines have had to stop this practice since after the Competition and Consumer Amendment (payment Surcharges) Act was passed in February 2016. See https://www.legislation.gov.au/Details/C2016A00009 (accessed 24.08.17). The UK will be doing the same from January 2018. See https://www.gov.uk/government/news/rip-off-card-charges-to-be-outlawed (accessed 24.08.17).

[12] Keeler (1989, p. 16) also questioned the practice on an ethical basis. He wrote: "But it is difficult to view this elimination of cross-subsidization as a bad thing, given its questionable basis in either economics or ethics."

[13] As Ghemawat (2009) notes, activity analysis is not new. It is another version of the McKinsey Business System or Porter's value chain. The original intent in the strategy literature, of using activity analysis, was to examine what Porter (1996) calls "strategic fit". Strategic fit (when activities complement strategy or competitive position) prevents imitation; firms can copy the parts but not the whole. Daft and Albers' (2013) notion of a business model includes the value chain as well as two other components which they call company core logic and assets. There are various definitions of a business model which is distinct from both strategy and tactics. Magretta (2002) refers to a business model as a system or how the pieces of a business fit together. Teece (2010) and Casadesus-Masanell and Ricart (2010) refer to it as the logic of the firm or how a firm creates and captures value.

Allegiant and Spirit are both classified as ULCCs and they describe themselves as serving underserved markets (Allegiant Travel Company, 2017; Spirit Airlines Inc., 2017). Yet, there are important differences in the choices these firms have made, which insulate both firms from competition. Allegiant links small and mid-sized cities to popular vacation destinations such as Orlando, Las Vegas, and Tampa. It provides limited-frequency point-to-point service using large, older aircraft (47 MD-80s, 34 A320s, and 4 B757s, ranging in age from 11 to 31 years) with meaningful remaining useful lives. Average block hours per day were 6.3 h per aircraft in 2016. Using older aircraft reduces capital costs, but also increases reputational risks around safety. Since frequency is limited and aircraft are old, there is sufficient time to fix them. It unbundles pricing by selling air transport on a stand-alone basis and air-related as well as third-party products as ancillary services. It outsources activities such as maintenance, ground handling, and baggage services and schedules services so that crew return to base every night. The average fare for scheduled service was $68.47 in 2016 and average total fare, including ancillary services, was $117.95. Data (T-100) from the Bureau of Transport Statistics (BTS) for the year 2016 show that Allegiant faces competition on only three of its top 20 routes.

Spirit, on the other hand, describes its underserved market as price-sensitive travelers who pay for their own travel. It explicitly states that it uses the ULCC model, offering base fares and removing components that are traditionally included in the fare. It uses a uniform fleet of A320s and utilizes opportunistic outsourcing. It has the youngest fleet of any major carrier and high aircraft utilization (12.4 h per day). In addition, it uses high-density seating and serves large markets in the United States as well as some vacation destinations in Latin America and the Caribbean. Although it charges for ancillary services, it competes based on total price, except customers can see what they paid for. In 2016, average ticket revenue per passenger flight segment was $55.54 and ancillary revenue was $51.87 per passenger. Unlike Allegiant, Spirit dominates only three of its top 20 routes. On the remaining routes, it has a small market share and competes with all major carriers. Its largest network overlap is with Southwest. Spirit sees no value in market share and aggressively monitors the profitability of routes. It seeks out routes where fares can be reduced by at least 25% and which have a stimulated demand of at least 200 or more passengers each way. It estimated that there were at least 300 large, unflown, high-fare markets in the United States in 2012 (Spirit Airlines Inc., 2012). This focus on routes, small scale, and the availability of many growth opportunities explains the exit by ULCCs from routes that do not meet the profit and volume criteria.

The US domestic aviation market has been disrupted by LCCs and ULCCs and has become commoditized and fragmented. The market is large and allows for many ways of segmenting. Legacy carriers have added another by "class" of travel by introducing basic transportation fares on domestic routes and premier economy on international routes. Those that do not want to cheapen their brand have introduced low-cost subsidiaries as "fighting brands". This is now being popularized in the literature as "an airline within an airline" although in most instances subsidiaries are run independently and therefore no different from airline-holding companies such as IAG or Singapore

Airlines Group. Other ways to segment include competing on price in major markets (Spirit) or connecting small unserved or underserved communities with vacation destinations (Allegiant).

Much of the economics literature discussed above focusses on the evolving competitive landscape in aviation and on the price impacts of changes in market structure. While this is both important and useful, there is scant discussion of what has remained the same. While Morrison (2001) was troubled by the large size of the Southwest effect, strategy scholars have long celebrated Southwest as an example of sustained competitive advantage or of profitable growth—the holy grail of business. Porter (1996, p. 4) illustrated the notion of competitive strategy by using Southwest as an example. Southwest deliberately chose a different set of activities from the incumbents at the time "to deliver a unique mix of value". Porter (1996) described Continental and Continental Lite as a straddle, or an example of a firm where activities were incompatible—an example of poor strategic fit. Ghemawat (2009, p. 98) used Southwest as an example of sustained superior performance, stating that it was "by far the largest creator of economic value in the airline industry since deregulation."

Ghemawat (1991) defines strategy as commitment to sticky (durable and firm-specific) resources. These allow firms to outperform competitors or prevent mean reversion by sustaining within-industry differences in profitability. 2016 was the 44th consecutive year of profitability for Southwest, with a return on invested capital of 30% (Southwest Airlines Co., 2017). In 2015, Southwest stock had delivered 17.5% average annual returns since 1997 when it was listed on the New York stock exchange, whereas the broader market performance had been 11% (Tully, 2015). Changes in industry structure and regulations do matter, as do jet fuel price hikes, wars, rising security costs, and financial crises; Southwest appears to be immune to these shocks and has beaten the market despite operating in an unattractive industry. A 2005 report by the United States Government Accountability Office (GAO) indicates that between 1978 and 2005 there were 162 bankruptcies in the airline industry and that the business failure rate in this industry was three times higher than the overall business failure rate in the United States. It also suggests that some of this is structural, since airlines have high fixed costs and assume debt to purchase equipment. Demand is cyclical, and yields have declined due to competition. These factors, combined with the numerous external shocks, lead to poor financial performance and higher debt.

Southwest has clearly evolved and made some changes to its way of doing business, however some choices have remained the same. These include a unified fleet of B737s which reduces pilot training and maintenance costs as well as allows for easy redeployment of aircraft. No charges for ticketing (including by phone or in person at the last minute) or changing itineraries. Passengers who cancel a flight can get full credit for another trip. Two pieces of checked baggage are included in the ticket price and Southwest does not sell food on-board; there are always "free" nonalcoholic beverages, peanuts, and pretzels or snack packs on longer flights. In addition, Southwest has simplified the boarding procedures and a fast turn and high aircraft utilization. Southwest avoids adding activities, whereas legacy carriers have kept their activities, but are charging customers for them—a clear case of value appropriation. Southwest could start serving hot meals and charging for them, but this would add to the turnaround time, which would lead to higher costs as it would have to purchase more aircraft to serve its existing routes. The choices that legacy carriers have made prevent them from imitating some of what airlines like Southwest do. The hub and spoke system is their sticky and durable asset or their strategic choice, which prevents them from using a uniform fleet and since they have various "classes" of service, they cannot eliminate hot meals.

Southwest attributes its performance to its customer service and employees, who are its sticky and firm-specific asset. The rapid turnaround requires "relational coordination" across functions pilots, mechanics, gate agents, ramp agents, etc. Southwest's departure process is characterized by "frequent, timely, problem-solving communication between functions, supported by relationships of shared goals, shared knowledge and mutual respect …" (Gittell and Bamber, 2010, p. 169). High levels of relational coordination leading to high productivity is attributed to Southwest's distinctive hiring process. Southwest hires for attitude and relational competence and not just for skills. It looks for what it describes as a warrior spirit (desire to excel and act with courage), a servants heart (putting others first), and not taking oneself too seriously or a fun-"luving" attitude (Southwest's spelling) (Weber, 2015).[14] Southwest also avoids layoffs as a matter of choice and seeks to cut all costs except wages and benefits and profit sharing.[15] Southwest is committed to its employees and treats unions as partners, whereas Ryanair controls employees and avoids relationships with unions. Gittell and Bamber (2010) call the Southwest approach the "high-road" and the Ryanair approach the "low-road" and suggest the former approach to human resource management leads to superior performance in the long run.

Beckenstein and Campbell (2017) suggest that Southwest's business model has five pillars: positive culture, product simplicity, high frequency, operational efficiency, and low fares. It is important to note that low fares are a result of low costs, which come from high labor and capital productivity as well as hedging fuel costs. These allow Southwest to lower fares. The legacy carrier model is different as despite bankruptcy reorganization they have a higher cost base. Bankruptcy has allowed them to offload underfunded pension plans to the Pension Benefit Guaranty Corporation (PBGC). In 2005, United's four pension plans were underfunded by $10 billion and PBGC only received a consideration of $1.6 billion in the United bankruptcy; as a result, the pension plans cannot be restored. In addition to ex-employees losing $3.2 billion in benefits, current employees lose through layoffs and wage cuts as these contribute disproportionately to cost reductions (GAO, 2005).

Another source of cost reduction is capacity. Beckenstein and Campbell (2017) indicate that US legacy carriers have eliminated nearly all of their primarily

---

[14] In 2016, Southwest received 342,664 resumes and hired 7207 new employees, or about 2% of applicants. See https://www.swamedia.com/pages/corporate-fact-sheet (accessed 30.08.17). Weber (2015) also indicates that in a 2014 survey, 75% of Southwest employees felt that their job was "a calling" rather than "a stepping stone" or "just a job".

[15] Unlike other airlines, Southwest had no layoffs after 9/11 or in 2008 when fuel costs were very high.

domestic hubs and 95% of domestic traffic is now routed through international connecting gateways. This allows the three legacy carriers to leverage their mega-alliance opportunities and focus on international growth.[16] They indicate that in the second quarter of 2017, legacy carriers provided 25% lower domestic seat capacity compared to the year 2000, whereas LCCs and ULCCs increased theirs by 171% over the same period.[17] These cost reductions do not allow legacy carriers to match the cost base of LCCs and ULCCs and they face declining yields in the domestic market—the only way to make money is from international growth and by appropriating value from domestic passengers by charging for ancillaries. It is unlikely that this "straddle" is going to work in the long run. What is more likely is that imitating competitors is going to increase price competition in the domestic market and passengers who prefer bundled or semibundled products may move to carriers such as Southwest. At the same time, the international market could become more fragmented reducing profit opportunities. This is now evident in the North Atlantic market where low-cost long-haul capacity in summer 2017 was 6%, a doubling from the previous year.

That leaves two options for legacy carriers: they can abandon the domestic market, leaving it to LCCs and ULCCs and sign interline agreements with them to feed international gateways, or they can try "fighting brands" or "an airline within an airline", which will at least help them to simplify their domestic product offering to match that of LCCs or ULCCs. This is better than segmenting an aircraft. Otherwise, if the assessment of the GAO is correct, we should expect to see more bankruptcy filings in the future. Another lesson from the work of the GAO is that while the economics literature tends to focus on efficiency, entry, and prices after liberalization and deregulation, there are distributional effects. Bankruptcy, if it is a result of the change in market structure after deregulation, as some argue, has had a negative impact on current and previous employees of legacy carriers—many of them are worse off (Dempsey, 2008). However, there are also more employees working in the aviation sector as a result of market growth due to deregulation. Thus, the distributional outcomes have been between labor groups before and after deregulation rather than rents moving from labor to other factors of production.

Legacy carriers have chosen different approaches to meeting competition in domestic versus international markets from LCCs. In the United States, the major carriers were not successful in using the airline within an airline strategy to compete with LCCs in the late 1990s (Gillen and Gados, 2008). Instead, they have now chosen to use their revenue management systems to cover the full range of the demand function and compete with both LCCs and ULCCs. This approach is consistent with the capacity discipline strategy in domestic markets to pursue profit rather than market share. Legacy carriers have introduced "basic" fares to compete with the low fares of LCC

---

[16] This is the same strategy pursued by the three legacy carriers in Europe—Lufthansa Group, IAG, and KLM-Air France.

[17] The number drops to 16% if regional partners are combined with legacy carriers. Regionals increased their capacity by 108% between 200 and 2017.

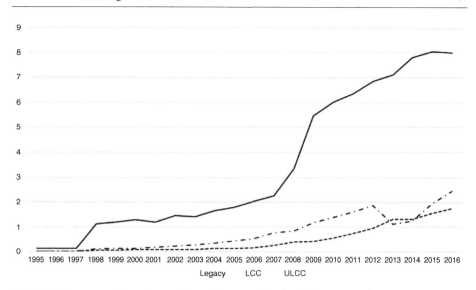

Exhibit 1 Revenues from charges for ancillary services in billions of US $ (U.S. Carriers). *Source*: MIT Airline Data Project. http://web.mit.edu/airlinedata/www/default.html (accessed 24.08.17). *Note*: These include baggage fees, cancellation fees, and miscellaneous operating revenues. See BTS Schedule P-1.2 for details.

and ULCC carriers in domestic markets. These "basic fares" represent transportation service that has stripped out nearly every ancillary or near bundled service; it is the cost of a seat. Such fares do not allow changes or cancellations nor is it possible to upgrade, board early, or request same day standby for a fee. All ancillary services are either not available or are available at a substantial fee.

US carriers, as those elsewhere, have unbundled their products to charge for all ancillary services. Price competition with LCCs and ULCCs in the domestic market was intense; in addition, the United States and much of the world had gone through the financial crises starting in 2008. It was at this point that legacy carriers introduced baggage fees and subsequently fees for other ancillary services.[18] Exhibit 1 illustrates the significant growth in revenue from unbundling. The legacy carriers did not begin in earnest until 2007–2008 and have increased revenues considerably. The LCCs and ULCCs have increased revenues as well but not nearly to the extent that of legacy carriers.

However, this is in part a sheer size effect; ancillary revenue as a percent of total revenue is much higher for LCC and ULCC carriers (Spirit 39%, Wizz 34%,

[18] Many airlines dropped meal service on domestic flights after 9/11. Delta started selling snacks in 2003, followed by United in 2005. See https://www.farecompare.com/travel-advice/airline-fees-bags-history/ (accessed 15.09.17). United introduced first bag fees on June 13, 2008, followed by American Airlines 2 days later and other carriers followed suit as the year progressed. See Brueckner et al., 2015, p. 466.

[19] 2015 data, see http://fortune.com/2015/07/14/airlines-highest-fees/ (accessed 15.09.17).

Exhibit 2 Long-Haul LCCs

Airline/Brand	Affiliation/Parentage	Launch Year
JetStar	Qantas	2006
AirAsia X	Air Asia*	2007
Scoot	Singapore Airlines	2012
Norwegian	Norwegian Air*	2012
Air Canada Rouge	Air Canada	2013
Cebu Pacific	Cebu Pacific Air*	2013
Jin Air	Korean Air	2014
Azul	Azul*	2014
Thai AirAsia X	Air Asia*	2014
NokScoot	Singapore Airlines & Nok Air*	2015
Lion Air	Lion Air*	2015
WestJet	WestJet*	2015
Beijing Capital	Hainan Airlines	2015
Eurowings	Lufthansa	2015
Wow Air	Wow*	2016
Level	IAG	2017

*Indicates LCC. For a list of LCCs, see: https://www.icao.int/sustainability/Documents/LCC-List.pdf (accessed 03.10.17).
Source: Adapted from CAPA (2017).

Allegiant 32%, Jet2.com 28%, Ryanair 25%, Tigerair 22%, Jetstar 21%, Flybe 21%, AirAsia 20%, and Volaris 19%).[19] LCCs have been particularly adept at obtaining ancillary revenue from passengers. In 2016, Spirit, Allegiant, and Frontier were the top three carriers in ancillary revenue per passenger ($49.89, $48.93, and $48.60, respectively).[20]

The "airline within an airline" model is pursued in international markets where market access is still regulated, to a large degree, through the international bilateral system. However, both legacy carriers and LCCs appear to adopt distinctive business models. For example, Air Canada's LCC "Rouge" competes only in international and many trans-border (Canada–United States) markets and only on lower yield leisure markets. It does not fly domestically. Eurowings, part of the Eurowings Group within the Lufthansa Group, flies in the EU to compete against LCCs and internationally. IAG has introduced LEVEL, and KLM-Air France will have "Boost" as their long-haul low-cost competitors but it is unclear whether they will pursue an Air Canada or Lufthansa type strategy. However, a large number of LCCs are also introducing long-haul service, generally under a different brand. As yet, no American legacy or LCC carrier has introduced a long-haul low-cost competitor. Exhibit 2 lists long-haul LCCs and their affiliated parentage.

---

[20] See http://www.ideaworkscompany.com/wp-content/uploads/2017/07/2016-Top-10-Airline-Ancillary-Revenue-Rankings.pdf (accessed 15.09.17).

3.4 Long-haul low cost

The low-cost model is also moving to the long-haul international markets. CAPA (2017) indicates that the launch of LEVEL (by IAG) represented the 15th low-cost long-haul operation since 2012. Seven of the 15 are affiliated with legacy carriers. AirAsia X leads in capacity (about 13,300 weekly seats) and frequency, whereas Norwegian leads in the number of routes (48) as well as distance (over 10,000 km). It is important to note, however, that legacy carriers have tried domestic low-cost affiliates and many have failed. AirAsia X's success thus far is often used as "proof" that "international" low-cost service is viable. It is important to note that much of that is driven by both geography and economics, rather than by a "new business model" or "strategy". AirAsia X is based in Malaysia which is one of the 10 members of the Association of Southeast Asian Nations (ASEAN). Two members, the Philippines and Indonesia, are archipelagos, the latter being the largest in the world. Others are small (Singapore and Brunei), and one is land-locked (Lao PDR). These countries are located between India and China with whom they have historical, cultural, and economic ties. Over the years, intra-ASEAN trade as well as trade with other Asian countries, particularly, China, has become more important relative to that with the EU or the United States.

Like geography, the level of prosperity also varies within ASEAN. Per-capita nominal GDP is above US $1000 in Cambodia and Myanmar, almost US $10,000 in Malaysia, and more than US $51,000 in Singapore. On a (purchasing power parity) PPP basis, the Asia Pacific region accounts for 45% of world GDP. Europe accounts for 21% and the United States for about 18%. Recent IMF data indicate that (annual) real GDP growth was 5.3% in Asia Pacific as well as East Asia, 4.9% in Southeast Asia, and 6.9% in South Asia. Both Europe and North America grew at around 2% and Australia and New Zealand at around 3%.[21]

It is because of geography that most 2-h flights within ASEAN are "international"; this applies equally to all carriers operating in this region and not just LCCs. LCCs, however, benefit more from economic growth and low- and middle-income populations, since legacy carriers are likely unaffordable for many ASEAN residents. Their "first flight ever", either domestic or international, is likely to be on an LCC. The increasing size of the middle class as well as the deep economic linkages between ASEAN countries and with their large and faster growing neighbors such as India and China provide growth opportunities for all ASEAN carriers but again more so for LCCs. It is not surprising then that a majority of AirAsia X's long-haul (about 6000 km) routes link ASEAN with China and India and indeed it is Australia's proximity to this vibrant region that explains some of the success of JetStar. Most of its international routes link Australia to ASEAN and other Asian countries.

Other exogenous factors that have made the long-haul LCC model possible include low fuel prices as well as more fuel-efficient aircraft such as the B787, the B737 Max,

---

[21] The economic data are the most recent available from the April 2017 IMF World Economic Outlook web site. See http://www.imf.org/external/datamapper/datasets/WEO (accessed 15.09.17).

and A320neo. The narrow bodies make it possible to serve thin long-haul markets. Indeed, aircraft technology has had a significant impact on change in aviation but only when it coupled with regulatory/policy change; there has been a continual interplay between technology and liberalization of airline markets.[22]

3.5   Summary and conclusions

This chapter has reviewed some of the changes that have taken place in the aviation industry over the last decade and a half. In particular, it focused on the competitive impacts of the strategic developments as well as the changes in strategic responses and the evolution of business models. The first issue we examined was the changing nature of price competition in the US aviation market. Legacy carriers have reduced capacity and reorganized in order to become more profit-focused. They are appropriating value from consumers by charging for ancillary services, just like some LCCs and ULCCs. LCCs and ULCCs, on the other hand, have added capacity and are setting prices in a commoditized and fragmented market. Legacy carriers have become the fringe. They provide muted competition to each other and to low-cost providers. LCCs and ULCCs continue to provide price competition to each other and to legacy carriers. As a result, both average prices and price dispersion have declined. While the "Southwest effect" may have declined, it has not disappeared as Southwest continues to exert a larger competitive effect on fares than other LCCs. It also remains the only example of sustained competitive advantage or profitable growth in the US aviation market since deregulation, delivering above (market) average returns for 44 consecutive years. We expect that legacy carriers will have to focus more on international markets for future growth as LCCs and ULCCs continue to grow in profitable segments of the domestic market.

The second issue we examined is the evolution of the airline business model, in particular, the LCC model and the emergence of the more radical ULCC model. The introduction, development, and evolution of the LCC model are well documented in the academic and trade literature (Mason and Morrison, 2008). Deregulation was instrumental in allowing differing airline business models to emerge. This model has been introduced in every deregulated airline market in the world with varying degrees of success for different reasons. Southwest is held up as the quintessential example of the LCC and is one that for the most part has been true to the original LCC model. Ryanair, the European LCC, is another example of a highly successful LCC which has been true to the LCC principles of simplicity in organization, fare structure, and service composition.

Under regulation, legacy carriers had ignored the elastic portion of the demand curve and had essentially foreclosed air travel to the majority of people. With the potential for market competition, the LCC model was a consequence of the need to

---

[22] Emirates' success at exploiting 6th Freedoms was dependent on Airbus 340, Boeing 777, and Airbus 380. Boeing 737 and Airbus 320 fueled the expansion of the LCCs.

be able to charge low fares to attract price-sensitive passengers (revenue management was still rudimentary). The key underlying drivers to achieve these low costs were increased productivity, lower factor input costs, and reduced complexity in every aspect of the organization. Each of these was of different importance depending on the LCC and whether it was located in the United States, Europe, Canada, or elsewhere. The key sources of cost savings were reduced distribution costs by using direct sales, eliminating global distribution system (GDS) fees, and having no commissions on ticket sales, while the second important source of cost savings were the use of secondary airports which not only reduced fees and charges but facilitated faster turnarounds which increased productivity of aircraft and crew.[23]

However, sustaining the cost advantage required the LCC firm (airline) to ensure that there was a strategic fit between its activities, or the activities were organized in a manner which reinforced its competitive position in the market. In the matter of the growth of the LCC model, the objective of low costs could be achieved through multiple channels including increased productivity of high-value assets such as aircraft and crew. To achieve this require first that the product offered should not be complex. But what is also needed is the use of secondary airports and the design of an activity that cannot be easily copied since it is firm-specific. As an example, Southwest has one of the faster turnarounds between flights; this is an activity which complements its low-cost strategy. Southwest can achieve this because they have a system in place in which the personnel culture of Southwest plays an important role (Gillen and Lall, 2004). Southwest has significantly more departures per gate than other carriers, whether LCCs or legacy. This is a result of being able to turn aircraft faster than other carriers and ability to turn a flight at a gate or preparing for a departure involves coordination of up to 12 different functional groups. The ability to coordinate is a result of pursuing a systems approach with the vertical relations between processes based on simplicity of service. This leads to simplicity in processes and simplicity of organization. This is fundamental to high productivity and lower costs. The key point is operational efficiency is not a strategy but follows from it; operational effectiveness complements the business model to achieve lower costs through simplicity of product design, processes, and organization. This culture is related to hiring and training practices and a no layoff policy.

We have seen a convergence of the legacy and LCC model. LCC costs have increased over time as variants of the basic LCC model have emerged that have differing product, network, and organizational features. Legacy carriers have also shed costs and improved productivity. They have significantly improved their revenue management systems to increase load factors and compete with LCCs especially in the middle range of fares. The increased competitiveness together with an economic downturn in 2008 led to a tactical shift to unbundling the airline service product and the use of ancillary fees to increase revenues. The legacy carriers have done remarkably well in

---

[23] Lower distribution charges provided 15% of the difference in the cost per available seat kilometer between LCCs and legacy carriers in the EU and use of secondary airports provided 21% of the cost difference. Other sources of cost savings were lower labor costs, increased utilization, and higher seating density; see Franke, 2004, p. 17).

increasing revenue and profit. The LCC have as well but face stiffer competition from the newer ULCC sector. It is important to recognize that there are limits to growth of mature LCCs due to higher costs of investment in aircraft and equipment as well as rising labor costs. Between 2000 and 2016, total labor and related expanse per equivalent seat mile increased by 1.05 cents for legacy carriers in the United States, by 1.41 cents for LCCs, and by 0.09 cents for ULCCs.[24]

A troubling outcome of unbundling is that over time econometric work on price competition and its impacts as we have discussed is going to become less representative of what is really going on and probably already is because BTS (DB1B ticket) data only include the price of transport, cancellations, and bags—and not all ancillaries—which are obviously becoming more important for all airlines. The fact that the United States was the one market for which there was detailed price data that permitted extensive and important third-party assessments of industry performance is no longer be true.

Acknowledgements

We thank an anonymous reviewer for their helpful comments and suggestions.

References

Airbus, 2017. Global market forecast 2017–2036. Airbus, commercial aircraft. http://www.aircraft.airbus.com/market/global-market-forecast-2017-2036/ (accessed 30.08.17).

Allegiant Travel Company, 2017. Allegiant travel company 10-K form. http://ir.allegiantair.com/phoenix.zhtml?c=197578&p=irol-sec (accessed 24.08.17).

Bachwich, A.R., Wittman, M.D., 2017. The emergence and effects of the ultra-low cost carrier (ULCC) business model in the U.S. airline industry. Journal of Air Transport Management 62, 155–164.

Beckenstein, A.R., Campbell, B.M., 2017. Public benefits and private success: the southwest effect revisited. https://papers.ssrn.com/sol3/papers.cfm?abstract_id=3016047 (accessed 02.09.17).

Bin Salam, S., McMullen, B., 2013. Is there still a southwest effect? Transportation Research Record: Journal of the Transportation Research Board 2325, 1–8.

Boeing, 2017. Current market outlook 2017–2036. Boeing, commercial airplanes. http://www.boeing.com/resources/boeingdotcom/commercial/market/current-market-outlook-2017/assets/downloads/2017-cmo-6-19.pdf (accessed 30.08.17).

Bowen, J.T., 2016. "Now everyone can fly"? Scheduled airline services to secondary cities in Southeast Asia. Journal of Air Transport Management 53, 94–104.

Brueckner, J.K., Lee, D., Singer, E.S., 2013. Airline competition and domestic US airfares: a comprehensive reappraisal. Economics of Transportation 2 (1), 1–17.

---

[24] See MIT Airline Data Project. http://web.mit.edu/airlinedata/www/default.html (accessed 24.08.17). Total labor and related expense per equivalent seat mile in 2016 was 5.13 cents for legacy carriers, 3.56 for LCCs, and 2.74 for ULCCs.

Brueckner, J.K., et al., 2015. Product unbundling in the travel industry: the economics of airline bag fees. Journal of Economics & Management Strategy 24 (3), 457–484.

Bryan, V., 2017. Ryanair seizes Lufthansa's crown as Europe's biggest airline by passengers. https://uk.reuters.com/article/uk-lufthansa-traffic-idUKKBN14U1P4 (accessed 24.08.17).

Call, G.D., Keeler, T.E., 1985. Airline deregulation, fares, and market behavior: some empirical evidence. In: Daughety, A.F. (Ed.), Analytical Studies in Transport Economics. Cambridge University Press, Cambridge, UK, pp. 221–247.

CAPA, 2017. Airline Leader, Issue 40, May–June.

Casadesus-Masanell, R., Ricart, J.E., 2010. From strategy to business models and onto tactics. Long Range Planning 43 (2–3), 195–215.

Daft, J., Albers, S., 2013. A conceptual framework for measuring airline business model convergence. Journal of Air Transport Management 28, 47–54.

Daft, J., Albers, S., 2015. An empirical analysis of airline business model convergence. Journal of Air Transport Management 46, 3–11.

Dempsey, P.S., 2008. The financial performance of the airline industry post-deregulation. Huston Law Review 45 (2), 422–485.

Doganis, R., 2006. The Airline Business, Second ed Routledge, Taylor and Francis Group, London.

Dresner, M., Lin, J.-S.C., Windle, R., 1996. The impact of low-cost carriers on airport and route competition. Journal of Transport Economics and Policy 30 (3), 309–328.

Fageda, X., Suau-Sanchez, P., Mason, K.J., 2015. The evolving low-cost business model: network implications of fare bundling and connecting flights in Europe. Journal of Air Transport Management 42, 289–296.

Franke, M., 2004. Competition between network carriers and low-cost carriers—retreat battle or breakthrough to a new level of efficiency? Journal of Air Transport Management 10 (1), 15–21.

GAO, 2005. Commercial aviation: bankruptcy and pension problems are symptoms of underlying structural issues. GAO-05-945. http://www.gao.gov/assets/250/248034.pdf (accessed 02.09.17).

Ghemawat, P., 1991. Commitment. Simon and Schuster, The Free Press, New York.

Ghemawat, P., 2009. Strategy and the Business Landscape, Third ed Prentice-Hall, New York.

Gillen, D., Gados, A., 2008. Airlines within airlines: assessing the vulnerabilities of mixing business models. Research in Transportation Economics 24 (1), 25–35.

Gillen, D., Lall, A., 2004. Competitive advantage of low-cost carriers: some implications for airports. Journal of Air Transport Management 10 (1), 41–50.

Gittell, J.H., Bamber, G.J., 2010. High- and low-road strategies for competing on costs and their implications for employment relations: international studies in the airline industry. The International Journal of Human Resource Management 21 (2), 165–179.

Goolsbee, A., Syverson, C., 2008. How do incumbents respond to the threat of entry? Evidence from the major airlines. The Quarterly Journal of Economics 123 (4), 1611–1633.

Hollander, A., 1987. On price-increasing entry. Economica 54 (215), 317–324.

Hüschelrath, K., Müller, K., 2012. Low cost carriers and the evolution of the U.S. airline industry. Competition and Regulation in Network Industries 13 (2), 133–159.

Hüschelrath, K., Müller, K., 2014. The value of bluer skies—how much do consumers gain from entry by JetBlue airways in long haul U.S. airline markets? International Journal of Transport Economics XLI (1), 131–157.

Keeler, T.E., 1972. Airline regulation and market performance. The Bell Journal of Economics and Management Science 3 (2), 399–424.

Keeler, T.E., 1989. Airline deregulation and the market performance: the economic basis for regulatory reform and lessons from the US experience. http://www.escholarship.org/uc/item/2pd5k8d3 (accessed 26.08.17).

Kwoka, J., Hearle, K., Alepin, P., 2016. From the fringe to the forefront: low cost carriers and airline price determination. Review of Industrial Organization 48 (3), 247–268.

Lieshout, R., et al., 2016. The competitive landscape of air transport in Europe. Journal of Transport Geography 50, 68–82.

Lohmann, G., Koo, T.T.R., 2013. The airline business model spectrum. Journal of Air Transport Management 31, 7–9.

Magretta, J., 2002. Why business models matter. Harvard Business Review 80 (5), 86–92.

Mason, K.J., Morrison, W.G., 2008. Towards a means of consistently comparing airline business models with an application to the "low cost" airline sector. Research in Transportation Economics 24 (1), 75–84.

Morrison, S.A., 2001. Actual, adjacent, and potential competition: estimating the full effect of southwest airlines. Journal of Transport Economics and Policy 35 (2), 239–256.

Porter, M.E., 1996. What is strategy? Harvard Business Review 74 (6), 61–78.

Scotti, D., Dresner, M., 2015. The impact of baggage fees on passenger demand on US air routes. Transport Policy 43, 4–10.

Sengupta, A., Wiggins, S.N., 2014. Airline pricing, price dispersion, and ticket characteristics on and off the internet. American Economic Journal: Economic Policy 6 (1), 272–307.

Southwest Airlines Co., 2017. Southwest airlines reports fourth quarter and record annual profit. 44th Consecutive Year of Profitability. Southwest Airlines Newsroom, https://www.swamedia.com/releases/release-eba09dc2b45876b76f05a1143e0ca048-southwest-airlines-reports-fourth-quarter-and-record-annual-profit-44th-consecutive-year-of-profitability (accessed 24.08.17).

Spirit Airlines Inc., 2012. Spirit airlines: run like a business. http://files.shareholder.com/downloads/ABEA-5PAQQ9/0x0x555011/f7a2957c-7392-4666-98d0-d842e3223532/Maxim_Growth_-_Spirit_Airlines_3.26.12.pdf (accessed 24.08.17).

Spirit Airlines Inc., 2017. Spirit Airlines Inc. 10-K form. http://files.shareholder.com/downloads/ABEA-5PAQQ9/5049368863x0xS1498710-17-44/1498710/filing.pdf (accessed 24.08.17).

Tan, K.M., 2016. Incumbent response to entry by low-cost carriers in the U.S. airline industry. Southern Economic Journal 82 (3), 874–892.

Teece, D.J., 2010. Business models, business strategy and innovation. Long Range Planning 43 (2–3), 172–194.

Tully, S., 2015. How Southwest airlines is disrupting business travel. Fortune. http://fortune.com/2015/09/23/southwest-airlines-business-travel/ (accessed 24.08.17).

van Ryzin, G.J., Talluri, K.T., 2005. An introduction to revenue management. Emerging Theory, Methods, and Applications. INFORMS Tutorials in Operations Research. INFORMS, 142-194, https://pubsonline.informs.org/series/educ.

Weber, J., 2015. How southwest airlines hires such dedicated people. Harvard Business Review, https://hbr.org/2015/12/how-southwest-airlines-hires-such-dedicated-people (accessed 30.08.17).

Williams, G., 1994. The Airline Industry and the Impact of Deregulation, Second ed Routledge, London, UK.

Wittman, M.D., 2014. The effects of capacity discipline on smaller U.S. airports: trends in service, connectivity, and fares. MSc Thesis. Massachusetts Institute of Technology. https://dspace.mit.edu/handle/1721.1/90076 (accessed 24.06.17).

Wittman, M.D., Swelbar, W.S., 2013. Evolving trends of U.S. domestic airfares: the impact of competition, consolidation and low cost carriers. http://dspace.mit.edu/bitstream/handle/1721.1/79878/ICAT-2013-07.pdf (accessed 24.06.17).

Further Reading

Pension Benefit Guaranty Corporation, 2017. Why PBGC cannot restore the United Airlines' pension plans. Pension Benefit Guaranty Corporation, Washington, DC, U.S. https://www.pbgc.gov/wr/large/united/united-airlines-plan-restoration (accessed 02.09.2017).

Mergers, efficiency, and productivity in the railroad industry: an attribute-incorporated data envelopment analysis approach

4

Rolf Färe*, Taylor K. McKenzie**, Wesley W. Wilson**, Wenfeng Yan†
*Oregon State University, Corvallis, OR, United States; **University of Oregon, Eugene, OR, United States; †Symantec, Mountain View, CA, United States

Chapter outline

Dedication

Virtually all who work in transport economics has been touched in some form by Professor Keeler and his work. In the early 1980s, when I started out, one of the very first papers I read was "Railroad Costs, Returns to Scale, and Excess Capacity," which was published in the *Review of Economics and Statistics* in 1974. It remains a paper that I require students working on railroads to read. His book titled *Railroads, Freight, and Public Policy* published in 1983 by Brookings is and remains a classic book, and I regularly cite it and reference it on regulatory issues on railroads. Over the years, I have read many of his works, and his works with his students and colleagues. Many of these students and colleagues have shaped transportation economics as practiced over the last several decades. It was not until the early 1990s that I met Professor Keeler when he visited the

Transportation Policy and Economic Regulation. http://dx.doi.org/10.1016/B978-0-12-812620-2.00004-3

University of Oregon and gave a seminar. I was very much astounded by his energy and knowledge
of the industry, which are attributes shared by most of the students of his that I have encountered.
All are grateful for their interactions with him as am I, and all hold him with great respect.

Wesley W. Wilson
University of Oregon

4.1   Introduction

After nearly 100 years of regulation, the railroad industry was in dire straits in the
1970s. Many point to the effects of regulation, new modes of transportation, and new
products that were transported to help explain the downward spiral of the industry
for example, Keeler (1983). Since passage of the Staggers Act of 1980,[1] the US railroad industry has experienced a tremendous increase in productivity and decreases in
rates and costs.[2] The Act allowed railroads some degree of pricing flexibility, which
allowed them to be responsive to changes in market conditions without a long and
lengthy rate review case. The Act also allowed multicar pricing as well as confidential
contract pricing with the result that railroads could price larger movements lower and
facilitate larger shipment sizes. The Act also streamlined abandonment regulations
and merger regulations. Because of the former, the network held by large Class I railroads has been reduced tremendously, and of the latter, the industry has consolidated
from 40 Class I carriers in 1980 to only 7 today.[3]

Mergers can lead to the realization of scale economies and cost savings due to
improvements in productivity. But, mergers can also result in gains to the market
power of the surviving firm, which leads to rising prices and a loss of social welfare
(Williamson, 1968).[4] In this study, we focus on the measurement and level of firm-
level efficiencies, and how efficiency and productivity have been affected by mergers.
The bulk of the related literature has examined these effects using a cost function and

[1] In 1980, the railroad industry was partially deregulated by the Staggers Act, which removed most price
controls and gave railroad firms the power to merge with one another and increase profitability.

[2] In the post-Staggers Act period, railroad productivity, measured by total factor productivity, increased by
163% from 1980 to 2007 (American Association of Railroads [AAR], 2008). The Rail Rate Index falls
from 1985 to 2000, flattens out until 2004, and, since 2005, rates have begun to go up (Surface Transportation Board (STB), 2009).

[3] Railroad firms in the United States are separated into three categories based on their annual revenues: Class I
for freight railroads with annual operating revenues above $346.8 million (in 2006 dollars), Class II for freight
railroads with revenues between $27.8 million and $346.7 million (in 2006 dollars), and Class III for all other
freight railroads. These classifications are set by STB. Studies differ in the number of Class I railroads in
1980. This information is consistent with Wilson (1997), Bitzan and Wilson (2007), and AAR (1980, 2010).

[4] For discussions of the relationship between deregulation and rates, efficiency, and innovation, see Berndt
et al. (1993), Wilson (1994), Wilson (1997), Gallamore (1999), Ellig (2002), Bitzan and Wilson (2007),
Waters (2007). For discussions of the relationship between deregulation and productivity growth, see
Bitzan and Keeler (2003) and Winston (2005). See Smith (1983) and Wilner (1997) for the summary of
railroad mergers and policy.

have generally found large effects.[5] In contrast, we use Data Envelopment Analysis (DEA). While there are a few studies of rail efficiency and productivity that use DEA for example, Lim and Lovell (2008, 2009), we differ from these in that we use an attribute-incorporated Malmquist productivity index (AMPI). Unlike other studies, this allows the frontier to vary across firms and through time in terms of measurable attributes, for example, average length of haul, miles of road, and so on.

The AMPI version of DEA allows us to specify the level of productivity and evaluate the sources and changes of productivity by decomposing the AMPI into the technical, efficient, and attribute components. This is particularly important in the railroad industry, because operating conditions are significantly different across railroads. In the application, we develop efficiency measures over time, estimate the effects of mergers on efficiency and productivity performance, and identify the real sources of productivity growth. We find that (1) the technical efficiency of each of the seven survivor firms grows gradually through time; (2) the mergers overall do not lead to a significant technical efficiency (TE) and scale efficiency (SE) gains, but three merged firms experience significant technical efficiency increases after mergers; (3) the mergers that happened in the 1980s have a higher impact on efficiency change than those in the 1990s; and (4) the productivity gains are mostly explained by network and operation attributes changes and technology improvement during this period. Overall, mergers do not have a material impact on the efficiency gains or losses in the long run.

This chapter is organized as follows. In Section 2, we provide a brief overview of the literature with regard to productivity. In Section 3, we develop the models we use, and in Section 4 describe the data. In Section 5, we present the empirical models and display the results along efficiency performance, merger effect, and productivity change lines. Finally, Section 6 presents a summary and the conclusions. A detailed description of AMPI is in an appendix.

4.2 Productivity and efficiency

In the 1970s and early 1980s, many transport industries were fully or partially deregulated. A unifying theme underlying deregulation is that regulation had either introduced inefficiencies or impaired firm incentives to innovate. Since then, there have been several advancements in techniques to study productivity, productivity growth, and efficiency, as well as several studies that apply the various techniques. In this section, we briefly describe productivity and the various approaches to measure productivity and productivity gains.

Productivity is concerned with how well inputs can be transformed into outputs. Productivity growth measures how productivity changes over time. Beginning with Solow's (1957) classic work, there has been considerable work on productivity to tie productivity growth to growth in economies and convergence of productivities

[5] See, for example, Berndt et al. (1993), Wilner (1997), Wilson (1997), Ivaldi and McCullough (2001), Gallamore (1999), Bitzan and Keeler (2003), Bitzan and Wilson (2007), Lim and Lovell (2008, 2009).

in developed and undeveloped countries (Jorgenson and Nishimizu, 1978; Munnell, 1990; Nadiri, 1970; Nishimizu and Page, 1982; Solow, 1957). There has also been significant work on productivity and inefficiency (Farrell, 1957), research and development (Griliches, 1979), the role of returns to scale (Chan and Mountain, 1983), as well as technological characteristics such as separability, homotheticity, homogeneity, and Hicks neutral technological change (Caves et al., 1980).

A variety of indices of total factor productivity have been developed by Christensen et al. (1973), Kendrick (1973), Diewert (1976), Caves et al. (1980), and others. Notably, the pioneering work of Caves et al. (1981) provided a method of getting estimates of productivity growth that emanate directly from a cost function, and therefore avoid issues relating to productivity growth as reflecting changes in scale or movements away from or toward equilibrium. In their analysis, the time derivative of the cost function provides two measures of total factor productivity growth (TFP)—one holds the set of inputs fixed and finds the increase in output, and one that holds the outputs fixed and finds the reduction in inputs needed to produce it as technology improves. Other developments have focused on efficiency levels.[6] Aigner et al. (1977) and Meeusen and van Den Broeck (1977) introduced the stochastic frontier approach, which isolates the influence of inefficient behavior from other sources of productivity gains. Charnes et al. (1978) introduced DEA, which provides a nonparametric approach to estimating the frontier along with related inefficiency measures. These approaches have been widely used.

The cost function approach has been widely used in railroad research to examine efficiency, productivity, and the effects of mergers. Before the 1980s, a wide range of studies, including Borts (1952), Friedlaender (1971), Keeler (1974), and Harris (1977), used the classic cost and production method.[7] Later, Brown et al. (1979), Caves et al. (1980, 1981), and Friedlaender and Spady (1981) started to estimate railroad costs using translog cost functions.[8] More recently, a number of the papers, including Berndt et al. (1993), Friedlaender et al. (1993), Wilson (1997), Ivaldi and McCullough (2001), Ivaldi and McCullough (2005), Bitzan and Keeler (2003, 2007), Bitzan and

---

[6] On the definition of efficiency, McCullough (2007) made a comprehensive study about railroad efficiency measure. He pointed out that there were two economic aspects of efficiency: productive efficiency (PE) and allocative efficiency (AE). PE occurs when an economy cannot produce more of one good or service without producing less of another, and AE occurs when the economy cannot raise one consumer's satisfaction without lowering another's. PE generally occurs when firms produce at minimum average total cost. AE occurs when price signals to consumers are based on marginal costs. In Ellig (2002), PE refers dynamic efficiency, and author describes that dynamic efficiency occurs when firms find ways to lower their costs (shift the production function), improve quality (shift the demand curve), or services (create a new demand curve). Although different studies have slightly different definitions of efficiency, in this chapter, we use the distance function-based efficiency definition, and pay attention on the technical and AE components.

[7] For example, Friedlaender (1971) estimated short- and long-run cost functions for railroads, Keeler (1974) used a Cobb-Douglas production function to model railroads.

[8] Translog cost function was first used by Christensen et al. (1973). A translog cost function can be used to estimate the properties of a technology without the functional form placing a priori restrictions on the technology. For example, Caves et al. (1980, 1981) used a translog production structure to estimate the productivity growth in railroad industry, and found that the productivity growth was more different from the previous studies that used index procedures.

Wilson (2007), explored the effects of partial deregulation on costs, productivity, and mergers.[9]

The DEA approach provides an alternative approach, and it has been applied to a wide range of industries. The primary advantage of the DEA approach is that it does not assume specific parametric functional forms for the production frontiers and avoids the use of distributional assumptions on the disturbance term in econometric models. It also provides a measure of inefficiency. Another advantage of the DEA model is that it can easily accommodate multiple outputs and multiple inputs simultaneously thereby avoiding inappropriate aggregation of multiple outputs and inputs which are common in service industries such as transportation.

DEA analyses use index numbers. As discussed in Diewert (1998), in the index number theory literature, measures are usually classified into indicators (differences) and indexes (ratios) (Diewert, 1998).[10] Accordingly, the DEA applications on efficiency measurement use either the difference-based index approach or the ratio-based index approach.[11] As noted by Cross and Färe (2008), the indicator decomposition difference approach, however, lacks "an axiomatic framework for the difference-based indicator," and as such, it cannot fully explore the sources of productivity changes.

In applications to the rail market, two papers by Lim and Lovell (2008, 2009) used an indicator approach to model changes in costs and profits to identify how productivity change contribute to changes in costs and profits over time and across railroads.[12] In their analyses, the measures are developed given the technology is the same for all railroads. They decompose changes in costs or profits from changes in prices, inputs, and outputs. In our application, we adopt a ratio-based index number and AMPI introduced by Färe et al. (1995).[13] This allows identification of observable differences in technologies and operational characteristics across firms, and the contributions of efficiency change to productivity. It also allows us to assess historical trends in efficiency and productivity, to examine the effects of merger activity on efficiency, and to identify the major factors associated with productivity growth in the US railroad industry during the period 1983–2008.

[9] For example, Bitzan and Wilson (2007) estimated a translog cost function of firm by a three-stage-least squares approach with miles of road (MOR) and revenue ton mails (RTM) treated as endogenous, and then use the results to estimate the cost effects of mergers. They focused on the efficiency gains of 14 mergers that took place between 1983 and 2003, and found that consolidation in industry level accounts for about an 11.4% reduction in costs.

[10] See Kumbhakar (1988), Chapin and Schmidt (1998), Coelli and Perelman (2000), Atkinson et al. (2003), Lan and Lin (2005), and Lim and Lovell (2008, 2009).

[11] The indicator (decomposition) model associates with the difference-based index number, which is the difference of prices, quantities, or values comparing two time periods or two points in time.

[12] This model was built on difference-based Bennet input price and quantity indicators. See Bennet (1920) for the definition of Bennet input price and quantity indicators.

[13] A ratio-based index number is a percentage ratio of prices, quantities, or values comparing two time periods or two points in time. The time period that serves as a basis for the comparison is called the base period and the period that is compared to the base period is called the given or current period.

4.3   Conceptual framework

An alternative to the production/cost function approach is the DEA approach, and in this section, we illustrate the DEA approach with an analysis of mergers, efficiencies, and productivity in the US rail industry. We focus on the measurement and level of firm level efficiencies, how efficiency and productivity have been affected by merger activity, and the sources of efficiency gains using a DEA approach, which is in contrast to the bulk of the literature.[14] As discussed earlier, there are a few studies of rail efficiency and productivity that use DEA. We differ from these in that we introduce, to this literature, an AMPI that allows the frontier to vary across firms and through time in terms of measurable attributes, for example, average length of haul, miles of road, and so on.

We begin with the notion of an input distant function and the Malmquist productivity index (MPI), which are the tools used to measure efficiency and productivity change. We then describe the linear programming DEA method to compute the distance function, the measures of technical efficiency (TE) and scale efficiency (SE). The final subsection introduces our main analysis framework—the AMPI method.

4.3.1   General setting and the distance function

Economic efficiency has technical and allocative components. The technical component refers to the ability to avoid waste, either by producing as much output as technology and input usage allow or by using as little input as required by technology and output production. Thus, the analysis of TE can have an output augmenting orientation or an input conserving orientation. The AE component refers to the ability to combine inputs and/or outputs in optimal proportions. Optimal proportions satisfy the first-order conditions for the optimization problem assigned to the firm.

Debreu (1951) and Farrell (1957) introduce a measure of TE. With an input conserving orientation, their measure is defined as (one minus) the maximum equiproportionate reduction in all inputs that is feasible with given technology and outputs. With an output augmenting orientation, their measure is defined as the maximum radial expansion in all outputs that is feasible with given technology and inputs. To define the Debreu-Farrell input-oriented measure of TE, the distance function needs to be introduced.

In general, we set up the production technology on the input and output subspace. Assume that a vector of inputs $x = (x_1, \cdots, x_N) \in R_+^N$ produces a vector of output $y = (y_1, \cdots, y_M) \in R_+^M$, and production technology can be represented by the production set $T = \{(x, y) : x \text{ can produce } y\}$. Technology can also be represented by input sets $L(y) = \{x : (x, y) \in T\}$ and output sets $P(x) = \{y : (x, y) \in T\}$. Shephard (1953) introduces the input distance function to provide a functional representation of production technology, and Shephard's (1970) output distance function provides another functional representation of production technology.[15] The input distance function is

$$D_i(y, x) = \max\{\lambda : (x / \lambda) \in L(y)\},$$

---

[14] See, for example, Berndt et al. (1993), Wilner (1997), Wilson (1997), Ivaldi and McCullough (2001), Gallamore (1999), Bitzan and Keeler (2003), Bitzan and Wilson (2007), Lim and Lovell (2008, 2009).

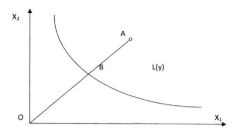

Figure 4.1 The input distance function.

for $\in L(y)$, $D_i(y,x) \geq 1$, and for $x \in I(y)$, where $I(y) = \{x : x \in L(y), \lambda x \notin L(y) \text{ if } \lambda < 1\}$ is the input isoquants, $D_i(y,x) = 1$.[16]

Fig. 4.1 shows that the value of the distance function for point A is equal to the ratio OA/OB. Given standard assumptions on T, the input distance function $D_i(y,x)$ is nonincreasing in y and is nondecreasing in x, homogeneous of degree +1, and convex in x. From now, using the formal interpretation as the value of the function, the Debreu-Farrell input-oriented measure of TE is $TE_i(y,x) = \min\{\lambda : \lambda x \in L(y)\}$ and it follows that $TE_i(y,x) = 1 / D_i(y,x)$.

The distance function (or the Debreu-Farrell measure TE), which has often served as a theoretical device for efficiency measurement, has been widely computed using the linear programming method. Furthermore, to explore the SE aspect, we establish the technology frontier model under assumptions of constant returns to scale (CRS) and variable returns to scale (VRS). The calculation of SE can be expressed as $\dfrac{TE_i(y,x \mid C)}{TE_i(y,x \mid V)}$ using the CRS and VRS efficiency scores.[17] SE can be used to determine whether a given producer is operating at decreasing, increasing, or CRS (see, for instance, Färe et al., 1985). If $\dfrac{TE_i(y,x \mid C)}{TE_i(y,x \mid V)} = 1$, the producer is operating under CRS and is scale efficient; if $\dfrac{TE_i(y,x \mid C)}{TE_i(y,x \mid V)} < 1$, the producer is operating under increasing or decreasing returns to scale. To determine which, see Färe et al. (1985).

---

[15] We illustrate the theoretical framework and result using the input-oriented distance function. But, the derivation and results are similar in output-oriented situation.

[16] For a system introduction of distance function and its properties, please refer to standard textbook, for instance, Färe and Primont (1995).

[17] The optimal scale size is a constant mix of inputs and outputs. In a single input single output context, optimal scale size is offered by the unit(s) offering maximum output to input ratio (i.e., maximum average product). The distance of the scale size of an input output bundle from optimal bundle is reflected in its SE. This measure is defined in either an input or an output orientation as the ratio between technical (i.e., CRS) efficiency and pure technical (i.e., VRS) efficiency. Another way to see SE is as a measure of the distance between the CRS and VRS boundaries at the scale size of the bundle. The larger the divergence between VRS and CRS efficiency ratings, the lower the value of SE and the more adverse the impact of scale size on productivity.

4.3.2   Malmquist productivity index

In 1982, Caves et al. (1982) introduce the MPI, which measures productivity as the ratio of input/output distance functions. Färe et al. (1994a) suggest using MPI and its decompositions to measure the productivity changes between two periods of activities. Using the period t benchmark technology, the period $t + 1$ input-oriented MPI is defined as

$$M_i^{t+1}(y^{t+1}, x^{t+1}, y^t, x^t) = \frac{D_i^{t+1}(y^{t+1}, x^{t+1})}{D_i^{t+1}(y^t, x^t)} = \frac{TE_i^{t+1}(y^t, x^t)}{TE_i^{t+1}(y^{t+1}, x^{t+1})}. \tag{1}$$

Färe et al. (1994b) specify that the MPI can be decomposed into two components: efficiency change (catch-up effect, or technical efficiency change) and technology frontier shift (technological change).

$$\begin{aligned} &M_i^{t+1}(y^{t+1}, x^{t+1}, y^t, x^t \mid C, S) \\ &= \text{EFFCH}(y^{t+1}, x^{t+1}, y^t, x^t \mid C, S) \cdot \text{TECH}(y^{t+1}, x^{t+1}, y^t, x^t \mid C, S) \end{aligned} \tag{2}$$

Efficiency change measures the ratio of how "close" to its frontier an observation is at each time period, that is,

$$\begin{aligned} \text{EFFCH}(y^{t+1}, x^{t+1}, y^t, x^t \mid C, S) &= \frac{TE_i^t(y^t, x^t \mid C, S)}{TE_i^{t+1}(y^{t+1}, x^{t+1} \mid C, S)} \\ &= \frac{TE_i^t(y^t, x^t \mid v, w)}{TE_i^{t+1}(y^{t+1}, x^{t+1} \mid v, w)} \cdot \frac{SE_i^t(y^t, x^t)}{SE_i^{t+1}(y^{t+1}, x^{t+1})} \cdot \frac{CO_i^t(y^t, x^t)}{CO_i^{t+1}(y^{t+1}, x^{t+1})} \end{aligned}, \tag{3}$$

where the first term $\dfrac{TE_i^t(y^t, x^t \mid v, w)}{TE_i^{t+1}(y^{t+1}, x^{t+1} \mid v, w)}$ measures change in purely technical efficiency; the second term $\dfrac{SE_i^t(y^t, x^t)}{SE_i^{t+1}(y^{t+1}, x^{t+1})}$ measures change in scale efficiency; the third term $\dfrac{CO_i^t(y^t, x^t)}{CO_i^{t+1}(y^{t+1}, x^{t+1})}$ measures change in congestion.[18]

Technology frontier change measures the change in the frontier over two periods, that is,

$$\text{TECH}(y^{t+1}, x^{t+1}, y^t, x^t \mid C, S) = \sqrt{\frac{TE_i^{t+1}(y^{t+1}, x^{t+1} \mid C, S)}{TE_i^t(y^{t+1}, x^{t+1} \mid C, S)} \cdot \frac{TE_i^{t+1}(y^t, x^t \mid C, S)}{TE_i^t(y^t, x^t \mid C, S)}} \tag{4}$$

The capital letters C, V, W, and S in the above expressions stand for the technology assumptions of CRS, VRS, weak disposability of input and strong disposability of input respectively.[19]

---

[18] The decomposition operations are based on Färe et al. (1994a).

[19] The definitions of CRS, VRS, weak disposability, and strong disposability can refer to any standard productivity textbook, for instance, Färe et al. (1985).

4.3.3 Data envelopment analysis

DEA is a mathematical programming approach, which constructs the frontier and measures the efficiency relative to the constructed frontiers. It does envelop the data, but it makes no accommodation for noise. Moreover, subject to certain assumptions about the structure of production technology, it envelops the data as tightly as possible. DEA was proposed by Charnes et al. (1978), which generalized the single input/output efficiency measures into the multiple cases by constructing a relative efficiency score as the ratio of single virtual output to single virtual input.

In this study, the distance function is mainly employed as a computational tool, so here we give the $\mathrm{TE}_i(y,x)$ or $\mathrm{D}_i(y,x)$ version of DEA method.

First the technology can be described by input requirement set as:

$$L^t(y^t \mid C,S) = \left\{ (x_1^t, \cdots, x_N^t) : \right.$$

$$y_{k,m}^t \le \sum_{k=1}^{K} z_k^t y_{k,m}^t \quad m = 1, \cdots, M$$

$$\sum_{k=1}^{K} z_k^t x_{k,n}^t \le x_{k,n}^t \quad n = 1, \cdots, N$$

$$z_k^t \ge 0 \quad k = 1, \cdots, K \bigg\}.$$

Then the Debreu-Farrell input measure of TE model is:

$$\mathrm{TE}_i^t(y_k^t, x_k^t \mid C,S) = \min_{\mathrm{g}} \lambda$$

$$\text{s.t. } y_{k,m}^t \le \sum_{k=1}^{K} z_k^t y_{k,m}^t \quad m = 1, \cdots, M$$

$$\sum_{k=1}^{K} z_k^t y_{k,n}^t \le \lambda x_{k,n}^t \quad n = 1, \cdots, N$$

$$z_k^t \ge 0 \quad k = 1, \cdots, K \bigg\}. \tag{5}$$

4.3.4 Attributes-incorporated Malmquist productivity index

As pointed out by Ray (1995), any change in the quality of output(s) without any change in the input-output quantities implies a corresponding change in productivity. Therefore, productivity indices unadjusted for attributes changes are misleading. To solve this problem, Färe et al. (1995) extends the productivity index in Färe et al. (1992) to incorporate attributes into the technology in a productivity analysis of Swedish pharmacies. In the application, the attributes are used together with ratios of distance functions to measure the service quality of each pharmacy. In our study, some major network and operation attributes are treated as the quality output variables as in Färe et al. (1995), which makes it possible to include those attributes into our conventional analysis of railroad productivity changes. The AMPI is an extension of MPI, and can be measured by distance function and DEA. In our AMPI model, three network and operation attributes are incorporated into the technology to study the relationship between productivity growth and these major attributes.

The main decomposition result of AMPI (in simplest form) can be expressed as:

$$AMPI = ACH \cdot EFFCH \cdot TECH$$

where the first term of left hand of formula ACH measures attribute change, the second part EFFCH measures efficiency changes, and the last part TECH indicates technical changes. It means that the productivity progress can be seen as the result of joint action of adjusting attributes, changing technical efficiency, and shifting of the technology frontier. For more details, see Appendix 3.B.

4.4   Data sources

The data used in this study come primarily from Class I railroad annual reports to the Interstate Commerce Commission and its successor, the STB. The panel data set is firm specific, consist of all class I railroad firms from 1983 to 2008. This period covers most of the mergers that took place after regulation, and a sufficient time thereafter to capture the effects of mergers.

On the selection of input and output variables, we follow most recently studies, for instance, Wilson (1997), Bitzan (1999), Bitzan and Keeler (2003, 2007), and Bitzan and Wilson (2007). Revenue ton-miles (RTM) is used as a measure of output.[20] Labor (LABOR), fuel (FUEL), equipment (WE), materials and supplies (WM), and investment in miles of road (INVR), are chosen as inputs.

RTM, the movement of a ton of freight over one mile for revenue, is the preferred measure for the output, which is actually demanded by shippers, and used by most railroad authorities. LABOR is measured by the average number of total employees; FUEL is measured by the total gallons of diesel oil consumed; WE is a weighted measure of total locomotives and freight cars in services[21]; MW is measured by expenditures on input.

To properly reflect operating and network characteristics in the railroad industry, most recent cost analysis models consider the attribute variables, namely, miles of road (MOR), unit train percentage (UTP), average length of haul (ALH), and so on. These variables capture differences in firm operating and network characteristics. MOR is

---

[20] Revenue ton-miles are the ton-miles that produce revenues. It is a commonly used measure of output. In some studies, these are indexed in a hedonic framework with a set of observables, while in other studies, the technology is indexed by a set of observables. These include: percentage of bulk traffic, unit train traffic, average length of haul, and a variety of others. We follow this latter approach in our analysis.

[21] We follow Bitzan and Wilson (2007) by calculating total expenditures on locomotives and cars and associated prices. The price of equipment was a weighted average of cars and locomotives (by cost shares). WE is then defined by the expenditures divided by the price of equipment.

a common variable in specifications and represents the size of the network (in terms of the aggregate length of road, excluding yard tracks, sidings, and parallel lines). Unit trains are considered the least costly of the different types of activities used to produce ton-miles; UTP is an indicator of low short-run costs. As the average number of miles a ton of freight travels (ALH), given all else constant, increases, total costs are expected to decline. Hence, in this study, the above three network and operating attribute variables—UTP, MOR, and ALH—are included. We expect that mergers can have a sizable impact on these variables, and meanwhile, these impacts may explain partial efficiency and productivity evolutions of railroad firms.

In 1983, there were 28 Class 1 firms. During the 1983–2008 time period, six firms were declassified as Class 1 firms, but continue to operate. The remaining firms have largely been consolidated into seven firms, which we label as BN, CN, CSX, KCS, NS, SOO, and UP[22] firms in the postmerger period (2001–2008). In total, there are 319 firm year observations in the data to form the technology frontier, and we use 182 firm year observations to compute the MPI and AMPI.

Because the time series data for survivor firms are preferable to detect the impact of mergers on efficiency and productivity, in data processing, we use the "mother firm" approach (MFA) to represent the data of railroads over time.[23] MFA approach can be described as following: we use the final merged firms' name over all the period, in the premerger year, data were calculated by summing up those two or more "mother firms" that merged to form the corresponding firms operating in the postmerger period. Therefore, factors used to measure efficiency and productivity were assumed to be additive.

4.5 Empirical application

The primary interest of this study is to evaluate the effects of industry and firm-level consolidation activities and the different sources of efficiency and productivity changes. There are two primary ways to deal with unbalanced panel data within the context of DEA. One is to treat the panel as a single cross-section (each firm year being considered as an independent observation) and pool the observations. This way, a single frontier is computed, and the relative efficiency of each firm in each period is calculated by reference to this single frontier (Atkinson et al., 2003; Chapin and Schmidt, 1998). Another possibility is to compute a frontier for each period and compare the efficiency of each firm relative to the frontier in each period (Kumbhakar, 1988; Odeck, 2008). We employ both approaches in our study, to emphasize that the different research routes give consistent results. The single technology output-oriented model is chosen because it is an efficient way to evaluate the efficiency change mode for the whole industry and the effect of firm-level mergers; the dynamic (time series) technology model is chosen because it helps us understanding the different causes which lead

---

[22] The abbreviations of railroad firms are provided in Appendix A along with a disposition of firm names and consolidation over time based on Bitzan and Wilson (2007).

[23] This approach was used in Odeck (2008) to study the mergers impact on efficiency and productivity of public transport services.

the productivity changes. More important, the MPI, and hence AMPI is built on and analyzed by the dynamic CRS model (Färe et al., 1994b).

4.5.1   Efficiency performance

Using the inputs and outputs data of all Class I railroad firms in the United States from 1983 to 2008, the technology and scale efficiencies were calculated by solving the linear programming problems in Section 3 under the single technology setting. The summary of values of TEs and SEs of survivor firms are displayed in Table 4.1. The TE and SE scores show each firm's annual technology and scale efficiency performance in the whole period, and we use them to analyze the efficiency effect of all the mergers that happened during the 1983 through 2008 time period.

We also visualize the evolutions of the TE and SE in Figs. 4.2 and 4.3.

In Fig. 4.2, the TE scores for the seven survivor firms have been plotted over time. Since our survivor firms' data have included all the information of their predecessors,[24] the change of efficiency score reflects the evolution of railroad industry TE performance. There is an obvious increasing trend on the average values of the TE (output distance function) for all the survivor firms during the period 1983–2003, the average values of the TE grow from 0.587 to 0.869, the geometric average growth rate is 1.1579 percent. The ranking among survivor firms is relatively stable; BN, SOO, and UP hold the top three places for almost all the years, the average efficiency scores are 0.851, 0.752, and 0.737. On the other hand, NS, CSX, and CN are the firms with lowest average efficiency score. Although the average efficiency scores of CN are low, CN shows a strong increasing trend during this period, it reached the efficient level in 2008. NS always has a relatively low efficiency performance, especially after 2000.

In Fig. 4.3, we present the evolution of the SE for the seven survivor firms during the period 1983–2008. There is an obvious characteristic—all the firms' scores are almost stagnant all over time. The average value of SE is 0.929 in 1983 and 0.917 in 2008; the geometric average growth rate is −0.0005 percent. The SE ranking among survivor firms is also relatively stable. BN and UP hold the top two places almost for the whole period; the average efficiency scores are 0.997 and 0.966. Since SE describes the divergence of the decision-making units from the most productive scale size, the small change of SE reflects that the railroads maintained a relatively stable size through time (after using the MFA procedure).

4.5.2   The mergers effect on the efficiency performance

Merger Effect Model (Single Technology Model): The single technology frontier output-oriented model is chosen to capture the merger effect on the evolution of efficiency performance of the industry and specific firms. In this model, we use only one output technology setting to calculate the efficiency scores for each firm during 1983–2008 period.

---

[24] But the information provided in Table 4.1 is still not absolutely complete; there are six firms (include BLE, BM, DH, DMIR, FEC, and PLE) lost class I status during 1983–1989. Those firms are out of our research scope.

Table 4.1 Summary of efficiency scores

Year	Efficiency score (CRS)								Scale efficiency							
	BN	CN	CSX	NS	SOO	UP	KCS	Mean	BN	CN	CSX	NS	SOO	UP	KCS	Mean
1983	0.710	0.400	0.530	0.560	0.460	0.710	0.740	0.587	1.000	1.000	0.964	0.966	0.836	1.000	0.740	0.929
1984	0.760	0.440	0.550	0.560	0.510	0.700	0.780	0.614	1.000	1.000	0.948	0.966	0.911	1.000	0.780	0.944
1985	0.660	0.440	0.530	0.600	0.540	0.660	0.720	0.593	0.985	1.000	0.946	0.714	0.844	1.000	0.720	0.887
1986	0.680	0.430	0.500	0.490	0.550	0.630	0.670	0.564	1.000	0.896	0.926	0.907	0.873	1.000	0.670	0.896
1987	0.730	0.420	0.520	0.500	0.700	0.620	0.670	0.594	1.000	0.913	0.929	0.909	0.875	0.984	0.670	0.897
1988	0.760	0.420	0.530	0.510	0.700	0.640	0.660	0.603	1.000	0.894	0.898	0.895	0.864	0.985	0.660	0.885
1989	0.790	0.530	0.540	0.500	0.740	0.640	0.630	0.624	0.988	0.964	0.857	0.893	0.881	0.985	0.630	0.885
1990	0.770	0.540	0.550	0.540	0.760	0.650	0.650	0.637	0.987	0.947	0.833	0.857	0.874	0.985	0.650	0.876
1991	0.780	0.590	0.550	0.530	0.770	0.700	0.680	0.657	1.000	0.967	0.797	0.828	0.865	0.946	0.680	0.869
1992	0.800	0.580	0.560	0.530	0.760	0.730	0.700	0.666	1.000	0.951	0.812	0.828	0.864	0.936	0.700	0.870
1993	0.800	0.620	0.580	0.530	0.760	0.750	0.690	0.676	1.000	0.969	0.773	0.883	0.800	0.938	0.690	0.865
1994	0.850	0.630	0.600	0.570	0.680	0.750	0.550	0.661	1.000	0.969	0.789	0.851	0.773	1.000	0.647	0.861
1995	0.890	0.680	0.620	0.590	0.910	0.760	0.590	0.720	1.000	0.971	0.785	0.843	0.910	0.950	0.711	0.881
1996	0.890	0.680	0.590	0.580	0.850	0.770	0.580	0.706	1.000	0.971	0.831	0.829	0.867	0.975	0.682	0.879
1997	0.870	0.670	0.600	0.600	0.780	0.710	0.600	0.690	1.000	0.957	0.822	0.833	0.839	0.922	0.674	0.864
1998	0.900	0.690	0.600	0.580	0.720	0.700	0.630	0.689	0.989	0.972	0.822	0.829	0.878	0.897	0.700	0.870
1999	0.920	0.720	0.630	0.640	0.720	0.730	0.640	0.714	0.989	0.911	0.913	0.914	0.847	0.924	0.727	0.889
2000	0.950	0.760	0.640	0.660	0.770	0.740	0.650	0.739	0.990	0.884	0.941	0.892	0.819	0.937	0.714	0.882
2001	0.990	1.000	0.700	0.620	0.770	0.790	0.640	0.787	0.990	1.000	0.897	0.849	0.786	0.963	0.681	0.881
2002	0.910	0.720	0.690	0.610	0.790	0.810	0.650	0.740	1.000	0.947	0.873	0.847	0.790	0.988	0.722	0.881
2003	0.920	0.760	0.690	0.620	0.810	0.830	0.650	0.754	1.000	0.950	0.885	0.838	0.818	0.988	0.722	0.886
2004	0.970	0.760	0.740	0.660	1.000	0.810	0.630	0.796	1.000	0.938	0.914	0.868	1.000	0.976	0.733	0.918
2005	1.000	0.770	0.720	0.650	0.970	0.810	0.660	0.797	1.000	0.951	0.867	0.844	0.980	0.953	0.710	0.901
2006	1.000	0.860	0.730	0.640	0.980	0.830	0.830	0.839	1.000	0.966	0.859	0.831	0.980	0.965	0.830	0.919
2007	1.000	0.940	0.740	0.630	1.000	0.860	0.790	0.851	1.000	0.979	0.851	0.829	1.000	0.966	0.806	0.919
2008	1.000	1.000	0.760	0.640	0.930	0.930	0.820	0.869	1.000	1.000	0.835	0.821	0.959	0.969	0.837	0.917
Geometric mean	0.851	0.633	0.610	0.580	0.752	0.737	0.670	0.694	0.997	0.956	0.866	0.859	0.872	0.966	0.709	0.890

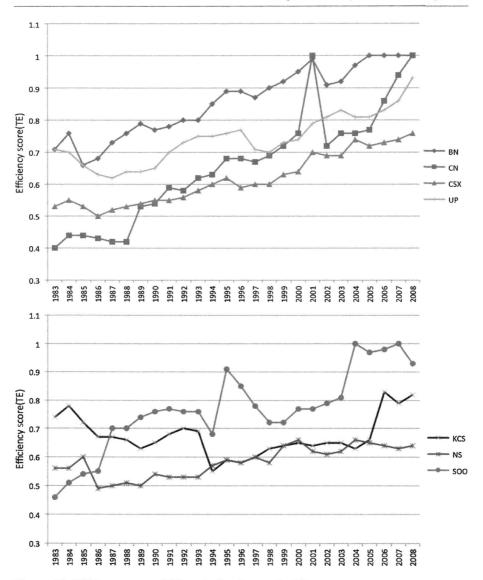

Figure 4.2 Efficiency scores (TE) evolution for survival firms.

To test the effects of mergers on the industry, we regress the TE and SE on a constant, a time trend, and a dummy variable indicating whether the firm has experienced a merger. Many of the unobserved and observed variables are highly correlated with time, the time trend allows for the possibility that efficiency has increased during the period for reasons other than mergers. On selecting a nonlinear time trend specification, there are three considerations. First, from the real TE data trend in Table 4.1 and Fig. 4.2, we observe many firms experience a distinct efficiency gain after merger and slowdown after several years (i.e., SOO merges MILW in 1985, UP merges SSW in

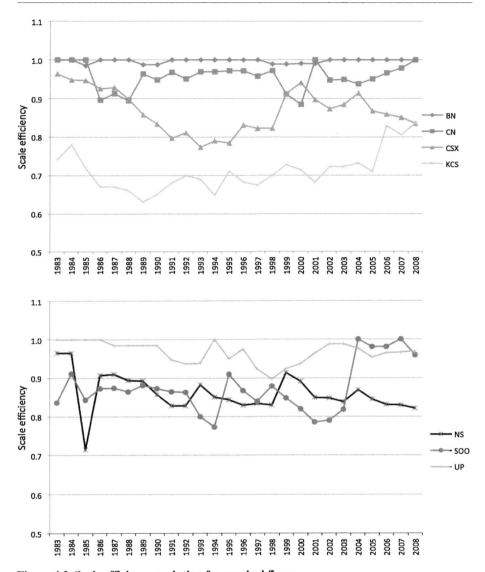

Figure 4.3 Scale efficiency evolution for survival firms.

1990, and CSX merges CR in 1999). Second, the average TE score also shows a waning rising trend during periods 1990–1995 and 2000–2008, which are the periods after each merger waves (1980s and 1990s). Finally, as discussed by Winston (1998) and used in Wilson and Wilson (2001), the effect of mergers on efficiency may smooth in over time. Following Wilson and Wilson (2001) and Chapin and Schmidt (1998), we use a nonlinear specification including interaction terms. The time trend is given by:

$$\text{trend} = \beta_{2,m} * \text{time} + \beta_{3,m} * (\text{time} / (\text{time} + 1)) * \text{merger}_m.$$

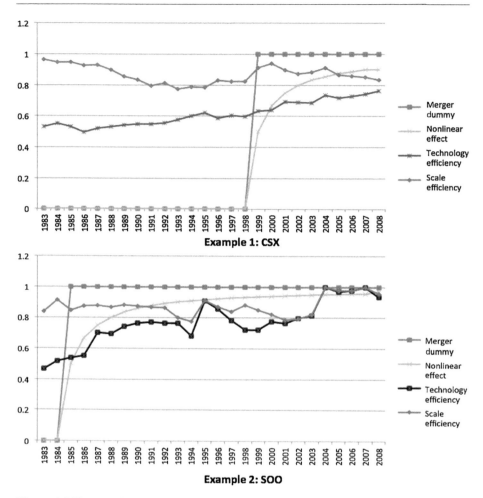

Figure 4.4 Two nonlinear time trend examples.

In Fig. 4.4, we give two examples of the nonlinear time trends for firm CSX and SOO.

And the regressions take the form:

$$y_m = \beta_{0,m} + \beta_{1,m} * \text{time} + \beta_{2,m} * (\text{time} / (\text{time} + 1)) * merger_m + \varepsilon_m,$$

where the suffix m stands for the specific merger which has happen during 1983–2008, y_m stands for the TE and SE, $merger_m$ is the dummy variable, and the time variable takes a value of 1 in the year merger happened, and 2, 3,… and -1, -2,… to indicate the years after merger and before merger.

One of the primary purposes of this study is to investigate the efficiency impact of mergers from 1983 to 2008. In examining mergers, we use a total 16 years data for

Table 4.2 **Efficiency effect of all mergers results**

Estimation period: 1983–2008		Intercept	Linear time trend	Nonlinear time trend	R square
All mergers	Efficiency score (CRS)	0.69784***	0.01937***	−0.09787	0.1338
		(0.02611)	(0.00550)	(0.06059)	
	Scale efficiency	0.93356***	0.0004275	−0.02425	0.0123
		(0.01370)	(0.00288)	(0.03170)	
Mergers in the1980s	Efficiency score (CRS)	0.60479***	0.01767**	−0.09817	0.1076
		(0.03274)	(0.00768)	(0.07400)	
	Scale efficiency	0.94682***	−0.00934**	−0.022	0.2787
		(0.01962)	(0.00460)	(0.04434)	
Mergers in the1990s	Efficiency score (CRS)	0.72999***	0.0157***	−0.02488	0.2791
		(0.02680)	(0.00547)	(0.06388)	
	Scale efficiency	0.92176***	0.00153	0.00453*	0.0173
		(0.01721)	(0.00351)	(0.04103)	

Note: The standard errors are in parentheses.
*, **, and *** indicate statistical significance at the 90, 95, 99% levels, respectively.

each merger, 6 years data before merger and 10 years after merger. If the interval of two mergers is less than 10 years, we repeatedly use those overlapping time data. We pool the data for all mergers of railroads that occurred between 1983 and 2008. The regression results are presented in Table 4.2, which utilizes the nonlinear time trend we described earlier.

We find that the industry level mergers do not have a significant effect on the efficiency performance, neither for the TE scores, nor the SE. However, the linear time trend for the TE is significant, with an estimated value of 0.01937, meaning an annual average 2% increase in technical efficiency. However, the time trends for the SEs are not statistically important—a result consistent with our observations from Table 4.1. The most likely reason that the SEs maintain relatively stable levels is we have applied the MFA procedure on the data of survivor firms, which keeps the size of firm stable even if the firm experiences mergers. A consequence of this treatment is that the effect of the mergers on scale cannot be identified.

Next, consider the different impacts between two merger groups. We divide the whole sample into two subsamples, one is the 1980s subsample, which includes seven merger activities that happened in 1980s, and the other is 1990s subsample, which also includes seven merger activities that happened in 1990s. When we use TE as regressand, as we expect, the estimation of time trend for both subsamples are positive and significant; the estimated parameter for the 1980s is 0.01767 and 0.0157 for 1990s, which shows that efficiency time trend effect for the 1980s is slight stronger than those in the 1990s. However, the effects of mergers are not statistically significant for either subsample. When we use SE as regressand, almost all the regressions results are not significant. In general, we get the results that the mergers do not affect the average efficiency performance for the industry during this period, and the efficiency time trend for 1980s mergers are high relative to those for 1990s.

Of special interest is the effect of each merger on individual firms. We select six main mergers for six survivor firms based on the total quantity of RTMs of firms involved in consolidation.[25] On these regressions, we use the total 26 years of data for each firm. No matter which year the merger occurred, we use a nonlinear time trend to catch the impact of the merger. The regression results are presented in Table 4.3.

In this table, each merger was regressed by both Efficiency Score (TE under CRS) and SE. First, the TE regression results show that these models have a high level of fitness; the smallest R square value is 0.6926. The intersection terms and time trend terms are both significant and positive, but estimations of the effects of the merger terms are not unified; half of the six firms show the merger has a significant and positive impact on efficiency change, including NS, CSX, and SOO. When we use SE as regressand, half of the time trend terms and almost all the nonlinear time trends are not significant. As a comparison, the results for KCS have significant results for both regressands and all the terms, which shows that the efficiency performance gains may not be a result of mergers.

4.5.3 Decomposition of productivity

Productivity Decomposition Model (Dynamic Technology Model): In this empirical model, we take the network and operation attributes into account. Three network and operation attributes (UTP, MOR, and ALH), which capture various dimensions of network characteristics, are treated as attributes in the DEA models.

To detect the impact of mergers on efficiency and productivity, we use MFA processing. The summing up of units in the premerger period is a necessary condition for making comparisons between the two periods, and is also an efficient way to apply our AMPI analysis model. Moreover, using the MFA processing, our unbalanced panel data becomes a balanced panel data set, which is a basic data requirement for employing MPI and AMPI performance evaluation models.

Under the above setting, first the effect of network and operation attributes will be estimated by a comparison of the single output DEA model and an attribute-incorporated multioutput DEA model. Furthermore, by computing each firm's AMPI from 1983 to 2008, and decomposing AMPI into attribute change, efficiency change (catch-up effect, or technical efficiency change) and technical change (technology frontier shift) components, the mergers effect on efficiency and productivity will be conveniently evaluated. The AMPI indices and their decompositions were calculated using the method showed in Section 3.3.4 and Appendix B for those seven survivor firms, using a balanced panel data from 1983 to 2008 and MFA data procedure. The values of the AMPI and its decompositions are displayed in Table 4.4; these results are

---

[25] There is no consolidation activity on KCS during 1983–2008, but the firm KCS is still included in Table 4.3 for comparison.

Table 4.3 Survival firms efficiency effect of mergers

Firm	Merger year	Regressand	Intercept	Linear time trend	Nonlinear time trend	R square
BN	1996	Efficiency score (CRS)	0.85685*** (0.01629)	0.01258*** (0.00194)	0.01725 (0.03446)	0.9243
		Scale efficiency	1.00089*** (0.00281)	0.0005647 (0.00033447)	−0.00914 (0.00594)	0.1103
CN	1999	Efficiency score (CRS)	0.7354*** (0.03317)	0.0219*** (0.00340)	−0.00864 (0.06441)	0.8771
		Scale efficiency	0.99701*** (0.00128)	0.00010479 (0.00015132)	−0.00103 (0.00532)	0.0073
CSX	1999	Efficiency Score (CRS)	0.61417*** (0.00941)	0.00657*** (0.000096458)	0.07772*** (0.01831)	0.9528
		Scale efficiency	0.7571*** (0.01649)	−0.01211*** (0.00169)	0.22343*** (0.03206)	0.7001
NS	1999	Efficiency Score (CRS)	0.57466*** (0.01590)	0.00294* (0.00163)	0.05855* (0.03092)	0.6926
		Scale efficiency	0.81815*** (0.02423)	−0.00567** (0.00248)	0.07233 (0.04710)	0.2075
SOO	1985	Efficiency Score (CRS)	0.49358*** (0.04954)	0.01184*** (0.00264)	0.18237** (0.07703)	0.7787
		Scale efficiency	0.8939*** (0.04156)	0.00546** (0.00221)	−0.09438 (0.06462)	0.2134
UP	1997	Efficiency Score (CRS)	0.77175*** (0.02111)	0.01084*** (0.00240)	−0.03895 (0.04317)	0.7628
		Scale efficiency	0.9603*** (0.01454)	−0.00185 (0.00165)	0.00927 (0.02972)	0.1425
KCS		Efficiency Score (CRS)	0.60485*** (0.03203)	0.00398* (0.00196)	0.34728*** (0.12194)	0.2687
		Scale efficiency	0.61394*** (0.01722)	0.00622*** (0.00105)	0.3139*** (0.06555)	0.6256

Note: The standard errors are in parentheses.
*, **, and *** indicate statistical significance at 90, 95, and 99% levels, respectively.

Table 4.4 Attribute-incorporated Malmquist productivity index and decomposition

Year	BN				CN				CSX				KCS			
	AMPI	ACH	EFFCH	TECH	AMPI	ACH	EFFCH	TECH	AMPI	ACH	EFFCH	TECH	AMPI	ACH	EFFCH	TECH
1983–1984	1.11	0.99	1.00	1.12	1.14	1.01	1.03	1.10	1.12	1.04	1.04	1.04	1.09	1.07	0.98	1.04
1984–1985	0.99	1.02	1.00	0.97	1.22	0.99	1.22	1.01	0.96	1.01	0.90	1.06	1.05	1.09	0.95	1.01
1985–1986	1.07	1.05	1.00	1.02	0.98	0.99	1.06	0.93	0.93	0.94	1.13	0.88	1.01	1.06	0.99	0.96
1986–1987	1.14	1.02	1.00	1.12	0.88	0.89	0.85	1.16	1.13	0.99	0.98	1.16	1.00	1.00	0.86	1.16
1987–1988	1.06	1.01	1.00	1.05	1.21	1.13	1.01	1.06	1.02	0.98	0.98	1.06	1.01	1.06	0.90	1.06
1988–1989	1.01	1.01	1.00	1.00	0.97	0.99	0.98	1.00	1.06	1.03	1.03	1.00	1.01	1.03	0.98	1.00
1989–1990	1.01	1.03	1.00	0.98	1.11	1.05	1.08	0.98	1.03	1.03	1.03	0.97	1.06	1.03	1.05	0.98
1990–1991	1.01	1.04	1.00	0.97	1.02	0.90	1.16	0.98	0.91	0.97	0.98	0.96	1.03	1.00	1.05	0.98
1991–1992	1.09	1.07	1.00	1.02	1.01	1.03	0.94	1.04	1.04	1.05	0.93	1.07	1.00	1.00	0.96	1.04
1992–1993	1.09	1.07	1.00	1.02	1.08	0.99	1.07	1.02	0.98	1.00	0.90	1.09	0.95	0.95	0.98	1.02
1993–1994	1.08	1.02	1.00	1.06	0.98	0.98	0.95	1.05	0.98	0.95	0.97	1.06	0.94	0.94	0.95	1.05
1994–1995	1.14	1.06	1.00	1.08	1.09	0.98	1.03	1.08	1.04	1.01	1.03	1.00	1.01	0.99	0.94	1.08
1995–1996	1.00	1.01	1.00	0.99	0.96	1.04	0.93	0.99	1.02	1.05	0.92	1.06	1.05	1.05	0.99	1.01
1996–1997	1.10	1.12	1.00	0.98	1.02	1.02	1.02	0.98	1.05	1.00	1.19	0.88	1.20	1.15	1.08	0.97
1997–1998	1.19	1.11	1.00	1.07	0.97	0.93	1.00	1.04	0.95	0.95	0.93	1.08	1.08	0.94	1.10	1.04
1998–1999	1.04	1.00	1.00	1.04	1.06	0.96	1.06	1.04	0.96	1.01	0.92	1.03	0.74	0.78	0.90	1.05
1999–2000	1.02	1.02	1.00	1.00	1.05	0.99	1.08	0.98	1.06	1.05	1.03	0.98	0.86	0.89	0.95	1.02
2000–2001	1.00	1.01	1.00	0.99	1.05	1.07	0.97	1.01	1.10	1.05	1.04	1.01	0.85	0.93	0.94	0.97
2001–2002	0.99	1.02	1.00	0.97	0.81	1.05	0.78	0.99	0.99	1.00	0.98	1.01	0.97	1.00	1.00	0.97
2002–2003	1.03	1.01	1.00	1.02	0.91	1.00	0.89	1.02	0.97	0.95	1.00	1.02	1.01	1.00	0.99	1.02
2003–2004	1.02	1.01	0.99	1.02	0.92	1.00	0.93	0.99	1.24	1.04	1.00	1.19	0.98	1.02	0.94	1.02
2004–2005	1.09	1.03	1.00	1.06	1.04	1.04	1.02	0.98	0.93	1.05	0.95	0.93	1.00	1.00	0.99	1.01
2005–2006	1.11	1.03	1.00	1.08	1.16	1.10	1.01	1.04	0.93	1.00	1.01	0.92	1.10	1.05	1.08	0.97
2006–2007	1.03	1.04	1.00	0.99	1.15	1.06	1.06	1.02	1.10	1.02	1.05	1.03	1.14	1.15	0.95	1.04
2007–2008	1.09	1.07	1.00	1.02	1.03	0.97	1.08	0.98	1.03	0.99	1.00	1.04	1.13	1.10	0.98	1.05
Geometric mean	1.059	1.034	1.000	1.025	1.027	1.005	1.004	1.018	1.019	1.006	0.995	1.019	1.005	1.008	0.978	1.020

Year	NS				SOO				UP				Industry average			
	AMPI	ACH	EFFCH	TECH	AMPI	ACH	EFFCH	TECH	AMPI	ACH	EFFCH	TECH	AMPI	ACH	EFFCH	TECH
1983–1984	1.07	1.00	1.02	1.05	1.09	1.02	0.96	1.11	1.18	1.10	1.01	1.06	1.128	1.035	1.014	1.075
1984–1985	0.93	1.02	0.84	1.09	1.04	1.08	0.97	0.99	0.86	0.78	1.00	1.10	0.956	0.949	0.963	1.046
1985–1986	0.95	0.96	1.11	0.89	1.03	0.99	1.02	1.02	0.79	1.01	0.87	0.90	0.939	1.000	1.005	0.934
1986–1987	1.02	1.01	0.87	1.16	1.28	1.03	1.15	1.08	1.15	1.01	0.98	1.16	1.120	1.006	0.970	1.146
1987–1988	0.99	0.94	0.99	1.06	0.99	1.01	0.95	1.03	1.04	1.03	0.95	1.06	1.036	1.004	0.977	1.056
1988–1989	0.98	0.96	1.02	1.00	0.96	0.94	1.03	0.99	1.07	1.04	1.03	1.00	1.033	1.015	1.018	1.000
1989–1990	1.14	1.02	1.15	0.97	1.30	1.21	1.10	0.98	1.10	1.07	1.06	0.97	1.069	1.045	1.050	0.974
1990–1991	0.95	1.02	0.97	0.96	0.98	0.99	1.01	0.98	1.14	1.07	1.11	0.96	1.024	1.029	1.032	0.964
1991–1992	1.03	1.02	0.94	1.07	1.05	1.02	0.99	1.04	1.17	1.09	1.01	1.06	1.095	1.063	0.980	1.050
1992–1993	0.99	0.97	0.93	1.10	0.95	0.94	0.99	1.02	1.16	1.06	1.00	1.09	1.075	1.035	0.974	1.067
1993–1994	1.02	0.93	1.03	1.06	1.01	1.08	0.89	1.05	1.07	1.01	1.00	1.06	1.045	0.991	0.995	1.059
1994–1995	1.04	1.02	1.03	0.99	1.29	1.06	1.13	1.08	1.07	1.06	1.00	1.01	1.088	1.044	1.011	1.031
1995–1996	1.12	1.10	0.96	1.06	1.04	1.04	0.99	1.01	0.93	0.88	1.00	1.06	0.998	0.983	0.980	1.035
1996–1997	0.99	0.97	1.16	0.88	1.01	0.99	1.05	0.97	0.86	0.98	1.00	0.88	0.995	1.030	1.055	0.917
1997–1998	0.94	0.97	0.90	1.08	1.00	1.07	0.90	1.04	1.07	1.09	1.00	1.08	1.071	1.052	0.948	1.074
1998–1999	0.85	0.92	0.90	1.03	1.19	1.10	1.03	1.05	1.16	1.06	0.91	1.03	1.038	1.008	0.995	1.034
1999–2000	1.01	0.99	1.04	0.98	1.11	1.06	1.03	1.02	0.89	0.88	1.06	0.98	0.981	0.972	1.021	0.988
2000–2001	1.12	1.02	1.11	0.99	1.26	1.21	1.07	0.97	0.98	0.98	1.03	1.01	1.026	1.011	1.016	1.000
2001–2002	0.91	0.93	1.01	0.97	0.99	0.99	1.03	0.97	1.11	1.09	0.99	1.01	1.016	1.031	0.995	0.990
2002–2003	0.99	1.02	0.95	1.02	0.96	1.03	0.91	1.08	1.02	1.00	1.01	1.02	1.007	0.999	0.989	1.020
2003–2004	0.94	0.94	0.93	1.08	1.12	1.01	1.03	1.08	1.07	1.00	1.00	0.96	1.058	1.003	1.022	1.033
2004–2005	1.06	0.97	1.03	1.06	0.94	0.94	0.99	1.01	0.97	1.00	1.11	1.06	1.022	0.986	1.000	1.037
2005–2006	0.88	0.99	0.90	0.99	1.06	0.99	1.05	1.02	1.04	0.91	1.01	0.98	1.036	1.033	0.992	1.011
2006–2007	1.03	1.01	0.96	1.06	0.93	0.99	0.90	1.04	1.03	1.06	1.00	1.01	1.044	1.032	0.999	1.012
2007–2008	1.02	1.00	1.16	0.88	1.06	0.98	1.03	1.05	0.93	1.03	1.01	1.01	1.024	0.997	1.023	1.004
Geometric mean	0.996	0.987	0.993	1.017	1.060	1.029	1.006	1.024	1.028	1.005	1.004	1.019	1.036	1.014	1.001	1.021

ACH, Attribute change; *AMPI*, attribute-incorporated Malmquist productivity index; *EFFCH*, efficiency changes; *TECH*, technical changes

used to analyze the productivity change over time and the real sources of productivity improvement.

As in the results from the Merger Effect Model, we still do not find any efficiency effects of merger activity. More precisely, the effects of mergers are idiosyncratic. Although three firms' mergers have positive and significant effects on the TE scores, the overall merger data does not lend any support to the notion that mergers have improved efficiency. According to AAR (2008), overall the productivity of the US railroads Class I have improved for 163% from 1980 to 2007, or an average 3.1% increase rate annually. Using our Productivity Decomposition Model (AMPI model), as displayed in Table 4.4, we observe that the average (geometric mean) railroad industry growth rate in AMPI is 3.6%, the network attribute change rate is 1.4%, the technology growth rate is 2.1%, but the efficiency change rate (catch-up effect) is almost stagnant with only a 0.1% annual growth. We do note that the AMPI index is not the real Productivity index. Rather, it is a Malmquist productivity index that incorporates several network and operation attributes.

Because adjusting the network and operation attributes come at a cost, railroads may not have sufficient incentives to improve their network attributes. Some firms (like BN and SOO) have high growth in productivity due to attribute changes during 1982–2008, yet others (NS) have low growth due to attribute change. In fact, as most attributes are also measures of operating and management levels of firms, these network and operation attribute changes are also impacted by the change of technology efficiency performance.

From Table 4.4, the AMPI on average has positive growth, except for some periods (1984–1986, 1995–1997, and 1999–2000). Not only the AMPI, but also two of its components (ACH and TECH) grow modestly. From the volatility perspective, the ACH is the smallest, which shows that the network attributes growth for the whole industry gradually. The average growth rate of TECH is 2.1, which is another explanation of the time trend effect on the efficiency scores in Merger Effect Model.

In summary, in this section we focused on the sources of productivity change in the industry. Our findings point to three results. First, the largest source of productivity improvement is changes in the technology frontier. It is the largest source of productivity gains in the industry, accounting for about two-thirds of the AMPI growth rate. Second, there have been significant changes in network and/or operational characteristics over time, and with these changes, there have been substantial changes in efficiency. Third, the effects of mergers, long held to have substantial effects on efficiency, are not found to have significant effects (in magnitude or statistically) on productivity.

4.6   Summary and conclusions

To analyze the efficiency impact of consolidation activity in an industry, attention must be paid to the correlative industry characteristics; a pure input-output production system is just a simplified model of industry reality. The incorporation of network and operation attributes into the production system or productivity index analysis provides an operational and managerial perspective of railroad industrial activity.

This study offers an analysis of railroad economic performance using the US railroad industry and firm level annual data. In this chapter, we use a nonparametric approach (DEA) to specify and estimate the technical inefficiency for the US railroad industry. The approach allows mergers to impact efficiency. We found that the efficiency performance changes are not the result of mergers. This conclusion is similar to the result of Bitzan and Wilson (2007), which found that the efficiency gains of 14 mergers in the railroad industry accounts for about an 11.4% reduction in industry cost, and Berndt et al. (1993), which found that mergers explain only 10% of cost changes under partial deregulation. The major explanations of the slight differences between our results and those from the Bitzan and Wilson (2007) and Berndt et al. (1993) are the different assumptions of the production technology and a different measurement method of efficiency.

There are several contributions from this chapter. First, our study adopts both fixed and dynamic technology frontiers, which makes it easy to compute and analyze the efficiency impacts and productivity change sources. Second, by adoption of the mother firm approach data process, we are able to generate an integrated panel data set. This allows for a dynamic technology mode that is used to track the efficiency changes over time. Third, the distance function and Malmquist index method does not need the prices of the inputs and outputs, which avoids the impact of big fluctuations on some factors' prices during study period. Finally, to bring our DEA more in line with the frequently used cost analysis approach, we introduce the AMPI into railroad efficiency change and productivity growth analysis in terms of important network and operation attributes.

We find that the TE performances of railroad firms grow through the period 1983–2008, and that mergers do not have significant effect on the TE and SE gains. We also find that the productivity improvement was mostly attributed to changes in major network and operation attributes and technology improvement. Our findings indicate that railroad efficiency improvement is highly dependent upon the improvement of industry technology and on adjusting of network and operation attributes. Mergers are natural consequences of business activities, and the linkages between efficiency and mergers are weak. Other possible reasons for the efficiency improvement may originate from deregulation, with the passage of the Staggers Act of 1980.

4.7 Appendix A

Railroad firms and acronym

Firm name	Abbreviation	Note
Atchison, Topeka & Santa Fe Railroad	ATSF	Merged with BN in 1996
Bessemer and Lake Erie	BLE	Lost Class I Status in 1985
Boston and Maine	BM	Lost Class I Status in 1989
Burlington Northern	BN	
Baltimore & Ohio Railroad	BO	Merged with CO and SCL to form CSX
Canadian National Railway	CN	

Firm name	Abbreviation	Note
Chicago & Northwestern	CNW	Merged with UP in 1995
Chesapeake & Ohio Railway	CO	Merged with BO and SCL to form CSX
Consolidated Rail Corporation	CR	Merged with CSX in 2000
CSX Transportation	CSX	
Delaware and Hudson	DH	Lost Class I Status in 1988
Duluth, Missabe, and Ironton	DMIR	Lost Class I Status in 1985
Denver & Rio Grande Western Railroad	DRGW	Merged with SP in 1994
Detroit, Toledo & Ironton	DTI	Merged with GTW in 1984
Florida East Coast	FEC	Lost Class I Status in 1992
Grand Trunk Western Railroad	GTW	Merged with DIT in 1984
Kansas City Southern	KCS	
Milwaukee Road	MILW	Merged with SOO in 1985
Modesto & Empire Traction	MET	Merged with UP in 1988
Missouri Pacific	MP	Merged with UP in 1986
Norfolk Southern	NS	
Pittsburgh, Lake Erie	PLE	Lost Class I Status in 1985
Seaboard Coast Line	SCL	Merged with BO and CO to form CSX
Soo Line	SOO	
Southern Railway	SOU	Merged with NW to form NS
St. Louis Southwestern Railway	SSW	Merged with UP in 1990
Union Pacific	UP	
Western Pacific	WP	Merged with UP in 1986

Source: http://www.trainweb.org/rosters/marks.html.

4.8   Appendix B

4.8.1   *Attributes-incorporated Malmquist productivity index*

We denote inputs by $x^t = (x_1^t, \cdots, x_N^t) \in R_+^N$, outputs by $y^t = (y_1^t, \cdots, y_M^t) \in R_+^M$ and attributes by $a^t = (a_1^t, \cdots, a_J^t) \in R_+^J$, then production technology at time t can be represented by the production set $T^t = \{(x^t, y^t, a^t) : x^t \text{ can product } y^t \text{ with } a^t\}$. The input distance function is $TE_j^t(y^t, a^t, x^t) = \inf\{\lambda : (x^t / \lambda, y^t, a^t) \in T^t\}$.

The attribute change index between time t and $t + 1$ is defined as:

$$ACH_i^{t,t+1}(y^{t+1}, a^{t+1}, x^{t+1}, y^t, a^t, x^t) = \sqrt{\frac{TE_i^t(y^t, a^t, x^t)}{TE_i^t(y^t, a^{t+1}, x^t)} \cdot \frac{TE_i^{t+1}(y^{t+1}, a^t, x^{t+1})}{TE_i^{t+1}(y^{t+1}, a^{t+1}, x^{t+1})}}.$$

AMPI between period t and $t + 1$ can be expressed as:

$$MA_i^{t,t+1}(y^{t+1}, a^{t+1}, x^{t+1}, y^t, a^t, x^t) = \sqrt{\frac{TE_i^t(y^t, a^t, x^t)}{TE_i^t(y^{t+1}, a^{t+1}, x^{t+1})} \cdot \frac{TE_i^{t+1}(y^t, a^t, x^t)}{TE_i^{t+1}(y^{t+1}, a^{t+1}, x^{t+1})}}.$$

As in Section 3.2.2, this expression can be decomposed into technology change and efficiency change components:

$$MA_i^{t,t+1}(y^{t+1},a^{t+1},x^{t+1},y^t,a^t,x^t)$$

$$= \frac{TE_i^t(y^t,a^t,x^t)}{TE_i^{t+1}(y^{t+1},a^{t+1},x^{t+1})} \cdot \sqrt{\frac{TE_i^{t+1}(y^{t+1},a^{t+1},x^{t+1})}{TE_i^t(y^{t+1},a^{t+1},x^{t+1})} \cdot \frac{TE_i^{t+1}(y^t,a^t,x^t)}{TE_i^t(y^t,a^t,x^t)}}$$

The AMPI can also be decomposed as:

$$MA_i^{t,t+1}(y^{t+1},a^{t+1},x^{t+1},y^t,a^t,x^t)$$

$$= ACH_i^{t,t+1}(y^{t+1},a^{t+1},x^{t+1},y^t,a^t,x^t) \cdot \sqrt{\frac{TE_i^t(y^t,a^{t+1},x^t)}{TE_i^t(y^{t+1},a^{t+1},x^{t+1})} \cdot \frac{TE_i^{t+1}(y^t,a^t,x^t)}{TE_i^{t+1}(y^{t+1},a^t,x^{t+1})}} \quad (6)$$

If we impose a separability assumption on the distance functions, that is, $TE_i^t(y^t,a^{t+1},x^t) = R^t(a^{t+1}) \cdot TE_1^t(y^t,x^t)$ and similarly for the other time distance functions, where $R^t(a^{t+1})$ is the separability variable. In this case, Eq. (6) can also be expressed as

$$MA_i^{t,t+1}(y^{t+1},a^{t+1},x^{t+1},y^t,a^t,x^t)$$

$$= ACH_i^{t,t+1}(y^{t+1},a^{t+1},x^{t+1},y^t,a^t,x^t) \cdot \sqrt{\frac{\overline{TE_i^t(y^t,x^t)}}{\overline{TE_i^t(y^{t+1},x^{t+1})}} \cdot \frac{\overline{TE_i^{t+1}(y^t,x^t)}}{\overline{TE_i^{t+1}(y^{t+1},x^{t+1})}}} \quad (7)$$

The second part in the right hand of above expression is exactly the same with Malmquist productivity index. Hence, we have

$$MA_i^{t,t+1}(y^{t+1},a^{t+1},x^{t+1},y^t,a^t,x^t) = ACH_i^{t,t+1} \cdot EFFCH^{t,t+1} \cdot TECH^{t,t+1} \quad (8)$$

The first part of right hand side of Eq. (8) measures attribute change, the second part shows the efficiency change and the last part indicates the technical change. A note on the computation of $R^t(a^{t+1})$, $TE_1^t(y^t,x^t)$ and other similar expressions in Eq. (7) is that we need to solve the following problem for each observation k',

$$\overline{TE_i^t}(y_k^t,x_k^t \mid C,S) = \min_z \lambda$$

$$\text{s.t.} \, y_{k',m}^t \leq \sum_{k=1}^K z_k^t y_{k,m}^t \quad m=1,\cdots,M$$

$$\sum_{k=1}^K z_k^t y_{k,n}^t \leq \lambda x_{k',n}^t \quad n=1,\cdots,N$$

$$z_k^t \geq 0 \qquad k=1,\cdots,K \}.$$

References

Aigner, A., Lovell, C.A.K., Schmidt, P., 1977. Formulation and estimation of stochastics frontier production function models. J. Econ. 86, 21–37.

Association of American Railroads, 1980. Railroad Facts (formerly titled Yearbook of Railroad Facts). Association of American Railroads, Washington, DC.

Association of American Railroads, 2008. Freight Railroads: A Historical Perspective. , http://www.aar.org/IndustryInformation/~/media/AAR/BackgroundPapers.

Association of American Railroads, 2010. Class I Railroad Statistics. , http://www.aar.org/pub-common/documents/abouttheindustry/statistics.pdf.

Atkinson, S.E., Färe, R., Primont, D., 2003. Stochastic estimation of firm inefficiency using distance functions. South. Econ. J. 69, 596–611.

Bennet, T.L., 1920. The theory of measurement of changes in cost of living. J. Royal Stat. Soc. 83, 455–462.

Berndt, E., Friedlaender, A., Wang Chiang, J., Vellturo, C., 1993. Cost effects of mergers and deregulation in the U.S. rail industry. J. Prod. Anal. 4, 127–144.

Bitzan, J.D., 1999. The structure of railroad costs and the benefits. Res. Transport. Econ. 5, 1–52.

Bitzan, J.D., Keeler, T.E., 2003. Productivity growth and some of its determinants in the deregulated U. S. railroad industry. South. Econ. J. 70 (2), 232–253.

Bitzan, J.D., Keeler, T.E., 2007. Economies of density and regulatory change in the U.S. railroad freight industry. J. Law Econ. 50 (1), 157–179.

Bitzan, J.D., Wilson, W.W., 2007. Industry costs and consolidation: efficiency gains and mergers in the U.S. railroad industry. Rev. Ind. Org. 30, 81–105.

Borts, G.H., 1952. Production relations in the railway industry. Econometrica 20 (1), 71–79.

Brown, R.S., Caves, D.W., Christensen, L.R., 1979. Modelling the structure of cost and production for multiproduct firms. South. Econ. J. 46 (1), 256–273.

Caves, D.W., Christensen, L.R., Diewert, W.E., 1982. The economic theory of index numbers and the measurement of input, output, and productivity. Econometrica 50 (6), 1393–1414.

Caves, D.W., Christensen, L.R., Swanson, J.A., 1980. Productivity in U.S. railroads, 1951–74. Bell J. Econ. 11 (1), 166–181.

Caves, D.W., Christensen, L.R., Swanson, J.A., 1981. Productivity growth, scale economies, and capacity utilization in U.S. railroads, 1955–74. Am. Econ. Rev. 71 (5), 994–1002.

Chan, M.L., Mountain, D.C., 1983. Economies of scale and the Tornqvist discrete measure of productivity growth. Rev. Econ. Stat., 663–667.

Chapin, A., Schmidt, S., 1998. Do mergers improve efficiency? Evidence from deregulated rail freight. J. Transp. Econ. Policy 33 (2), 147–162.

Charnes, A., Cooper, W.W., Rhodes, E., 1978. Measuring the efficiency of decision making units. Euro. J. Oper. Res. 2, 429–444.

Christensen, L.R., Jorgenson, D.W., Lau, L.J., 1973. Transcendental logarithmic production frontiers. Rev. Econ. Stat. 55 (1), 28–45.

Coelli, T., Perelman, S., 2000. Technical efficiency of European railways: a distance function approach. Appl. Econ. 32, 67–76.

Cross, R.M., Färe, R., 2008. Value data and the Bennet Price and quantity indicators. Econ. Lett. 102 (1), 19–21.

Debreu, G., 1951. The coefficient of resource utilization. Econometrica 19 (3), 273–292.

Diewert, W.E., 1976. Exact and superlative index numbers. J. Econ. 4 (2), 115–145.

Diewert, W.E., 1998. Index Number Theory Using Differences Rather than Ratios, Department of Economics, UBC, Discussion paper No. 98–10.

Ellig, J., 2002. Railroad deregulation and consumer welfare. J. Regul. Econ. 21 (2), 143–167.

Färe, R., Grosskopf, S., Lindgren, B., Roos, P., 1992. Productivity changes in Swedish pharmacies 1980–1989: a nonparametric Malmquist approach. J. Prod. Annual, 85–101.

Färe, R., Grosskopf, S., Lovell, C.A.K., 1985. The Measurement of Efficiency of Production. Kluwer-Nijhoff Publishing, Boston.

Färe, R., Grosskopf, S., Lovell, C.A.K., 1994a. Production Frontiers. Cambridge University Press, Cambridge.

Färe, R., Grosskopf, S., Norris, M., Zhang, Z., 1994b. Productivity growth, technical progress, and efficiency change in industrialized countries. Am. Econ. Rev. 84 (1), 66–83.

Färe, R., Grosskopf, S., Roos, P., 1995. Productivity and quality changes in Swedish pharmacies. Int. J. Prod. Econ. 39, 137–144.

Färe, R., Primont, D., 1995. Multi-Output and Duality: Theory and Application. Kluwer-Nijhoff Publishing, Boston.

Farrell, M.J., 1957. The measurement of productive efficiency. J. Royal Stat. Soc. 120 (3), 253–281.

Friedlaender, A.F., 1971. The social costs of regulating the railroads. Am. Econ. Rev. 61 (2), 226–234.

Friedlaender, A.F., Berndt, E.R., Chiang, J.S.W., Showalter, M., Vellturo, C.A., 1993. Rail costs and capital adjustments in a quasi-regulated environment. J. Trans. Econ. Policy 27 (2), 131–152.

Friedlaender, A.F., Spady, R.H., 1981. Freight Transport Regulation. The MIT Press, Cambridge.

Gallamore, R.E., 1999. Regulation and innovation: lessons from the American railroad industry. In: Gomez-Ibanez, J., Tye, W.B., Winston, C. (Eds.), In Essays in Transportation Economics and Policy: A Handbook in Honor of John R. Meyer. Brookings Institution Press, Washington, DC, pp. 493–530.

Griliches, Z., 1979. Issues in assessing the contribution of research and development to productivity growth. Bell J. Econ., 92–116.

Harris, R.G., 1977. Economies of traffic density in the rail freight industry. Bell J. Econ. 8 (2), 556–564.

Ivaldi, M., McCullough, G.J., 2001. Density and integration effects on Class I U.S. freight railroads. J. Regul. Econ. 19 (200), 161–182.

Ivaldi, M., McCullough, G.J., 2005. Welfare tradeoffs in U.S. rail mergers. CEPR Discussion Paper No. 5000.

Jorgenson, D.W., Nishimizu, M., 1978. US and Japanese economic growth, 1952–1974: an international comparison. Econ. J. 88, 707–726.

Keeler, T.E., 1974. Railroad costs, returns to scale, and excess capacity. Rev. Econ. Stat. 56 (2), 201–208.

Keeler, T.E., 1983. Railroads, Freight, and Public Policy. Brookings Institution Press, Washington, DC.

Kendrick, J.W., 1973. Productivity trends. Bus. Econ., 56–61.

Kumbhakar, S., 1988. On estimation of technical and allocative inefficiency using stochastic frontiers functions: the case of US Class I railroads. Int. Econ. Rev. 3, 727–733.

Lan, L.W., Lin, E.T.J., 2005. Measuring railway performance with adjustment of environmental effects, data noise and slacks. Transportmetrica 1, 161–189.

Lim, S.H., Lovell, C.A.K., 2008. Short-run total cost change and productivity of US Class I railroads. J. Trans. Econ. Policy 42, 155–188.

Lim, S.H., Lovell, C.A.K., 2009. Profit and productivity of U.S. Class I railroads. Manag. Dec. Econ. 30, 423–442.

McCullough, G.J., 2007. U.S. Railroad Efficiency: A Brief Economic Overview, Research to Enhance Rail Network Performance,. Transportation Research Board.

Meeusen, W., van Den Broeck, J., 1977. Efficiency estimation from Cobb-Douglas production functions with composed error. Int. Econ. Rev., 435–444.

Munnell, A.H., 1990. Why has productivity growth declined? productivity and public investment. New Engl. Econ. Rev. (Jan), 3–22.

Nadiri, M.I., 1970. Some approaches to the theory and measurement of total factor productivity: a survey. J. Econ. Liter. 8, 1137–1177.

Nishimizu, M., Page, J.M., 1982. Total factor productivity growth, technological progress and technical efficiency change: dimensions of productivity change in Yugoslavia, 1965–78. Econ. J. 92 (368), 920–936.

Odeck, J., 2008. The effect of mergers on efficiency and productivity of public transport services. Transport. Res. Part A: Policy Prac. 42 (4), 696–708.

Ray, S.C., 1995. Productivity and quality changes in Swedish pharmacies: a comment. Int. J. Prod. Econ. 39, 145–146.

Shephard, R.W., 1953. Cost and Production Functions,. Princeton University Press, Princeton.

Shephard, R.W., 1970. Theory of Cost and Production Functions. Princeton University Press, Princeton.

Smith, D., 1983. The evolution of rail merger policy. Proc. Transport. Res. Forum 24, 558–565.

Solow, R.M., 1957. Technical change and the aggregate production function. Rev. Econ. Stat., 312–320.

Surface Transportation Board, 2009. Study of Railroad Rates: 1985–2007. , http://www.stb.dot.gov/econdata.nsf/142bd9233122e76285256605006100e0/e2dde951ff7a815a8525753e004e1236?OpenDocument.

Waters, W.G., 2007. Evolution of railroad economics. Dennis, S.M., Talley, W.K. (Eds.), Railroad Economics: Research in Transportation Economics, 20, Elsevier Science, Amsterdam, pp. 11–67.

Williamson, O.E., 1968. Economies as an antitrust defense: the welfare tradeoffs. Am. Econ. Rev. 58 (1), 18–36.

Wilner, F.N., 1997. Railroad Mergers: History Analysis Insight. Simmons-Boardman Books, Inc, Omaha.

Wilson, W.W., 1994. Market-specific effects of rail deregulation. J. Ind. Econ. 42 (1), 1–22.

Wilson, W.W., 1997. Cost savings and productivity gains in the railroad industry. J. Reg. Econ. 11, 21–40.

Wilson, W.W., Wilson, W.W., 2001. Deregulation, rate incentives, and efficiency in the railroad market. Starr McMullen, B. (Ed.), Research in Transportation Economics, 6, pp. 1–24.

Winston, C., 1998. U.S. industry adjustment to economic deregulation. J. Econ. Pers. 12 (3), 89–110.

Winston, C., 2005. The Success of the Staggers Rail Act of 1980. Brookings Institute, http://www.brookings.edu/~/media/Files/rc/papers/2005/10_railact_winston/10_railact_winston.pdf.

Policy in the deregulated and newly competitive railroad industry: a global analysis

Curtis M. Grimm*, Russell Pittman**
*University of Maryland, College Park, MD, United States; **U.S. Department of Justice, Washington, DC, United States

Chapter Outline

Dedication

I met Professor Ted Keeler soon after arriving in Berkeley as a PhD student in 1978. Berkeley Economics was a challenging and intellectually stimulating environment, but as a new PhD student was also somewhat impersonal and intimidating. Ted was friendly and encouraging from the start. I had previously worked on rail policy issues at the Wisconsin Department of Transportation. Ted was very interested in my work and invited me to attend and present at the Transportation Economics workshop. This provided connections with the strong network of PhD students working on transportation topics, many of whom I've stayed connected with over the years, and also led to financial support to conduct transportation economics research. Though I never had Ted as a professor in an actual class, I learned much more than in any class through my interaction with Ted in the workshop, in conversations, and in directed study.

Ted was an outstanding dissertation advisor as I proceeded in the program and chose a dissertation topic on competition issues in rail mergers. In addition, Ted linked me with Bob Harris, who had worked under Ted on rail policy issues and then taken a faculty position in Berkeley's Business School. Bob also provided excellent support and friendship throughout and after my PhD program. I am immensely grateful for Ted's profound positive influence on my transportation economics research and career.

Transportation Policy and Economic Regulation. http://dx.doi.org/10.1016/B978-0-12-812620-2.00005-5

5.1   Introduction

Rail reform began in the United States with heavily regulated railroads largely deregulated with the 4R Act and Staggers Rail Act in 1980. Researchers including Keeler had called for a change in public policy and predicted that there would be efficiency benefits in relying to a much greater extent on markets and competition to allocate resources. US rail deregulation provided a greater reliance on free markets to promote railroad profitability and public benefits. By increasing operating freedom and stimulating competition, deregulation spurred the railroad industry to shrink its physical plant and work force to better match available traffic (Grimm and Windle, 1999). As discussed by Grimm and Winston (2000): "The industry abandoned roughly one-third of its track and reduced crew sizes; used contracts to align cars and equipment with shippers' demand and to reduce its vulnerability to problems caused by overcapacity; and expanded the use of intermodal operations, double stack rail cars, and computer systems to provide faster, more reliable service. Real operating costs per ton-mile have fallen steadily, and, as of 1998, were 60% lower than when deregulation began. Some of the cost decline can be attributed to the long-run trend in rail's traffic mix to include a greater proportion of low-cost bulk traffic, but deregulation's contribution is substantial. Cost reductions and productivity improvements stemmed the long-run erosion in market share. And rail traffic grew. After reaching a postwar low in the mid-1980s, originating rail carloads have grown from 19.5 million in 1985 to 25.7 million in 1998. All of these factors have boosted profitability. During 1971–80, the industry's return on equity was less than 3%; during the 1990s the industry's return on equity averaged 10.7% (United States General Accounting Office, 1999)." Rail deregulation has clearly been a successful policy.

The movement to markets spread worldwide, primarily in the form of privatization of previously government-owned railroads. The common theme in the transformation of railroads was that markets and competition would provide better performance than government regulation and ownership. Indeed, the railroad industry was a microcosm of the fundamental economic reform throughout the global economy. In addition, the early US experience illustrating lower costs, enhanced efficiency, and revitalization of a moribund industry was also influential. In North America, the CN was moved to the private sector in 1995 (Wilner, 1997). In Mexico, the railroad was sold off in concessions. An important motivation, as in the United States, was increasingly high costs, poor service quality and decline in traffic. The Mexican railroad was split into three vertically integrated systems (TFM, FERROMEX, and Ferrosur), along with a terminal carrier, and a public bidding process ensued (Villa and Sacristán-Roy, 2013). Throughout Europe and the rest of the world, similar developments occurred (Mizutani and Uranishi, 2013; Pittman, 2004; Urdánoz and Vibes, 2013). These changes have been well documented; see for example, a recent survey by Laurino et al. (2015).

This paper will contribute to the literature by examining competition policy issues in the deregulated and privatized railroad industry. The next section examines these issues in the United States, with regard to both merger policy and competitive access. Keeler (1983) noted that rail merger issues would be prominent in the deregulated industry. Mergers would be expected both to rationalize excess capacity and align carriers optimally; accordingly, evaluation of competitive effects is of paramount importance when relying on competitive markets in lieu of regulation. Even 37 years after Staggers, competitive access issues remain salient, with pending proposals before the Surface Transportation Board (STB) to significantly expand competitive entry over rival carriers' tracks.

We then turn to competitive policy more broadly in North America, both merger and competitive access issues. Merger proposals and activity in Canada and Mexico have predominantly been end-to-end mergers with US railroads, raising some concerns about the possible denial of connecting traffic to independent railroads—that is, vertical foreclosure.[1] Competitive access continues to be important in both countries, with proposals to expand access now being considered. The fourth section of the paper examines competition policy issues outside North America, focusing on Europe and Russia. The paper ends with a summary of findings and conclusions.

5.2   US competition policy issues

5.2.1   Merger policy

Deregulation in the United States has been accompanied by substantial merger activity, as predicted by Keeler (1983); Table 5.1 provides a synopsis of Class I US mergers. The first merger wave occurred shortly after the 1980 Staggers Act. As discussed

Table 5.1 **Class I unification 1980–98**

Effective date of unification	Type of unification	Applicant railroads	Controlling railroad/company
6/2/80	Control	DT&I	GTW
12/1/80	Merger	SLSF	BN
9/23/80	Control	C&O/SCL	CSX
6/3/81	Control	Maine Central	Guilford
1/1/82	Merger	BN/C&S/FW&D	BN
6/1/82	Consolidation	SOU and N&W	NS
12/22/82	Merger	UP/MP/WP	UP
1/1/83	Consolidation	Family Lines/L&N	Seaboard System
7/1/83	Control	Boston & Maine	Guilford
1/5/84	Control	D&H	Guilford
2/19/85	Control	SOO/CMSP&P	SOO
3/26/87	Control	CR-government	CR-private
8/12/88	Merger	UP/MKT	UP
10/13/88	Control	SP/SSW/DRGW	DRGW
4/27/95	Purchase	UP/C&NW	UP
9/22/95	Merger	BN/ATSF	BNSF
9/11/96	Merger	UP/SP	UP
6/20/98	Control	NS/CSX/CR	NS and CS

Source: Railroad Mergers by Frank N. Wilner and AAR *Railroad Ten-Year Trends*.

---

[1] "End-to-end" rail mergers combine one railroad carrying traffic from A to B with a second railroad carrying traffic from B to C, resulting in a combined firm carrying traffic from A to C.

by Grimm and Winston (2000): "Chessie System and Seaboard Coast Line formed CSX, Norfolk and Western and Southern Railroad formed Norfolk Southern, Missouri Pacific and Western Pacific became part of Union Pacific, and the St. Louis-San Francisco Railroad along with Colorado Southern and Fort Worth Denver formed part of Burlington Northern." In accordance with ICC rail merger policy in the 1980s and early 1990s, the mergers were primarily end-to-end. As discussed by Pittman (1990), the ICC turned down the Santa Fe/Southern Pacific merger based on significant horizontal competitive impacts. The first merger wave resulted in three large railroads in the Eastern half of the US (CSX, NS, and Conrail) and four large carriers in the West (BN, UP, Santa Fe, and Southern Pacific).

A second US rail merger wave took place in the mid 1990s. As detailed by Grimm (2008): "The starting point was a battle between the UP and BN for control of the Santa Fe; BN was the successful suitor. Union Pacific subsequently merged with the Southern Pacific. In the East, NS and CSX vied for acquisition of Conrail; the end result was a joint takeover by the two railroads of Conrail. Thus the Burlington Northern-Santa Fe and Union Pacific-Southern Pacific mergers left only two major railroads in the western United States while Norfolk Southern's and CSX's joint acquisition of Conrail left only two major railroads in the east. Thus US railroad structure has remained largely stable since the mid-1990s, with two dominant systems in the East and West."

This second wave of US rail mergers involved more horizontal competitive effects and made salient the challenging issue of how to analyze such effects using a traditional structural approach, as developed, for example in the DOJ Horizontal Merger Guidelines. The guidelines evaluate transactions in broader economic and strategic terms and provide a more refined assessment of the impact of a transaction on market structure, as opposed to merely delineating "2-1" shippers at a specific station or even a specific shipper facility. Such an approach is commonplace for assessing mergers in other industries and other countries. While this paper focuses on evaluating competitive impacts from rail mergers, Gallamore and Meyer (2014) provide a more comprehensive discussion of rail mergers, including potential service and efficiency benefits.

As discussed in more detail in Grimm (2008), a starting point is that a railroad's "products" consist of the transportation of commodities between specific origin-destination pairs. A railroad is truly a multiproduct firm, in that each origin-destination and type of commodity shipped can properly be regarded as a unique product. One issue in defining the market is how to handle truck and other intermodal competition. Motor carriers certainly provide strong competition for some movements, but may be less effective competitors for bulk products and/or longer hauls. Accordingly, a focus on rail intramodal competition is appropriate in the initial analysis. When focusing on potential reduction of intramodal competition, a next step is whether to only consider carriers actually serving shippers at particular points as competitors, or to define relevant markets as rail traffic in broader origin-destination corridors. Thus a critical market definition issue is the scope of the geographic market. A key point here, as discussed in more detail in Grimm and Winston (2000), is that shippers captive to one railroad with another nearby benefit from indirect competition in many ways, such as truck transloading or threats to build out to another carrier's line. Accordingly a geographic market definition of origin-destination pairs of US Department of Commerce Business Economic Areas ("BEAs") is often or even usually appropriate, though for some commodities a smaller geographic area such as a county is arguably more appropriate (Pittman, 1990).[2]

Shippers could also enjoy railroad competition in some cases through product or geographic competition. For example, an industrial site served only by Railroad A in a given market may be able to use a substitute product shipped from a different origin by Railroad B. Furthermore, the destination portion of an origin-destination pair served by a monopoly railroad could obtain the same product from an alternative origin served by Railroad B; likewise, the origin portion of an origin-destination pair served by a monopoly railroad could ship its product to different destinations served by railroad B. Research by James MacDonald on grain shipments in the Midwestern US (1987, 1989) demonstrated the effectiveness of geographic competition in disciplining the railway rates. Mexico relied largely on geographic competition in its railways restructuring (Pittman, 2007, 2017a).

A final issue in defining rail markets is the complexity that many long-haul movements entail coordination by more than one carrier. It is common for connecting carriers to submit a single competitive bid for the entire movement. Therefore competition is greatly enhanced when the alternative, fully-independent routings are available. If one firm participates on all routings, competition can be greatly hampered. The STB and previously the Interstate Commerce Commission has clearly stated that independence of routings is critical:

> *Competition between railroads generally requires the presence of two or more independent routes, that is, routes having no carriers in common. When a single carrier is a necessary participant in all available routes, i.e., a bottleneck carrier, it can usually control the overall rate sufficiently to preclude effective competition. Consolidated Papers, Inc., et al. v. Chicago and North Western Transportation Co., et al, 7 I.C.C. 2d 330, 338 (1991).*

Accordingly, in evaluating the potential 2-1 impacts of a merger transaction, we focus attention on instances where the number of independent railroad routings is reduced from 2-to-1. The ICC's and STB's notion of independent routes set forth can be illustrated in Table 5.2.

Prior to the UP/SP merger, there were five rail routings in the Memphis to San Antonio market, but only two independent options. Either UP or SP becomes a bottleneck carrier—that is, as noted above, "a single carrier [that] is a necessary participant in all available routes"—for each of the five routes, leaving two independent competing options premerger. After the UP/SP merger only one independent option remains, as UP/SP participates in each of the routes. Thus this BEA pair constitutes a 2-to-1 market with regard to the UP/SP merger.

---

[2] A further complication is that both counties and BEA's vary a great deal in size. As always, the details of a particular situation matter.

Table 5.2 **Memphis to San Antonio routes and market shares**

Current rail routes	Market share for route
SP direct	17%
UP direct	31%
BN—UP	4%
CSXT—UP	26%
NS—UP	22%

The examination of types of shippers impacted by a loss of competition, as discussed above, supports a definition of rail markets as narrowly defined origin-destination pairs, most often using Business Economic Areas (BEAs). A BEA-BEA market definition also follows that of the Justice Department in the SP/SF and UP/SP cases, in particular that of Witness Pittman in his testimony and academic writings related to the SP/SF case, defining markets as flows between origin and destination BEA's for all but the most bulky commodities. In the SF/SP case, the ICC supported this definition of markets, but the STB found it too broad in the UP/SP case. A similar approach as described earlier was recently accepted by the STB in determining horizontal competitive effects of Norfolk Southern's acquisition of certain rail lines of the Delaware and Hudson Railway Co. (Grimm, 2014). Of course, any market definition applied to all rail traffic does not perfectly depict the competitive circumstances of each shipper. Accordingly, the methods described here should be combined with more detailed analyses of circumstances of individual shippers who raise concerns regarding competitive harms. This approach was followed by the STB to determine horizontal competitive effects of Norfolk Southern's acquisition of certain rail lines of the Delaware and Hudson Railway Co. (Grimm, 2014).

As discussed in more detail in Grimm and Plaistow (1999), there were significant 2-to-1 competitive impacts across three mergers: SP/SF, BN/SF, and UP/SP. In particular, the total revenues from rail traffic switching from two to one independent routes because of the merger exceeded $2 billion. The DOJ's comparable structural approach found 2-1 competitive effects of $1.5 billion. Nonetheless, this merger was approved, with trackage rights as negotiated by the parties of record to ameliorate competitive harms, as opposed to divestitures as advocated by other parties.

As discussed in Grimm (2008), another key issue was the conclusion by the STB that there would not be competitive harm in markets where the UP/SP reduced the number of rail carriers from three to two (approximately $5 billion in rail freight revenues). "In many of these markets UP and SP were the dominant two carriers before the merger. UP and SP had a combined market share of 70% or greater in around $2 billion of the 3-2 markets. For example, Houston was the originating or terminating point in a significant amount of 3-2 traffic in the UP/SP merger case. Very little of that traffic was intermodal, or automotive, with chemicals accounting for a large percentage of the 3-2 traffic. Thus the STB ruled out on a blanket basis any competitive harms in 3-2 markets regardless of the market shares of the two merging carriers or the degree to which truck competition might provide a competitive alternative in a particular market (Grimm, 1996)." As detailed in Grimm (2008), there exists both theoretical and empirical evidence of negative competitive impacts in situations where the number of rail carrier independent alternatives within a corridor would be reduced by a merger from three to two (Grimm, 1985; Kwoka and White, 1998; Levin, 1981; MacDonald, 1987, 1989; Winston et al., 1990).

A final key issue in evaluating competitive harms in railroad mergers is the design of conditions to ameliorate competitive harms. The STB has broad powers to condition merger approval, and so can potentially further the public interest through amelioration of competitive harms in the event a merger is otherwise in the public interest. The issue of how best to condition mergers with serious horizontal effects was most salient in the UP/SP merger. The Department of Justice (DOJ), along with a number of other public agencies and shippers, recommended divestiture in markets where UP and SP had parallel lines and were the only railroads in these markets. The merger applicants proposed that rival railroad BN be given trackage rights in these 2-1 markets to preserve a second competitor. The STB opted for the trackage rights "fix" to the merger (Kwoka and White, 1998).

5.2.2   Recent US proposals to expand competitive access

Arguably linked to reduction in competition as discussed earlier, shippers for many years have been pushing for greater competitive access both in new legislation and in STB proceedings. The STB moved ahead with a competitive access proposal in Ex Parte 711, more specifically a proposal by the National Industrial Transportation League (NITL) to sharply increase competitive access. In a Notice Of Proposed Rulemaking ("NPR") issued by the STB on July 27, 2016, the Board invited interested parties to submit comments on its proposal to require an incumbent serving railroad to "switch" the shipper's traffic at unspecified rates to the nearest actual or potential working interchange with another railroad, as long as that working interchange was within a reasonable distance of the facility seeking such access. If a shipper or a competing carrier could meet one of two tests—a "practicable and in the public interest" test or a "necessary to provide competitive rail service" test—the serving railroad would be required to provide this "switch" to the other railroad.

As with similar previous proposals, the STB's version of the NITL mandatory switching rule has evoked sharp negative reactions from the class I railroads as well as their trade association, the Association of American Railroads (AAR), who uniformly have evoked the prospect of "reregulation" and the spectre of the state of the railroad sector preStaggers to warn against the harms likely from the imposition of any statutory or regulatory protections for "captive shippers" beyond those currently in place.[3]

The shippers community, on the other hand, has complained that as a result of the merger wave of the 1990s, they are typically served by two major railroads at most, and that the eastern and western duopolists have learned in the 10–20 years since the mergers

---

[3] Readers of a literary or political bent may be reminded of the frequent riposte of the newly powerful pigs in George Orwell's *Animal Farm* to complaints from the other animals: "Surely you don't want Jones back!"

that their lives are quieter and more prosperous if they do not compete too strenuously for each other's customers. As evidence the shippers have pointed to data from the two Christensen Associates reports commissioned by the STB (2009, 2010) as well as the AAR's own tables, which showed that rates charged to shippers, after falling continuously for 25 years after Staggers, now exhibit a 10-year upward trend. The Christensen Associates reports further showed that the class I railroads, in sharp contrast to their preStaggers experience of profit rates in the low single digits, are now earning much higher rates of return, very much in the neighborhood defined by the STB as "revenue adequate"—that is, sufficient to support the heavy investment requirements of this capital-intensive industry—so that this particular goal of deregulation has been achieved.[4]

The shippers have also pointed to the arguments of Pittman (2010b) and others that the primary regulatory tool designed for the protection of captive shippers, the stand-alone-cost test, which caps the rate to the level that would be charged by a hypothetical railroad built for the purpose of serving that route, is cumbersome and expensive and in practice provides little protection to shippers, while alternative tools designed by Congress and the regulator in response to these concerns such as the simplified stand-alone-cost test[5] and the "three benchmarks" test[6] have been little used and similarly ineffective in providing protection (TRB, 2015).

As of this writing:

- A study by a committee formed by the Transportation Research Board of the National Academy of Sciences (TRB, 2015) has echoed many of the complaints of captive shippers and circulated a paper written by two of its members (Wilson and Wolak, 2017) to replace the stand-alone-cost test with price ceilings based on the rates charged to noncaptive shippers;
- A study by the consulting firm InterVISTAS (2016) commissioned by the STB has also echoed many of the complaints of captive shippers but overall defended the toolkit of the stand-alone-cost test, simplified stand-alone-cost test, and three benchmarks test, and declined to endorse major changes in that regime; and
- The record in STB proceeding Ex Parte 711, "Reciprocal Switching," remains open, without a Board decision one way or the other regarding the final status of its proposed new switching regime.

Defenders of the stand-alone-cost test continue to argue, *contra* Pittman (2010b), that the test is grounded in the fundamental economics of contestability theory.[7] In

---

[4] The shortage of funds for investments that resulted from the preStaggers regulatory regime was what Keeler (1983) termed the "railway problem."

[5] "The simplified SAC procedure is conceptually the same as the full SAC procedure. It is streamlined by replacing the design of a hypothetical stand-alone railroad and postulation of its customer base with the apparently less demanding requirement of estimating the SAC of providing the current service with its current traffic on the actual railroad involved." (TRB, 2015, at 132).

[6] This test compares the revenue-to-variable-cost ratio (R/VC) of the disputed traffic (using the far-from-perfect Uniform Rail Costing System of the STB) with (1) the R/VC "of the portion of the defendant railroad's other 'potentially captive' traffic that has an R/VC higher than 180 percent;" (2) "the average R/VC of the railroad's traffic that most resembles that of the traffic at issue with regard to such characteristics as commodity type, carload size, and travel distance;" and (3) "the average markup that the railroad is presumed to need on all of its potentially captive traffic to make the railroad revenue adequate." (TRB, 2015, at 133).

[7] See, for example, ICC (1985) and Faulhaber (2005). See Decker (2015) for a broader discussion.

addition, critics of the TRB and Pittman alternative proposals have argued that with so much money at stake in rate cases, there is no effective way to avoid rent-seeking and rent-dissipating behavior by both sides, meaning that the cost and disruption of abandoning the status quo would yield little actual benefit.

One weakness of proposals for mandatory switching regimes that has been almost completely overlooked in the debates has been the requirement for the complaining shipper to have an offer from a second railroad to switch the traffic at attractive rates.[8] If under the current duopoly situation one railroad is not willing to compete aggressively to poach customers from the other, as the shippers allege, why would the same railroad be willing to offer a low rate for traffic to be switched? The NITL proposal also is much more costly and burdensome from a regulatory perspective, compared to the Canadian model where interswitching occurs automatically if the connecting railroad is within 30 km. Rates are prescribed based on number of cars and length of switching, so that the need for interswitching and the appropriate rates do not need to be determined on a case-by-case basis.[9] As discussed by Grimm (2004), another issue to be addressed with mandatory switching proposals is the asymmetry in size and bargaining power between the "Big 4" Class 1s in the United States and the remainder of the industry. Operating revenues in 2014 for these four were: Union Pacific—$23.9 billion; BNSF—$23.0 billion; CSX—$12.3 billion; and NS—$11.6 billion. Each of the other railroads in the United States has annual revenues under $4 billion. For example KCS, the smallest Class 1, had 2014 operating revenues of $1.3 billion. Because of this, Grimm (2016) argues that the smaller Class 1s as well as regional and shortline railroads should be exempt from any mandatory switching requirements.

5.2.3   Antitrust exemption to expand competitive access?

One frequently made proposal for strengthening the protections offered shippers, especially captive shippers, vis-à-vis the increasingly concentrated railroad industry is to remove the partial exemption enjoyed by the railroad companies from the US antitrust laws. Under first the Interstate Commerce Act (1887) and then the Interstate Commerce Commission Termination Act (1995), a good deal of commercial activity of railroad companies, including mergers, is subject to the "exclusive" jurisdiction of the STB, and other state and federal laws, including the antitrust laws, are accordingly "preempt[ed]." (Criminal cartel activity subject to Section 1 of the Sherman Act is not included in the exemption.) The shippers community has argued that this exemption in favor of an allegedly railroad-friendly regulator has contributed to the high rates and poor service of which they complain.

---

[8] This issue was noted by the Alliance for Rail Competition in its filing before the STB in this proceeding on October 26, 2016: "[T]here is the possibility that access to a second railroad would not always result in improved service or reduced rates. A shipper gaining access to a second railroad could find that it now has the choice of two railroads, both of which impose excessive rates and charges, provide poor service, and force the shipper to absorb burdens and costs formerly borne by the rail carriers." (pp. 3–4).

[9] Note that the Canadian regulatory regime also requires the participation of a willing second railroad to carry the traffic. See Cairns (2013) and TRB (2015, at 136–140) for detailed discussions of the Canadian regime, including both advantages and disadvantages vis-à-vis the existing US regime.

In fact it is not clear how much difference such a legislative change would make, especially with a railroad industry concentrated by previous mergers (Pittman, 2010a). As discussed below, the STB in 2001 expressed its skepticism regarding the benefits of further industry concentration, changing its merger standard to require (in part) not just a showing of no significant harm to competition but an actual improvement in competitive conditions. Furthermore, while the STB did permit both the UP/SP and BN/ATSF mergers in the face of some opposition from the DOJ, it did impose conditions on both, ordering trackage rights regimes to protect shippers who would otherwise have been faced with a newly created monopoly railroad; likewise, and in agreement with DOJ, it blocked the earlier ATSF/SP merger proposal. Third, DOJ would face its own constraints and limitations in seeking to block a future merger of class I railroads:

- DOJ cannot block any merger on its own, but must bring litigation in federal district court seeking to convince a judge that the merger would harm competition in violation of Section 7 of the Clayton Act; and
- DOJ's jurisdiction for seeking to block a merger is limited to competition issues (though these may be broadly defined), whereas the STB can block mergers under a broader "public interest" standard. This particular difference may be potentially most important in the case of a proposed end-to-end, trans-continental merger, which in the current state of the North American railway industry seems likely to trigger one or two similar mergers, creating a much more concentrated national railroad industry as a result. Indeed, it may well be the case that approval of such mergers would be easier if merger authority were shifted from the STB to DOJ. According to press reports, STB concerns about vertical foreclosure competition issues were expected with regard to proposed CP/NS merger in 2016 and may have played a role in that merger not moving forward (Klobuchar, 2016; Sparkman, 2016).

Besides mergers, the principal hope of those urging the removal of the partial antitrust exemption for railroads is a series of judicial rulings that would basically mirror the compulsory switching regulations that the same parties are proposing: they propose that shippers could challenge "refusals to deal"—refusals of the serving railroad to either allow the trains of a second railroad to serve shippers located on the tracks of the first or to agree to carry only a short haul and switch the traffic to the second railroad—as a violation of Section 2 of the Sherman Act, which prohibits monopolization or attempted monopolization of a market.

As one of us has discussed elsewhere (Pittman, 2010a), though such a change in the legal regime might indeed provide an additional weapon for shippers to use in challenging rail rates, the plaintiff shippers would likely face a number of steep hurdles in actual litigation. The Supreme Court has stated that in general a seller "has a right to deal, or refuse to deal, with whomever it likes, as long as it does so independently"— though in a separate decision it noted that "Under certain circumstances, a refusal to cooperate with rivals can constitute anticompetitive conduct and violate § 2."[10]

In particular, refusals to deal have generally been found unlawful only when they have been part of a broader scheme to reduce competition—for example, to enforce an

---

[10] Respectively, Monsanto Co. v. Spray-Rite Serv. Corp., 463 U.S. 752, 761 (1984) (citations omitted), and Verizon Commc'ns v. Law Offices of Curtis V. Trinko, LLP, 5540 U.S. 398, 408 (2004).

illegal tying arrangement—rather than simply because the "deal" refused would have been more advantageous to the buyer than the one offered. A further complication is that these would be unusual refusal-to-deal cases, because the complaining shipper would be seeking not only compulsory "deals" between itself and the defendant, serving railroad but also between the defendant and its competitor railroad.

5.3   Competition policy issues in North America

5.3.1   Vertical competitive effects in North American rail mergers

Now looking more broadly at rail competition policy issues in North America, with regard to mergers a critical issue has been the evaluation of vertical foreclosure issues arising from end-to-end mergers of US carriers with Canadian or Mexican railroads.[11] The issue arose in 1999 in the context of a proposed merger between Canadian National and BNSF. A number of Class 1 carriers objected to the merger, raising what were in essence vertical foreclosure concerns. Vertical foreclosure in the rail context arises when a carrier uses a monopoly position in one segment to gain advantage in the broader origin-destination market. The merger proposal to consolidate the BNSF and Canadian National was stymied by the STB with the establishment of an 18 month moratorium on mergers (Phillips, 2000). The STB subsequently promulgated new railroad merger guidelines, which clearly had the effect of making approval of future end-to-end mergers between Class 1 carriers more difficult (McArthur, 2001; Depalma, 2001). Included in the rules (49 CFT 1180.1—General policy statement for merger or control of at least two Class 1 railroads) was a stipulation that future mergers would result in *increased* competition: "To offset harms that would not otherwise be mitigated, applicants should explain how the transaction and conditions they propose would enhance competition." Vertical foreclosure concerns were clearly enunciated: "Applicants shall also explain how they would at a minimum preserve competitive and market options such as those involving the use of major existing gateways, build-outs or build-ins, and the opportunity to enter into contracts for one segment of a movement as a means of gaining the right separately to pursue rate relief for the remainder of the movement."

As discussed in Grimm and Harris (1983) and Grimm et al. (1992), vertical foreclosure concerns arise in end-to-end rail mergers. We first note that this can appear counterintuitive, as mergers of firms in the same industry are generally considered horizontal. To clarify, Fig. 5.1 depicts three rail carriers. Carrier 1 serves the A-B market, while Carriers 2 and 3 serve the B-C market. Carrier 1 acquires Carrier 3, providing an example of an end-to-end merger as transportation from A to B and then B to C is analogous to successive stages in a production process or an upstream/downstream relationship. Accordingly, postacquisition Carrier 1–3 is now "vertically integrated" from A to C. Vertical foreclosure concerns can arise with respect to Carrier 2. For

---

[11] Vertical foreclosure is not the only possible anticompetitive outcome from an end-to-end rail merger, one where carriers connect at one or more junction points. See, for example, Pittman (2017b).

Figure 5.1 One carrier serving market A-B and two carriers serving market B-C.

example, for traffic originating at A and terminating at C, Carrier 1–3 may prefer to retain the long-haul over A-C and could refuse to interchange traffic with Carrier 2 at B. Another foreclosure concern is that Carrier 1–3 could "price squeeze" Carrier 2 in the negotiations for revenue divisions on A-C interline traffic.

Vertical foreclosure issues were at the heart of the STB evaluation of the 2003 KCS-TFM consolidation, raising key questions for the STB to resolve: What framework should the Board use in assessing claims of vertical foreclosure arising in rail consolidations? More broadly, how should the Board proceed in implementing its merger guidelines in future cases involving two Class 1 carriers? One possible framework to address vertical foreclosure issues is the Chicago view, which maintains that an efficient unintegrated firm will never be foreclosed, because that would "leave money on the table"—similar to the Coasian view discussed later that in many circumstances private bargaining should lead to efficient solutions. Revenues would be divided between the integrated and unintegrated carrier such that both would have an incentive to move traffic over the efficient interline route.

The following example (with reference to Fig. 5.2), drawn from Grimm (2008), elucidates the Chicago view: "Assume that $200 was the maximum rate obtainable for a unit of traffic in the A-C market. Further assume that marginal costs (MC) for the unit of traffic are as follows: Railroad 1's MC for the A-B segment and Railroad 1's MC for the BC segment are each $50; railroad 2's MC for the B-C segment are $45. Railroad 2 is therefore the more efficient carrier over the B-C segment. If Railroad 1 handles the traffic over the entire AC route, it obtains a profit of $100. Railroad 1, however, can obtain a higher profit by interchanging with Railroad 2, so long as 1 receives a revenue division greater than $150. Railroad 2 would be willing to participate if its revenues were greater than its MC, that is, at least $45. The two railroad's revenue requirements define a negotiating range such that 1's division would be between $150 and $155 while 2's would be between $45 and $50. As long as Railroad 2's costs

RAILROAD 1

          RAILROAD 1   --
     A --------------------------------------- B   C

RAILROAD 2

Figure 5.2 One railroad serving market A-B and market B-C, and one railroad only serving market B-C.

are lower on the B-C segment, there will be a division such that both 1 and 2 have an incentive to interline over the more efficient route. The Chicago view concludes that there is no need for regulatory intervention to prevent Railroad 1 from vertically integrating to obtain this leverage over 2 and no need for intervention in determining revenue divisions between 1 and 2."

Grimm and Harris (1983) and Grimm et al. (1992) discuss the Chicago view in more detail along with limitations in applying the Chicago view to rail mergers. To briefly summarize, given the large fixed costs associated with railroads, an unintegrated carrier could well be able to cover its incremental but not its fixed costs if it were forced to accept low margins. Importantly, divisions on interline traffic are generally governed by standard industry division rules, which have an efficiency basis given the transaction costs involved in negotiating rates for each interline movement. The integrated carrier may also be concerned with the prospect of STB regulatory or DOJ antitrust intervention if it used a monopoly link as leverage to force an uneven division. Therefore the integrated carrier may well prefer to foreclose its rival rather than execute a price squeeze. Consistent with this view, the testimony of Grimm in the KCS-TFM consolidation endorsed the STB's more activist approach to vertical foreclosure in end-to-end mergers, as enunciated in the new rail merger guidelines, and recommend that the Board should evaluate vertical foreclosure concerns on a case-by-case basis with careful attention to the bargaining power of rival railroads.

More specifically, a case-by-case approach would assess vertical foreclosure concerns based on specific facts regarding the likelihood of foreclosure, the ability of a potentially foreclosed railroad to protect itself, and the likelihood that shippers may ultimately pay in higher prices or inferior service. Concerns in end-to-end mergers could arise if an unintegrated carrier's bargaining position over divisions was substantially weakened and that carrier had no countervailing power, for example, if a short line or small railroad lost a friendly connection in conjunction with a consolidation of two mega-railroads. For vertical foreclosure to be exercised, the integrated carrier must have superior power in the vertical relationship with rival railroads as well as the ability to force shippers to favor its routings.

This proposed approach can be illustrated with reference again to Fig. 5.1. Carriers 1, 2, and 3 are initially independent, with Carrier 1 serving the A-B market and Carriers 2 and 3 serving the B-C market. Carrier 1 acquires Carrier 3, and a potential vertical foreclosure issue arises with respect to Carrier 2. The key initial question is: Can Carrier 2 protect itself against foreclosure? There are a number of means available in most rail situations. Carrier 2 may have options other than Carrier 1 to reach point A. Carrier 2 may originate or terminate captive traffic on its B-C line. Or, the situation may be reversed in other markets, with a Carrier 2 single-line routing in competition with a Carrier 1–3 interline one. The crux of the issue is the relative bargaining power and leverage between Carriers 1 and 2 following the merger. Note that the fact that the merger of Carriers 1 and 3 may alter the leverage between Carriers' 1 and 2 is not in itself germane. The key is whether the postmerger leverage between the two carriers allows the unintegrated carrier to protect itself.

More specifically, the conclusion of Grimm's testimony in the KCS-TFM consolidation was that UP's argument that they will be vertically foreclosed at the Laredo gateway was without merit. The current status quo provided Union Pacific with enormous leverage and bargaining power with regard to interline relationships in the US–Mexico rail market. While a consolidation of KCS with Tex-Mex and TFM arguably improved the position of TFM (postmerger called "NAFTA Rail") vis-à-vis UP, UP would still maintain a dominant position in the balance of power. There are many factors which provided Union Pacific substantial leverage and vertical power in its vertical relationships with NAFTA Rail and which provided ample protection versus any KCS vertical foreclosure attempts. First, Union Pacific is the largest of the Class I carriers, accounting for over one-fourth of total rail industry revenue and almost one-fifth of total rail industry track miles. NAFTA Rail, in its entirety, would have less than one-eighth the revenues of UP. This size mismatch provides UP with enormous leverage in negotiations over rate divisions. Second, UP dominates cross-border traffic. For example, UP's market share for Laredo Northbound traffic is 91% based on 2001 data; UP's share for Laredo Southbound traffic is 71%. This virtual monopolization of traffic in the US portion of these intercountry movements provides UP with substantial leverage. Additionally, UP has alternative gateways to Mexico and can thus protect itself against foreclosure by shifting traffic or threatening to do so. For all traffic to and from the United States and Mexico, UP carriers 90% of the Northbound traffic and 79% of the Southbound traffic, with access at all six rail gateways. In addition, UP owns 26% of Ferromex, TFM's competitor in Mexico. UP has a great deal of US–Mexico traffic tied up under long-term contracts, so that shifts in routing or divisions for quite some time are not even an option. UP has many captive shippers and extensive network coverage for US–Mexico traffic. And added to all these factors which amply protect UP's market position, Tex Mex must operate over UP's infrastructure to connect TFM with KCSR. As such, NAFTA Rail's ability to compete with UP at Laredo depends largely upon the dispatching, maintenance and investment practices of UP.

In sum, when evaluating outcome in the interline relationships following an end-to-end merger, the key is the bargaining power of the carriers following the merger, not the change in bargaining power from the merger. An appropriate approach to vertical foreclosure issues involves careful assessment on a case-by-case basis of the likelihood of foreclosure and the ability of rival railroads and shippers to protect themselves. In its KCS-TFM merger decision, the STB, while applying the spirit of the new merger guidelines with a more activist approach to vertical foreclosure issues, found that there was no basis for Board intervention in this case in fixing divisions or intervening in interline negotiations as UP had recommended.

Especially if there are practical limitations on the ability of the connecting railroads to come to an efficient negotiated solution—sometimes termed a "Coasian" solution after the Coase (1959) argument that there are incentives for contracting parties to reach an efficient solution regardless of the initial allocation of property rights—there is a second perspective on the issue that supports concerns regarding postmerger foreclosure: the "vertical arithmetic" that has become increasingly popular in antitrust analyses of vertical mergers and restraints (Pittman, 2017c). Under the "vertical arithmetic" framework there are three crucial parameters that determine whether it will be in the interest of the newly vertically integrated firm—in this case, the railroad following its end-to-end merger—to refuse to interchange traffic with its nonintegrated, downstream former interchange partner. These three parameters are the profit margin earned by Railroad 1 on the AB leg of the journey, the profit margin earned by Railroad 1 on the BC leg of the journey, and the "diversion ratio" from Railroad 2 to Railroad 1, defined as the percentage of the traffic that would be retained by Railroad 1 (rather than lost by the railroads collectively—to other modes, for example) if Railroad 1 were to foreclose Railroad 2 by insisting on handling all the ABC traffic.

A simple arithmetical exercise (Riordan and Salop, 1995; Pittman, 2017c) shows that foreclosure will be profitable if and only if the diversion ratio D_{21} exceeds the ratio $M_{AB}/(M_{AB} + M_{BC})$, where M_{AB} and M_{BC} are the respective profit margins earned by Railroad 1 on the two legs of the journey. If we assume that for most bulk shippers, the identity of the delivering railroad is not particularly important in their modal choice, then the diversion ratio should be close to one, and foreclosure will often be a profitable strategy.

A separate issue regarding end-to-end rail mergers concerns the efficiencies claimed for them. As with other vertical mergers, proponents claim efficiencies from the elimination of "double marginalization"—that is, the reduction in output that results from the upstream firm adding a margin to the price that it charges the downstream firm, with the downstream firm then adding its own margin.[12] Since the presence of double marginalization imposes costs on both the two suppliers and their customers, it is another area where efficient, "Coasian" bargaining might be expected to take place in the absence of a merger to reduce the costs and thereby make all parties better off. One example of a strategy that might achieve this would be multipart tariffs—that is, second degree Pigouvian price discrimination.

A recent paper co-authored by one of us (Pittman) finds evidence in favor of an efficient bargaining solution for end-to-end railroads. Alexandrov et al. (2017) use the confidential, "unmasked" waybill data from the STB to test whether a vertically integrated railroad carrying traffic—in this case, coal—from A through B to C charges a lower rate than the combined rates of separate railroads carrying an interchanged movement from A to B and then from B to C. Using hedonic pricing regressions designed to mimic those used by MacDonald (1989) and Christensen Associates (2009, 2010) and performing separate tests for both before and after the BN/ATSF merger of 1996 and for a panel of coal shipments in 2001–03, the authors are unable to reject the hypothesis of no difference between the rates charged by integrated and nonintegrated carriers.

A direct implication of these findings is that independent railroads interchanging freight over an end-to-end line are able—through negotiations, through multipart tariffs, through repeat interactions, through some other means—to achieve an efficient pricing solution, so that in today's nationally concentrated freight railways sector, further end-to-end mergers are unlikely to result in significant efficiencies. An indirect implication might be that if negotiations between interchanging railroads are efficient, negotiations between vertically integrated railroads and their unintegrated actual and potential interchange partners are also able to achieve efficient solutions, so that at least the most wasteful of the foreclosure behaviors identified by Grimm and Harris (1983) and Grimm et al. (1992) no longer take place.

---

[12] Spengler (1950). See also, for example, Martin (2010), at 366–367.

5.3.2   Recent proposals in Mexico and Canada to expand competitive access

As in the United States, expanding rail competitive access is a salient regulatory issue in both Canada and Mexico. Canada's proposed Transportation Modernization Act would extend interswitching from the current 30 km limit to include long-haul interswitching. Mexico has recently established a Railway Regulatory Agency with power to require trackage rights for competitive access. The Mexican Federal Competition Commission issued a preliminary report in March 2017 finding a lack of effective competition for interconnection trackage rights between KCSM, Ferromex, Ferrosur, and Ferrovalle. A final report is expected later this year.

5.4   Competition policy issues outside North America

The past few decades have seen a worldwide movement toward the reform and creation of competition in what were traditionally monopoly, state-owned railways, especially but not exclusively in Europe. The United Kingdom and Sweden were pioneers, but subsequent directives from the European Commission—both the Competition and the Transport Directorates—have led to progress in that direction in both freight and passenger rail transport and in both long-time EU member states and newer members and applicants.

The pioneering reforms of the United Kingdom and Sweden took a particular form that strongly influenced subsequent reform discussions, especially in Europe: vertical separation (VS). This may be understood as a specific instance of a reform that is an often discussed option in discussions regarding the reform of state-owned monopoly "public utility" providers more broadly: unbundling (Newbery, 2000; Pittman, 2003). Under VS, the sector is opened to entry by new train operating companies (TOC's), while the train operations of the incumbent railway are organizationally separated from infrastructure (track) operations, a strategy intended to remove any incentives or tendencies for the infrastructure operator to discriminate in favor if the incumbent train operator. While the incumbent, now separated train operating company may be privatized, typically the infrastructure operator remains state-owned. The EC Competition and Transportation Directorates have made it clear that VS is their desired long-term solution for EU railways (Nash, 2006; Knieps, 2013).

An alternative, related reform strategy favored by some European countries is generally termed "third party access" (TPA): as in VS, train operations are opened to entry by new train operating companies, but in TPA the incumbent infrastructure operator continues to operate its own trains as well. The advantage of TPA is that it creates competition for the incumbent freight and passenger train operations without eliminating the economies of scope enjoyed by the vertically integrated incumbent; the disadvantage is that it does not remove the incentive for the same vertically integrated incumbent to discriminate against independent, nonintegrated TOC's (Pittman, 2005). Examinations of the European experience with reform to date support the contention of TPA advocates that this strategy has often been successful at achieving the competition-creating benefits of VS without the necessity of bearing its costs (Mizutani and Uranishi, 2013; Mizutani et al., 2015; Nash et al., 2014).

As in other "public utilities" sectors, the VS option has been a favorite among economists and competition-friendly reformers, who often cite the example of the US government's break-up of the vertically integrated AT&T telephone system as a successful model (Brennan, 1987). A minority faction of reformers have sought to avoid the unpalatable alternatives of incentives for discriminatory access versus of the loss of economies of scope by urging an alternative strategy often termed "horizontal separation." This regime mimics the long-standing arrangements of the United States and Canada as well as the original organization form of the United Kingdom railways: privately owned, vertically integrated railway companies run their own trains over their own infrastructure, competing for business either along "parallel" routes—that is, both railways serving the same origin-destination pair—or in the form of the "source" or "destination" competition discussed above—that is, two railways competing to carry good X from origin O to different destinations, or two railways competing to deliver good X at destination D from different origins (Pittman, 2007). The horizontal separation strategy was adopted by both Mexico and Brazil as they restructured their railways in the 1990s, and is the regime adopted in some parts of the Australian railway system (Castelar and Azevedo, 2016; Estache et al., 2001; Perkins, 2016; Sampaio and Daychoum, 2017; Villa and Sacristán-Roy, 2013).

Interestingly, the Russian Federation, holding one of the largest and most important railways in the world, has debated all three of these popular reform options and chosen, at least for now, a fourth: privatization of logistics organization and of rolling stock ownership and repair, but not of infrastructure, (most) locomotive ownership, or (most) train operations (ECMT, 2004; Pittman, 2013; RUIE, 2013). The incumbent state-owned monopolist RZhD remains vertically integrated between infrastructure and train operations and operates virtually all freight trains on that infrastructure. Current law and regulation permits private "operators"—freight forwarders and owners of rolling stock—but, in general, not private "carriers"—companies owning their own locomotives and running their own trains on the RZhD infrastructure. The two exceptions are some luxury passenger train companies and some oil exporters (Polikarpov, 2015).

The results have been—thus far—disappointing for reformers. A 2009 report by the Federal Antimonopoly Service (FAS), "On the state of competition in the Russian Federation," lists in its chapter on freight rail the following goals that remain unmet:

- "Competition in the transport of goods—… no new carriers… [to challenge] the monopoly OAO RZD on the transport of goods;"
- "Tariffs for infrastructure services—the main financial instrument for the formation of independent goods[haulers] have not been developed;"
- "Develop[ing] private property in the main line locomotives;"
- "Improving the regulatory framework for access by all interested users to infrastructure services;"
- "Develop[ing] and implement[ing]… the regulatory framework of the operators of rolling stock."

In addition, RZhD remains mandated by the government to continue the operation of significant cross-subsidies within the system, both supporting passenger operations from freight revenues (though progress has been made in this regard) and supporting some freight movements—especially long-distance coal movements—with revenues from other freight movements.

Accordingly, the FAS has accused RZhD of violating the provisions in the competition law prohibiting the abuse of a dominant position on the market with some regularity over the past twelve years, including the following reported specifics:

- Discrimination against the owners of private rolling stock in the provision of rolling stock repair services (2005, 2008, 2009);
- Discrimination against the owners of private rolling stock for carrying beer, thus artificially encouraging use of the services of RZhD daughter company Refservice (2005, 2007);
- Refusal to service privately owned rolling stock at RZhD stations (2006);
- Refusal to reload private containers, thus artificially encouraging use of the services of RZhD daughter company TransContainer (2006);
- Refusal to provide weighing services to privately owned rolling stock (2006); and
- Discrimination against the owners of private rolling stock in the allocation of return traffic to avoid empty hauls (2010).

5.5   Summary and conclusion

This paper has discussed competition policy issues in the United States, North America, and in newly competitive rail industries worldwide. US rail deregulation provided a greater reliance on free markets to promote railroad profitability and public benefits. Three key competition policy issues have emerged in the wake of this regulatory reform. The first is competitive impacts of rail mergers. Following the 1980 Staggers Act, a wave of rail mergers ensued. These mergers were predominantly end-to-end and in the industry conditions at that time did not generally raise significant horizontal merger concerns. However, a second US merger wave took place in the mid 1990s. These mergers contained significant horizontal elements and made salient the challenges in applying traditional merger analysis to the rail industry. Issues such as how to define a relevant rail market, the competitive impacts of moving from three to two carriers in a market, and the role of conditions to ameliorate competitive harms are discussed in the paper.

The paper then turns to recent US proposals to expand competitive access. As of this writing, a proposal by the NITL is pending at the Surface Transportation Board. Under certain conditions, the proposal would require an incumbent serving railroad to "switch" the shipper's traffic at unspecified rates to the nearest actual or potential working interchange with another railroad, as long as that working interchange was within a reasonable distance of the facility seeking such access. Input to the STB has been sharply divided, with the shipper community generally in favor of the proposal based on reduction of rail competition since Staggers. The Class I railroads, on the other hand, are strongly opposed to the proposal. The discussion of US competition policy issues finishes with an evaluation of the impacts of removing the partial antitrust exemption of rail carriers under the US antitrust laws. While this could provide shippers with additional avenues to challenge railroad rates and actions impacting rates, the discussion provides reasoning that such an exemption might have limited impacts.

Influenced by US rail deregulation, the movement to markets spread worldwide, primarily in the form of privatization of previously government-owned railroads. The paper next turns to competition policy issues in North America, first examining vertical competitive effects in North American rail mergers. The issue first arose in 1999 in the context of a proposed merger between Canadian National and BNSF. The merger proposal to consolidate the BNSF and Canadian National was stymied by the STB with the establishment of an 18 month moratorium on mergers, due largely to what were in essence vertical foreclosure concerns raised by a number of Class I carriers. Vertical foreclosure concerns were also raised by UP and BNSF in the cross-border KCS-TFM consolidation. The paper discusses in some detail a recommended approach to addressing vertical foreclosure issues arising in this context. More specifically, the authors endorse the STB's more activist approach to vertical foreclosure in end-to-end mergers, as enunciated in the new rail merger guidelines, and recommend that the Board should evaluate vertical foreclosure concerns on a case-by-case basis with careful attention to the bargaining power of rival railroads. This section of the paper ends with discussion of recent proposals in Mexico and Canada to expand competitive access. The final section of the paper briefly addresses competition policy issues outside North America.

While many years have passed since initial deregulation and privatization of railroads globally, competitive access issues are still very prominent. This underscores the challenge of devising and implementing competitive policy in the railroad industry. As with other network industries such as electricity and telecommunications, attempts to inject greater competition raise many complex challenges regarding competitive access and competitive policy. It is likely that competitive access issues will remain prominent in the global railroad industry for many years to come.

Acknowledgments

The excellent research assistance of Kate Ren and Laharish Guntuka is gratefully acknowledged.

The views of the authors do not represent the views of the U.S. Department of Justice.

References

Alexandrov, A., Pittman, R., Ukhaneva, O., 2017. Royalty stacking in the U.S. freight railroads: Cournot versus Coase, unpublished paper presented at Third Annual Research Colloquium. The Economics and Regulation of the Freight Rail Industry. Georgetown University, Mc Donough School of Business, Washington, DC.

Brennan, T.J., 1987. Why regulated firms should be kept out of unregulated markets: understanding the divestiture in United States v. AT&T. Antitrust Bull 32, 741–793.

Cairns, Malcolm, 2013. Expansion of regulated access to railway infrastructure in North America: Implications from practices and recent experiences with regulated access overseas. Res. Transp. Bus. Manage. 6, 31–44.

Castelar, Armando, Azevedo, Luísa, 2016. Rail regulation in Brazil. Network Ind. Q. 18.

Coase, R.H., 1959. The federal communications commission. J. Law Econ. 2, 1–40.

Decker, Christopher, 2015. Modern Economic Regulation: An Introduction to Theory and Practice. Cambridge University Press, Cambridge, UK.

Depalma, C., 2001. New Merger Rules Force Railroads to Give Assurance of Competition. New York Times.

ECMT, 2004. Regulatory Reform of Railways in Russia. European Conference of Ministers of Transport, Paris.

Estache, A., Goldstein, A., Pittman, R., 2001. Privatization and regulatory reform in Brazil: the case of freight railways. J. Ind. Comp. Trade 1, 203–235.

Faulhaber, G.R., 2005. Cross-subsidy analysis with more than two services. J. Compet. Law Econ. 1, 441–448.

Gallamore, R.E., Meyer, John R., 2014. American Railroads: Decline and Renaissance in the Twentieth Century. Harvard University Press, Cambridge.

Grimm, C., 1985. Horizontal competitive effects in railroad mergers. Keeler, Theodore E. (Ed.), Research in Transportation Economics, 2, JAI Press, pp. 27–53.

Grimm, C., 1996. "Verified Statement," on behalf of the Kansas City Southern Railroad. Union Pacific-Southern Pacific Merger.

Grimm, C., 2014. "Verified Statement," On Behalf of Norfolk Southern Railroad, STB Docket No. 35873.

Grimm, C., 2004. Testimony to U.S. House of Representatives Committee on Transportation and Infrastructure Subcommittee on Railroads.

Grimm, C., 2016. "Verified Statement," On Behalf of the Kansas City Southern Railroad, STB Docket No. EP 711.

Grimm, C., 2008. Merger analysis in the post-Staggers railroad industry. In: Carstensen, Peter C., Farmer, Susan Beth (Eds.), Competition Policy and Merger Analysis in Deregulated and Newly Competitive Industries. Edward Elgar Publishing.

Grimm, C., Harris, R., 1983. Vertical foreclosure in the rail freight industry: economic analysis and policy prescriptions. ICC Pract. J. 50 (5), 508–531.

Grimm, C., Plaistow, J., 1999. Competitive effects of railroad mergers. J. Transp. Res. Forum 38 (1), 64–75.

Grimm, C., Winston, C., 2000. Competition in the deregulated railroad industry: source, effect and policy issues. In: Peltzman, S., Winston, C. (Eds.), Deregulation of Network Industries: The Next Steps. Brookings, Washington, D.C, pp. 41–72.

Grimm, Curtis M., Windle, Robert, 1999. The rationale for deregulation. In: James Peoples (Ed.), Regulatory Reform and Labor Markets. Kluwer Press.

Grimm, C., Winston, C., Evans, C., 1992. Foreclosure of railroad markets: a test of Chicago leverage theory. J. Law Econ. 35, 295–310.

ICC, 1985. Coal Rate Guidelines Nationwide." U.S. Interstate Commerce Commission, Ex parte No. 247 (sub no. 1).

Keeler, T.E., 1983. Railroads, Freight, and Public Policy. Brookings.

Klobuchar, A., 2016. Washington: Klobuchar Statement on Canadian Pacific Ending Merger Efforts with Norfolk Southern. US Official News: LexisNexis Academic.

Knieps, Günter, 2013. Competition and the railroads: a European perspective. J. Compet. Law Econ. 9, 153–169.

Kwoka, J., White, L., 1998. Manifest destiny? The Union Pacific-Southern Pacific Merger (1996). In: Kwoka, J., White, L. (Eds.), The Antitrust Revolution. third ed. Oxford University Press.

Laurino, Antonio, Ramella, Francesco, Beria, Paolo, 2015. The economic regulation of railway networks: A worldwide survey. Transp. Res. Part A 77, 202–212.

Levin, Richard, 1981. Railroad rates, profitability, and welfare under deregulation. Bell J. Econ. 12, 1–26, Spring.

Martin, S., 2010. Industrial Organization in Context. Oxford, UK.

McArthur, K., 2001. U.S. to Release New Rail Merger Rules; Most Observers Say the Big Six Railways in; North America Will Ultimately Become Two. The Globe and Mail (Canada). LexisNexis Academic.

MacDonald, James M., 1987. Competition and rail rates for the shipment of corn, soybeans, and wheat. Rand J. Econ. 18.

MacDonald, James M., 1989. Railroad deregulation, innovation, and competition: effects of the staggers act on grain transportation. J. Law Econ. 32 (April), 63–95.

Mizutani, Fumitoshi, Smith, Andrew, Nash, Chris, Uranishi, Shuji, 2015. Comparing the costs of vertical separation, integration, and intermediate organisational structures in European and East Asian Railways. J. Transp. Econ. Policy 49.

Mizutani, Fumitoshi, Uranishi, Shuji, 2013. Does vertical separation reduce cost? An empirical analysis of the rail industry in European and East Asian OECD Countries. J. Regul. Econ. 43 (1), 31.

Nash, Chris, 2006. Europe: alternative models for restructuring. In: Gómez-Ibáñez, José, de Rus, Ginés (Eds.), Competition in the Railway Industry: An International Comparative Analysis. Edward Elgar, Cheltenham, UK.

Nash, Chris, Smith, Andrew, van de Velde, Didier, Mizutani, Fumitoshi, Uranishi, Shuji, 2014. Structural reforms in the railways: incentive misalignment and cost implications. Res. Transp. Econ.

Newbery, D.M., 2000. Privatization, Restructuring, and Regulation of Network Industries, Cambridge, MA.

Perkins, Stephen, 2016. Regulation, competition and performance of Mexico's freight railways. Network Ind. Q. 18.

Phillips, D., 2000. Railroad Merger in Doubt After Court Upholds Moratorium. The Washington Post. LexisNexis Academic.

Pittman, Russell, 1990. Railroads and competition: the Santa Fe/Southern Pacific merger proposal. J. Ind. Econ.

Pittman, R., 2003. Vertical restructuring (or not) of the infrastructure sectors of transition economies. J. Ind. Comp. Trade 3, 5–26.

Pittman, Russell, 2004. Russian railways reform and the problem of non-discriminatory access to infrastructure. Ann. Public Cooperative Econ. 75 (2), 167–192.

Pittman, R., 2005. Structural separation to create competition? The case of freight railways. Rev. Network Economics 4, 181–196.

Pittman, Russell, 2007. Options for restructuring the state-owned monopoly railway. Dennis, Scott, Talley, Wayne (Eds.), Railroad Economics (Research in Transportation Economics), 20, Elsevier, Amsterdam.

Pittman, Russell, 2010a. The economics of railroad 'captive shipper' legislation. Admin. Law Rev. 62, 919–936.

Pittman, Russell, 2010b. Against the stand-alone-cost test in U.S. freight rail regulation. J. Regul. Econ. 38, 313–326.

Pittman, Russell, 2013. Blame the switchman? Russian railways restructuring after ten years. In: Alexeev, Michael, Weber, Shlomo (Eds.), The Oxford Handbook of the Russian Economy. Oxford, UK.

Pittman, Russell, 2017a. Reforming and restructuring Ukrzhaliznytsia: a crucial task for Ukrainian reformers. Sci. Transp. Progr. (Bulletin of the Dnipropetrovsk National University of Railway Transport) 67, 34–50, http://stp.diit.edu.ua/article/view/92775/92558.

Pittman, Russell, 2017b. The strange career of independent voting trusts in U.S. rail mergers. J. Compet. Law Econ. 13, 89–102.

Pittman R., 2017c. Three Economist's Tools for Antitrust Analysis: A Non-Technical Introduction. U.S. Department of Justice, Antitrust Division, Economic Analysis Group Discussion Paper 17-1. Available from: https://www.justice.gov/atr/three-economist-s-tools-antitrust-analysis-non-technical-introduction.

Polikarpov, Alexander, 2015. Russian railfreight market at a crossroads. Int. Railway J.

Riordan, M.H., Salop, S.C., 1995. Evaluating vertical mergers: a post-Chicago approach. Antitrust L.J. 63, 513–568.

RUIE, 2013. Evaluation of Most Feasible Infrastructure and Transportation Operations Integration Model in the Frame of Destination Freight Transportation Services Market Model Implementation Until 2015. Russian Union of Industrialists and Entrepreneurs, Transport and Transport Infrastructure Committee (Institute of Natural Monopolies Research), Moscow.

Sampaio, Patrícia Regina Pinheiro, Daychoum, Mariam Tchepurnaya, 2017. Two decades of rail regulatory reform in Brazil (1996–2016). Util. Policy.

Sparkman, 2016. STB throw monkey wrench into possible CP-NS merger while opposition grows. Mater. Handling Logist.

Spengler, J.J., 1950. Vertical integration and antitrust policy. J. Pol. Econ. 58 (4), 347–372.

TRB, 2015. Modernizing Freight Rail Regulation, Committee for a Study of Freight Rail Transportation and Regulation. Transportation Research Board of the National Academy of Sciences, Special Report 318.

United States General Accounting Office, 1999. Railroad Regulation: Changes in Railroad Rates and Service Quality Since 1990.

Urdánoz, Miguel, Vibes, Catherine, 2013. Regulation and cost efficiency in the European railways industry. J. Productivity Anal., 1–14.

Villa, Juan Carlos, Sacristán-Roy, Emilio, 2013. Privatization of Mexican railroads: fifteen years later. Res. Transp. Bus. Manage. 6, 45–50.

Wilner, Frank N., 1997. Railroad Mergers: History Analysis Insight.

Winston, C., Corsi, T., Grimm, C., Evans, C., 1990. The Economic Effects of Surface Freight Deregulation. Brookings Institution, Washington, D.C.

Wilson W.W., Wolak F.A., 2015. Demonstration of competitive rate benchmarking to identify unusually high rates. In: TRB, Modernizing Freight Rail Regulation, Committee for a Study of Freight Rail Transportation and Regulation. Transportation Research Board of the National Academy of Sciences, Special Report 318.

Further Reading

Campos, Javier, 2001. Lessons from railway reforms in Brazil and Mexico. Transp. Policy 8 (2), 85–95.

Ciccantell, Paul S., 2002. Building the NAFTA railway: Kansas City Southern Railway in the North American Economy. Latin Am. Bus. Rev. 3 (2), 85–110.

Gallamore, R.E., 1999. Regulation and Innovation: lessons from the American railroad industry. In: Gomez-Ibanez, Jose, Tye, William B., Winston, Clifford (Eds.), Essays in Transportation Economics and Policy: A Handbook in Honor of John R. Meyer. Brookings, Washington.

Grimm, C., 1984. An evaluation of economic issues in the UP–MP–WP railroad merger. Logist. Transp. Rev. 20 (3), 239–259.

Grimm, C., Harris, R., 1985. The effects of railroad mergers on industry performance and productivity. Transp. Res. Rec. 1029, 9–17.

Harris, Barry C., 1997. "Verified Statement," STB Finance Docket No. 33388, CSX/NS.

National Research Council (U.S.), 2015. Committee for a Study of Freight Rail Transportation and Regulation. Modernizing Freight Rail Regulation. Transportation Research Board Special Report 318. Transportation Research Board, Washington, D.C.

Orenstein, Jeffrey, 1990. United States railroad policy: Uncle Sam at the throttle.

Designing future merger policy in north american rail: lessons from the past?

James F. Nolan, Eric T. Micheels, Lindsay A. Pollard
University of Saskatchewan, Saskatoon, Saskatchewan, Canada

Chapter Outline

Dedicati on—James Nolan

Two degrees of separation lie between myself and Ted Keeler. The first time I heard of Ted's work was as a student at UC Irvine in the mid-1990s. I was taking a graduate field course in transportation economics offered by John Ying (U. Delaware). John was a student of Ted's at UC Berkeley and had already coauthored several very good papers with him on transportation-related topics. At that time, John was on sabbatical, but teaching this two quarter course sequence at UCI to an eager group of transportation economists and engineers. I have always thought that had I taken the course with one of the extant UCI faculty working in transportation economics, it would have been markedly different because almost all of the transportation research being done at UCI at that time was passenger mode focused, including my own doctoral dissertation.

Instead, the material we covered in John's course sequence (much of which still crops up in my own teaching) was I now know very much Ted Keeler, including the theory of natural monopoly, regulatory economics, pricing models, efficiency measurement, etc. with nearly equal coverage of both passenger and freight modes of transportation as examples. The latter was my first exposure to issues of interest in freight transportation, which I found especially fascinating. Without knowing it at the time, the die was cast. In effect, these courses and their Ted Keeler-inspired content helped cement my eventual career path focusing mostly on freight transportation research. For that, I surely owe a debt of professional gratitude not only to John Ying, but also to his mentor at UC Berkeley, Dr. Ted Keeler.

Transportation Policy and Economic Regulation. http://dx.doi.org/10.1016/B978-0-12-812620-2.00006-7

6.1   Introduction

In the spirit of this tribute volume, we believe that considering Prof. Keeler's career body of transportation and particularly rail research, he would find the present situation in the North American rail sector of considerable interest. After nearly 20 years of relative industry stability under deregulation, once again, the rail industry finds itself in a state of flux. From the extensive service disruptions that occurred in 2013–2014, combined with uncertainty over the future of coal shipments as well as more recent efforts to initiate mega-mergers in the industry, it is very likely that the industry will soon be undergoing considerable regulatory change. The direction and magnitude of the regulatory policies that may be brought into use to help address these issues are still unclear at this time.

In the post-Staggers era through the 1980s and 1990s, a number of large US railroad mergers were approved, and each of these helped to define the scope of the remaining major carriers in the rail industry of today. Key among the approved mergers include the 1995 Burlington Northern Santa Fe (BNSF) merger (Conant, 2004a) as well as the 1996 Union Pacific Southern Pacific (UPSP) merger (Conant, 2004b). In fact, it was a series of operational problems stemming from the latter merger that led to shipper calls for increased diligence in assessing any future rail merger attempts (Kwoka and White, 1999).

In spite of the latter problems, Class 1 railroads were not quite done with mergers. While preliminary talks on a proposed merger began as early as 1994 (Madar, 2002), in 1999 the recently privatized Canadian National (CN) railway offered formal merger terms to the BNSF Railway (Wall Street Journal, 1999). The resultant cross-border railway (hereafter called CNBN) would have been by far the largest Class 1 carrier even by today's standards, possessing the holy grail of both East–West and North–South coverage across a significant portion of North America. While CN was the merger aggressor in this particular case, both railways were fully supportive of the proposed deal.

A series of public hearings describing the relative benefits and costs of the proposed merger were overseen by the Surface Transportation Board (STB) through the following year. While lengthy hearings had been conducted by the ICC/STB for previous merger proposals that proved controversial (including the rejected Santa Fe—Southern Pacific merger attempt of 1987, see Pittman, 1990), in light of the described difficulties encountered with the most recent major merger, the CNBN hearings were especially lengthy, producing thousands of pages of testimony from shippers, carriers, and other interested parties associated with the rail industry. The review process passed through several stages, as the STB made considerable efforts to garner input from all relevant parties. As we now know, the STB not only blocked the CNBN merger attempt, but also did something it had not done since deregulation. The STB imposed a moratorium on future rail mergers that, while effectively lifted in 2005, went essentially unchallenged until 2015.

In 2015, another cross-border rail merger was proposed between the Canadian Pacific (CP) and Norfolk Southern (NS) railroads. This time, the primary impetus for the merger deal manifested through one individual, Mr. Hunter Harrison. A peripatetic railroad icon and at the time the CEO of the CP railway, Harrison possessed and still possesses a considerable reputation as an industry visionary, a professional following that helped sustain these merger discussions after so many years of inactivity.

While there were never any formal hearings on the CP–NS proposal, ultimately Canadian Pacific (or more specifically, Mr. Harrison) dropped its pursuit of NS. With CP as the clear merger aggressor in this case—unlike the previous CNBN merger proposal—as we shall see it was never completely clear if NS ever had any real interest in the merger. Ultimately, the outcome seems to have affected Mr. Harrison to the point where eventually left CP to take his current position as CEO of another Class 1 carrier, CSX ("Chessie Seaboard X") Rail (Financial Post, 2016b).

Given the historical rail merger narrative and considering the current state of the industry in North America, there is growing uncertainty among shippers about the possibility of new rail mergers and consequently how merger policy in rail will be informed moving forward. To this end, we examine a previously untapped source of information that may help shed light on issues arising with respect to potential future mergers in the rail industry.

Relying upon what we believe is the complete set of (digitized) 1999–2000 public submissions for the CNBN merger hearings, we employ qualitative analysis software (NVivo) to search and mine the submissions for crucial phrases of interest as communicated by stakeholders in association with that proposed merger. Qualitative analysis essentially creates a frequentist mapping of text, whereby heavily used words or phrases found in documentation can be distilled out and examined. Once complete, we then use the generated results to help clarify the current regulatory and merger situation in the North American rail sector.

To this end, we render comparisons between the most frequent phrases raised in the CNBN merger hearings against various public statements and information we found about the failed CP–NS merger proposal. Given the breadth and depth of the CNBN submissions, this qualitative analysis very likely "spans the space" of crucial issues brought up at that time by industry stakeholders regarding rail mergers. While we acknowledge that there have been significant operational changes in the industry in the intervening years, we hope the reader agrees that with respect to rail mergers, the more things change, the more they stay the same. In this light, we offer that this perspective on the CNBN merger hearings will help to better inform merger policy moving into the future.

After almost two decades of relative silence, the prospect of additional rail mergers in North America now seems to be inevitable. The failed CNBN merger attempt in 2000 led to new regulations—both in Canada and the United States—to both govern as well as to assess the viability of any future mergers. Without question, the failed CNBN merger was a watershed moment in the rail deregulation movement that had significantly changed the US industry up to that point. For this reason, we feel that the event is worthy of further study placed in the context of what is occurring in the industry today.

6.2   The turning point—an overview of the (failed) CNBN merger

Economic and competition issues regarding mergers and associated regulations have been extensively examined with respect to the US rail system. Seminal research on this topic includes the work of Pittman (1990), Gallamore (1999), Kwoka and White (1999), and most recently, Winston et al. (2011). Regarding the proposed 1999–2000 merger of the BNSF and the Canadian National (CN) railways, Madar (2002) examined the impact of deregulation and merger policy (or lack thereof) from the Canadian perspective. In turn, he suggested that changes in the regulatory environment in both the United States and Canada for surface transportation, particularly related to rail, allowed railways to reconsider key operational decisions such as line abandonment and rate setting. He concluded that prior changes in the North American regulatory environment, along with the underlying economics of railway ownership and operations that support large economies of scale and encourage further consolidation, helped lead to greater scrutiny of the CNBN merger (see Fig. 6.1).[1]

Some of the issues for shippers raised during the merger review included "high rates, poor service, and arbitrary treatment" (Madar, 2002, p. 153). Among the proposed remedies by some shipper representatives, greater trackage rights were suggested for remaining railways in the belief that it would help buttress contestability in potentially underserved markets. The issue of maintaining contestability through some form of trackage rights was most relevant for shippers of bulk commodities, many of whom are often geographically constrained (Vachal and Bitzan, 2005). In effect, we know that commodity producers cannot really choose where to locate a coal mine or a major grain-growing region. To date, in spite of the regulatory rejection of the CNBN merger, in fact none of the proposed remedies have been enacted on the scale envisioned by their proponents. And while rail rate regulations across the border differ, on most movements railways have considerable freedom to price as they see fit.

Due to the breadth and scope of the proposed CNBN merger, along with those one would consider typical participants at rail merger hearings, the CNBN merger hearings also gave rise to several varied and unusual submissions by interested but not directly involved parties to the proposed merger. For example, Nobel prize winning economist Kenneth Arrow (who, to the authors knowledge, never conducted research on railroads) made a submission essentially supporting future rail mergers. In their submission, the now defunct Enron Corp. asked the STB for permission to establish a procedure for industry participants to develop a system of tradable rail capacity rights,

---

[1] Rail "economies" come in several related forms. It is still an unresolved empirical issue as to just what is the most efficient size of general freight railroad in North America. But why might already large railroads want to merge? Aside from benefitting from economies of scale (where even greater outputs generate lower average costs), network-based transportation industries can also benefit from related economies of density and economies of size (see Boyer, 1997 for comparative explanations of these terms). Each of these sources of economies could be a reason for a large railroad to want to merge with another large railroad. For example, and considering potential service levels, a railroad might want to merge with another to gain economies of density, meaning that it can offer more frequent and varied (i.e. better) service to shippers due to the presumably more dense and extensive track network that typically results from a merger.

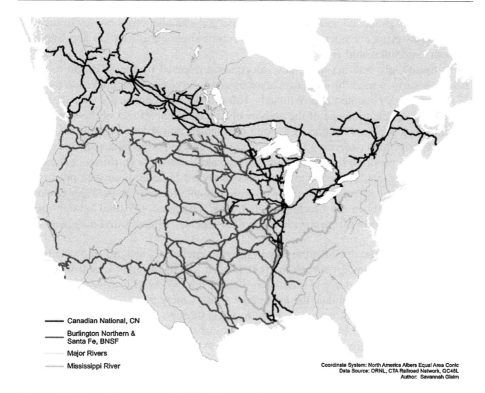

- Canadian National, CN
- Burlington Northern & Santa Fe, BNSF
- Major Rivers
- Mississippi River

Coordinate System: North America Albers Equal Area Conic
Data Source: ORNL, CTA Railroad Network, GC48L
Author: Savannah Gleim

Figure 6.1 Map of the current CNBN rail networks.

similar to prior work Enron did in the energy sector. These are but two of the hundreds of submissions examined, but are strongly indicative of the broader interest at that time in this particular set of merger hearings.

The CNBN merger proposal, and the consequences that ultimately came of it, was a something of watershed moment for the rail industry in North America. The moment passed with regulatory changes limited mostly to merger policies in the sector, leaving many important issues raised at that time by concerned parties effectively unresolved. And as we shall highlight later in our analysis, it seems that the more the rail industry changes, the more it stays the same.

6.3   Qualitative data and analysis

Like many other modern organizations, the STB maintains an updated web site (www.stb.gov) that posts current rulings and/or hearings pertaining to their regulatory actions. However, back in 2000, things were somewhat different on the information dissemination front. Subsequent to the extensive STB hearings on the proposed CNBN merger, the STB released for purchase every submission that was considered as part of the proposed merger. Since the merger was also cross-border in jurisdiction, there were a considerable number of submissions both from US and Canadian shippers and interested groups.

In those early Internet days, any information released by the STB had to be ordered by surface mail through a separate business services provider. While the work of Madar (2002) counted approximately 160 submissions considered over the 4 days of hearings, at the time one of the authors obtained a complete set of the written submissions (on paper, as well as converted or scanned into Adobe Acrobat and loaded onto a CD-ROM) concerning the proposed merger. Given the nature of this qualitative data, we presume that these now 16-year-old documents constitute a somewhat unique dataset that has not been heretofore analyzed in detail. Our data presumably also includes any interested parties who were not able to show up in Washington and participate directly in the hearings at that time. There are 449 total submissions in our dataset, stemming from a wide range of shippers, carriers, individuals, and other interested parties.

We offer that the documentation will provide interesting insights into whether the concerns about rail mergers back in 2000 differ in any meaningful way from the concerns that were voiced a few months ago about the efforts of Canadian Pacific and Hunter Harrison to formulate the next major Class 1 merger.

While it is possible for an individual to wade through this amount of documentation and garner some essential points and foci of the statements being made, given the number of submissions in the data we decided to utilize the power of qualitative software to mine the documents for key points and phrases pertaining to the topic of rail mergers. NVivo is a modern and powerful software package used in a number of research fields (particularly in the legal profession) to help collate and categorize large amounts of written information so as to track common trends and identify links among documentation. Research using NVivo applied to transportation policy include Jeffcott et al. (2006) who examined safety culture in UK railways, and Chaney (2013) who studied the relationship between politics and public transportation policy in the UK. From the NVivo web site:

> *NVivo is software that supports qualitative and mixed methods research. It's designed to help you **organize, analyze and find insights in unstructured, or qualitative data** like: interviews, open-ended survey responses, articles, social media and web content ... importantly, completing this kind of research without software can make it very hard to discover connections in your data and find new insights that will give you an edge. (http://www.qsrinternational.com/nvivo-product)*

While NVivo can be programmed to mine digitized documentation for words and phrases, we decided as an initial run for this analysis to check for a number of key terms from the rail merger discussions of that era and see which emerge from the STB submissions. Using a variety of references, we broke down our search terms into five broad categories covering what seemed to be the primary concerns at that time with the issue of rail competition, the economics of mergers, rail, transportation and miscellaneous (other) possible categories. The latter we felt was important to include

Table 6.1 **Keywords, by Category (with Terminology References where Necessary)**

Competition	Economics	Rail terms	Transportation terms	Other
Intermodal competition	Standalone cost (STB, 1996)	Captive shippers (Vachal and Bitzan, 2005)	Capacity constraints	Sovereignty
Geographic/source competition (Grimm and Winston, 2000)	Economies of scale, density, or size	"Two-to-one" markets (Majure, 1996)	Bottleneck	Border
Intramodal competition	Merger efficiency	"Three-to-two" markets (Tye and Horn, 2005)	Trackage rights (Madar, 2002)	Class 1
Inter-rail competition	Free trade	Improved service	Congestion	International trade

because of other issues at hand in the CNBN merger attempt, including the cross-border nature of the proposal, which would have been a first for both countries.

This process led us to generate the following matrix of rail "phrases", comprising the overall category set that was used for this preliminary NVivo search of the extensive STB submission data (see Table 6.1).

Once search terms are determined, NVivo facilitates the manipulation of key phrases or terms for search. After file conversion because of the age of the scanned Acrobat files, each individual submission was then loaded into NVivo. Depending on the application, the software produces quantitative measures drawn from the qualitative data, for example, it can produce counts of a specified word or phrase as found within the documentation data.

In this analysis, we are mostly interested in obtaining a more frequentist sense of what issues were paramount on the minds of the interested participants over the somewhat controversial 2000 CNBN merger proceedings. It is this qualitatively explored output that will be examined against the more recent news-based material available regarding the failed talks between Canadian Pacific and its US Class 1 merger suitors. This is as far we can go with the current analysis since the latest merger talks were just that and never transitioned to a formal review process through the STB.

6.3.1 Interpreting qualitative information from the CNBN merger submissions

To start, we list the matching tabulations identified in the 1999–2000 STB merger submission database. The software is limited by its users and its inputs, for example, we cannot track word context, nor at this stage did we try to identify words or phrases that might be associated or linked with another given word or phrase. To this end, in

Table 6.2 **Key Phrase Frequencies (Phrase Occurrences/Phrase Source Count)**

Competition	Economics	Rail Terms	Transportation Terms	Other
Inter-modal competition 6/3	Standalone cost 7/4	Captive shippers 118/23	Capacity constraints 18/14	Sovereignty 0/0
Geographic/source competition 3/3	Economies of scale, size, density, or scope 23/18	"Two-to-one" markets 0/0	Bottleneck 0/0	Border 0/0
Intra-modal competition 37/15	Merger efficiency 0/0	"Three-to-two" markets 0/0	Trackage rights 42/22	Class 1 533/96
Inter-rail competition 1/1	Free trade 10/5	Improved service 54/39	Congestion 0/0	International trade 35/17

Table 6.2, we list not only the raw phrase frequencies, but also show the number of sources or submissions where the phrase was used. We do this because it is possible that a single document could have multiple occurrences of a single phrase, a situation that can lead to a biased impression of the importance of that particular phrase in the overall analysis. Therefore, listing the source count as well gives a better sense of the overall breadth of an issue related to the selected key phrases.

We must remind the reader that most of the submissions were simply letters written to the STB, in many cases composed by individuals or interested parties who may or may not have been overly familiar with either economic- or rail-specific terminology. For example, we suspect that some technical terminology describing declining rail competition in a market subject to a merger (i.e. phrases like "two-to-one" and "three-to-two") may not have been well known at that time by various shipper interests, especially among smaller shippers who may or may not have had any prior dealings with the STB or rail research. Please also keep in mind that while we attempted to input what we felt was the most common written form of a particular phrase, it is entirely possible some phrase occurrences may have been missed due to slight variations in wording within a given submission.

Staying mindful of these caveats, examining Table 6.2, it is interesting to note that the most commonly found phrase among those we entered as part of our qualitative analysis (aside from the validation search of the generic term "Class 1" for railways) was that of "captive shippers" (with 118 occurrences in 23 documents), and the next most commonly found phrase was "improved service" (with 54 occurrences in 39 documents). Although these phrases are clearly linked with respect to possible merger-related service issues in the industry, the former is noteworthy because at the time it was becoming a well-established terminology among a variety of railway customers. The rail captivity issue was in fact predicted by several researchers to be one that was not likely to disappear with deregulation and railway pricing freedoms (Burton, 2009; MacDonald, 2013). Finally, the next most frequently occurring phrase in the submissions ("trackage rights") is also a specialized rail term but one that seems to have gained some traction among interested parties at that time. Essentially, it refers to the ability and extent of a competing railway to operate on the tracks of a host railway in order to access traffic on the host railway (Karikari et al., 2002). As we shall see, in its tone, this phrase implies a rail competition mechanism surprisingly similar to the set of competitive access provisions offered by Hunter Harrison and Canadian Pacific with respect to their proposed CP–NS merger.

One caveat worth highlighting is that of potential selection bias in this data. Although a potentially useful technique to help better understand regulatory and legal processes that rely on written inputs or testimony, qualitative analysis is constrained by the fact that in many cases (and this analysis is no exception), qualitative data is not truly random. There will often be some level of inherent bias in qualitative findings since in the case of a merger hearing, for example, it is likely only the most interested parties who will submit documentation. Although we know submissions came from a very wide range of commercial and even personal interests, those with a vested interest in the rail industry (i.e. many shippers and fewer carriers) surely dominated the submissions and our data. As rail shippers vastly outnumber rail carriers, shipper phrases expressing negative impressions about mergers must outnumber any positive impressions about the merger process that would likely characterize railway or rail industry submissions.

We conclude that a broad inspection of keywords identified in the 1999–2000 STB merger hearings indicate there was significant interest in both shipper captivity and associated service levels, as well as the possibility for improving competition in the rail sector (via trackage rights). These focal points stemming from the preliminary qualitative findings led us to speculate about the potential for geographic trends or linkages among the identified submitters.

For example, *a priori* a shipper based in a rail hub like Chicago should be far less concerned about the effects of a possible rail merger on captive shippers than a shipper located in a region or state served by one or few railways. In this light, we used the subset of phrase data (ordered here by phrase source count) to identify the location/source associated with that individual submission. We next aggregated this information up to the state/provincial level, which led to the tabulations found in Table 6.3.

Although not apparent in our very random visual scans of some of the merger documentation, it seems that many of the submissions we identified using rail-related terminology were dominated by industry specialists or lobbyists. We mention this because Washington, DC, was the most frequently listed location of the submitter for each of our primary key phrases. Although there were a number of submissions originating from potentially affected states and regions under the proposed merger, this surprising finding is most likely explained by submitters' use of consulting/law firms representing various shipping interests to prepare formal documentation, while in turn these firms often have offices in the important national capital region.

Examining Table 6.3 further, it is interesting that a handful of the "improved service" occurrences among the submissions in fact originated from Canada, whereas the other highest ranked phrases we identified in this analysis were based exclusively in

Table 6.3 **Key Phrase "Improved Service" (54 Occurrences, 39 Sources)**

State/Province	# Times Referenced/# of Sources
Idaho	1/1
Ontario (Canada)	3/2
North Dakota	1/1
Nebraska	2/1
Washington, DC	19/13
Texas	5/8
California	2/2
Kansas	1/1
New York	3/2
British Columbia (Canada)	5/3
Massachusetts	1/1
Saskatchewan (Canada)	1/1
Iowa	1/1
Quebec (Canada)	2/2
Washington State	1/1
Illinois	2/1
Ohio	1/1

Key Phrase "Captive Shippers" (118 Occurrences, 23 Sources)

Colorado	2/1
Washington, DC	34/9
Illinois	1/1
New York	2/2
Ohio	3/3
Ontario (Canada)	55/1
Texas	4/2
Virginia	7/2
Montana	9/1
Nebraska	1/1

Key Phrase "Trackage Rights" (42 Occurrences, 22 Sources)

California	3/2
Colorado	3/1
Washington, DC	20/12
Illinois	1/1
Nebraska	7/2
Ohio	2/1
South Dakota	2/1
Virginia	1/1
Montana	3/1

the United States. Considering the relative lack of experience on the part of Canadian-based shippers with mergers in rail, this finding seems to indicate that primary concerns in Canada at that time about the proposed merger were less about eventual rail market structure but more about the nature of future rail service under a merger. It may be that Canadian interests at that time were projecting the potential benefits to them stemming from a large-scale North American rail merger (e.g. improved Canadian access to US markets, more single line service, etc.), so this phrase in effect highlights some level of shipper support for the potential cross-border merger.

Next, the term "captive shipper" was most frequently found in submissions originating in the states of Ohio and New York, whereas the term "trackage rights" was most frequently listed by a couple of submissions from California. Since we did not identify many submissions that originated directly from regions where these issues might be of greatest importance, we conclude that shipper lobbying interests seem to have been a key component of these particular merger proceedings. Among the numerous Washington, DC, originating merger documentation, we acknowledge that a more detailed (possibly visual) inspection of each submission will be needed in order to try to identify various working locations of shippers represented in the submissions.

6.4   Comparing merger information from yesterday to today

It has been said that generals fight their last war (Warner, 1934; Millett, 1949), meaning they try to win the next battle by implementing the lessons learned during the previous conflict. Millett (1949) offered that economists do the same thing with respect to fighting the last depression, whereas Warner (1934) cautioned business owners against selling goods based on conditions of the previous business cycle. Given the public comments (highlighted below) by Mr. Harrison, this truism may also fit with CEOs of Class 1 railways interested in negotiating the first successful merger of Class 1 railways since the STB moratorium was lifted.

In this section, we offer the reader some informal comparisons between our qualitative analysis of the 1999 merger data against what we uncovered through media coverage of the most recent rail merger discussions. We use the term "informal" due to the nature of the information we are able to obtain about the 2015 CP–NS merger proposal, which as we now know never progressed to a more formal stage (e.g. was placed under review by the STB) in any sense of the word.

We initiate this analysis and comparison of rail merger concerns through time by referencing back to the three most frequently identified operational phrases we uncovered in the 1999 data in Table 6.2. These operational phrases were (by descending number of occurrences); (i) captive shippers, (ii) improved service, and (iii) trackage rights.

Subsequently, we reference back to our prior description of the CP–NS merger proposal as formulated by Mr. Harrison. Considering the latter, we propose the following. It seems very likely that all three of the highlighted operational concepts/phrases must have motivated Mr. Harrison's formulation of the novel merger conditions, such as he believed might be rendered acceptable to both Norfolk Southern as well as the STB. To wit, by suggesting the creation of a regulated access rights regime (i.e. addressing trackage rights) applicable to any cost-efficient railroad competitor over his merged railroad, Mr. Harrison surely was trying to mitigate concerns of shippers (i.e. addressing captive shippers) over possible reductions or changes in rail output (i.e. addressing improved service) in a postmerger rail market.

6.4.1 Overview of rail merger concerns, as voiced today

To the present, we now provide some discussion about the most recent proposal for a Class 1 railway merger in North America. The "move to merger" effectively began in 2012 when Hunter Harrison was installed as CEO of Canadian Pacific Railway following a shareholder proxy fight led by Bill Ackman. Mr. Harrison is well known in the North American rail industry as a shaker who has been able to consistently identify operational efficiencies through the reorganization and modernization of each Class 1 railway he has run (Canadian Pacific, 2016). Some writers and rail pundits refer to Mr. Harrison as a "legend" (Financial Post, 2016c) and it is clear that he as an individual believes he has the clout to enact significant change in the railroad sector (see Fig. 6.2).

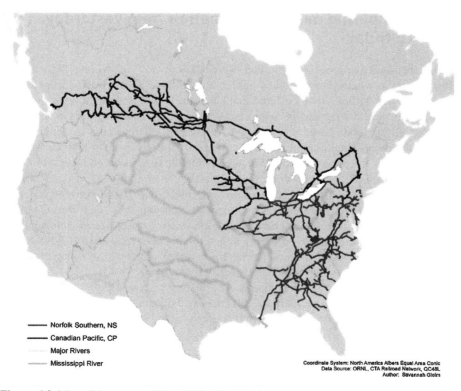

Figure 6.2 Map of the current CP and NS rail networks.

By output measures, Canadian Pacific is one of the two smallest Class 1 railways (Railway Age, 2015). Mr. Harrison had taken Canadian Pacific in just a few years from being one of the least efficient Class 1 railways to being one of the most efficient. CP operates track in both Canada and the United States, but is unique (along with CN) in North America in having very strong East–West, coast-to-coast connectivity. With this strength in mind, the first serious discussions of Class 1 mergers since 2000 began in early October 2014 when Canadian Pacific proposed a bid for CSX Railway, a major Class 1 railway predominantly operating in the Southern and Eastern United States (Wilner, 2014). However, these discussions were short-lived, as by mid-October of that year CSX effectively rejected the Canadian Pacific merger bid and all was dropped before any formal regulatory intervention. But Mr. Harrison was not finished. Perhaps emboldened by reaction to his prior efforts, by November 2015 Mr. Harrison and CP had put together a US $28 billion offer for Norfolk Southern Railway.

Unlike several previous Class 1 rail merger proposals, this merger attempt was destined to become more hostile and financial in structure. Early discussions revolved around the nature of the buyout that CP would try to put together to NS shareholders, but after resistance on the part of NS's head office, Harrison seems to have considered a slight change of tactics. By this CP began openly discussing a basket of operational concessions they were willing to make in order to facilitate merger approval on the part of the STB (Railway Age, 2015). What made this all the more surprising was that this basket included provisions for the potential merged railway to be obliged to offer some form of regulated track access to competitors. Of course, the idea of open or competitive access in North American rail has been around for some time, but since their deregulation under Staggers, the very idea has always been strongly opposed by every Class 1 railway.

It seems CP and Hunter Harrison, in particular, were willing to back up their belief that the merged railway would become so massively cost efficient (with export coverage for most major populated regions of North America) that they were effectively daring anyone else to get onto their tracks and move freight more cheaply than the merged railway. It was a bold tack and one which appealed to a spectrum of rail competition supporters who maintain that without such provisions, market power from merged Class 1 railways will almost certainly offset any efficiency gains available to shippers (Tye and Horn, 2005).

But the idea that an "American" railway would somehow fall under "foreign" control, raising possible questions about military sovereignty, was a point raised previously by the US Army in the formal CNBN merger hearings. In the midst of the merger talks between CP and NS, this issue came to light once again. Early in April 2016, in a surprising public commentary, the US Army once again voiced opposition to a proposed rail merger. In their view, the merged CP–NS railway would own hundreds of miles of "strategic" railway lines across the United States, a situation that was simply not acceptable on account to military logistics, planning, and national security (Financial Post, 2016a).

Given the continued high-level opposition to the merger, and in spite of the proposal never getting beyond the concept stage nor being formally reviewed by the STB, in April 2016, Mr. Harrison and CP finally abandoned their bid for NS (Financial Post, 2016b). In the meanwhile, on March 17, 2017, Mr. Harrison accepted an offer from CSX to be their CEO (as reported by *Trains.com*). Only time will tell whether or not the merger genie is once again out of the bottle in North American rail.

In summary, since the onset of industry deregulation, US railroads mostly followed a strategy of growing through acquisitions, while improving efficiency as well as increasing single line service (Gallamore, 1999). A series of major US rail mergers in the post-Staggers era culminated in the attempt by CN and BNSF to formulate what would have been the largest rail merger to that time.

After extensive hearings on the topic, the STB ultimately concluded that railroads' traditional strategy to improve efficiency was no longer working for either customers or the railroads. In rejecting the merger, what resulted was a moratorium on future mergers imposed by the STB (STB, 2001). Initially targeted for 15 months, the tone of the STB decision in fact led to a long period where no mergers were even proposed among the Class 1 railroads. This lasted until the recent ruminations of Hunter Harrison and CP to merge initially with CSX, followed by the very public discussions about a possible merger with NS, neither of which came to fruition.

Railroading is one of the oldest and most established industries in North America. While its relative importance to GDP has declined over time, moving bulk freight across regions and for export is still critical to our modern industrial economy. Under major deregulation, freight rail has embraced various technology changes to become more "lean and mean", while in turn gradually stabilizing its overall market share in the North American surface freight market relative to its primary competitors (truck and barge). In spite of this and considering certain inescapable realities about the railroad sector including the presence of various economies associated with firm size, perhaps it is not surprising that effectively we find that the more rail seems to change and adapt to the times, the more it stays the same. To this end, we conclude that the wide-ranging concerns voiced most frequently back in 1999 over the failed CNBN merger seem to be almost precisely the same concerns that surely motivated certain specific conditions added by Mr. Harrison to his 2015 merger proposal. While we believe a more extensive search of the 1999 data is needed, the consistency of the 1999 and 2015 merger descriptions and information was unexpected.

6.5 Conclusions

In his continued efforts to develop data-based analyses in order to help shed light on contentious issues in the railroad industry, we offer that Prof. Keeler would find this analysis of considerable interest. We employ both a novel dataset and technique of analysis to highlight concerns of those parties who commented on the 1999–2000 CNBN merger attempt. While of interest on its own, we also find that many of the concerns raised at that time were similar to those which have been raised (at least informally) in the most recent discussions on mega-mergers in the rail sector. While the industry has certainly evolved in the last 15 years, we wonder if the industry is truly destined to have the past repeat itself.

The other purpose of this chapter is to motivate qualitative analytics that will hopefully allow past decisions to be more formally compared to what the future might hold. In future research, the authors are trying to locate similar style documentation concerning the failed SFSP merger of 1987. We hope to again formally examine how merger concerns and policy evolved through the decade separating that failed merger with the CNBN attempt and uncover whether the key phrases/concepts across these failed mergers are as similar or different as compared to what we identified through the current analysis.

Epilogue

On December 16, 2017, shortly after this chapter was accepted for publication, Mr. Hunter Harrison, most recently the CEO of CSX Corp., passed away after a short illness. He was 73 years old. Considering the discussion contained in the latter part of the chapter, it is clear that Mr. Harrison has left a legacy of railroad operations and management style that will continue to shape the sector for some years to come. Even so, it remains to be seen how aggressively Class 1 railroads will pursue future mergers now that Mr. Harrison is no longer around to serve as a catalyst for this particular growth strategy.

References

Boyer, K., 1997. Principles of Transportation Economics. Addison Wesley, New York.
Canadian Pacific, 2016. Precision railroading: using the CP model to build a leading transcontinental railway. http://cpconsolidation.com.
Conant, M., 2004a. Burlington Northern–Santa Fe merger. Research in Transportation Economics 7, 103–116.
Conant, M., 2004b. Union Pacific merger of Southern Pacific. Research in Transportation Economics 7, 117–133.
Financial Post, 2016a. U.S. army opposes CP Rail's proposed Norfolk Southern takeover due to national security concerns. http://business.financialpost.com/news/transportation/u-s-army-opposes-cp-rails-proposed-takeover-of-norfolk-southern-due-to-national-security-concerns.
Financial Post, 2016b. Canadian Pacific railway drops pursuit of merger with Norfolk Southern Corp. http://business.financialpost.com/news/transportation/canadian-pacific-railway-drops-pursuit-of-merger-with-norfolk-southern-corp.
Financial Post, 2016c. Why hunter Harrison's status as a 'legend' remains untarnished by the CP Rail-Norfolk Southern merger failure. http://business.financialpost.com/news/transportation/why-hunter-harrisons-status-as-a-legend-remains-untarnished-by-the-cp-rail-norfolk-southern-merger-failure.
Gallamore, R., 1999. CT Regulation and innovation: lessons from the American railroad industry, Chapter 15. In: Gomez-Ibanez, J., Tye, W., Winston, C. (Eds.), Essays in Transportation Economics and Policy: A Handbook in Honor of John R. Meyer. Brookings, Washington, DC, pp. 221–247.
Grimm, C., Winston, C., 2000. Competition in the deregulated railroad industry: sources, effects and policy issues, Chapter 2. In: Peltzman, S., Winston, C. (Eds.), Deregulation of Network Industries: What's Next. AEI-Brookings Joint Center for Regulatory Studies, Washington, DC.

Jeffcott, S., Pidgeon, N., Weyman, A., Walls, J., 2006. Risk, trust, and safety culture in UK train operating companies. Risk Analysis 26, 1105–1121.

Karikari, J., Brown, S., Nadji, M., 2002. The Union Pacific/Southern Pacific railroads merger: effect of trackage rights on rates. Journal of Regulatory Economics 22, 27–285.

Kwoka, J., White, L., 1999. Manifest destiny? The Union Pacific and Southern Pacific railroad merger (1996). In: Kwoka, J., White, L. (Eds.), The Antitrust Revolution: Economics, Competition and Policy. Oxford University Press, New York.

MacDonald, J., 2013. Railroads and price discrimination: the roles of competition, information and regulation. Review of Industrial Organization 43, 85–101.

Madar, D., 2002. Rail mergers, trade, and federal regulation in the United States and Canada. *Publius:* The Journal of Federalism 32 (1), 143–159.

Majure, W., 1996. Verified statement (redacted). US Department of Justice.

Millett, J.D., 1949. Post-war trends in public administration in the United States. The Journal of Politics 11 (4), 736–747.

Pittman, R., 1990. Railroads and competition: the Santa Fe/Southern Pacific merger proposal. The Journal of Industrial Economics 39, 25–46.

Railway Age, 2015. NS to CP: Proposed merger a poor combination. http://www.railwayage.com.

STB, 2001. Decision STB Ex Parte No. 582 (Sub No.1). Major rail consolidation procedures, service date June 11.

Tye, W., Horn, J., 2005. Transportation mergers: the case of the US railroads, Chapter 27. Button, K., Hensher, D. (Eds.), Handbook of Transport Strategy, Policy and Institutions, 6, Elsevier, New York.

Vachal, K., Bitzan, J., 2005. Protecting the captive railroad shipper, Chapter 28. Button, K., Hensher, D. (Eds.), Handbook of Transport Strategy, Policy and Institutions, 6, Elsevier, New York.

Wall Street Journal, 1999. Burlington Northern to merge with Canadian National Rail.

Warner, E.P., 1934. Present conditions under the NRA. American Marketing Journal 1 (1), 6–14.

Wilner, F. 2014. What lurks behind the door Hunter Harrison opened? Personal commentary, Railway Age Magazine.

Winston, C., Maheshri, V., Dennis, S., 2011. Long-run effects of mergers: the case of U.S. Western railroads. Journal of Law and Economics 54, 275–304.

Further Reading

Burton, M., 2014. The economics of evolving rail rate oversight: balancing theory, practice and objectives. Journal of Transportation Law, Logistics and Policy 81, 267–293.

Chaney, P., 2014. Mixed-methods analysis of political parties' manifesto discourse on rail transport policy: Westminster, Scottish, Welsh and Northern Irish elections 1945–2011. Transport Policy 35, 275–285.

Ivaldi, M., McCullough, G., 2005. Welfare trade-offs in U.S. rail mergers, CEPR Discussion Paper No. 5000. SSRN: https://ssrn.com/abstract=772646.

STB, 2006. Decision STB Ex Parte No. 646 (Sub No. 1). Simplified standards for rail rate cases, decided July 26.

Ocean container shipping

7

Wayne K. Talley
Old Dominion University, Norfolk, VA, USA

Chapter Outline

Dedication

I have been in the company of Professor Keeler only once, that is, in 1981 whilst an Industry Economist at the Interstate Commerce Commission in Washington, DC. Professor Keeler and I had lunch together in the cafeteria of the Interstate Commerce Commission's building. Curt Grimm was also at this luncheon. Professor Keeler and Curt met earlier in the day to discuss Curt's progress on his railroad dissertation for which Professor Keeler was the advisor. My research in railroads has greatly benefited from my readings of Professor Keeler's research in the area. Also, I have benefited over the years from professional interactions with several of Professor Keeler's former Ph.D. students—James Peoples with whom I have coauthored articles and book chapters and Curt Grimm and Starr McMullen with whom I have had discussions at numerous transportation academic meetings.

7.1 Introduction

Ocean shipping is the transportation of goods over ocean waterways and is the primary means by which goods are transported in global markets. Participants in ocean shipping include: (1) shipper exporters that provide export goods for shipment over

Transportation Policy and Economic Regulation. http://dx.doi.org/10.1016/B978-0-12-812620-2.00007-9

ocean waterways, (2) origin truck, rail, and vessel intermodal carriers that transport export goods from their shipper locations to origin ports, (3) origin ports that load the export goods onto berthed ships of shipping lines, (4) shipping lines that transport export goods on their ships over ocean waterways to destination ports, (5) destination ports that receive these ships, unload the goods (now imports) from the ships and then load the goods onto the trucks, railcars, and vessels of destination truck, rail, and vessel intermodal carriers, respectively, (6) destination intermodal carriers that transport the import goods to their consignee importer locations, and (7) consignee importers that receive the import goods. For a discussion of the business of shipping, see Heidbrink (2012).

Ocean shipping utilizes three types of chains (or spatial networks): (1) maritime transport chain—"a network over which carriers, ports, and shippers are involved in the movement of cargo" (Talley and Ng, 2013, p. 311; Talley, 2014, p. 174). The choice of a maritime transport chain is a function of the: chain profit of the wth water carrier, the chain profit of the lth land carrier, the chain cargo throughput of the pth government-owned port, and the chain logistics cost of the sth shipper; (2) port service chain—"a service network utilized by a port's service providers in the provision of the port's services that accounts for the quality-of-service relationships among the services" (Talley et al., 2014, p. 236); and (3) hinterland transport chain—"a transport network over which cargo imported into a hinterland from a seaport to the importer and exported from the hinterland from an exporter to a seaport is transported by an intermodal transport carrier" (Talley and Ng, 2017, p. 179). A port hinterland is the landward side of a port and a port foreland is the seaside of a port (Rodrigue and Nottebom, 2010).[1]

Ocean container shipping is ocean shipping of goods stored in standardized boxes (or containers).[2] This mode of transport has grown rapidly due to the adoption of containers of standard sizes and the "awareness of industry players of the advantages and cost savings resulting from faster vessel turnaround times in ports, a reduction in the level of damages and associated insurance fees, and integration with inland transport modes such as trucks, barges and trains" (Notteboom, 2012, pp. 230–231). In addition to the use of a standardized container, the growth in ocean container shipping has also benefited from government investments and international trade policies. "Container transportation has revolutionized the ocean transportation of general cargo and is comparable in impact to the introduction of the steam engine in water transportation and the jet engine in air transportation" (Talley, 2010, p. 134) and "has gone hand in hand with the creation of the modern intermodal transport systems, facilitating dramatic increases in shipping capacities and reductions in delivery time through intermodal cargo movements between ships, trains and trucks" (Bernhofen et al., 2016, p. 36).

This chapter presents a detailed discussion of ocean container shipping that can be described by the contents of the chapter's sections: Section 7.2 presents an historical

---

[1] The academic disciple of maritime economics consists of the two major areas—shipping economics and port economics. A collection of major works in maritime economics is found in Talley (2017). Economic theories of maritime carriers and ports are found in Talley (2012a, b), respectively.

[2] For a comprehensive history of the shipping container, see Levinson (2006).

overview of ocean container shipping—the early years of ocean container shipping, a comparison of ocean breakbulk, and container shipping, world's 20 largest container shipping lines in 2007 and 2017, government investments that have benefited (or will benefit) ocean container shipping (e.g. Suez Canal, Panama Canal, Nicaragua Canal, Northern Sea Route (NSR), and One Belt One Road), international trade policies that have benefited ocean container shipping (e.g. GATT—The General Agreement on Tariffs and Trade, NAFTA—The North American Free Trade Agreement, and CAFTA—The Central America Free Trade Agreement) and economic effects of ocean container shipping.

Section 7.3 presents business strategies used by ocean container shipping lines for improving their financial conditions—larger containerships, mergers and acquisitions, and alliances. Section 7.4 presents ocean containerization in the United States—double-stack train service, transportation regulatory reform acts, dockworkers, exporters, importers, and the US Jones Act (cabotage).

7.2   An historical overview of ocean container shipping

Ocean transportation carriers transport general and bulk goods that are classified as: breakbulk (general cargo on pallets), container (general cargo stored in standardized containers), dry bulk (loose dry bulk cargo such as coal and grain), liquid bulk (liquid cargo such as petroleum products), and neobulk (cargo of uniform sizes and weights shipped as loose or nonpackaged cargo such as automobiles, steel, and lumber) cargoes. General cargoes are manufactured goods of various sizes and weights transported as packaged (breakbulk or container) cargoes. Bulk (dry and liquid) and neobulk cargoes are cargoes other than general cargoes that are transported as loose or nonpackaged cargoes.

Through the 1950s, general cargo was handled as breakbulk cargo, that is, general cargo on pallets that was hoisted from port docks into the holds of berthed ships via the ships' cargo nets and cranes. The pallets would then be positioned precisely in the ships' holds and braced to protect them from damage during ocean crossings. This process was performed in reverse at the other end of the voyage, making the ocean transportation of breakbulk general cargo a labor-intensive, slow, and an expensive process.

The ocean shipping of general cargo began to change in 1955 when Malcom McLean, the owner of a North Carolina trucking company, believing that general cargo needed to be handled only twice, that is, at its origin when stored in a standard sized box and at its destination when unloaded from the standard sized box, purchased a small tanker company, renamed it Sea-Land, and adapted its vessels to transport truck trailers (Chadwin et al., 1990; Talley, 2000). The first voyage of a containership occurred on April 26, 1956, when a Sea-Land containership left Newark, New Jersey for Puerto Rico. Confrontations with railroads, shipping lines, and unions, however, delayed Sea-Land's maiden international voyage to Rotterdam in 1966. With this voyage, the containerization of international trade had begun.

In the years that followed, truck trailers were replaced with standard sized boxes (or containers) without wheels, generally 20- or 40-ft long, eight feet wide, and eight or eight-and-a-half feet high. The 20-ft standardized container became to be known as a TEU (a twenty-foot equivalent unit) and the 40-ft standardized container became to be known as an FEU (a forty-foot equivalent unit). With locking mechanisms at each corner, a TEU and an FEU could be secured to a truck chassis, a railcar, a crane, or other TEUs and FEUs inside a ship's hold or on its deck.

Containerships were designed to be nonself-sustaining, that is, without cranes aboard unlike breakbulk ships. Consequently, containerships had to rely on container ports to provide cranes for the loading and unloading of containers. Breakbulk ports aspiring to become container ports had to become more capital-intensive—not only investing in dockside cranes but also in infrastructure and mobile capital. The finger piers of breakbulk ports (that extended into the water and perpendicular to port berths for the loading/unloading of breakbulk ship cargo) were eliminated and the berths of breakbulk ports were redesigned so that containerships could dock parallel to the berths (for easier loading/unloading of containers via dockside cranes). Breakbulk cargo warehouses, where breakbulk cargo was stored for protection from the weather, were eliminated and the land cleared for the storage of containers. If land was plentiful, containers were stored on truck chassis for easy movement to and from ships; if not, containers were stacked on land one upon another, several containers high.

In 1980, the global trade carried in containers was 100 million metric tons and in 2015 it was 1.7 billion metric tons.[3] "The growth in world trade appears to have coincided with the genesis of the global container era which can be dated to 1966" (Bernhofen et al., 2016, p. 36).

Ocean container shipping "became an essential driver in reshaping global supply chain practices, allowing global sourcing strategies of multinational enterprises, pull logistics solutions and the development of global production networks" (Notteboom, 2012, p. 231). The cost of shipping general cargo by ocean container shipping is lower than shipping general cargo by ocean breakbulk shipping due to the: lower loading/unloading costs, lower cargo theft, and damage costs (from protection against theft and damage by containers) and lower inventory holding costs (from faster delivery and thus faster transactions) for ocean container shipping than for ocean breakbulk shipping.[4]

With cranes and various types of mobile equipment being used to move containers in a container port, the amount of labor utilized by container ports is significantly less than that used by breakbulk ports. The losses in port jobs attributable to ocean container shipping have ranged from 40% to 60% in many countries (Zarocostas, 1996). In the United Kingdom, dockworker jobs fell from 80,000 in 1967 to 11,400 in 1986 and further declines of 44% occurred between 1989 and 1992 (Talley, 2000). However, the productivity of dockworkers that remained "improved by a factor of at least 15".[5]

---

[3] Source: https://www.statista.com/topics/1367/container-shipping/ (accessed 30.06.17).

[4] Source: https://people.hofstra.edu/geotrans/eng/ch2en/conc2en/table_impacts_early_containerization. html/ (accessed 25.06.17).

A gang of 20 dockworkers can load 20 tons of cargo per hour on a breakbulk ship, whereas on a containership, one crane and perhaps half as many dockworkers can load 400–500 tons per hour (Chadwin et al., 1990, p. 3). A breakbulk ship often took a week to unload and reload; a containership might be in port for only 12 h for the same amount of cargo.

Although general cargo is the primary type of cargo shipped in ocean containers, neobulk, dry bulk, and liquid bulk cargoes are also on occasion shipped in containers, for example, expensive automobiles (neobulk cargo) to protect them from the weather of ocean crossings, grains (dry bulk cargo) shipped in empty containers when general cargo is not available for shipment in empty containers and specialized liquid-bulk cargo (e.g. acids) shipped in containers with inserts.[6]

The world's 20 largest container shipping lines as of August 2007 (ranked by a line's fleet-ship TEU-carrying capacity or the number of TEUs that a line's fleet of ships can carry) appear in Table 7.1. Maersk Line was the world's largest container shipping line in August 2007 with 19% of the fleet-ship TEU-carrying capacity of the world's 20 largest container shipping lines, followed by Mediterranean Shipping and CMA CGM, ranked second and third, with TEU-carrying capacities of 12.7% and 8.5%, respectively.

The world's 20 largest container shipping lines as of April 2017 (ranked by a line's fleet-ship TEU-carrying capacity) appear in Table 7.2. Maersk Line was the world's largest container shipping line as of April 2017 with 18.7% of the fleet-ship TEU-carrying capacity of the world's 20 largest container shipping lines. The world's second and third largest container shipping lines as of April 2017 were Mediterranean Shipping and CMA CGM with TEU-carrying capacities of 16.9% and 12.4%, respectively, of the fleet-ship TEU-carrying capacity of the world's 20 largest container shipping lines. Note that no US container shipping line appears in Tables 7.1 and 7.2. Furthermore, a comparison of information reported in these tables reveals a nontrivial increase in the TEU-carrying capacity of the world's 20 largest container shipping lines from 8,967,000 TEUs in 2007 to 17,805,000 TEUs by 2017. Such an increase in TEU-carrying capacity underscores the significance of the world's 20 largest container shipping lines in transporting container cargo.

Despite evidence presented in Tables 7.1 and 7.2 indicating container shipping's importance to the transportation of international cargo, "transportation is largely ignored in the economics trade literature" (Blonigen and Wilson, 2013, p. 634). One plausible explanation is that international trade data do not contain specific information on the transportation service (e.g. ton-miles) provided in the transportation of trade. However, UNCTAD's seaborne trade data do include information on the transportation service (in ton-miles) in transporting seaborne trade between countries. "Seaborne trade excludes transshipment cargoes (transferred from one ship to another ship at the same seaport) and cabotage cargoes (loaded on a ship and unloaded from a ship of a nondomestic flag carrier at seaports in the same country)" (Talley, 2018). In addition

---

[5] Source: https://people.hofstra.edu/geotrans/eng/ch2en/conc2en/table_impacts_early_containerization. html/ (accessed 25.06.17).

[6] For a discussion of the earnings differentials of US dockworkers and seafarers, see Talley (2008).

Table 7.1 **The world's 20 largest container shipping lines (August 2007)**

Rank	Shipping Line	Fleet-Ship TEU-Carrying Capacity, 1000s (% of total)	Headquarters
1.	Maersk Line	1700 (19.0)	Denmark
2.	Mediterranean Shipping	1140 (12.7)	Switzerland
3.	CMA CGM	765 (8.5)	France
4.	Evergreen Line	609 (6.8)	Taiwan
5.	Hapag-Lloyd	479 (5.3)	Germany
6.	China Ocean Shipping Company (COSCO)	440 (4.9)	China
7.	China Shipping Container Lines	423 (4.7)	China
8.	APL	364 (4.1)	Singapore
9.	NYK Line (Nippon Yusen Kaisha)	343 (3.8)	Japan
10.	OOCL (Orient Overseas Container Line)	340 (3.8)	Hong Kong
11.	Hanjin Shipping Company	322 (3.6)	South Korea
12.	Mitsui O.S.K. Lines	306 (3.4)	Japan
13.	Kawasaki Kisen Kaisha (K Line)	284 (3.2)	Japan
14.	Yang Ming Marine Transport	273 (3.0)	Taiwan
15.	Compania Sud Americana de Vapores	251 (2.8)	Chile
16.	Zim Integrated Shipping Services	243 (2.7)	Israel
17.	Hamburg Sud	235 (2.6)	Germany
18.	Hyundai Merchant Marine	175 (2.0)	South Korea
19.	Pacific International Lines	154 (1.7)	Singapore
20.	Wan Hai Lines	121 (1.4)	Taiwan
	Total	8967	

Source: http://www.lloydslist/ (accessed 29.08.07).

Table 7.2 The world's 20 largest container shipping lines (April 2017)

Rank	Shipping Line	Fleet-Ship TEU-Carrying Capacity, 1000s (% of total)	Headquarters
1.	Maersk Line	3328 (18.7)	Denmark
2.	Mediterranean Shipping	3015 (16.9)	Switzerland
3.	CMA CGM	2216 (12.4)	France
4.	China Ocean Shipping Company (COSCO)	1733 (9.7)	China
5.	Hapag-Lloyd	1025 (5.8)	Germany
6.	Evergreen Line	1010 (5.7)	Taiwan
7.	Orient Overseas Container Line (OOCL)	648 (3.6)	Hong Kong
8.	Nippon Yusen Kaisha (NYK Line)	592 (3.3)	Japan
9.	Yang Ming Marine Transport	576 (3.2)	Taiwan
10.	Hamburg Sud	568 (3.2)	Germany
11.	Mitsui O.S.K. Lines (MOL)	509 (2.9)	Japan
12.	United Arab Shipping Company (UASC)	486 (2.7)	Middle East
13.	Hyundai Merchant Marine	437 (2.5)	South Korea
14.	Kawasaki Kisen Kaisha (K Line)	374 (2.1)	Japan
15.	Pacific International Lines	371 (2.1)	Singapore
16	Zim Integrated Shipping Services	311 (1.7)	Israel
17	Wan Hai Lines	239 (1.3)	Taiwan
18	X-Press Feeders Group	144 (1.0)	Singapore
19	KMTC	123 (1.0)	South Korea
20	SITC	100 (1.0)	Singapore
	Total	17,805	

Source: http://www.alphaliner.com/top100/ (accessed 16.04.17).

to the technology benefits of ocean container shipping, the growth in container trade has also benefited from government investments and international trade policies.

7.2.1 Government investments

Government investments in waterways have improved the quality of the service of ocean container shipping by reducing the travel times of containerships between origin and destination ports that, in turn, reduce the inventory costs incurred by the owners of the transported general cargo, thereby promoting the growth of international trade. Waterways include artificial waterways (i.e. canals) such as the Suez Canal and Panama Canal and the proposed Nicaragua Canal and nonartificial waterways with navigational improvements (e.g. the NSR and the One Belt One Road).

7.2.1.1 Suez Canal

The Suez Canal is an artificial sea-level waterway in Egypt, connecting the Mediterranean Sea to the Red Sea through the Isthmus of Suez. The canal is owned and maintained by the Suez Canal Authority of Egypt and was officially opened on November 17, 1869. It is 120.1 miles in length. In 2012, 17,225 vessels traversed the canal.[7] The canal provides vessels with a shorter-distance waterway in traveling between the northern Indian and North Atlantic oceans via the Mediterranean and Red seas. In the summer of 2014, work on the expansion of the width of the canal began and the expanded Suez Canal opened on August 6, 2015. The expansion allows ships to transit the canal in both directions, simultaneously, thereby reducing the travel times of ships between their origin and destination ports via the Suez Canal.

7.2.1.2 Panama Canal

The Panama Canal is an artificial 48-mile waterway in Panama that connects the Atlantic Ocean with the Pacific Ocean and was officially opened on August 15, 1914. The Panama Canal greatly reduces the times incurred by ships in traveling between the Pacific and Atlantic Oceans and avoids the hazardous, lengthy Cape Horn route around the southernmost tip of South America via the Strait of Magellan or Drake Passage.[8]

  The Panama Canal is owned by the Panamanian government and operated by the Panama Canal Authority (ACP). Unlike the Suez Canal, the Panama Canal has locks at each of its two ends—one to lift ships up to the Gatun Lake (an artificially created lake used in the operation of locks) and one to lower ships down from the Gatun Lake.[9]

  An expanded Panama Canal with a third set of locks began its commercial operation on June 26, 2016, allowing for larger-sized (wider) ships to pass through the canal. Prior to the expansion, the largest-sized containership that could transit the Panama Canal was a containership with a carrying capacity of 5000 TEUs. With the expansion, the largest sized containership that can pass through the Panama Canal

---

[7] Source: https://en.wikipedia.org/wiki/Suez_Canal/ (accessed 17.06.17).

[8] Source: https://en.wikipedia.org/wiki/Panama-Canal/ (accessed 19.06.17).

[9] The impact of the Panama Canal expansion is found in Pagano et al. (2016).

has more than doubled, that is, a containership with a carrying capacity of approximately 13, 500 TEUs.

7.2.1.3   Suez Canal Versus Panama Canal

The ship route from Hong Kong to New York via the Suez Canal is 11,589 nautical miles versus 11,206 nautical miles via the Panama Canal and depending on where the cargo originates in Asia, a "containership slow-steaming at an average rate of 16 knots (takes) only 24 h longer to travel that route via the Suez than via Panama" (Leach, 2013, p. 12). A fully loaded 4800-TEU containership transiting the Suez Canal is assessed Suez Canal tolls as high as $480,000 versus $450,000 in transiting the Panama Canal. Cargo insurance costs for shippers of cargo transiting the Suez Canal are higher, for example, from paying war-risk insurance, attributable to the risk of piracy in the Gulf of Aden.

7.2.1.4   Nicaragua Canal

In July 2014, the government of Nicaragua approved plans for a canal linking the Pacific Ocean and the Atlantic Ocean via the Caribbean Sea. The Nicaragua Canal would compete with the Panama Canal, since they would be less than 300 miles apart.

Construction of the US $50 billion Nicaragua Canal Project is expected to start in 2017. In addition to the canal itself (171 miles long and between 251 and 306 yards wide), the Nicaragua Canal Project will also include the construction of two ports, an airport, two artificial lakes, two locks, and tourist facilities.[10]

7.2.1.5   Northern Sea Route

The NSR (also known as the Northeast Passage) is a shipping route between the Atlantic and Pacific Oceans along the Russian coast of Siberia and the Far East. Russia officially opened the route for commercial shipping in the early 1990s. "Shipping through the Arctic Ocean via the NSR allows for the saving of about 40% in the sailing distance from Asia (Yokohama) to Europe (Rotterdam), compared to the traditional route via the Suez Canal" (Liu and Kronak, 2010, p. 434), but at greater costs (Pruyin, 2016) from having to use ice-classed cargo ships, ice breaker service, and the nonregularity of service caused by variable weather and ice conditions.

In response to the growth in polar traffic, the International Maritime Organization (IMO) has proposed a Polar Code that would establish safety and environmental protocols for ships traversing the waters around the two poles (Gupta, 2014). The Polar Code would classify ships based on their ability to travel through ice-choked waters.

7.2.1.6   One Belt One Road

The One Belt One Road is an initiative by China to address recent declines in its economic growth and to "push for growth driven by domestic consumption rather than by

---

[10] Source: https://www.freshfruitportal.com/news/2017/01/30/work-to-begin-on-nicaragua-canal-in-first-quarter-of-2017/ (accessed 04.07.17).

infrastructure and exports" (Knowler, 2015a, p. 14). The One Belt One Road will link China's Yangtze River Delta, Pearl River Delta, and Bohai Sea economic zones to European economies via "the development of unblocked road and rail networks between China and Europe" (Knowler, 2015b, p. 44). The One Belt One Road "brings together the Silk Road Economic Belt and Maritime Silk Road developments aimed at linking China with Europe and Africa, and the countries in between" (Knowler, 2015a, p. 14).

The international transportation routes of the One Belt One Road will connect China with Central Asia, Russia, and the Baltic region of Europe by running from China's coast to Europe through the South China Sea and the Indian Ocean on one route and from China's coast through the South China Sea to the South Pacific on the other (Knowler, 2015a). One-Belt-One-Road ports and maritime facilities from the Pacific Ocean to the Baltic Sea will also be constructed (Knowler, 2015b, p. 44).

International trade is the exchange of merchandise and services between countries. Seaborne trade is merchandise international trade that is transported by ship from a seaport in country A to a seaport in country B. "Sea transport handles over 80% of the volume of global trade" (United Nations, 2012, p. 44). Government investments in canals and improvements in ship waterways have contributed to the growth in seaborne trade.

7.2.2   International trade policies

International trade policies such as GATT, NAFTA, and CAFTA have reduced or eliminated trade barriers, thereby increasing international trade and, in turn, the growth in ocean container-shipping among the participating countries.

GATT is a "legal agreement among many countries, whose overall purpose was to promote international trade by reducing or eliminating trade barriers such as tariffs or quotas."[11] GATT was signed by 23 countries in Geneva on October 30, 1947, taking effect on January 1, 1948, and remained in effect until April 14, 1994 when 123 countries signed the Uruguay Round Agreements, establishing the World Trade Organization (WTO) on January 1, 1995, the so-called successor to GATT. Estimates of increases in members' trade flows attributed to GATT "range from 16% to 277%" (United States International Trade Commission, p. 26).

While GATT is a world multilateral trade agreement, NAFTA is a trilateral trade agreement that came into effect on January 1, 1994, following signatures by Canada, Mexico, and the United States to the agreement, thereby "creating a trilateral trade block in North America." NAFTA sought to eliminate tariff trade barriers to investment and trade between Canada, Mexico, and the United States as well as eliminating nontariff trade barriers. NAFTA also sought to protect the intellectual property rights of traded goods. Within 10 years of NAFTA's implementation, all US–Mexico tariffs were eliminated except for tariffs on US agricultural exports to Mexico. However, these were phased out during the following 15 years. "Most economic analyses indicate that NAFTA has been a small net positive for the United States, large net positive for Mexico and had an insignificant impact on Canada." "Estimates of the impacts of

[11] Source: https://en.wikipedia.org/wiki/General_Agreement_on_Tariffs_and_Trade/ (accessed 19.06.17).

NAFTA on the US economy vary by state and industry" (United States International Trade Commission, p. 26).

CAFTA is a free trade agreement among the United States and the Central American countries of Costa Rica, El Salvador, Guatemala, Honduras, and Nicaragua. When the Dominican Republic joined CAFTA in 2004, CAFTA was renamed CAFTA-DR and is the first free trade agreement between the United States and a group of developing countries. The goal of CAFTA-DR is to be a free trade area that is similar to NAFTA.[12] Following passage of CAFTA, approximately 80% of the tariffs on US exports to the participating countries were immediately eliminated; with the addition of the Dominican Republic, CAFTA-DR has become the second-largest Latin American export market for US producers (behind only Mexico).[13]

7.2.3 Economic effects of ocean container shipping

Since several modes (water, rail, and truck) are used in the transportation of containerized cargo, intermodal freight transportation is a creation of ocean container shipping. The modern container port (also a creation of ocean container shipping) provides for the removal of the land–sea interface bottleneck in the transportation of general cargo. With general cargo being shipped in a closed container, the pilferage, damage, and theft of containerized cargo are less than that for general cargo shipped as breakbulk cargo. "The ability for land and sea carriers to handle each other's containers in different locations set the foundation of global container adoption around the globe" (Bernhofen et al., 2016, p. 40).

7.3 Ocean container shipping lines' business strategies in a changing economic environment

Ocean container shipping accelerated in the 1980s with the addition of the Asian container shipping lines—Evergreen, Hanjin, Orient Overseas Container Line (OOCL), and Yang Ming. By 1987, Evergreen was the world's largest ocean container shipping line (Chadwin et al., 1990, p. 6). By 1988, the Asian container shipping lines operated 30% of the world's container fleet (Chadwin et al., 1990, p. 7). The largest and second largest US flag container shipping lines were Sea-Land and American President Lines (APL), respectively. Between 1983 and 1988, "the deadweight tonnage of containerships deployed in the Far East-North American trade more than doubled" and in 1988, this tonnage "increased by 25% when the Danish Maersk Line and American Sea-Land Service entered this trading route" (Talley, 2010, p. 138).

Container shipping lines have adopted various service strategies, for example, the load-center strategy of calling at only one or two ports in a range of ports or the multiport strategy of calling at several ports along the same coast. Some lines main-

---

[12] Source: https://en.wikipedia.org/wiki/North-American-Free-Trade-Agreement (accessed 15 7 17).

[13] Source: https://ustr.gov/trade-agreements/free-trade-agreements/cafta-dr-dominican-republic-central-america-fta/ (accessed 07.07.17).

tained their service over highly competitive routes between North America, Europe, and Asia, while others focused on less-competitive North–South routes. Sea-Land provided door-to-door service, utilizing its own facilities and equipment, while other lines contracted for truck, rail, and intermediary services. Evergreen, Nedlloyd, and Senator Lines provided round-the-world services with Evergreen using large ships in continuous eastbound and westbound circuits.

By the late 1990s, container shipping lines were experiencing financial difficulties. The estimated collective losses of the lines operating in the transpacific, transatlantic, and Europe/Far Asia trades in 1996 were $411 million (Porter, 1996). The continuing excess supply of containership TEU-carrying capacities (and subsequent declining freight rates) contributed to the losses. The market supply of containership TEU-carrying capacities exceeded the market demand. Finding it difficult to raise freight rates, container shipping lines sought to improve their financial conditions by reducing costs by using larger containerships, undertaking mergers and acquisitions, and forming alliances.

7.3.1 Larger containerships

The rationale for a container shipping line in using larger containerships to reduce costs is that containerships exhibit economies of ship size at sea (Talley, 2009, p. 63), that is, the cost per TEU transported at sea by a containership decreases as the size of the ship increases, all else held constant.

A 4000 TEU ship has a 30%–40% per TEU transportation cost saving over a 2500 TEU ship and a 6000 TEU ship has an 18%–24% per TEU transportation cost saving over a 4000 TEU ship (Talley, 2000). A 12,000 TEU ship has a 11% per TEU transportation cost saving over an 8000 TEU ship (Notteboom, 2004). From the above percentages, it is apparent that the marginal TEU transportation cost savings in using larger and larger containerships at sea decrease as the ships increase in size.

Alternatively, containerships exhibit diseconomies of ship size in port, that is, "ship cost per TEU loaded on and unloaded from a ship in port increases as ship size increases" (Talley, 2009, p. 63). The reason is that larger containerships have a greater number of TEU slots from which and to which containers are moved than smaller containerships (Talley, 2009, p. 63), thereby requiring container ports to assign a greater number of cranes, etc. for moving containers to and from larger containerships than for smaller containerships, all else held constant. Larger containerships also require: (1) port channel widths with sufficient vessel turning circles, (2) port channels with deeper depths so that larger ships will not run aground[14], (3) port shoreside container cranes with longer outreach, greater loading capacity and lift height, (4) greater port terminal storage capacity, and (5) larger truck and railroad port facilities.

As of June 2015, the container shipping industry had 67 containerships on order with TEU-carrying capacities of 19,000 TEUs or more; Maersk line had 11 containerships on order with TEU-carrying capacities of 19,630 TEUs (Tirwchwell, 2015). Containerships with carrying capacities exceeding 10,000 TEUs accounted for 55% of

---

[14] See Talley (2007) for a discussion of port dredging.

the delivered capacity in 2015; 24 ships with carrying capacities greater than 17,000 TEUs joined the world fleet in 2015 (Staff, 2016). For further discussion of container-ships, see Talley (1986, 1990).

7.3.2   Mergers and acquisitions

P&O (a British carrier) and Nedlloyd (a Dutch carrier) on January 1, 1997, announced that they would merge to create the world's largest container shipping line, P&O Nedl-loyd. The estimated cost savings from the merger was US $200 million—65% of which would be immediate from eliminating duplicate overhead costs (Tirwchwell, 1997; Wastler, 1997). In April 1997, APL and NOL (of Singapore) agreed to merge. The es-timated annual cost savings from the merger was US $130 million from consolidating container, inland, and vessel services and reducing information and marine terminal expenses (Tirwchwell, 1997).

In 1999, Maersk acquired Sealand for US $800 million. The acquisition created the world's largest container shipping line, Maersk-Sealand. During 2000–2003, sev-eral major container shipping lines acquired smaller container shipping lines to in-crease their presence on specific trade routes, for example, acquisitions were made by Maersk-Sealand, P&O Nedlloyd, CP Ships, CSAV, Hamburg Sud, CMA-CGM, and Wan Hai. In 2005, Maersk-Sealand acquired P&O Nedlloyd, creating Maersk Line (the world's largest container shipping line at the time), followed by the acquisition of CP Ships by Hapag Lloyd. Hapag-Lloyd acquired the container shipping line CSAV in December 2014 and Hamburg Sud acquired Compania Chilena de Navegacion in June 2015 (Salisbury, 2015).

In 2016, the Chinese container shipping lines, COSCO and China Shipping, merged and Hanjin had a financial collapse. The three Japanese container shipping lines—K Line, MOL, and NYK—agreed to a merger on April 1, 2018, that would create the fifth largest container shipping line in the world, the Ocean Network Express (ONE). The three Taiwanese container shipping lines—Evergreen, Yang Ming Line, and Wan Hai Lines—have agreed to a merger at a future date.

7.3.3   Vessel-sharing alliances

In forming vessel-sharing alliances, the ships of one alliance shipping line can be used to transport the cargo of other shipping lines of the alliance. That is to say, if an alli-ance ship is in port and cargo space is available on the ship, the cargo of an alliance line partner can be loaded onto this ship for transport. By sharing ships (i.e. form-ing vessel-sharing alliances), container shipping lines can reduce their ship operating costs without sacrificing ship frequency of service. An alliance line's saved ship capac-ity, in turn, can be diverted to new service routes or to an increase in the frequency of port calls on existing routes.

As of August 1995, four major container-shipping-line alliances were in existence (Talley, 2009), that is, the: (1) Sealand/Maersk Alliance of Sealand and Maersk Line; (2) Tricon Alliance of Cho Yang Shipping Company, DSR-Senator Lines, Hanjin Ship-ping Company, and the United Arab Shipping Company; (3) Global Alliance of APL,

OOCL, Mitsui OSK Line, and Nedlloyd; and (4) Grand Alliance of Peninsular and Orient Line (P&O), Hapag Lloyd Line, Neptune Orient Line (NOL), and NYK Line.

As of August 2016, the four major container-shipping-line alliances that were in existence (Knowler, 2016) include: (1) 2M (Maersk Line and Mediterranean Shipping), (2) CKYHE (Cosco, K Line, Yang Ming, Hanjin, and Evergreen), (3) G6 (APL, Hapag-Lloyd, Hyundai, MOL, NYK, and OOCL), and (4) Ocean Three (China Shipping, CMA-CGM, and United Arab Shipping). Changes in the names of alliances and the shipping-line members of alliances from August 1995 to August 2016 are due in part to the relatively large number of mergers among container shipping lines during the time period.

Alliances and mergers, however, do not address the container shipping industry's fundamental problem—ship overcapacity. "At least 12% of the ship capacity needs to be taken out … but even the initial removal would only offer temporary relief. Once container lines see strengthening rates – many likely would bring back ideal capacity, plunging the industry back into overcapacity" (Szakonyi, 2016, p. 14).

The following section focuses on ocean container shipping in the United States. In addition to the first container shipping line being a US flagged line and the first international voyage by a containership was between the United States and Rotterdam, the world's first container double-stack train service (containers stacked two high transported by rail cars) was also provided in the United States. In addition to United States double-stack train service, the following section discusses US transportation regulatory reform acts, US dockworkers, US exporters and importers, and the US Jones Act.

7.4   Containerization in the United States

Prior to the 1980s, containerships from Asian ports, transporting container cargo destined for a US East Coast port, would sail across the Pacific Ocean, transit the Panama Canal and then sail to the US East Coast Port (where the cargo would be unloaded). However, the width of the Panama Canal constrained the size of the containerships that could transit the Panama Canal.

7.4.1   US double-stack train service

In April 1984, this began to change—when an APL containership (carrying container cargo destined for the US East Coast) departed an Asian port, sailed across the Pacific Ocean and stopped at a US West Coast Port, where a US railroad was contracted to transport the ship's cargo by a double-stack train to the intermodal rail facility in Chicago—from which the cargo would be distributed by truck and rail to their US East-Coast destination markets.[15] By the late 1980s, most of the container cargo from Asia bound for the US East Coast did not arrive by ship, but rather was discharged on the US West Coast, and transported by double-stack trains across the continent, thereby placing US West Coast container ports in competition with East Coast container ports.

---

[15] A discussion of intermodalism is found in Fan et al. (2012).

Double-stack rail cars are specifically designed to transport containers stacked two high. The appeal of double-stack trains (consisting of double-stack railcars) is their cost advantage over conventional container-on-flat car (COFC) trains, that is, for slightly more locomotive power, the same labor and slightly more fuel, 200 containers can be transported on a double-stack train as opposed to 100 containers on a COFC train (Talley, 2009). Rail freight service using double-stack trains is also referred to as rail land-bridging. Today, shipping lines contract with railroads for transportation of their containers via double-stack trains to and from ports on both the US West Coast and the US East Coast.

Double-stack trains have height passage requirements, that is, the heights of rail tunnels must be high enough for the passage of double-stack trains through rail tunnels. If not, the tunnels would have to be heighted or their bases lowered. Such was the case for rail tunnels of Norfolk Southern (NS) railroad (on the US East Coast) used in the provision of double-stack train service between Norfolk, Virginia, and Chicago. In response, the "Heartland Corridor" project was initiated to raise the heights of mountain railway tunnels in the state of West Virginia so that NS double-stack trains could travel between the Port of Virginia and Chicago. A side benefit of this project was the reduction in the rail distance via NS double-stack trains between the Port of Virginia and Chicago.

Impacts of US double-stack (container) train service include:

(1) Container shipping lines were able to utilize larger containerships in transiting the Pacific Ocean than those constrained by the width of the Panama Canal (i.e. containerships not exceeding 5000 TEUs in size) and, in turn, due to containerships exhibiting economies of ship size at sea could lower their unit TEU cost at sea.

(2) Double-stack train service (rail land-bridging) between a US West Coast Port and the US East Coast is 5–6 days faster than all-water transportation service. As a consequence, the related cargo-inventory cost of double-stack train service is less than that for all-water transportation service, all else held constant, but the transportation cost of double-stack train service is higher than that for all-water transportation service.

(3) Rail land-bridging has promoted the growth of US West Coast container ports (in particular, the Ports of Los Angeles and Long Beach) to the detriment of US East Coast container ports. In the mid-1980s, US East Coast ports captured 22% of Asian containerized cargo, but this percentage had declined to 15% by 1997 (Mongelluzzo, 1998). The decline would have been worse if not for the Asian trade via the Suez Canal.

(4) Economies of ship size at sea for larger containerships (using the Suez Canal) made the Suez Canal trade somewhat competitive with the rail land-bridging trade of US West Coast Ports, that is, the all-water service via the Suez Canal from Singapore to the Port of New York/New Jersey, a 9000-nautical mile route, takes 22 days, one to two days longer than transit across the Pacific Ocean to the Ports of Los Angeles and Long Beach and then rail land-bridged to the US East Coast. Container cargo received by US East Coast ports via all-water Asian trade using the Suez Canal grew from zero in 1991 to 6% of all-water container service between Asia and the US by mid-1996 (Talley, 2000).

(5) The large volume of containers moving from US West Coast container ports to the US East Coast via double-stack trains has resulted in significant increases in highway congestion for US West Coast container port cities. This problem for the port cities of Los Angeles and Long Beach was addressed with the construction of the $2.4 billion Alameda Corridor, the largest intermodal construction project in US history (Talley, 2009).

The Alameda Corridor is a 20-mile, high-capacity grade-separated intermodal rail corridor (trench) that consolidated more than 90 miles of rail lines to link the Ports of Los Angeles and Long Beach to eastward rail service in the Los Angeles area; the construction of the Alameda Corridor eliminated 200 street-level railroad crossings.

7.4.2   US Transportation Regulatory Reform Acts

The US Shipping Act of 1916 Act legalized shipping liner conference agreements by granting them immunity from antitrust legislation. The US Shipping Act of 1984 amended the US Shipping Act of 1916, reducing US economic regulation of ocean transportation. The 1984 Act permitted independent rates (i.e. independent of conference rates) and legalized service contracts between shippers and carriers/conferences as well as door-to-door (intermodal) as opposed to just port-to-port rates (Chadwin et al., 1990; Cassavant and Wilson, 1991).

By leaving the port-of-call choice to the shipping line, the Shipping Act of 1984 provided shipping lines with the opportunity to: (1) utilize larger ships, thus reducing their ship transportation cost at sea (due to economies of ship size at sea) and (2) charge door-to-door rates. The use of door-to-door rates enabled container shipping lines, utilizing larger ships to transport large volumes of container cargo and to bargain for and obtain lower rates from US inland transportation carriers. The Shipping Act of 1984 also "permitted steamship lines to set rates without regulatory review and approval" and "could offer intermodal service anywhere" (Prince, 2006, p. 48A).

The US Ocean Shipping Reform Act of 1998 amended the US Shipping Act of 1984. The major provisions of the 1998 Act include: (1) a confidential contract provision that allows for the first time, "confidential one-on-one contracts by shipping lines, but not conferences, with their customers" and (2) "ocean carriers engaged in confidential arrangements with big shippers must disclose contractual information regarding specific dock and port movements to longshore unions" (Peoples et al., 2006, p. 223). The principal goal of the 1998 Act was to "provide shippers and ocean carriers with greater choice and flexibility in entering into contractual relationships with shippers for ocean transportation and intermodal services" (Lewis and Vellenga, 2000, p. 29). Shippers benefited from the 1998 Act by being "able to tailor ocean/intermodal transportation rates and services to individual requirements and circumstances" (Peoples et al., 2006, p. 223). For a discussion of international shipping regulatory issues, see Talley (2005).

7.4.3   US dockworkers

In the 1960s, containerization—the foremost port labor-saving technology—was introduced to US ports. Under containerization, breakbulk ports often became container ports, replacing port labor with port capital, resulting in significant losses in dockworker jobs (Talley, 2009). In 1950, there were 100,000 full-time US dockworkers; by 2003, the number of US dockworker jobs had declined to 10,500 jobs (Greenwald, 2004).

The major dockworker unions in the United States are the International Longshore-men's Association (ILA) on the East Coast and the International Longshore and Ware-house Union (ILWU) on the West Coast. In the 1920s, there was an excess supply of US dockworkers with both union and nonunion dockworkers competed for daily work assignments. In 1937, the West Coast dockworkers broke away from the ILA to form the ILWU (Talley, 2018).

The ILA responded to the losses in dockworker jobs by negotiating for dockworker local guaranteed annual income (GAI) plans and "work preservation" schemes. In 1965, the Port of New York/New Jersey provided ILA GAI agreements of 1600 paid hours per year to fully registered longshoremen. To qualify, dockworkers had to have worked 700 or more hours in a given fiscal year. In exchange, the ILA agreed to reduce gang sizes and provide greater flexibility in work practices (Talley, 2018).

In the 1970s, the union wages of US rail engineers and dockworkers were compa-rable. After 1984, the union wages of rail engineers declined relative to those of dock-workers, that is, a negative union hourly wage gap of 6.9% for rail engineers versus dockworkers (Talley, 2004). The primary reason for the relative decrease in union rail engineer wages versus union dockworker wages is the change in the relative bargain-ing power among the occupations. For railroads, there was a shift in the balance of power in wage negotiations from unions to management.

US truck drivers (as for US rail workers) loss bargaining power in the postderegula-tion period, but occurred much sooner than for rail workers. The union wages of US truck drivers and dockworkers were comparable in the 1970s. After 1984, the union wages of truck drivers declined relative to those of dockworkers, that is, a negative union hourly wage gap of 22.7% for truck drivers versus dockworkers (Talley, 2004). The primary reason for the relative decrease in union truck driver wages versus union dockworker wages is the change in the relative bargaining power among the occupa-tions. For truck carriers, there has been a shift in the balance of power in wage negotia-tions from unions to management.

Unlike US railroad and truck-carrier union workers, the bargaining power of US union dockworkers increased in the postderegulation period from a shift in the balance of power in wage negotiations from management to unions (Talley, 2018). This shift in power is attributed to the: "(1) increase in the demand for dockworkers; (2) decrease in the likelihood that dockworker employers will chance a strike; and (3) increase in port capital-labor ratios" (Talley, 2002, p. 462). Employers of US union dockworkers at container ports have become reluctant to chance a strike due to the fear that if a strike occurs, they might lose ship calls and cargo to competing ports. Also, port labor cost as a percentage of total port cost for container ports has declined, thereby increasing the likelihood that container ports would be willing to agree to higher dockworker wages in labor negotiations.

7.4.4 US importers and exporters

This section reveals that some of the largest US retail companies rely heavily on ocean container shipping for importing retail cargo (that is eventually placed for sale in their retail stores). The major US product that is exported as containerized cargo is paper.

In Table 7.3, the top-10 ranked US importers of ocean containerized cargo for 2014 are found. The top-ranked US importer, Wal-Mart Stores, imported 775,400 TEUs in 2014, followed by the second-ranked importer (Target) that imported 521,300 TEUs in 2014. The TEU imports of Wal-Mart Stores were more than twice those of Home Depot, the third-ranked US importer of TEUs of containerized cargo.

In Table 7.4, the top-10 ranked US exporters of ocean containerized cargo for 2014 are found. The top-ranked US exporter, American Chung Nam, exported 335,400 TEUs, followed by the second-ranked exporter, Koch Industries, that exported 239,800 TEUs. As revealed in Table 7.4, paper products are the primary products exported by the top-10 ranked US exporters of containerized cargo. The exporters are also export chemicals, grains, feeds and metals as containerized cargo.

In 2014, the total number of TEUs of US imported containerized cargo imported by the top-10 ranked US importers of containerized cargo is 2,869,900 TEU (see Table 7.3) and the total number of TEUs of US exported containerized cargo exported by the top-10 ranked US exporters of containerized cargo is 1,388,200 TEUs (see Table 7.4). Hence, in 2014, the top-10 ranked US importers of TEUs of containerized cargo imported more than twice the number of TEUs of containerized cargo exported by the top-10 ranked US exporters of TEUs of containerized cargo.

Table 7.3 **Top-10 US importers of ocean containerized cargo (2014)**

Rank	Importer	TEUs (1000s)	Product	Headquarters
1.	Wal-Mart Stores	775.4	Retail	Arkansas
2.	Target	521.3	Retail	Minnesota
3.	Home Depot	342.4	Retail	Georgia
4.	Lowe's	249.0	Retail	North Carolina
5.	Dole Food	199.6	Food	California
6.	Sears Holding	179.0	Retail	Illinois
7.	Chiquita Brands International	171.0	Fruit/vegetables	North Carolina
8.	Heineken USA	149.7	Beverages conglomerate	New York
9.	Samsung America	147.4	Conglomerate items	New Jersey
10.	Family Dollar Stores/Dollar Tree	135.1	Retail	Virginia

Source: Staff (2015a, b) JOC TOP 100 Importers, U.S. Foreign Trade, J. Commerce June 1: 46.

Table 7.4 **Top-10 US exporters of ocean containerized cargo (2014)**

Rank	Exporter	TEUs (1000s)	Product	Headquarters
1.	American Chung Nam	335.4	Paper	California
2.	Koch Industries	239.8	Conglomerate Items	Kansas
3.	International Paper	157.3	Paper	Tennessee
4.	Delong	111.9	Grains, Feeds	Wisconsin
5.	Denison International	104.4	Paper	California
6.	Dupont	102.5	Chemicals/Plastics	Delaware
7.	Meadwestvaco/Rock-tenn	93.8	Paper	Virginia
8.	Sims Metal Management	84.4	Metals	New York
9.	Newport Ch International	80.5	Paper	California
10.	Potential Industries	78.2	Paper	California

Source: Staff (2015a, b) JOC TOP 100 Exporters, U.S. Foreign Trade, J. Commerce June 1: 36.

7.4.5   US Jones Act

Section 27 of the US Jones Act requires "that all goods transported by water between US ports be carried on US flag ships, constructed in the United States, owned by US citizens and crewed by US citizens and US permanent residents".[16] Maersk Line Limited and Matson, Inc. are US Jones Act shipping lines. As US flag shipping lines, they can load cargo on their ships at one US port and unload the cargo from the same ships at another US port. Maersk Line Limited transports cargo utilizing container, tanker and multipurpose ships. Matson, Inc. provides shipping services over the Pacific Ocean to and from the Hawaiian Islands.

Cabotage is the transportation of cargo between two locations in the same country by a transportation carrier from another country. The US Jones Act thus prohibits the cabotage of non-US flagged container shipping lines from loading cargo on their ships at one US port and then unloading the cargo from these ships at another US port. Prohibiting cabotage is found in a number of countries in addition to the US, for example, China. While economic liberalization and regulatory reform have contributed to the growth of ocean container shipping in the US, limitations still remain, for example, the

[16] Source: https://en.wikipedia.org/wiki/Merchant_Marine_Act_of_1920/ (accessed 30.06.17).

prohibition of cabotage that protects US flag container shipping lines from competition from foreign-flag container shipping lines.

7.5 Conclusion

Ocean container shipping is the ocean transportation of cargo in a standardized container (or box). Malcom McLean purchased a small tanker company, renamed it Sea-Land, and adapted its ships for the transportation of truck trailers and subsequently the transportation of containers. The first voyage of a containership occurred on April 26, 1956 when it departed from Newark, New Jersey for the destination of Puerto Rico. The first international voyage of a Sea-Land ship was in 1966 from Newark, New Jersey to the Port of Rotterdam. In comparison to ocean breakbulk shipping, the costs incurred by shippers in shipping their general cargo by ocean container shipping are lower, for example, lower cargo theft and damage costs (from protection against cargo theft and damage provided by containers) and lower cargo inventory holding costs (from faster delivery and thus faster transactions), all else held constant.

Since several modes (rail, truck, and water) are used in the transportation of containerized cargo, ocean container shipping created intermodal freight transportation. The container port is also a creation of ocean container shipping; without the container technology (e.g. ship-to-shore cranes) of a container port, the passing through of containerized cargo through a noncontainer port would be more labor-intensive.

Global trade carried in containers increased from 100 million metric tons in 1980 to 1.7 billion metric tons in 2015. This growth is not only attributable to the container technology used in ocean container shipping but also to government investments and international trade policies. Government investments that have shortened the waterway travel distances in the transportation of global trade are the constructions of the Suez Canal and the Panama Canal (and proposed construction of the Nicaragua Canal) and the NSR and the proposed One Belt on Road initiative that will connect China with Central Asia, Russia, and the Baltic region of Europe. The international trade policies of GATT, NAFTA, and CAFTA have also enhanced the growth in containerized global trade by promoting global trade among the perspective countries and providing global trade cargo to be transported by ocean container shipping.

By the late 1990s, container shipping lines were experiencing financial difficulties from an excessive supply of containership TEU-carrying capacity, that is, the supply of the carrying capacity exceeded its demand. With the difficulty of raising rates, the lines sought to improve their financial conditions by reducing costs via investing in larger containerships, undertaking mergers and acquisitions, and forming vessel-sharing alliances. However, the excess supply of containership TEU-carrying capacity still remains.

Prior to the 1980s, containerships from Asian ports destined for a US East Coast port would sail across the Pacific Ocean, transit the Panama Canal and then sail to the US East Coast Port for the unloading of their cargo. By the mid-1980s, containerships might stop at a US West Coast Port, where a US railroad was contracted to transport the ship's cargo by a double-stack train to the US East Coast, where the cargo would be dispersed by truck and rail carriers to their US East-Coast destination markets. Double-stack train (or rail land-bridging) service between a US West Coast Port and the US East Coast is five to six days faster (but more expensive) than all-water transportation service. Rail land-bridging has promoted the growth of US West Coast container ports (in particular, the Ports of Los Angeles and Long Beach) to the detriment of US East Coast container ports.

Ocean container shipping has revolutionized the ocean transportation of general cargo. Its impact is comparable to the introduction of the jet engine in air transportation and the steam engine in water transportation.

Appendix A

The world's 20 largest container ports in 2015, ranked by number of TEUs handled, appear in Table A1. Note that nine of these ports are found in China.

Table A1 **World container port rankings (2015)**

Rank	Port	Country	TEUs (000s)
1	Shanghai	China	36,516
2	Singapore	Singapore	30,922
3	Shenzhen	China	24,142
4	Ningbo	China	20,636
5	Hong Kong	China	20,073
6	Busan	South Korea	19,469
7	Qingdao	China	17,323
8	Guangzhou	China	17,097
9	Dubai Ports	United Arab Emirates	15,585
10	Tianjin	China	13,881
11	Rotterdam	Netherlands	12,235
12	Port Kelang	Malaysia	11,887
13	Kaohsiung	Taiwan	10,264
14	Antwerp	Belgium	9654
15	Dalian	China	9591
16	Xiamen	China	9215
17	Hamburg	Germany	8821
18	Tanjung Pelepas	Malaysia	8797
19	Los Angeles	United States	8160
20	Long Beach	United States	7192

Source: http://www.aapa-ports.org/Industry/content.cfm?ItemNumber=900 (accessed 17.04.17).

The common features of a container port are the: (1) wharf, (2) berth, (3) apron, (4) container yard, and (5) inland interchange gate. A wharf is a structure alongside a waterway to which ships are moored for the loading and unloading of cargo. A berth is the water area alongside a wharf, where a ship sits for cargo loading and unloading. The apron is an area of the wharf, where containers are staged. Inland from the apron is the container yard, where containers are stuffed and stripped. Inland interchange gates are gates for the entry and departure of containers by land (or inland waterways) to and from the port. Larger containerships require: (1) channel widths to have sufficient vessel turning circles; (2) the size of shore-side container cranes to have longer outreach and greater loading capacity and lift height; (3) greater terminal storage capacity; and (4) larger truck and railroad facilities.

Port multiservice congestion occurs when port users of two or more different services (i.e. multiservices) provided at the same port node or over the same port link within a port's service chain interfere with one another to the extent that they experience service congestion at the shared node or over the shared link (Talley and Ng, 2016a, b). For derivation of a port economic cost function, where the choice variables in the derivation are port quality of service variables, see Talley and Ng (2016a, b).

References

Bernhofen, D.M., El-Sahli, Z., Kneller, R., 2016. Estimating the effects of the container revolution on world trade. Journal of International Economics 98, 36–50.

Blonigen, B., Wilson, W., 2013. The growth and patterns of international trade. Maritime Policy and Management 40, 618–635.

Cassavant, K.L., Wilson, W.W., 1991. Shipper perspectives of the shipping Act of 1984. Transportation Quarterly 45, 109–120.

Chadwin, M.L., Pope, J.A., Talley, W.K., 1990. Ocean Container Transportation: An Operational Perspective. Taylor & Francis, New York.

Fan, L., Koehler, M.M., Wilson, W.W., 2012. Intermodalism and new trade flows. In: Talley, W.K. (Ed.), The Blackwell Companion to Maritime Economics. Wiley Blackwell, Oxford, UK, pp. 21–137.

Greenwald, R.A., 2004. Working the docks: labor, management and the new waterfront. Shah, S.K. (Ed.), Review of Business, 25, pp. 16–22.

Gupta, S., 2014. IMO Developing Polar Code to Govern Voyages Through Icy Waters. Professional Mariner, May 10.

Heidbrink, I., 2012. The business of shipping: an historical perspective. In: Talley, W.K. (Ed.), The Blackwell Companion to Maritime Economics. Wiley-Blackwell, Oxford, UK, pp. 34–51.

Knowler, G., 2015a. China's expanding trade tentacles. Journal of Commerce, 14–16, May 4.

Knowler, G., 2015b. One belt, one road and one new terminal. Journal of Commerce 42, 44, October 5.

Knowler, G., 2016. Forwarders brace for alliance pain. Journal of Commerce, 16–17, August 8.

Leach, P.T., 2013. Two canals. Journal of Commerce, 10–14, April 15.

Levinson, M., 2006. The Box: How the Shipping Container Made the World Smaller and World Economy Bigger. Princeton University Press.

Lewis, I., Vellenga, D.B., 2000. Ocean Shipping Reform Act. Transportation Journal, 27–34.

Mongelluzzo, B., 1998. Work stoppages again disrupt West Coast ports. Journal of Commerce, July 15, 1A, 14A.

Notteboom, T.E., 2004. Container shipping and ports: an overview. In: Talley, W.K. (Ed.), The Industrial Organization of Shipping and Ports, Rev. Network Econ. 3, 86–106.

Notteboom, T.E., 2012. Container shipping. In: Talley, W.K. (Ed.), The Blackwell Companion to Maritime Economics. Wiley-Blackwell Publishing, Oxford, UK, pp. 230–262.

Pagano, A., Wang, G., Sanchez, O., Ungo, R., Tapiero, E., 2016. The impact of the Panama Canal expansion on Panama's maritime cluster. Maritime Policy and Management 43, 164–178.

Peoples, J., Talley, W.K., Thanabordeekij, P., 2006. Shipping deregulation's wage effect on low and high wage dockworkers. In: Cullinane, K., Talley, W.K. (Eds.), Port Economics: Research in Transportation Economics. Elsevier, Amsterdam, pp. 219–249.

Porter, J., 1996. Continued losses swamp container lines in Sea of Red. Journal of Commerce, August 1, 2B.

Prince, T., 2006. 50 years of containerization. Journal of Commerce, April, 48A.

Pruyin, J.F.J., 2016. Will the Northern Sea Route ever be a viable alternative? Maritime Policy and Management 43, 661–675.

Rodrigue, J.-P., Nottebom, T., 2010. Foreland-based regionalization: integrating intermediate hubs with port hinterlands. Research in Transportation Economics 27, 19–29.

Salisbury, M., 2015. Slow-go for US container growth. Journal of Commerce 21, 20, September.

Staff, 2015a. JOC TOP 100 exporters, U.S. foreign trade. Journal of Commerce, 36, June 1.

Staff, 2015b. JOC TOP 100 importers, U.S. foreign trade. Journal of Commerce, 46, June 1.

Staff, 2016. Mega-ships losing luster in global container trades. Journal of Commerce, 7, April 18.

Szakonyi, M., 2016. The great alliance shuffle. Journal of Commerce, May 16, 10–13.

Talley, W.K., 1986. A short-run cost analysis of ocean containerships. The Logistics and Transportation Review 22, 131–139.

Talley, W.K., 1990. Optimal containership size. Maritime Policy and Management 17, 65–175.

Talley, W.K., 2000. Ocean container shipping: impacts of a technological improvement. Journal of Economic Issues 34, 933–948.

Talley, W.K., 2002. Dockworker earnings, containerization and shipping deregulation. Journal of Transport Economics and Policy 36, 447–467.

Talley, W.K., 2004. Wage differentials of intermodal transportation carriers and ports: deregulation versus regulation. In: Talley, W.K. (Ed.), The Industrial Organization of Shipping and Ports, Rev. Network Econ. 3, 207–227.

Talley, W.K., 2005. Regulatory issues: the role of international Maritime institutions. In: Hensher, D.A., Button, K.J. (Eds.), Handbook of Transport Strategy: Policy and Institutions. Elsevier, Amsterdam, pp. 421–433.

Talley, W.K., 2007. Financing port dredging costs: taxes versus user fees. Transportation Journal 46, 53–58.

Talley, W.K., 2008. Earnings differentials of U.S. dockworkers and seafarers. International Journal of Transport Economics 35, 169–184.

Talley, W.K., 2009. Port Economics. Routledge, Abingdon, UK.

Talley, W.K., 2010. Shipping. In: Hoel, L.A., Giuliano, G., Meyer, M.C. (Eds.), Intermodal Transportation: Moving Freight in a Global Economy. Eno Transportation Foundation, Washington, DC, pp. 133–159.

Talley, W.K., 2018, Second ed. Port Economics. Routledge, Abingdon, UK.

Talley, W.K., 2012a. Maritime carriers in theory. In: Talley, W.K. (Ed.), The Blackwell Companion to Maritime Economics. Wiley-Blackwell Publishing, Oxford, UK, pp. 89–106.

Talley, W.K., 2012b. Ports in theory. In: Talley, W.K. (Ed.), The Blackwell Companion to Maritime Economics. Wiley-Blackwell Publishing, Oxford, UK, pp. 473–490.

Talley, W.K., 2014. Maritime transport chains: carrier, port and shipper choice effects. International Journal of Production Economics 151, 174–179.

Talley, W.K., 2017. Maritime Economics: Critical Concepts in Economics. Vols. 1 and 2—Shipping Economics, Vols. 3 and 4—Port Economics. Routledge, Abingdon, UK.

Talley, W.K., Ng, M., 2013. Maritime transport chain choice by carriers, ports and shippers. International Journal of Production Economics 142, 311–316.

Talley, W.K., Ng, M., 2016a. Port multi-service congestion. Transportation Research Part E 94, 66–70.

Talley, W.K., Ng, M., 2016b. Port economic cost functions: a service perspective. Transportation Research Part E 88, 1–10.

Talley, W.K., Ng, M., 2017. Hinterland transport chains: determinant effects on chain choice. International Journal of Production Economics 185, 175–179.

Talley, W.K., Ng, M., Marsillac, E., 2014. Port service chains and port performance evaluation. Transportation Research Part E 69, 236–247.

Tirwchwell, P., 1997. NOL-APL: what now? Journal of Commerce, April 15, 1A, 4B.

Tirwchwell, P., 2015. The mega-ship malaise. Journal of Commerce, 86, June 15.

Wastler, A.R., 1997. Alliances: not so grand? Journal of Commerce, April 16, 3B.

Zarocostas, J., 1996. Port industry jobs worldwide continue to decline, study says. Journal of Commerce, May 12, 8B.

Further Reading

Lakshmi, A., 2016. UNCTAD: Seaborne Shipments Reach Record. MarineLink, December 18, p. 1.

Mongelluzzo, B., 2014. Will alliances measure up? Journal of Commerce, 36–37, March 15.

Peoples, J., Talley, W.K., 2004. Owner-operator truck driver earnings and employment: port cities and deregulation. Peoples, J., Talley, W.K. (Eds.), Transportation Labor Issues and Regulatory Reform: Research in Transportation Economics, 10, Elsevier, Amsterdam, pp. 191–213.

Staff, 2006. From a vision to a revolution. Journal of Commerce, April 17, 6A–7A.

Talley, W.K., Russell-Riggs, S., 2018. Trade logistics and seaborne transportation. Blonigen, B., Wilson, W. (Eds.), Handbook of International Trade and TransportationEdward Elgar, Cheltenham, UK.

United States International Trade Commission, 2016. Economic impact of trade agreements implemented under trade authorities procedures, 2016 report. Government Printing Office, Washington, DC.

Evolution of transportation policy and economics

B. Starr McMullen
Oregon State University, Corvallis, OR, United States

Chapter Outline

Dedication

As a new graduate student at U.C. Berkeley in 1973, I found that I was woefully underprepared for graduate theory courses in Economics (not to mention one of the handful of women in the Department at that time.) It took me the entire first year to get up to speed, and a lot of intense work resulted in my receiving the top qualifying exam grade in Macroeonomics and one of the highest scores on the Micro exam. The powers that be decided that there must be something wrong with the qualifying exam as the students who had achieved high course grades did not do well (and I did?). Their "solution" was for me to retake the micro theory classes and increase my course grades to continue in the program before continuing. Ted Keeler was the first Micro instructor I encountered in the retake process and, after the first exam he asked why I was taking this course as I obviously had mastered the material. He negotiated a deal for me in which I would take the Industrial Organization sequence, including the qualifying exam in place of the repeat of the micro series (and thus not fall a year behind in my studies). I gladly accepted the offer, did well and decided rather than pursuing Macroeonomics, I really liked applied Micro. Ted suggested I apply for a Sloan Foundation Fellowship for research in transportation economics, which I received and became part of the interdisciplinary Sloan Transportation seminar at Berkeley that was led by Professors Ted Keeler and Daniel McFadden. This was a career changer for me. He essentially took the time and effort to help me out and encourage me in a direction that became the direction of my professional career.

Through the Sloan seminar I met and sustained lifelong professional ties with many transportation economists who were students or former students of Ted Keeler: Ken Small, Randy Pozdena, Steve Morrison, Cliff Winston, and John Bitzan to name a few. I have served the profession as president of both the Transportation and Public Utilities Group (TPUG) of the American Economic Association and the Transportation Research Forum (TRF). I have been the administrator of the

Transportation Policy and Economic Regulation. http://dx.doi.org/10.1016/B978-0-12-812620-2.00008-0

Joyce and Bill Furman Fellowships in Transportation Economics at Oregon State University and have followed Ted's example by teaching and encouraging students to study transportation economics and many have, as a result, become transportation professionals.

My entire professional career has been devoted to research (and teaching!) on various aspects of transportation: trucks, trains, boats, and planes—as Ted would say. First my research was directed towards predicting and then assessing the impacts of regulatory reform and deregulation on the transportation industries, especially in regard to costs, productivity, and competitive behavior. My interests later turned to more practical pricing and finance questions facing policymakers. In particular, questions surrounding infrastructure finance and learning to work with an interdisciplinary group of transportation researchers. Ted Keeler was a great influence on my choice of research topics as both of us have had a great interest not necessarily just in the development of theoretical concepts but also in applying economics to the immediate problems confronting society.

8.1   Introduction

The role of economics and economists in transportation has evolved as the transportation system first developed and then matured. This natural progression has changed the questions and issues that transportation economists are asked to address.

During most of the 20th century the major transportation industries (e.g., rail, trucking, and airlines) operated under the authority of governmental regulatory bodies (the Interstate Commerce Commission and the Civil Aeronautics Board). Regulatory authorities were required to make decisions regarding industry exit and entry, entry and exit to and from routes, and rate setting. Since the stated objective of regulators was to provide financially healthy industries while promoting competitiveness, economists were extensively consulted and employed by regulatory agencies as well as the regulated industries, to provide analyses supporting policy decisions.

Between the 1930's and regulatory reform and deregulation in the late 1970's and early 1980's (the Airline Deregulation Act of 1978, the Staggers Act of 1980, and the Motor Carrier Act of 1980), economists played an active role in policy. By the late 1970's the railroad industry was facing problems of deteriorating rail infrastructure and financial losses while at the same time the trucking industry, which used the highway system, was making what most economists considered to be excess profits.

Academic economists started questioning the need for government intervention in some transportation markets (especially air and motor carriage) by studying industry structure, industry competitiveness, and efficiency using advancing economic theory and econometric techniques. Much of this work followed in the path of the seminal study by Friedlander and Spady (1981) that simulated what would happen to rail and motor carrier prices, rates, and profits if first-best marginal cost pricing were to be implemented rather than the rates that prevailed under regulation. Douglas and Miller (1974) provided major policy information regarding these issues for the airline industry. Economists studied what would happen to prices, profits, and overall welfare in previously regulated transportation industries in a competitive market environment.

Data reporting required by regulatory agencies provided economists with the means to study pricing and industry structure empirically. Both the post-World War II refinement of economic concepts and statistical tools (Winston et al., 1990) and advances in computer technology facilitated research. Computing power allowed more complex statistical analysis and advanced real time data collection technologies created an explosion of data available for research using advanced econometric techniques. In 1960–80's provided some of the most extensive studies of transportation industries by economists and most observers agreed that it was one of the few empirical examples of economic research culminating in policy. The Airline Deregulation Act of 1978, the Motor Carrier Act of 1980, and the Staggers Rail Act of 1980 were major pieces of regulatory reform/deregulation that relied largely on evidence provided by economists.

Ted Keeler and his students played a major role in predicting the impacts of regulation and subsequent deregulation/regulatory reform on previously regulated transportation industries (Dorman, 1983; Harris and Winston, 1983; Keeler, 1972, 1983). Once these industries became deregulated another spate of studies concentrated on estimating the actual impacts of regulatory change and comparing them to what had been predicted (McMullen and Lee, 1999; McMullen and Stanley, 1988; Morrison and Winston, 1986, 1995; Winston et al., 1990; Ying and Keeler, 1991). Indeed, this was one of the few times that economists came close to having a controlled experiment observing the same industry in both regulated and fairly competitive market environments. Pre and postregulatory costs, rates, and productivity were examined and conclusion drawn—many of which are included in other chapters in this book.

The transition to the more competitive environment was more difficult for some carriers than for others. In most cases the need for studies of competitiveness lessened—although there was still involvement of economists in examining pricing and possible anticompetitive behavior in monopoly rail routes and in some cases on air routes. However, deregulation also led to a considerable reduction in data reporting requirements and the lack of available firm level data made industry level research more difficult. Policymakers came to rely less on economists as market forces determined outcomes and thus there was less need for economists to weigh in on these matters. What remains in this line of research on the transportation industries and competitiveness—the major thrust of 20th century economic research—is to examine the impact of proposed mergers and pricing agreements on competitiveness in airlines, motor carriage, and railroads. Much of the policy on this is conducted by the US Department of Justice now rather than by regulatory authorities.

In the meanwhile, the focus of economists and policymakers shifted from studying the transportation industries themselves, to issues regarding the transportation infrastructure. Railroads had been experiencing financial difficulties maintaining their infrastructure in the post-World War II era in which highway transportation thrived, a factor which played a role in rail's movement towards regulatory reform. The highway infrastructure was relatively newer and the Interstate Highway System was not even completed until the early 1990s. However, by the 1990s, it had become apparent that the interstate highway system itself had not been engineered for either the larger than expected increases in vehicle miles traveled (VMT) or truck configurations that were heavier and did more damage to the roads and bridges than originally predicted when the system was designed. Thus, roads and highways deteriorated faster than expected resulting in a system that had not only reached capacity in many places, but was increasingly in desperate need of maintenance and repair.

Revenues produced by state and national gas taxes traditionally provided a major funding source for roadways. The Highway Revenue Act of 1956 created the Highway Trust Fund (HTF) into which most of the revenues from Federal highway user fees were to be deposited to be used for highway expenditures. The Surface Transportation Assistance Act of 1982, which increased the gas tax also created the mass transit account within the HTF specifically dedicated to expenditures on mass transit. The HTF has stopped growing as rapidly as VMT as the vehicle fleet has incorporated more and more fuel-efficient vehicles. Projections are for continued decline and shortfalls in the HTF in the future. This declining revenue source has led state and federal departments of transportations (DOTs) to seek alternative funding sources including user fees, taking on debt to pay for road maintenance and construction, reallocating revenues from property taxes, sales taxes, bond finance, and so on (Kile, 2011; Wachs, 2003).

The combination of increases in VMT (and thus road damage) accompanied by declining HTF revenues led to the formation of the National Surface Transportation Infrastructure Finance Committee (NSTIFC), a bipartisan committee formed by Congress to study the problem. The Committee issued a final report in February 2009 that encouraged adoption of a user fee structure in which road users bear a larger portion of the full costs of the infrastructure they demand—including congestion, pollution, and other indirect impacts. The committee recommendations included removing barriers that prevented tolling and most critical was the need for a commitment to a more direct user fee based on VMT. This was seen as a major factor towards providing a sustainable financing system for highway infrastructure in the long-term.

At the same time that highway infrastructure was experiencing financial difficulties, policymakers were trying to design policy with multiple additional goals in mind, including providing access to economic opportunities for residents, promoting economic development, relieving congestion, and reducing pollution. It became increasingly clear that most of these goals require formulation of policy to deal with a national transportation system rather than standalone modes. Thus, policymakers now are facing a different question: how to decide where in the system to assign scarce resources so as to maximize the social benefit from the system. This requires some form of national multimodal decision-making—something that has been discussed and acknowledged in theory, but has yet to be fully operationalized. While multimodal investment decisions are often made in passenger transit, this is a new question for freight transportation—a mode that relies heavily on highway infrastructure.

Given the infrastructure and finance systems in the United States, promotion of an efficient, effective national transportation system is a particularly challenging task. Pricing implicit in the current system of fuel taxes plus an assortment of other taxes and fees used for road finance, is not optimal and has encouraged overuse of the highway system. The response, especially in regard to urban areas is to subsidize large investments in alternatives to the private auto (e.g., light rail, commuter rail, bus, bike lanes, etc.) However as long as highway users do not pay appropriate user fees, these massive subsidies to nonauto modes are not likely to achieve desired results of reducing vehicular traffic and congestion, and relieving stress on highway infrastructure. Thus, dealing with the long-term problems facing the mature US transportation system in the most efficient way possible will require pricing policy that better aligns user fees with user costs.

This chapter provides an introduction to some of the issues facing economists and policymakers regarding infrastructure and pricing for an efficient transportation system. The focus here will be on highway infrastructure, finance and pricing in particular. After providing a background of the problems facing highway finance, some research on highway pricing policy—a VMT tax in particular—is reviewed. Since roads and highways are an important component of passenger transportation, a section on transit research as it relates to pricing, and subsidies under current policy is included, followed by a short section on issues encountered when trying to make multimodal investment decisions for freight.

8.2   Highway infrastructure finance

The financial crisis for highways is the result of multiple factors. One, as mentioned previously, is the fact that driving simply has increased faster than expected and roads were not engineered to handle the traffic that they now face. This is an example of where past policy helped create the current transportation system in a way in which it may not have developed without government intervention and promotion. Indeed, the railroads have long argued that they were placed at a competitive disadvantage even under regulation because they had to price so as to cover the fixed (private) costs of their infrastructure whereas motor carriers had roads publicly provided and the user fees they do pay are variable costs rather than total costs. The result is that roads have not been optimally priced and since the price of driving has been kept below cost, users of the highway system drive more than they would have otherwise. The larger than expected VMT on highways is one consequence of underpricing the roads. Since damage to the roads is directly related to VMT, the result is that roads and highways have deteriorated faster, increasing maintenance, and repair costs. This is of particular concern in regard to heavy trucks as the damage done to the road surface increases exponentially with axle weights over 18,000 pounds and truck traffic growth has exceeded expectations (Merriss and Krukar, 1982).

Maintenance and repair costs gone up due to increases in VMT but also due to increases in the overall price level that have helped drive costs up over time. This places stress on the financing of roads as highway fuel taxes are set at a fixed amount per gallon (at both state and federal levels) and these rates change infrequently and do not keep pace with inflation.

Another factor adding to financial stress has been is the increasing disassociation between road use and fuel consumption. When fuel taxes were originally implemented, most automobiles had similar fuel economy so that they all paid approximately the same user fee per mile of driving. Recent trends in fuel efficiency and alternative fuel vehicles (promoted by other government policies such as CAFÉ standards, designed to reduce dependence on fossil fuels and emissions) have led to a reduction in the tax revenues collected per mile traveled. Perversely, the reduced operating costs per mile to drivers from more fuel-efficient vehicles can cause a rebound effect, increasing miles driven and the associated damage to roads, furthering weakening the link between fossil fuel taxes and VMT (Small and Dender, 2007). Because road damage from hybrid and electric vehicles is similar to that of fossil fuel vehicles, the gas tax no longer provides a user fee mechanism closely associated with the costs that users impose on the road. Specifically, more fuel-efficient vehicles are driving more, increasing damage to roads, and contributing to congestion expenses and other externalities, while paying *less* in user fees per mile since the fuel tax is charged per gallon of fuel. Thus, achieving the goals of energy independence and reduction in the use of petroleum products are being reached, but at the expense of contributing to financial stress for infrastructure.

A final factor considered here is the reduction in the share of HTF funds that are dedicated to highways as up to 25% of HTF expenditures are made for nonhighway purposes—the largest being the diversion of funds from highways to the Mass Transit Account and other nonhighway uses such as bike lanes and alternative transportation (Poole, 2010). The basic rationale for these diversions from the HTF has been made using the argument that development of alternative transportation modes will help ease traffic on roads in urban areas, thus reducing congestion and resultant decreases in traffic will reduce wear and tear on the road system (Litman, 2013). This result depends on considerable diversion of traffic from automobiles to public transit.

Pucher and Renne, (2003) examine the pattern of urban mode choice over time and find that despite the massive investment in public transit, the auto's share of daily, local travel rose from 81.8% of trips in 1969 to 86.4% in 2001, while public transit's share fell from 3.2% to 1.6% over the same period. Thus, despite massive subsidization and investment in public transit, the desired goal of diverting significant amounts of traffic from roads has not taken place. Indeed, Knutson (2009) examines road quality in states and finds that those states with the largest diversions of funds from user fee accounts to nonhighway purposes appear to have lower quality roads.

A major reason for the dominance of autos over public transit is continued underpricing the cost of driving, which encourages overuse of roads and highways. Continuing to increase investment in public transit to try and "even the playing field" just increases financial stress on infrastructure finance without getting desired results in terms of reducing VMT, emissions, congestion, and so on. Indeed, nonprice policies such as providing subsidies to continue to invest in public transportation will not likely succeed without movement towards optimal pricing of roads.

Thus, the NSTIFC (2009) suggestion of a VMT tax as policy tool to help provide sustainable funding could also be a first step in the direction of making public transit a more attractive alternative to driving.

Thus, economists have a major role to play in the formulation of comprehensive transportation infrastructure policy—starting with road pricing. Since the damage done to the road is based on usage, a VMT fee is a great example of the economic concept of user fees put into practice. Further, economists have argued that a VMT tax would be considerably more efficient in helping reduce emissions than a tax on fuel, even though it falls short of a true externality tax (Parry and Small, 2005; West, 2005).

Replacement of a fuel tax by an alternative funding mechanism such as the VMT has been an issue discussed at great length by policymakers at both state and Federal levels. Although most of the conversation has centered on the VMT tax for passenger vehicles, the basic concept has long been discussed for heavy vehicles. As far as heavy vehicles (those over 26,000 pounds) are concerned, the damage to the road goes up exponentially with the weight, even more specifically with equivalent single axle loads (ESALs). While fuel consumption goes up with weight, it does not go up nearly as much as the damage that increased truck weights inflict on the road. Recognizing this, Oregon has had a weight-distance tax on heavy vehicles since 1948 and now has an ESAL weight based schedule based on the cost of different truck configurations and weights impose on the road. The advantage of such a user fee system is that it provides a price mechanism where users can lower the price they pay per mile by adopting truck configurations with lower total ESALs that cause less damage to the road (Merriss and Krukar, 1982).

Small et al. (1989) provided the first in depth empirical analysis of optimal road pricing, showing how marginal cost pricing for heavy vehicles using ESAL based loads could not only encourage less damaging truck configurations, but if used along with in an optimizing investment model, could result in lower user fees in the long run and improve overall social welfare. They illustrated how alternative second best solutions such as optimal investment without optimal pricing of highways, or optimal pricing with current investment, could also result in significant social welfare increases. In fact, they show that simply by increasing weight limits for truck configurations that had 5 or 6 axles (less damaging configurations for the road) thus increasing their loads and diverting loads from more damaging truck configurations, would achieve about 88% of the social welfare gain achieved by optimal pricing and investment.

As it stands now, Oregon is the only state with an ESAL weight-mile tax for heavy vehicles although three others have some form of a weight-mile tax for heavy vehicles (New York, Kentucky, and New Mexico). In the late 1980s eleven states had some form of a heavy vehicle weight-mile tax, but all the others have been repealed after considerable pressure by the American Trucking Association. The (NSTIFC, 2009) also recommended increasing user fees on heavy trucks due to the fact that they underpay their share of highway costs, but they were not as specific as the tax structures suggested by Merriss and Krukar (1982) or Small et al. (1989).

To date, much research by DOTs regarding a VMT tax has concentrated on non-economic factors such as developing technologies to collect the data and implement a VMT tax, or public opinion polls as to the political acceptance of a VMT tax. Part of the reason for this is the fact that most government DOTs employ engineers and planners as opposed to the regulatory authorities of the 20th century that employed economists and conducted economic research. In the past that was fine as there was not a problem with finance—the gasoline/diesel taxes brought enough revenue into the HTF to fund expenditures and DOTs spent most of their time designing and building roads and bridges. It was an obvious choice—no one would (or should!) ask an economist to design a bridge or build a rail line.

Given the current problems with infrastructure finance, many of the issues that need to be addressed are more in the realm of social science and economics in particular. Some of these topics are addressed next in a review of the work economists have done regarding the expected impact of a VMT tax replacing a fuel tax. In many ways this exercise can be thought of as analogous to the transportation research that took place in the 1970s that tried to predict the impact of deregulation.

8.3   Impacts of a VMT tax

Implementation of a highway user fee/tax that reflects the actual costs that users impose on the system is an important first step in creating a more efficient and effective transportation system. In almost every case involving pricing, however, issues are raised regarding the impact on people and households in lower income groups. Accordingly, the most common issues regarding a VMT include the concern that a VMT will be regressive—imposing a higher cost of those in low income groups—and also that such a tax would impose higher costs on those in rural communities versus urban areas (McMullen et al., 2010).

The CBO (1990) has claimed that a VMT tax would be somewhat regressive in a way similar to the regressivity of gasoline taxes. The exact impact on those in lower income groups will depend on the distribution of the fuel economy of the vehicles driven by those in lower income groups. If, as West (2005) finds, those in lower income groups drive older, less fuel-efficient vehicles, an adverse impact may not be realized. There has also been concern expressed regarding the impact on rural versus urban households as those in rural areas often drive longer distances and have fewer alternatives to driving. Thus, the distribution of vehicles of different fuel economies amongst households in the groups where equity is a concern is an important factor in assessing the impact of a VMT tax.

Most analyses evaluate the impact of changing from a fuel tax to a revenue neutral VMT tax in place of a fuel tax by first considering the amount a household spends on the fuel tax and then determining the amount that the same household would pay if a vehicle mileage fee were imposed instead of the fuel tax. This follows the procedure used by the Congressional Budget Office (CBO) to evaluate the impact of changes in taxes. Research efforts that focus on the equity concerns include those done on Oregon (McMullen et al., 2010; Zhang et al., 2009), Nevada (Paz et al., 2014), Texas (Larsen et al., 2012), and the entire US (Weatherford, 2011). Interestingly, these studies show somewhat different results.

The data set used in all of these studies is the National Household Travel Survey (NHTS) for various years. DOT data collection has traditionally focused on size and weight data required to oversee truck size and weight limits. Increasingly GPS technologies have made it possible to collect vehicle specific data on trucks or vehicles that collect all sorts of data on location, speeds, and so on. Most of this data is available for urban areas and also for individual vehicles rather than firms or household units. Household level data must be collected via surveys which are much more costly, thus resulting in much smaller data sets. Further, the data collected in the household surveys is not always exactly what an economist would collect if they had designed the survey. NHTS data for individual states often consists of just a couple of hundred households. This is a result of the fact that the individuals designing these data collections are usually engineers and planners that need data for their simulation models as opposed to data that might be useful to economists for estimating elasticities of demand, cross-elasticities of demand between modes, and so on. That said, some states opt to add on their own state-specific questions to the NHTS survey and others have developed their own survey instruments, which are often more detailed, especially in regard to the location of households.

While some researchers follow the CBO (1990) and simply calculate the impact assuming that household driving behavior is unchanged by the tax change (the static model), most use a regression model (the dynamic model) to see how a change in the price per mile of driving (in addition to other determinants of driving behavior) impacts driving to determine the ultimate impact. Some even use a nested logit model to include vehicle choice decisions although most data sets are not rich enough to do this analysis (McMullen et al., 2010; Paz et al., 2014; Weatherford, 2011; Zhang et al., 2009). Although using a more complex model is preferred, McMullen et al. (2010) find that the resulting impact from the change in tax is virtually the same regardless of whether a static or dynamic model is used. Differences in the individual studies seem to arise from the data set used.

State-specific studies using NHTS data find slight increases in income regressivity when changing from a fuel tax to a VMT fee (Larsen et al., 2012; McMullen et al., 2010; Zhang et al., 2009) assuming a revenue neutral VMT replacement for the fuel tax. However, Weatherford (2011) used national data and found that a flat VMT fee would be slightly *less* regressive than a fuel tax. In most cases the change in annual taxes paid after switching to a VMT tax is found to be less than $20/year for higher income households who gain, and less than $10/year for lower income households that end up paying more under a VMT tax (McMullen et al., 2010). Interestingly, public criticism of a VMT tax has also centered on the fact that a flat, revenue neutral tax means that vehicles with higher than average fuel economy actually pay more whereas less efficient "gas guzzlers" pay less under a VMT tax. Accordingly, it has been suggested that a VMT tax structure be designed to charge higher per mile fees to vehicles with lower fuel economy. The impact of this graduated tax structure is to increase regressivity due to lower income households that own less fuel-efficient vehicles (McMullen et al., 2010; West, 2005). This is an example of conflicting goals where the intention to increase fuel efficiency and thus reduce dependence on fossil fuels and reduce emissions ends up placing a greater burden on those in lower income groups.

As far as the urban/rural impact of such a change in fee structure is concerned, McMullen et al. (2010) found that rural households benefit slightly from the change from a fuel tax to a flat VMT fee, a result largely attributable to the fact that rural households drive less fuel-efficient vehicles in Oregon. Paz et al. (2014) found that while a VMT fee would reduce VMT for both urban and rural households, rural households would end up paying slightly more due to the fact that they drive more miles than urban households (Paz et al., 2014). Using a nationwide data set Weatherford (2011) found that VMT fees shifted the tax burden from rural households to urban households.

The question of urban versus rural impacts from a change in road pricing policy remains an important topic of interest to policymakers. In particular, will a policy that works in one urban area to reduce VMT, for instance, work in others? McMullen and Eckstein (2013) use a standard regression techniques to examine the demand and determinants of VMT in a panel study using data from a cross section of 87 US urban areas over the period 1982–2009. The VMT data for urban areas was collected and published by the Texas Transportation Institute for use in their annual Urban Mobility Report (Texas Transportation Institute, 2011). Findings show determinants of driving, as measured by vehicle-miles per capita, differed across urban areas. In particular, urban areas with larger urban populations those located in the western part of the United States had higher per capita VMT than those in other regions of the country. Urban areas with higher transit ridership were found to have lower VMT per capita, a finding consistent across all model specifications and also with *a priori* expectations. This suggests that development of transit systems could play an important role in VMT reduction but more research is needed to be able to target transit investments towards places where there is the most potential for diversion from auto ridership if this is going to be most effective in reducing VMT. Their findings also suggest that the employment and the industry mix of an urban area may significantly impact VMT.

Ke and McMullen (2017) demonstrate how determinants of VMT can even vary across urban areas that are located in the same state (Oregon). They use a unique data set, the Oregon Household Activity Survey, which provided information on over 15,000 individual households (rather than less than 500 households in the NHTS Oregon sample) that provided exact location rather than the simple "Urban" or "Rural" designator for households in the NHTS. Their study also shows that VMT determinants can differ significantly between rural areas in the same state. Much of this has to do with geographic constraints (such as mountains, etc.) but there is also some evidence that social aspects, namely people's preferences, may influence behavior. For instance, in some Oregon communities owning a high fuel efficiency vehicle was associated with driving more (higher VMT) as predicted by the "rebound" effect. However, in the Portland area household driving a more efficient vehicle actually drove *less*—suggesting that households in that community may have different preferences. In one case it is the cost per mile of driving that is influencing the driving decision whereas is the other situation the household may place greater value on environmental aspects and thus select a more fuel-efficient vehicle and at the same time plan to drive less. Indeed, in some regions of the state the coefficient on price per mile was insignificant, indicating that it was not an important determinant of driving behavior.

Thus, it is important for policymakers to realize that a policy designed to affect VMT in one location might not succeed in another. Similarly, the economic impact from changing from a fuel tax to a VMT tax—which comes from the change in the price per mile of driving, may have little or no impact on driving behavior, depending on the location considered.

8.4   Transit investment and subsidies

Both federal and state governments have proposed reducing VMT to achieve policy objectives which include reduced congestion, reduced emissions, reduced dependence on fossil fuels, and so on. The Federal Surface Transportation Policy and Planning Act of 2009 set a directive to reduce national per capita VMT and to increase public transportation usage, intercity passenger rail services, and nonmotorized transportation. These goals are not new and, indeed, have been the goal of Federal policies ever since the Mass Transportation Act of 1964 first provided capital subsidies for investment in mass transit (first providing about 2/3 of the cost and later increasing the federal contribution to 80% of the cost of new projects) in the hope that it would divert traffic from autos to mass transit and create a more balanced transportation system.

Further, there are incentives in transit investment finance through matching funds, encouraging overinvestment in transit with the result that further subsidies are required to operate transit systems. Indeed, Pucher et al. (1983) found that as government subsidies of transit increased, the cost of producing urban transit increased as well. In fact, despite substantial investment in transit, especially rail, transit supply as measured by vehicle-miles increased by 35% between 1984 and 2006 whereas unlinked passenger trips increased by only 13.5% and the share of operating fares covered by fare revenue decrease from 39% in 1996 to 33% in 2006 (Guiliano, 2011).

Pucher and Renne, (2003) show that while much of the dollar value of investment in public transit that has been in rail systems, benefits those in higher income groups rather than those in lower income groups. Indeed, they argue that investments that promote walking may actually help the mobility of people in lower income groups—and could probably do so at a lower cost.

The idea that monies allocated to public transit could be spent more efficiently to produce desired goals of mobility, is not new. In particular, it has been argued that actually higher quality service in terms of service frequency, flexibility, and accessibility could be provided by a high speed bus system rather than investment in rail systems in urban areas—and at much lower cost (Henscher and Golub, 2008; Tirachini et al., 2010). Researchers also find that transit systems and modes run by private rather than public agencies can provide service at lower cost (McMullen and Noh, 2007; Pucher et al., 1983; Sava, 2002).

The net result is an economically inefficient outcome. What policymakers should be asking is where funds can be allocated to best achieve goals of mobility, and so on in the most efficient, lower social cost way possible.

Guiliano (2011) argues that as long as vehicles on roads are not required to pay the full cost of using the roads, funds directed into public transit and subsidies devoted to transit will not succeed in diverting traffic from roads. Parry and Small (2005) put the welfare gains from an optimized uniform toll on auto mileage in the United States at around $40 billion per year; welfare gains from differentiating the toll by region and time of day would be larger still. Such gains are on an entirely different scale from those achievable by merely reforming transit prices. Thus, policy toward transit could be formulated most effectively within a framework that explicitly incorporates revenue needs and the existence of other distorting taxes, especially highway taxes and pricing. Thus, to help transit, it is important for policymakers to formulate a long-term transportation plan that recognized the interdependence of pricing different modes.

8.5   Multimodal investment decision-making for freight

In times of tight budgets and trust funds that are running short of paying for maintenance of existing infrastructure, it is becoming increasingly apparent that investment decisions in transportation infrastructure need to be made in a way that best optimizes system efficiency. This differs somewhat from the current paradigm where investment decision-making is usually made by each mode separately (highway, rail, water. etc.) Some of the reason for this is due to funding sources that are mode-specific and cannot be used for other purposes.

However, when funds are fungible, it becomes incumbent on policymakers to examine system-wide impacts of potential transportation investments and develop ways to make "apple-to-apple" comparisons that will best optimize system efficiency and social welfare.

At the same time there is increased recognition of the externalities produced in the transportation sector—especially congestion and emissions (GHG) that need to be taken into consideration along with the explicit costs that have long been part of the planning process. One of the biggest problems inherent in such multimodal investment comparisons is how to account for differences in the energy/GHG "footprint" of alternative investments and the projection of the impact on congestion and thus traffic flows, travel time and the value of time.

To date, most analyses of the impact of highway infrastructure improvements on state transportation system performance have focused on the impact on passenger traffic or the total vehicle count. This is particularly true when it comes to the consideration of infrastructure improvements on congestion and time reliability. In assessing the value of reliability—or an increase in reliability—on freight transport, it becomes apparent that the matter is much more complicated than for passenger travel.

For passenger travel, the total value of a trip is calculated as the value to the driver and any passengers on board. The value to these occupants of the change in reliability is generally accepted to be their value of time multiplied by the change in transit time. There are debates about the appropriate value of time to use (i.e., is it the average hourly wage rate in the area—or should it be half of that for transit time, etc.), and whether the relationship between a reduction in reliability and social value is linear, but it is clear that these issues pertain to the occupants of the vehicle and thus are directly related to its operation.

Some have interpreted the valuation of time for freight transportation in a parallel fashion by valuing time using the hourly wage of the truck driver. However, wage reveals only part of the real value of time in a freight operation. Freight transport typically involves a shipper and a carrier (trucking firm). The value placed on a reduction in travel time differs considerably across shippers of different product, distance of the point-to-point shipment, transport mode, and so on. Shippers make their choice of transport mode based on a combination of service price and also service quality (of which travel time and reliability are but one component.) Carriers often change travel times and/or a route's offered capacity in response to factors that impact their costs, namely changes in time and reliability.

Thus, driver time cost savings can only be used as a lower bound for the value to freight transportation that derives from any increase in reliability/time savings due to a highway improvement. Alstadt and Weisbrod (2008) mention several specific reasons why the valuation of freight transportation travel time savings has been underestimated in the past:

1. Costs to carriers of transportation extend beyond the driver's wages, for example, wages of dock workers and other support costs.
2. Because shipments have an opportunity cost, benefits to the shipping firms from freight time reduction are not considered.
3. Logistical reorganization for shippers, such as the reduction in warehousing costs due to faster and more reliable networks, are ignored.

Methods for estimating modal shifts need to be improved to reflect actual shipper behavior. In almost every methodology currently being used by states to compare infrastructure investment alternatives between rail and highway choices, it is assumed that all new nonhighway capacity (usually rail) will result in an equal diversion of traffic from highway. Since all the congestion time saving and emissions reduction figures depend on the diversion of highway traffic to rail (or nonhighway mode) and the values used for diversion are the largest possible, these methodologies all result in *overestimation* of benefits/value of investment in nonhighway modes.

For instance the "benefits" of alternatives to highway transportation for freight are often calculated by estimating the potential new capacity of the alternative mode investment (say rail) and assuming that this is the amount of freight traffic that will be diverted from highways. This "estimate" is then used to calculate benefits for both GHG reductions. The studies themselves go into great depth explaining how they value time and place a value/quantity on emissions per mile; however they never seem to realize that the basic assumption—that all new capacity will divert an equal amount of traffic from roads—is faulty.

There is a real need to get realistic estimates of the mode shift potential from investment in these highway alternative modes. Even though rail is "greener", it is a misallocation of resources to invest in it if it does not actually produce enough net benefits to justify investing there instead of in a highway improvement.

This idea of investment for system-wide efficiency is something that needs to be explored more thoroughly—if only to make planners aware of the fact that their current methodologies are grossly overestimating benefits for highway alternative investment due to overestimation of mode-shifting.

8.6 Conclusions: the role of the economist

There is no shortage of topics for transportation economists in the postregulatory environment of the 21st century. The conceptual frameworks and theoretical and econometric tools continue to develop along with computer capacity and complexity of transportation systems. As Winston (1985) so aptly documented, the field of economics has an extensive repertoire of tools to apply to topics in transportation economics.

As our modern systems depend more and more on small, quick shipments, highway freight transportation will continue to be an important part of our national freight transportation network. Simply building more rail or improving waterway transportation—two modes that cause fewer GHG emissions—will not be enough to meet GHG reduction goals as the reality is that shippers will not divert enough traffic from highway to these alternate modes to make much of a difference. Economists, by studying freight behavior and distribution systems, can continue to explore mode choice and guide policymakers into those investments that are most effective in achieving the desired goals.

Similarly, in urban transportation systems, policymakers need to make investment decisions that reflect mode choice decisions actually made by passengers rather than assuming that alternatives to the automobile will automatically reduce highway travel. As historical data show, the automobile share of urban local traffic has grown while the transit share has fallen, despite large investments in public transport infrastructure. This is not to say that investment in public transport is useless, only that policymakers have to examine where such investment will yield the best results and act accordingly—even if such investment is in highway improvements/maintenance.

In all cases, most economists will agree that the first step towards creating a more efficient and effective transportation system is to get user fees and prices charged for the use of transportation systems in line with the costs that users impose on the system. The place to start is obviously in the realm of highway pricing. Since highway user fees have historically failed to recoup the costs that users impose on the system, the highway system is overused and this is one reason the current structure of user fees is not sufficient to maintain and improve the system. The fact that highway transport has essentially been subsidized by charging lower than optimal user fees—the current US gasoline tax is estimated to be about half of the optimal road tax (Parry and Small, 2005)—has also led to distortions in the pricing and investment in other modes, especially public transit. The result is a transportation system that is in desperate financial straits.

As policymakers move towards pricing closer to optimal pricing through, for instance, implementation of a VMT tax for highway vehicles, they need to work with economists to select appropriate prices realizing the different economic behaviors across locations and differences between passenger and freight modes of transportation. Successful pricing policy will need to consider these behavioral differences—which are the realm of economics and economists.

References

Alstadt, B.B., Weisbrod, G.E., 2008. A generalized approach for assessing the direct user impacts of multimodal transport projects. In: Presented at the Transportation Research Board.

Dorman, G.J., 1983. A model of unregulated airline markets considering schedule delay, frequency and stochastic delay. Res. Transp. Econ. 1, 131–140.

Douglas, G., Miller, III, R., 1974. Economic Regulation of Domestic Air Transport: Theory and Practice. The Brookings Institution.

Friedlander, A., Spady, R., 1981. Freight Transport Regulation: Equity, Efficiency and Competition in the Rail and Trucking Industries. MIT Press.

Guiliano, G., 2011. Transportation Policy: Public Transit, Settlement Patterns, And Equity in the United States. The Oxford Handbook of Urban Economics and Planning, (Online September 2012).

Harris, R.G., Winston, C., 1983. Potential benefits of rail mergers: an econometric analysis of network effects on service quality. Rev. Econ. Stat. 65 (1), 32–40.

Henscher, D.A., Golub, T., 2008. Bus rapid transit systems: a comparative assessment. Transportation 35 (4), 501–518.

Ke, Y., McMullen, B.S., 2017. Regional differences in the determinants of Oregon VMT. Res. Transp. Econ. 62, 2–10, Available online March 22, 2017..

Keeler, T., 1972. Airline regulation and market performance. Bell J. Econ. 3, 399–424.

Keeler, T.E., 1983. Railroads, Freight, and Public Policy. The Brookings Institution.

Kile, J., 2011. The Highway Trust Fund and Paying for highways. Testimony for Congressional Budget Office (CBO).

Knutson, R., 2009. Highway Finance and Impacts on Road Quality (unpublished Master's thesis in economics). Oregon State University.

Larsen, L., Burris, M., Pearson, D., Ellis, P., 2012. Equity evaluation of fees for vehicle miles travelled in Texas. Transportation Research Record: Journal of the Transportation Research Board, No. 2297. Transportation Research Board of the National Academies, Washington, D.C. pp. 11–20.

Litman, T., 2013. Whose Roads: Evaluating Bicyclists' and Pedestrians' Right to Use Public Roadways. Victoria Transport Policy Institute.

McMullen, B.S., Stanley, L., 1988. The impact of deregulation on the production structure of the motor carrier industry. Econ. Inquiry 26, 299–316.

McMullen, B.S., Lee, M.-K., 1999. Cost efficiency in the U.S. motor carrier industry before and after deregulation: a stochastic frontier approach. J. Transp. Econ. Policy 33 (Part 3), 303–318.

McMullen, B.S., Zhang, Lei, Nakahara, Kyle, 2010. Distributional distributional impacts of changing from a gasoline tax to a vehicle-mile tax for light vehicles: a case study of Oregon. Transp. Policy 17 (6), 359–366.

McMullen, B.S., Eckstein, N., 2013. Determinants of VMT in urban areas: a panel study of 87 US urban areas 1982–2009. J. Transp. Res. Forum 52 (3), 5–24, Fall.

McMullen, B.S., Noh, D., 2007. Accounting for emissions in the measurement of transit agency efficiency: a directional distance function approach. Trans. Res. Part D Transp. Environ. 12 (1), 1–9.

Merriss, J., Krukar, M., 1982. A proposal for an axle weight-distance road user charge. Transp. Res. Forum Proc. 23 (1), 405–411.

Morrison, S.A., Winston, C., 1986. The Economic Effects of Airline Deregulation. The Brookings Institution.

Morrison, S.A., Winston, C., 1995. The Evolution of the Airline Industry. The Brookings Institution.

National Surface Transportation Infrastructure Financing Commission (NSTIFC), 2009. Paying Our Way: A New Framework for Transportation Finance Final Report.

Parry, I.W.H., Small, K., 2005. Does Britain or the United States have the right gasoline tax? Am. Econ. Rev. 95 (4), 1276–1289.

Paz, A., Nordland, A., Veeramisti, N., Khan, A., Sanchez-Medina, J., 2014. Assessment of economic impacts of vehicle miles travelled fee for passenger vehicles in Nevada. Transportation Research Record: Journal of the Transportation Research Board, No. 2450. Transportation Research Board of the National Academies, Washington, D.C. pp. 26–35.

Poole, Robert, 2010. Federal Dollars for Federal Roads. The Washington Times.

Pucher, J., Renne, J.L., 2003. Socioeconomics of urban travel: evidence from the 2001 NHTS. Transp. Q. 57 (3), 49–77, Summer.

Sava, E.S., 2002. Competitive Contracting of Bus Service: A Better Deal for Riders and Taxpayers. Manhattan Institute for Policy Research, No. 30.

Small, K., Dender, V., 2007. Fuel efficiency and motor vehicle travel: the declining rebound effect. Energy J. 28 (1), 25–51.

Small, K.A., Winston, C., Evans, C.A., 1989. Road Work: A New Highway Pricing & Investment Policy. Brookings Institution.

Texas Transportation Institute, 2011. 2010 Annual Urban Mobility Report. http://mobility.tamu.edu/ums/.

Tirachini, A.D., Henscher, D.A., Jara-Diaz, S.R., 2010. Comparing operator and users costs of light rail, heavy rail and bus rapid transit over a radial public transport network. Res. Transp. Econ. 29 (1), 239–242.

US Congressional Budget Office (CBO), 1990. Federal taxation of tobacco, alcoholic beverages, and motor fuels: a CBO study. Washington, D.C.

Wachs, M., 2003. Improving Efficiency and Equity in Transportation Finance. The Brookings Institute.

Weatherford, B., 2011. Distributional implications of replacing the federal fuel tax with per mile user charges. Transportation Research Record: Journal of the Transportation Research Board, No. 2221. Transportation Research Board of the National Academies, Washington, D.C. pp. 19–26.

West, S., 2005. Equity implications of vehicle emissions taxes. J. Transp. Econ. Policy 39 (1), 1–24.

Winston, C., 1985. Conceptual developments in the economics of transportation: an interpretive survey. J. Econ. Lit. 23, 57–94.

Winston, C., Corsi, T.M., Grimm, C.M., Evans, C.A., 1990. The Economic Effects of Surface Freight Deregulation. The Brookings Institution.

Ying, J.S., Keeler, T.E., 1991. Pricing in a deregulated environment: the motor carrier experience. RAND J. Econ. 22 (2), 264–273, Summer.

Zhang, L., McMullen, B.S., Valluri, D., Vehicle, K., 2009. Mileage fee on income and spatial equity. Transportation Research Record: Journal of the Transportation Research Board, No. 2115. Transportation Research Board of the National Academies, Washington, D.C. pp. 110–118.

Further Reading

Kastrouni, E., Gkritza, K., Hallmark, S.L., 2013. Equity evaluation of fuel tax per gallon and VMT Fee. In: Transportation Research Board Annual Meeting.

Stedt, Pucher J.M., Hirshman, I., 1983. The impact of subsidies on the cost of urban transport. J. Transp. Econ. Policy.

Competing with the private sector: the welfare-maximizing response

Philip A. Viton
The Ohio State University, Columbus OH USA

Chapter Outline

I am grateful to an anonymous reviewer for catching a serious error in the initial version of this paper, as well as for valuable expository suggestions.

Dedication

Ted Keeler's blending of theoretical and empirical rigor has been a major influence on my own work. I first met him in the regulation part of the I–O sequence at Berkeley, where he astonished me one evening by apologizing for having to schedule an exam when the SF Symphony was playing Bruckner in town. But of course it was his invitation to join the Transportation Cost Study that determined the long-term course of my research. It was there that I first formulated a model of

Transportation Policy and Economic Regulation. http://dx.doi.org/10.1016/B978-0-12-812620-2.00009-2

bus-mode optimization, and the fact (as Ted gently pointed out) that it had already been done—and done much better—by Mohring didn't shake the realization that I had it in me to do original research. Participation in this study and having Ted as my thesis advisor were the formative events of my graduate studies. I know that Ted's interests have since shifted to health economics (see, e.g. Keeler et al., 1996) but I offer the present study, hearkening back to his early work, as a token of my admiration and gratitude.

9.1   Introduction

The Post Office competes with Federal Express; municipal power providers compete with private electric and gas suppliers; state-maintained secondary schools and universities compete for students with their private counterparts. In the transportation sector, we see that private transit can compete successfully with publicly provided services (Morlok and Viton, 1980), and privately operated highways compete with government-maintained roads (Viton, 1995). The increasingly parlous state of public-sector budgets, coupled with taxpayer reluctance to fund large deficits, has led to policies actively encouraging the private sector to compete in what were previously thought of as public-sector responsibilities, and there is every indication that this will only become more widespread in the future.

When competition does occur, the public provider must decide how to respond. One strategy is to do nothing, but if an entrant captures a significant portion of the market, the public operation may be left with large costs, a reduced customer base, and the need to finance an unacceptably large deficit from general taxes. A second strategy is to exit the market altogether, effectively privatizing the service, but if the private provider exploits its resulting market power, this may lead to social-welfare losses even if it reduces public-sector deficits. A third is deterrence: the public provider may preemptively change its pricing and service levels in an attempt to deny a potential entrant any niche in the market. But this too may have welfare costs, especially if the private sector has efficiency advantages, or could produce a differentiated service valued by a segment of the community. And a fourth is to remain in the market and attempt to compete head-to-head with the entrant.

Given the range of possibilities, what *should* a public provider do? It seems clear that the community expects public providers to do more than simply maximize net revenues (profits) or minimize costs. It expects them to take a broader view of what constitutes public service, a view that considers their decisions' impacts on the broader community. These broader impacts lead to what will be termed the *optimal* public-provider response, in which it reacts to private competition by setting its prices and service levels to maximize community welfare conditional on the entrant's behavior. The optimal response is interesting in its own right, but it also provides a benchmark against which to evaluate other responses. We focus on the case of urban bus transit, a market in which entry is easy and competition between public and private sectors is often observed (see Morlok and Viton, 1980 for empirical case studies), but the model's

---

[1] That is, as the consequences of product differentiation. See Viton (1981) for an approach under different behavioral assumptions; however, the welfare implications are not there explored, as they are here.

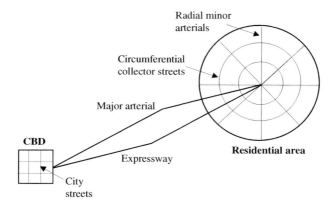

Figure 9.1 The transport corridor.

structure is applicable to any market in which consumers make discrete choices over alternatives that are described by prices and characteristics (levels of service). The model can be thought of as an attempt to ascertain the potential of competition to enhance community welfare. Alternatively, it can be viewed as an exploration of the consequences of introducing an innovative form of service—here, high cost high level of service—in transit.[1] At least in transit, such service need not be provided by a private entrant and indeed we observe instances (Morlok and Viton, 1980) where it is provided by the public agency itself in addition to its " standard" public transit offerings.[2]

9.2 The model

This section describes the model of private entry and public response as a system of Cournot–Nash competition by two transit providers in the presence of a competitive fringe (automobile travel).

9.2.1 Spatial setting

Consider a corridor connecting a circular residential area of radius r miles to a 1-mile-square downtown CBD (see Fig. 9.1). Within the residential area, minor arterials are laid out along the radii and collector streets circumferentially; in the CBD, city streets follow a grid pattern.[3] Two untolled L-mile roads, a major arterial and a limited-access expressway, connect the center of the residential area and the edge of the CBD. All travel is between these two areas and must use one of the two connecting roads. Road size (in lanes) is assumed fixed.

9.2.2 Commuters

There is a single time period, intended to represent the morning peak. During this period, N utility-maximizing, price- and quality-taking commuters per hour make one

[2] This interpretation was suggested by an anonymous referee.
[3] These street-layout assumptions are for convenience only and should not significantly affect the results.

trip between the origin and destination. The commuting population is made up of G homogeneous groups; group g is a proportion s_g of the total, so there are $N_g = Ns_g$ travelers from group g. We assume that there is no spatial segregation in the residential area and that commuters' origins are uniformly distributed over the minor arterials.

Commuters choose a single mode for their travel (where a mode is a road-plus-vehicle-type pair), so they face a discrete-choice decision problem. We assume that the conditional indirect utility (v_{gm}) that a representative member of group g obtains if mode m is chosen depends linearly on a vector x_{gm} of observable characteristics of mode m and on a random variable (ε_{gm}) representing all other (unobserved) determinants of choice, and we write $v_{gm} = x'_{gm}\beta_g + \varepsilon_{gm}$. We assume that the random variables are i.i.d, Type-1 extreme-value variates and study the probability P_{gm} of choosing mode m, which, under our assumptions (see, e.g. Domencich and McFadden, 1975), are given by the logit model:

$$P_{gm} = \Pr[v_{gm} > v_{gk} \text{ for all } k \neq m] \tag{9.1}$$

$$= \frac{e^{x'_{gm}\beta_g}}{\sum_k e^{x'_{gk}\beta_g}} \tag{9.2}$$

Thus, of the N_g commuters in group g, $N_g P_{gm}$ are expected to use mode m.

9.2.3   Entry and response

We distinguish $M = 4$ modes. The first two are auto-based, with mode 1 using the major arterial and mode 2 the expressway. Mode 3 is public bus transit using the arterial, and mode 4 is a potential private bus transit entrant using the expressway. The public sector operates both the highway system and public transit (mode 3). Since we shall be concerned with the optimal public transit response to entry, we assume that the costs of maintaining the highway network are independent of utilization and may be neglected.[4]

Competition between public and private transit is modeled as a repeated game between myopic Cournot–Nash (zero conjectural variation, i.e. where the participants do not attempt to anticipate each others' responses) players, the two transit providers. At each stage of the game, one of the transit operators takes the decision (the "operations plan", described in Section 9.2.6) of its rival and the characteristics of auto travel as given, and chooses its own operations plan. The difference between the two transit providers is in their goals: the private provider selects its plan to maximize profits, whereas the public provider chooses its plan to maximize aggregate social welfare in the corridor.

It is not possible to derive the resulting configuration (the equilibrium) in closed form; we therefore obtain it by tracing out the successive moves of the competitors: these moves are indexed by superscripts (with subscripts identifying the player). We

---

[4] With relatively few buses on the roads—autos do essentially no marginal road damage at current construction standards—ignoring road wear is not a significant limitation. See Small et al. (1989) for a model in which highway maintenance costs depend on the composition of the traffic stream.

start from a purely descriptive initial state (0) with three modes, the two automobile modes (1 and 2), with characteristics (as perceived by members of group g) x_{g1}^0 and, respectively, and public transit, with operations plan y_3^0. Corridor social welfare in the initial state is W^0. The game begins when private transit (mode 4) attempts to enter the market with an operations plan y_4^1 chosen to maximize its profits. We assume that entry and exit are costless. If the market cannot support two transit modes (i.e. if maximized private-sector profits are negative), the game ends. If entry succeeds, then public transit (mode 3) reacts, choosing y_3^1 to maximize social welfare conditional on the characteristics of the auto and private transit modes, and this is followed by the private transit's response, choosing y_4^2 to maximize profits, once again conditional on the decisions of the other players. This constitutes the end of iteration 1. Iteration 2 begins with the private sector's response to the public sector's decision and continues with the public sector's welfare-maximizing response to *that* decision. The game continues until neither competitor has any incentive to change its operations plan.[5] When the game ends,[6] we have the profit-maximizing operations plan of the private entrant and the welfare-maximizing plan of the public sector. If corridor social welfare, when the game ends, is W^*, a measure of the benefits of private entry with an optimal public sector response is $W^* - W^0$.

9.2.4   Profit maximization

The private provider (mode 4) is a profit maximizer. Let f_4^j represent its fare at stage j of the game; we assume that only nondiscriminatory (uniform) fares are permitted. The operations plans selected by both transit operators (together with auto costs and exogenous features of the transportation system) determine the stage-j modal characteristics x_{gm}^j perceived by group-g users, and hence the mode choice probabilities P_{gm}^j. If $C_4^j(y_4^j)$ is the total cost per hour of providing private transit's operations plan y_4^j, the entrant's profits per peak hour are:

$$\Pi^j = R_4^j - C_4^j(y_4^j) \tag{9.3}$$

where $R_4^j = f_4^j \sum_g N_g P_{g4}^j$ are fare revenues.

9.2.5   Social welfare maximization

The public transit provider responds to entry by choosing its iteration-j operations plan y_3^j to maximize corridor social welfare, which consists of user benefits from the transportation system, profits generated by the private entrant, and net public sector revenues. We assume that public sector deficits are financed by nondistortionary

---

[5] Each complete cycle of the game is a private-transit move followed by a public-transit response. In the empirical implementation, we need to decide when to stop iterating. In order to be conservative—to avoid stopping when additional iterations could result in the outcome's changing significantly—the game was played until successive sets of choice probabilities differed by less than 0.00001.

[6] In numerous runs of the model, the game ended after no more than five cycles: this makes the assumption of myopia reasonable, since it implies that there is little time for learning to take place. I do not know of any results to establish whether this iterative process may fail to converge to the equilibrium when it exists, or how existence would be affected by other response options besides Cournot–Nash.

taxation raised wholly within the corridor, that all net revenues are distributed within the corridor, and that there are no income-distributional considerations.[7]

Given the logit model of mode choice, a money measure of the user benefits for a representative member of group g in state j, generated by the operations plans of all providers, is:[8]

$$B_g^j = \frac{1}{\lambda_g} \ln \sum_m e^{x_{gm}^j \beta_g} \tag{9.4}$$

where λ_g is the marginal utility of income for a representative member of group g. The welfare of all users of transport services in the corridor at the end of iteration j is then $\sum_g N_g B_g^j$. Since we assume that highway costs are constant, we take the public sector's cost function to be its *transit* cost function $C_3^j(y_3^j)$. In later discussions, we will allow for the possibility that the public sector can levy fees (e.g. to internalize air pollution externalities) on other modes: thus, public sector revenues R_3^j are the fare revenues from its transit operation, plus any other fee revenues. Corridor social welfare in state j is therefore

$$W^j = \sum_g N_g B_g^j + (R_3^j - C_3^j) + \Pi^{j-1} \tag{9.5}$$

recalling that the public sector's iteration j takes the current level of private profits (Π^{j-1}) as given.[9]

9.2.6 Modal characteristics and operations plans

The modal characteristics faced by consumers are determined partly by exogenous features of the transport system (e.g. road size or auto operating costs) and partly by the operations plans of the transit operators. Anticipating the empirical results in Section 9.3, these characteristics are costs (fares for transit users), and travel times, which consist of in-vehicle, access. and wait times. In-vehicle times are determined by road size, which we take to be the number of standard-sized lanes in a given direction, and traffic volume, as discussed in Section 9.3.2. Auto costs are exogenous, and fares are set directly by the transit operators, so it remains to determine access and wait times for transit users.[10,11]

Recall that transit operates between a circular residential area of radius r miles and a downtown CBD. Suppose that access to the transit systems is by walking to the nearest bus stop at s_w miles per hour[12] and that transit system m provides service on E_m equally spaced radial routes along the minor arterials in the residential area (see Fig. 9.1). Given the uniform distribution of commuters, the average commuter lives

---

[7] That is, $1 in profits contributes $1 to corridor welfare no matter which group receives it.
[8] See Small and Rosen (1981) for a derivation of this benefits measure.
[9] Maximization of profits and welfare was carried out using the MINOS algorithm of the GAMS optimization package. See Brooke et al. (1988) for details.
[10] We assume that auto users face zero wait and access times.
[11] This model is based on Pozdena (1975). See also Keeler et al. (1975).
[12] Other access schemes are straightforward to add to the model.

midway between two of mode m's routes. If this commuter walks along a circumferential (collector street) path to the nearest route, and if we assume for simplicity that there is a bus stop there, then the average access time is

$$\text{Average access time} = \frac{\pi r}{2 s_w E_m} \text{ hours} \tag{9.6}$$

Next, suppose that transit system $m(m = 3, 4)$ runs buses at a headway (inter-bus interval) of ψ_m hours along each of its routes. If we assume that this interval is short enough for commuters not to attempt to time their arrivals at the bus stop (as is reasonable for the peak period considered here), then the average waiting time is given by the engineering rule-of-thumb " wait equals half the headway", and

$$\text{Average wait time} = \frac{\psi_m}{2} \text{ hours} \tag{9.7}$$

If the headway on each of E_m routes is ψ_m, then the transit system m contributes E_m / ψ_m vehicles per hour to the road connecting the residential area to the CBD.

Finally, we assume that transit operations plans are subject to a vehicle capacity constraint: buses have a maximum capacity, which we take to be 50 commuters per bus, which implies that transit mode m's operations plan must satisfy:

$$\psi_m \sum_g N_g P_{gm} \leq 50 \tag{9.8}$$

Thus, the characteristics on which commuters base their decisions, and hence their mode choice probabilities, are determined if we take transit system m's operations plan to consist of a choice of route coverage E_m, headway ψ_m, fare f_m and, in the case of the public sector, any additional user fees levied on other modes.

9.3   Empirical parameters

We turn now to the empirical details of the model.

9.3.1   Commuter choice and characteristics

Table 9.1 shows a logit model of individual choice taken from (Train, 1976) and estimated for work trips in the San Francisco Bay Area.[13] As Small and Rosen (1981) have shown, if an individual makes a single trip, an estimate of the marginal utility of income λ_g for a representative individual in group g—needed to compute user benefits B_g^j in Eq. (9.4)—is the negative of the estimated coefficient of cost, divided by the post-tax wage.

---

[13] Unfortunately, it appears that model coefficients are not transferable over urban areas, so this is a limitation on the generality of the results. See on this Small, 1992, pp. 34–35.

Table 9.1 Choice Model

Characteristic	Units[c]	Estd. Coefficient, β	t-Statistic
Cost ÷ post-tax wage	¢÷(¢/minute)	−0.372	6.84
In-vehicle time	minutes	−0.0322	4.45
Access + wait time[a]	minutes	−0.0338	6.58
Auto alternative dummy[b]		−0.0332	1.41

[a] Called " other time" in Train (1976).
[b] Variable is 1 for the auto mode, zero otherwise.
[c] Times and costs in round-trip units.

Table 9.2 Demographic Characteristics

Group	Proportion, s_g	Income ($/year)	Wage ($/hour)	Auto Cost ($/mile)	Auto Occupancy
1	0.60	12,198	5.98	0.31	1.13
2	0.40	61,945	30.37	0.31	1.13

We assume that there are $G = 2$ homogeneous groups of commuters.[14] Table 9.2 shows the assumed proportions (s_g) of each group in the population, as well as their incomes.[15] To simplify the analysis, we assume that, irrespective of income, all auto commuting uses compact cars, whose costs are shown in Table 9.2.[16] We also assume that auto occupancy is 1.13 persons per vehicle[17] and that all costs are divided equally among the automobile's occupants.

9.3.2 Travel times

There are five kinds of roads: minor arterials and collector streets in the residential area, city streets in the CBD, and the major arterial and the expressway connecting the two. We assume that travel times on all roads except the expressway are fixed and independent of the traffic on them. This is reasonable if traffic is light (as it would be on the residential roads) or if traffic generated by this corridor is a small portion of total traffic (as it would typically be in the CBD). On the major arterial, travel times depend primarily on public transit's stop pattern, as well as on features like traffic lights; assuming these to be given,

[14] See Small and Yan (2001) on the importance of heterogeneity in policy analyses.
[15] These values are derived from the income classes of United States Department of Commerce (1997), Table 530, attributing to each class the midpoint of the ranges in column 1 of the table; and to the final class (income greater than $1,000,000) a value of $2,000,000. Income taxes are based on the percentages shown in column 11, and the distribution of incomes on column 2. The conversion of annual income to an hourly wage assumes $255 \times 8 = 2040$ hours per year for both groups.
[16] See Winston and Shirley (1998, p. 25) (operating cost is 7.8¢ per seat mile) and note 13 (based on an occupancy of 4).
[17] Occupancy is based on Parody et al. (1987), reporting home-based work trips in Dallas in 1984.

Table 9.3 **Fixed Travel Times and Speeds**

Road Type	Travel Time (min/mile)	Speed (mile/h)	Average Trip Distance (miles)
Residential and city streets			r/2, 1/2
Autos	2.40	25	
Buses	6.67	9	
Major arterial			L
Autos	3.00	20	
Buses (public transit only)	4.00	15	

it is reasonable to assume that travel times on this road are also independent of traffic. Table 9.3 shows the assumed travel times per mile (and implied speeds) on these roads, which are intended to reflect conditions in larger urban areas during the peak period.

Travel times on the expressway, however, do depend on traffic (congestion). We measure this using the Bureau of Public Roads function[18]

$$\text{Travel time per mile (min)} = \alpha + \gamma \left(\frac{N_A}{c_A w} \right)^{\kappa} \tag{9.9}$$

where N_A is the number of "passenger-car equivalent" (PCE) vehicles per hour using the road, c_A is the capacity of a lane in PCEs per hour, and w is the number of high-way lanes. The parameter α is the travel time per mile under uncongested (free-flow) conditions, when the volume-to-capacity ratio is zero, and $\alpha + \gamma$ is the travel time per mile when the volume-to-capacity ratio equals 1. The upper part of Table 9.4 shows the

Table 9.4 **Determination of Expressway Travel Times**

Description	Symbol	Value
Free-flow travel time (min/mile)	α	1
At-capacity travel time (min/mile)	γ	2
Lane capacity (PCEs/lane/h)[a]	c_A	1800
Power law[b]	κ	4
Bus PCE factor		1.8
Assumed speeds (mph):		
At free-flow (volume-to-capacity ratio = 0)		60
At capacity (volume-to-capacity ratio = 1)		20

[a] Source: Small et al. 1989, Table 6.1.
[b] Small et al., 1989, note c to table 6.1, for additional discussion of this parameter.

[18] See, for example, United States Bureau of Public Roads (1964).

assumed values of these parameters, based on the speeds shown in the lower part of the table.

We assume that a compact car contributes 1 PCE to the traffic stream and that each bus contributes 1.8.[19] Based on the assumption of 1.13 persons per vehicle, and if the auto-on-expressway choice probability is P_{g2} for group g, the number of type-g autos is $N_g^* = N_g P_{g2} / 1.13$. If private transit's operations plan involves E_4 routes and headway ψ_4 on each route, the number of buses per hour on the expressway is E_4 / ψ_4; thus the total number of PCEs (recall that the public transit operator does not use the expressway) is

$$N_A = N_1^* + N_2^* + 1.8 \frac{E_4}{\psi_4} \tag{9.10}$$

To determine the number of expressway lanes, we make the assumptions shown in Table 9.4 about expressway speeds in the initial state (when there is no private transit) and solve the travel-time Eq. (9.9) for w.

9.3.3   Transit costs

The round-trip cost of providing public transit is assumed to depend on a cost per mile c_M and a cost per hour c_H; hence the cost per bus round trip is

$$C_3^* = 2[c_M (L + r + 1) + c_H (t_a L + t_r r + t_s)] \tag{9.11}$$

where t_a, t_r, and t_s are fixed travel times per mile on the major arterial, residential streets, and city streets, respectively, and we assume that each trip involves 1 mile on CBD streets.[20] Then the total public transit system cost per hour, with E_3 / ψ_3 buses operated, is

$$C_3(y_3) = \frac{E_3}{\psi_3} C_3^* \tag{9.12}$$

We assume that $c_M = \$0.2914$ and $c_H = \$47.0132$.[21]

Private transit's cost function $C_4(y_4)$ is similar except that the time-on-arterial term t_a is replaced by the corresponding time on expressway, which is determined

---

[19] See Garber and Hoel (1997, p. 374, Table 9.13): the value of 1.8 is for buses along a level 2-lane highway at level-of-service A.

[20] That is, buses go from one end of the CBD to the other before starting the return trip.

[21] Based on Viton (1977) updated to 1984 prices in order to allow a straightforward comparison between the results obtained here and those of Winston and Shirley (1998). We use the increase in transit maintenance costs per vehicle-mile over the period 1972–1995 to adjust cost per vehicle-mile, the increase in average hourly earnings for local and inter-urban passenger travel employees for wage costs per vehicle hour, and the increase in the producer prices of motor vehicles for the capital cost of buses, which are converted into a cost per hour assuming a 2-h peak in each of 250 days per year. Sources: maintenance costs in the passenger transit industry: United States Department of Commerce (1986, Table 1066) and United States Department of Commerce (1997, Table 1031). Hourly earnings: Tables 694 (1986) and 662 (1997). Producer prices: Tables 789 (1986) and 758 (1997).

Table 9.5 Characteristics of the Initial Situation

Descriptive			
Residential area radius (r)	2	Commuters per hour (N)	7500
Linehaul distance (L)	4		
Auto Travel		**Public Transit**	
Expressway speed (mph)	35	Headway (ψ_3^0, min)	15
Expressway lanes (w)	2.73	Route coverage (E_3^0)	8.0
Autos-on-expressway share (%)	57.2	Fare (f_3^0, \$/trip)	1.50
Autos-on-arterial share (%)	34.8	Share (%)	7.9

endogenously via Eq. (9.9). We can allow private transit to have an efficiency advantage by taking its costs per mile and per hour to be a given fraction of those in the public sector.

9.4   Results

We begin by constructing the characteristics of the initial state, intended to be representative of peak period commuting in congested corridors of the larger US cities. We take the number of commuters in the corridor to be $N = 7500$ per (peak) hour and assume that the linehaul distance is $L = 6$ miles, while the radius of the residential area is $r = 2$ miles. The in-vehicle portion of the average trip is thus 7.5 miles,[22] roughly consistent with observed commuting patterns. In the initial state, public transit is assumed to provide peak service at a headway of 15 min, over six equally spaced routes in the residential area, and at a fare of \$1.50 per trip. We assume that the peak-period speed on the expressway is 35 mph, implying that expressway is $w = 2.73$ lanes in each direction. Under these conditions, 7.9% of trips use transit, also consistent with observed patterns.[23] Autos-on-expressway's share is 57.2%, whereas autos-on-arterial accounts for the remaining 34.8%. Table 9.5 summarizes these initial characteristics.

9.4.1   Entry and response: the base case

In this setting, private entry is profitable, and we can break our analysis of its impact into two stages. First, what is the impact of entry alone, that is, a situation in which the public provider does not respond at all to entry (referred to earlier as Inaction)? The resulting equilibrium conditions are shown in panel A of Table 9.6. Private transit provides a service very similar to that provided by public transit, but because of its faster linehaul speed (recall that the public operator is constrained to use the arterial,

---

[22] The average in-vehicle distance is the linehaul distance, plus half the residential area radius, plus 1/2 mile in the CBD.

[23] For example, Winston and Shirley (1998, Tables 1–2) put transit's share of work trips in the 116 largest US urban areas at 8.7%, but this includes subway and rail transit, which are not included in this model.

Table 9.6 The Base Case

A. Equilibrium Characteristics: Entry + No Response (Inaction)				
	Auto Arterial	Auto Expressway	Public Transit	Private Transit
Share (%)	26.1	48.6	5.9	19.4
Toll/fare ($/trip)	–	–	1.50	1.43
Bus headway (min)	–	–	15.0	16.1
Bus routes	–	–	6.0	7.8
Highway speed (mph)	–	43.0	–	43.0

B. Equilibrium Characteristics: Entry + Optimal Response				
	Auto Arterial	Auto Expressway	Public Transit	Private Transit
Share (%)	19.8	40.0	25.8	14.3
Toll/fare ($/trip)	–	–	0.00	1.29
Bus headway (min)	–	–	13.5	18.7
Bus routes	–	–	9.3	6.7
Highway speed (mph)	–	50.8	–	50.8

C. Welfare Change: ¢ per Commuter-Mile			
	Due to Entry	Of Optimal Response	Total
User benefits	14.1	9.3	23.5
Private transit profits	1.7	−0.6	1.1
Public transit net revenues	−0.4	−3.2	−3.6
Total	15.5	5.5	21.0

while private transit uses the expressway) succeeds in capturing close to 20% of the market. Public transit sees its share drop slightly (from 7.9% to 5.9%), while the proportion of commuters using private cars drops from 92% to 75% and as a consequence highway speeds rise from 35 to 43 mph. One implication of this is that what is driving the switch to private transit is not its level of service but rather the faster service that it can offer; a second implication is that any welfare improvements of this could easily be obtained by the public sector's instituting what amounts to express-bus services, as indeed one observes in several urban areas.

The second stage of the analysis asks what changes if the public sector responds optimally (i.e. as a welfare maximizer) to entry. The resulting equilibrium (completed after four iterations) is shown in panel B of Table 9.6. The most striking feature of the equilibrium is that public transit offers free (zero-fare) service (Perrone, 2002). This contrasts with the recommendations in Winston and Shirley (1998) that an optimizing transit system should *increase* fares substantially.[24] Public transit also responds to

---

[24] In Winston and Shirley (1998, Table 4-2), optimal bus fares per mile rise by a factor of 4.2, to as much as 55¢ per mile.

entry by improving both its headway and route coverage. Private transit responds in turn by reducing its fare from $1.43 when the public sector does not respond to $1.29 (an almost 10% reduction) accompanied by a slight worsening of its nonfare level of service (headway and route coverage). Because of this, its share of the market falls from 19% to 14%, while, due primarily to its fare policy, public transit's share rises from 6% to almost 26%. Auto usage falls further, to 60% (as compared with 92% originally and 75% after private entry). With fewer auto users on the expressway, highway speeds continue to improve, reaching 51 mph.

The welfare implications are shown in panel C of Table 9.6, in cents per commuter per mile travelled ("cents per commuter-mile"). Private entry itself (i.e. the equilibrium in panel A) adds 14¢ to user benefits, and profits (which we are assuming are distributed in the corridor, with no additional welfare implications) add a further 1.7¢. Public transit net revenues decrease slightly (i.e. deficits increase) and overall the corridor experiences a welfare improvement of 15.5¢ per commuter-mile.

Entry followed by social-welfare-maximizing behavior on the part of the public provider adds a further 9.3¢ per commuter-mile to user benefits (a 35% increase), but profits fall, and of course public-sector deficits increase substantially, and it must be recognized that this may therefore be politically infeasible; we return to this question shortly. The total impact of entry and optimizing response, relative to the initial situation, is that the corridor experiences an improvement in social welfare valued at 21¢ per commuter-mile.

This raises two questions. First, as we have seen in Table 9.6, competition (entry) alone is responsible for close to 75% of the total welfare improvement generated by entry followed by an optimizing response by the public sector. It is, therefore, of interest to ask: how often can we expect entry to be possible? To answer this, Table 9.7 shows equilibria for a variety of structural settings deliberately chosen to be unfavorable to private entry. In only one case (F), when all unfavorable features are combined, is private entry impossible and, as cases (G) through (I) show, a single change in the environment is enough to restore the feasibility of entry. The social welfare improvement is greatest when the expressway is initially more congested[25] (case A) or when public transit is faster (case C), but is never negligible. In no case does public transit deviate from its zero-fare policy. Clearly, the benefits of competition can be expected to be widely available.

Second, how much of the welfare improvement in Table 9.6 would be possible by the public sector acting alone? That is, what would be the result if the public sector adopted a social-welfare-maximization policy and private entry did not occur (or was deterred, which we discuss later). Table 9.8 shows the resulting equilibrium and its welfare implications. A pure welfare-optimizing public sector provides free transit and improves service (headways and route coverage) over the initial situation (Table 9.5) but not as much as it is induced to do by competition. While this improves expressway speeds over the initial situation, traffic on the expressway is slower than it would be without competition. And deficits increase. The overall impact is that public-sector optimization alone yields just over 50% of the social-welfare improvement possible when optimizing

[25] More expressway congestion is unfavorable to private entry because we assume that the entrant must use the expressway.

Table 9.7 **Private Entry Under Unfavorable Conditions**

Case	Description	Transit Shares (%) Public	Private	Welfare Change[a]	% of Entry ± Optimiz.	% of Inaction
	Entry + optimization	25.8	14.3	21.0¢	100.0	135.5
A	More expwy congestion (initial speed 30 mph)	26.9	13.9	22.8	108.6	45.8
B	Shorter trips ($L = 4$ miles)	24.6	7.5	17.8	84.8	42.5
C	Faster public transit (art. speed 20 mph)	35.2	11.4	22.3	106.2	49.7
D	More rich commuters ($s_2 = .5$)	24.1	12.2	21.2	101.0	33.5
E	Fewer commuters ($N = 5000$/h)	24.3	12.2	17.9	85.2	32.3
F	All of the above	29.9	–	13.1[b]	62.3	83.9
G	All except (A)	27.7	3.4	15.7	74.8	54.2
H	All except (B)	33.0	7.0	20.7	98.6	58.1
I	All except (C)	22.6	3.9	15.1	71.9	50.3

[a] Welfare change in cents per commuter-mile from an initial situation which changes for each case.
[b] No entry is possible in this setting.

Table 9.8 **Public Transit Optimization without Private Entry**

A. Equilibrium Characteristics				
	Auto Arterial	Auto Expressway	Public Transit	Private Transit
Share (%)	23.0	44.6	32.4	–
Toll/fare ($/trip)	–	–	0.00	–
Bus headway (mins)	–	–	12.3	–
Bus routes	–	–	10.2	–
Highway speed (mph)	–	46.7	–	–

B. Welfare Change: ¢ per Commuter-Mile from Initial State		
	Entry + Optimization	Public Sector Optimization
User benefits	23.5	15.1
Private transit profits	1.1	–
Public transit net revenues	−3.6	−4.5
Total	21.0	10.6
Percent of entry + optimization	100.0	50.5
Percent of entry alone	135.4	68.4

Table 9.9 Private Transit with 15% Efficiency Advantage

A. Equilibrium Characteristics

	Auto Arterial	Auto Expressway	Public Transit	Private Transit
Share (%)	19.6	39.6	25.3	15.5
Toll/fare ($/trip)	–	–	0.00	1.30
Bus headway (mins)	–	–	13.6	17.4
Bus routes	–	–	9.3	7.2
Highway speed (mph)	–	51.0	–	51.0

B. Welfare Change: ¢ per Commuter-Mile from Initial State

	No Cost Advantage	15% Efficiency Advantage
User benefits	23.5	24.1
Private transit profits	1.1	1.3
Public transit net revenues	−3.6	−3.5
Total	21.0	21.9
% of no cost advantage	100.0	104.8

behavior by the public sector is spurred by the impetus of private-sector competition. And it yields 68% of the benefits that would be realized by private-sector entry alone.

Much of the interest in having the public sector compete with private enterprise comes from the expectation of substantial efficiency gains (cost savings), but whether such gains exist in transit is controversial. Viton (1996) compares the distribution of technical efficiency between public and private bus transit operators using a nonparametric methodology and finds no systematic differences. Winston and Shirley (1998, p. 91), on the other hand, (citing other sources) suggest that private operators may have up to a 15% cost advantage over the public sector.

To assess the impact of any efficiency gains, Table 9.9 shows the equilibrium when private transit has a 15% cost advantage over the public sector; all other parameters are at initial situation (Table 9.5) values. Lower costs enable the private entrant to improve its level of service, and its market share increases slightly. The optimal public transit response is essentially unchanged from the entry + optimization case in Table 9.6, panel B, and the benefits of private entry increase by 5.8%.

9.4.2 Deficits and the welfare costs of nonoptimal responses

Despite the gains in overall corridor social welfare, the optimal public-sector response significantly increases public sector deficits, and this might, as a practical matter, pre-

---

[26] If (as here) public sector provision succeeds in reducing uninternalized negative externalities, it could be argued that the marginal cost of public borrowing is less than 1—that $1 of public borrowing has a welfare impact valued at less than $1—and that deficits are therefore less of a problem than this suggests. But even if this is true, as a practical political matter, deficits are still likely to be a major concern.

Table 9.10 Consequences of Public Transit Exit

A. Equilibrium Characteristics				
	Auto Arterial	Auto Expressway	Public Transit	Private Transit
Share (%)	28.4	51.1	–	20.5
Toll/Fare ($/trip)	–	–	–	1.46
Bus Headway (mins)	–	–	–	15.6
Bus Routes	–	–	–	8.0
Highway speed (mph)	–	40.5	–	40.5

B. Welfare Change: ¢ per Commuter-Mile from Initial State		
	Base Case	Exit
User benefits	23.5	10.0
Private transit profits	1.1	1.9
Public transit net revenues	−3.6	1.1
Total	21.0	13.0
% of Base Case	100.0	61.9

vent public transit from responding optimally.[26] What other responses could it make to entry, and what are their welfare consequences?

As we have seen, one possibility is inaction: the public transit operator simply ignores the entrant and leaves its operations plan unchanged. The resulting equilibrium was shown in Table 9.6 where the results was a welfare improvement of 15.5¢ per commuter-mile over the initial situation. However, due to a loss of market share, deficits increase, if only slightly. So inaction is not a feasible strategy for deficit reduction.

A strategy that can solve the deficit problem is complete privatization: the public sector exits the corridor completely, leaving all mass transit to be provided by the private sector.[27] Depending on how public transit reallocates resources to other corridors, this could result in welfare improvements in the rest of the urban area, but here we consider only the local (corridor) impact. As shown in Table 9.10, a private transit monopolist[28] increases its fare to $1.46 per trip (from $1.29 with transit competition), improves service and captures 21% of the market, but fewer auto-on-expressway users are diverted and highway speeds improve to only 41 mph. But all transit deficits are eliminated, and private sector profits increase. Corridor social welfare improves by 13¢ per commuter-mile from the initial state, but this is only 62% of what is achievable by an optimal public-sector response to private entry and constitutes an opportunity cost of 8¢ per commuter-mile.

If private transit is more efficient, these opportunity costs can be somewhat reduced, but not eliminated entirely. With a 15% efficiency advantage, public-sector inaction yields 77% of the benefits achievable with an optimal response, while privati-

[27] This is the in effect the response recommended by Winston and Shirley (1998).
[28] Of course this is only a *transit* monopoly: the ability to exploit monopoly power is constrained by the auto sector.

Table 9.11 **Impact of Public Transit Charging Fares**

Public transit Fare	Reduction in Deficits	% of Optimal Corridor Welfare
$0.00	00.0%	100.0%
0.25	18.9	95.2
0.50	33.0	90.5
1.00	51.5	81.4
1.50	74.9	81.4

zation (exit) generates 66%. Inaction is therefore preferred on social welfare grounds (with or without efficiency gains), but of course exit is the most effective way to deal with deficits. It is also important to note that with transit always available in some form, no public-sector response reduces social welfare over the initial state: it is simply a question of the degree of improvement.

As we have seen, public transit's optimal response is always to provide free service, which of course induces large deficits. Another possibility to cope with these is to permit the public bus operator to charge a fare and set the other level-of-service parameters (headway and route coverage) to maximize (conditional) social welfare, allowing transit competition from the private sector. Table 9.11 shows the results for the case without a private-sector cost advantage relative to the Entry + Optimization case in Table 9.6. On the one hand, a 25¢ fare has a relatively small impact on corridor welfare, but it also reduces deficits by less than 20%. A fare of $1.50 succeeds in substantially reducing deficits (by 75%) but achieves only 81% of what is attainable with a zero fare, an opportunity cost of about 20%. Interestingly, while reducing the fare from $1.50 to $1.00 worsens the deficit situation, it does not result in any noticeable improvement in social welfare. If deficits are a significant problem for public transit, then it is probably better to maintain a fare of $1.50 and let competition and level of service mitigate these effects, rather than reducing the fare to $1.00 even if that is in the direction of optimality.

Finally, could the public operator act so as to deter competition altogether? This strategy is of potential interest because, as noted, it seems likely that the public sector could offer a private-sector-like express-bus service imitating the offering of the public entrant. For the case shown in Table 9.6, doing so would actually result in a profit for the public sector (assuming that the express operation was run as an independent division, and the arterial service was arranged to maximize welfare conditional on the expressway division's action). However, this would require deterring a potential entrant, and this seems effectively impossible. Even if public transit halved its headways and doubled its route coverage, private entry remains possible. Only if fewer than 3500 commuters per (peak) hour travel in the corridor does deterrence become feasible, but even then the 15-fold increase in public-sector deficits is probably enough to rule it out as a practical matter.

Table 9.12 **Equilibrium with Internalized Externalities**

A. Equilibrium Characteristics (Externalities included)				
	Auto Arterial	**Auto Expressway**	**Public Transit**	**Private Transit**
Share (%)	12.0	25.4	42.6	20.4
Toll/fare ($/trip)	–	0.00	0.00	1.50
Bus headway (mins)	–	–	10.9	15.8
Bus routes	–	–	11.6	7.9
Highway speed (mph)	–	56.5	–	56.5

B. Welfare Change: ¢ per Commuter-Mile from Initial Situation		
	Externalities Included	**Inaction**
User benefits	40.2	23.4
Private transit profits	3.2	5.4
Public transit net revenues	−10.5	−2.1
Externality revenues	6.6	−4.0
Total	26.4	22.8
% of externalities included	100.0	86.4

9.4.3 Externalities

All transportation gives rise to important negative externalities, but thus far they are dealt with only indirectly, via public transit's operations plan. We now investigate the possibility of more direct responses.

No transport mode currently faces the direct marginal costs of accident and air pollution externalities. Suppose that the public authorities can internalize them in the initial state (i.e. before any private entry occurs) via a system of user fees on autos and buses (also assumed to be costless to administer). We follow Winston and Shirley (1998) in estimating accident costs per vehicle-mile at $0.155 for autos and $1.12 for buses.[29] Auto air pollution costs are estimated by Small and Kazimi (1995) at 3¢ per vehicle-mile, and Winston and Shirley (1998) note that bus costs are about twice that. Thus, accident and pollution external costs per vehicle-mile are 18.5¢ for autos and $1.18 for buses.[30]

When auto users must bear these external costs of their choices, public transit becomes substantially more attractive in the initial state: even at its initial (nonoptimal) operations plan,[31] its share is 22% and it realizes profits of $506 per peak hour. The

---

[29] Winston and Shirley (1998) estimate bus accident costs at $0.124 per passenger-mile: we convert to a cost per vehicle-mile using the average ratio of passenger-miles to vehicle-miles, 9, reported in their Table 2-1.

[30] We assume that public and private bus operations give rise to the same levels of these external costs. In addition, we adjust the number of highway lanes so that initial speeds are still 35 mph.

[31] A fare of $1.50 per trip, a headway of 15 min, and 6 equally spaced routes in the residential area.

externality fees charged to autos add $7138, so the transport sector as a whole returns $7644 per peak hour to society.

Nevertheless, private entry remains feasible, and Table 9.12 shows the equilibrium when the public sector responds optimally. Both transit modes attract many more users, and the share of autos on the expressway falls from 40% to 25%. Fully 63% of commuting now takes place on some form of mass transportation, and highway speeds increase to 57 mph from 35 mph relative to the initial (no competition) state and from 51 mph when externalities are not priced. The welfare-maximizing transit operations plan incurs a deficit of $5900 per peak hour and private profits only partially offset this, but overall, the impact of the improved transit service is an increase in social welfare of 26.4¢ per commuter-mile over the initial state.[32] If deficits make the welfare-maximizing response infeasible, a strategy of inaction succeeds in reducing deficits significantly, while achieving 86% of the benefits of optimization, but exit—leaving all transit to the private sector—eliminates deficits but generates only 58% of the benefits of optimization.

9.5 Conclusions

Faced with competition from the private sector, a public provider must decide how to respond. We have focused on its welfare-maximizing response, in which it configures its service to maximize community (here, corridor) welfare, given the decisions of the private entrant. With this standard as a benchmark, we can also assess the impacts of other responses. This paper has studied these questions for the case of public transit in a congested urban corridor, where competition via private entry is generally feasible.

When entry occurs, public transit's optimal response is to differentiate itself from the entrant, primarily by large fare reductions (in our case, to zero). The result is a significant increase in social welfare and a dramatic reduction in highway traffic congestion. However, this substantially increases public transit's deficits. In light of this, several second-best strategies for limiting public-sector deficits were studied. Inaction (not responding to entry and keeping to its preentry service levels) is preferable on social welfare grounds to complete privatization (exit), even though privatization could eliminate the public sector's deficits entirely and could perhaps be justified on that basis. Another possibility is for the public provider to resile from a low-fare policy, while optimizing the other components of its level of service. This is preferable to both inaction and exit on social-welfare grounds, but, in the case studied here, only a fare of $1.50 also makes a significant contribution to reducing the deficits induced by optimal behavior.

A second interpretation of these results stresses the importance of product differentiation, since about 75% of the total welfare benefits of entry and reacting to it occur due to entry alone, and the differentiated service the entrant provides (see Table 9.6). In the context of public transit, this is important because it appears that the service provided by the private entrant could equally well be provided by a division of the

---

[32] Since social welfare in the initial situation is changed by internalizing externalities, a direct comparison with Table 9.6 is not relevant and therefore is not shown in the table.

public provider, though it is questionable whether a somewhat schizophrenic set of behavioral motivations could coexist in the same public-sector organization, and we have not studied the contribution to welfare that would be made by instituting profitable (but not profit-maximizing) service. At the same time, it must be reiterated that private entry is widely possible and deterrence by the public provider is likely to be unacceptably costly.

Public-sector providers of public services will always tend to view the possibility of competition from the private sector with alarm. However, at least in the context studied here, from a social-welfare standpoint, this alarm is misplaced: competition is always beneficial. This fact can be seen as supporting the idea of an implicit " public–private partnership" in which the public and private sectors strive together to provide that degree of product differentiation that maximizes social welfare. It is hoped that the present paper has provided some guidelines as to how such partnerships could work in practice.

References

Brooke, A., Kendrick, D., Meeraus, A., 1988. GAMS: A User's Guide. The Scientific Press, Redwood City, California.

Domencich, T., McFadden, D., 1975. Urban Travel Demand: A Behavioral Analysis. North-Holland, New York.

Garber, N.J., Hoel, L.A., 1997. Traffic and Highway Engineering, Second ed PWS Publishing Company, Boston, MA.

Keeler, T.E., Small, K.A., Viton, P.A., Mere-Witz, L.A., Pozdena, R.J., 1975. The full costs of urban transport, III, Monograph 21. Institute of Urban and Regional Development, University of California, Berkeley.

Keeler, T.E., Hu, T-w., Barnett, P.G., Manning, W.E., Sung, H.-Y., 1996. Do cigarette producers price-discriminate by state? Journal of Health Economics 15, 499–512.

Morlok, E.K., Viton, P.A., 1980. Self-sustaining public transportation services. Transport Policy and Decision-Making 1, 169–194.

Parody, T.F., Levinson, H.S., Brand, D., 1987. Characteristics of urban transportation demand: an updated and revised handbook. Transportation Research Record (1139), 39–47.

Perrone, J.S., 2002 October. Advantages and disadvantages of fare-free transit policy. Technical Report NCTR-473-133.

Pozdena, R.J., 1975. A methodology for selecting urban transportation projects, Monograph 22. Institute of Urban and Regional Development, University of California, Berkeley.

Small, K.A., 1992. Urban Transportation Economics. Harwood Academic Publishers, Chur, Switzerland.

Small, K.A., Kazimi, C., 1995. On the costs of air pollution from motor vehicles. Journal of Transport Economics and Policy 29, 7–32.

Small, K.A., Rosen, H.S., 1981. Applied welfare economics with discrete choice models. Econometrica 49, 105–130.

Small, K.A., Yan, J., 2001. The value of "value pricing" of roads: second-best pricing and product differentiation. Journal of Urban Economics 49 (2), 310–336.

Small, K.A., Winston, C.M., Evans, C., 1989. Road Work. The Brookings Institution, Washington, DC.

Train, K.E., 1976. Work trip mode split models. Unpublished working paper. Institute of Transportation Studies, Travel Demand Forecasting Project, Berkeley.

United States Bureau of Public Roads, 1964. Traffic Assignment Manual. GPO, Washington, DC, Technical Report.

United States Department of Commerce, 1986. Statistical Abstract of the United States. U.S. Government Printing Office, Washington, DC.

United States Department of Commerce, 1997. Statistical Abstract of the United States. U.S. Government Printing Office, Washington, DC.

Viton, P.A., 1977. Equilibrium of supply and demand in urban transportation. Department of Economics, University of California, Berkeley, Working Paper SL-7706.

Viton, P.A., 1981. On competition and product differentiation in urban transportation: the San Francisco Bay Area. Bell Journal of Economics 12 (2), 362–379.

Viton, P.A., 1995. Private roads. Journal of Urban Economics 27B (5), 401–412.

Viton, P.A., 1996. Technical efficiency in multi-mode bus transit: a DEA production frontier analysis. Transportation Research 31B (1), 13–29.

Winston, C.M., Shirley, C., 1998. Alternate Route: Toward Efficient Urban Transportation. Brookings Institution, Washington, DC.

Devolution of transportation: reducing big-government involvement in transportation decision making

Randall Pozdena[1,2]
QuantEcon, Incorporated, ECONorthwest, Incorporated

Chapter Outline

[1] This report was authored by Randall Pozdena President of QuantEcon Inc.and Senior Director of ECONorthwest Inc. both of which are Oregon-based consultancies. He received his BA in Economics with Honors from Dartmouth College and his PhD in economics from the University of California Berkeley. Former positions held by the author include professor of economics and finance, senior economist at the Stanford Research Institute (now SRI International) and research vice president of the Federal Reserve Bank of San Francisco. He also served on numerous public non-profit and private boards and investment committees. He is a member of the CFA Institute and the Portland Society of Financial Analysts.

[2] The author wishes to thank the Cascade Policy Institute for its kind financial support of this research. The Cascade Policy Institute is a nonprofit, nonpartisan public policy research and educational organization. The analysis and opinions presented in this paper are solely the responsibility of the author and were not influenced by the Institute or any other entity. The author wishes to thank John Bitzan and James H. Peoples, Jr., for their kind editorial advice.

Transportation Policy and Economic Regulation. http://dx.doi.org/10.1016/B978-0-12-812620-2.00010-9

Dedication

I met Professor Ted Keeler while I was preoccupied with completing the theory sequence at Berkeley in 1970. It was a refreshing change to be discussing applications of microeconomic theory in contrast to the abstract substance of the theory coursework. I recall his own work's focus vein on the possibility of self-financed passenger rail at a time when passenger rail was on its way to being nationalized. He was challenging the accepted wisdom of the day that passenger rail was inherently not able to be financially self-sustaining. He had articulated an approach that involved increasing seat density to airline levels and reforming the heavily featherbedded labor agreements in place at that time. Having already embraced a neophyte but strong private market philosophical bent, it was refreshing to see his work and his articulation of it reflecting that posture. At that time, intrastate trucking and intrastate air travel in California markets was heavily regulated. His skepticism about the appropriateness of such regulation also resonated with me. Later on, working with Ted, classmate Ken Small, and others attached to Mel Webber's Institute for Urban and Regional Development, drew my attention to provision of urban transportation services. Ultimately, this led to my dissertation topic in that area, and development of a quadratic programming approach to transportation project selection. The sparse computer resources of the day necessitated representation of the study region as a skeletal network, but laid the groundwork for my interest in mathematical modeling of transportation markets. In 1976, with my dissertation behind me 2 years before, I was appointed to the Governor's Transportation Policy Plan Task Force. All of the seeds that Ted had planted sprouted in a chapter of California's first transportation policy plan that introduced the concepts of road pricing, deregulation of air and truck transport, and other then-radical reforms. Although teaching, consulting, a 14-year stint as a research vice president of the Federal Reserve Bank of San Francisco intervened, as did other, nontransport topics, I continue to this day to work significantly in this field. The simple, skeletal network models of my dissertation have grown up to include a proprietary Toll Optimization Model that solves for optimal tolls on urban freeway networks that adopt high-occupancy toll policy on a portion of their lanes. The model has been applied in over 70 studies on networks that have thousands of links and employs complex stochastic representations of link traffic profiles and user values of time. Although I still yearn for the day when roads will be appropriately and ubiquitously priced, Ted's work, counsel, and encouragement lives on in this and other elements of my professional life.

10.1   Introduction: the role of government in transportation

This chapter addresses the issue of the appropriate role of governments in transportation. In particular, we discuss the potential for devolution of decision-making authority from those government entities whom currently have it to some lower level of government or even to the private sector and its private constituents and agents.

The distribution of authority among levels of government is a very important issue. In the United States, revenues of approximately half-a-trillion dollars each year are collected by federal, state, and local government and funneled through complex allocation procedures to fund transportation activities. The allocation of the funding involves a complex thicket of formulae, programs, trust funds, grants, subsidies, cross-subsidies, and political gerrymandering that is opaque to the average citizen. The gross pattern of sources and uses of transportation funding is, nonetheless, revealing.

Using the most recently available (2012) data on government involvement in transportation pricing and investment, we find that spending on highway, transit, and air modes represents 98% of government spending on transportation. These are the most "socialized" modes, in the sense that government spending decisions weigh most heavily on these modes. In contrast, rail, pipeline, and water modes receive relatively little government spending in absolute terms. This is due to their more privatized status (in the case of rail and pipeline) and local public operation of ports in the case of water transport.[1]

The nexus between modal and geographical sources and uses is weak, at best. Approximately half of all government transportation spending uses revenues raised in a manner that has absolutely no link to the level activity in the various transport modes. These so-called "supportive" revenues are generated by broad-based taxation of incomes, property, payrolls, sales, and other sources. Approximately half of the spending *does* use funds that are raised within the transportation sectors themselves. Even these so-called "own-source" funds, however, are typically not levied on the basis of the use of the various modes, let alone the costs occasioned by that use. Rather, own-source revenue mechanisms often have attributes of broad-based taxation.[2] Additionally, another $20 billion of transportation total funding is diverted to nontransportation uses altogether.

Large modal cross-subsidies further confound the allocation process, most notably from highways to public transit. Fully 13% (approximately $15 billion annually) of federal, state, and local "own-source" revenue from highways is diverted to transit. The $17 billion of "supportive revenue" currently received annually for the air mode goes to the FAA where geographical and other allocations get made in a centralized fashion. The FAA spends about 50% on air traffic control (ATC) operations, 20% on ATC investments and research, 8% on safety regulation and certification, and only the small, remaining share to the Airport Improvement Program (AIP) to state and local governments for airport development. The $8.5 billion in supportive revenue for the

---

[1] Pipelines remain rate-regulated, in contrast to rail.
[2] See a more thorough discussion of this in Pozdena (2014).

water mode is used mainly for building and maintaining infrastructure for seaports and waterways, much through the Army Corp of Engineers. Most of the funding goes toward dredging harbors and rivers, developing and maintaining locks and channels on rivers, etc. In the case of seaports, at least, though dominated by public ownership, the ownership is mainly by lower levels of government—state and/or local authorities—and mostly supported by own-source revenue.

The federal footprint in transportation funding is large. Across all modes of transport, 32% of all funding (own-source and other) flows through federal processes. In both the highway and transit modes, approximately 25% of funding is directly federal in origin with weak or no links to activity or costs. The federal share of public funding is 60% in air, 73% in water, and 100% in rail and pipelines, although the absolute level is smaller than other modes.

The pattern of sources and uses from which these statistics are derived is presented in Exhibit 1. Unfortunately, the flow-of-funds information in Exhibit 1 for the nation cannot be replicated for individual states, limiting the ability to construct such a table for our example state of Oregon. The pooling of revenues in trust vehicles, the heavy use of broad-based taxation in finance, and the opacity of the allocation processes make this impossible—as federal transportation officials readily admit.[3] It is possible, however, to measure the relative importance of many of the federal programs to a state. It is also possible to measure the extent to which a state's funding allocations are reflective of a disproportionate reliance on, and concession to, federal authority and funding for local or regional transportation services. These measurements are made for illustration purposes for the state of Oregon.

As Exhibit 2 reveals, Oregon has received significant Federal funding allocations for highway, transit, and air modes. These allocations are, in many cases, larger than the state's share of US population (1.2% in 2014). This is partly serendipitous due to the computations used in the federal agency program allocation formulae, but also due to differences in political influence on federal agencies among states and local areas.

For some modes, the lack of justification for federal funding involvement is more obvious than others. For example, urban transit has de facto characteristics that cause the potential beneficiaries of transit to be exclusively local in geography, but funding for this mode flows selectively among the various urban areas. In addition, the federal government in this case serves as a conduit for cross-subsidization from payments made by automobile and truck users to transit.

The imbalance in the Oregon shares in Exhibit 2 comes significantly, on average, at the expense of other taxpayers both within Oregon, and across other states. This is a legacy of Neil Goldschmidt, a former mayor of Portland and governor of Oregon, whose ascent to US Secretary of Transportation in 1979 established the political

---

[3] "State-specific statistics: The GTFS 2014 provides Federal, State, and local government transportation revenue and expenditures. While the data for State and local governments are reported at the aggregate level, data are lacking for individual State and local governments. That is due to the fact that no consolidated and consistent data are available from a single source that provides comprehensive financial statistics by State for all modes of transportation. Additionally, Federal grants are only available at the aggregate level by mode" (USDOT Bureau of Transportation Statistics, 2014, Chapter 4).

Exhibit 1 Sources and Uses of Transportation Funding, All Levels of Government, 2012 ($ billion)

Mode and Type of Revenue		Transportation Uses by Mode								Nontransportation Uses		
		Highway	Transit	Rail	Air	Water	Pipeline	General Support	Total	General Fund	Other Uses	Total
Highway	Own-source revenue	35.252	–	–	–	–	–	0.008	40.265	–	–	–
	Supporting revenue	15.268	–	–	–	–	–		15.268	–	–	–
	Diverted to other uses	–	–	–	–	–	–	–	–	1.486	0.771	2.257
Transit	Own-source revenue	–	12.256	–	–	–	–	–	12.256	–	–	–
	Supporting revenue											
	Diverted to other uses	–	–	–	–	–	–	–	–	0.084	–	0.084
Rail	Own-source revenue	–	–	2.295	–	–	–	–	2.295	–	–	–
	Supporting revenue											
	Diverted to other uses	–	–	–	–	–	–	–	–	2.302	0.004	2.305
Air	Own-source revenue	–	–	–	12.796	–	–	–	12.796	–	–	–
	Supporting revenue	–	–	–	17.649	–	–	–	17.649	–	–	–
	Diverted to other uses	–	–	–	–	–	–	–	–	1.072	3.272	4.345
Water	Own-source revenue	–	–	–	–	2.246	–	0.047	2.293	–	–	–
	Supporting revenue	–	–	–	–	8.541	–	–	8.541	–	–	–
	Diverted to other uses	–	–	–	–	–	–	–	–	–	–	–
Pipeline	Own-source revenue	–	–	–	–	–	0.090	–	0.090	–	–	–
	Supporting revenue	–	–	–	–	–	0.091	–	0.091	–	–	–
	Diverted to other uses	–	–	–	–	–	–	–	–	0.316	0.000	0.316
General support	Own-source revenue	–	–	–	–	–	–	0.031	0.031	–	–	–
	Supporting revenue	–	–	–	–	–	–	1.276	1.276	–	–	–
	Diverted to other uses	–	–	–	–	–	–	–	–	0.451	–	0.451
	Own-source revenue	74.915	9.846	–	–	–	–	–	84.761	2.072	–	2.072

Federal sources by mode

(Continued)

Exhibit 1 Sources and Uses of Transportation Funding, All Levels of Government, 2012 ($ billion) *(cont.)*

State and Local Sources by Mode

Mode and Type of Revenue	Transportation Uses by Mode								Nontransportation Uses		
	Highway	Transit	Rail	Air	Water	Pipeline	General Support	Total	General Fund	Other Uses	Total
Highway											
Supporting revenue	85.648	—	—	—	—	—	—	85.648	—	—	—
Diverted to other uses								—	8.042	—	8.042
Transit											
Own-source revenue	—	17.607	—	—	—	—	—	17.607	—	—	—
Supporting revenue	—	25.054	—	—	—	—	—	25.054	—	—	—
Diverted to other uses	—	—	—	—	—	—	—	—	—	—	—
Rail											
Own-source revenue	—	—	—	—	—	—	—	—	—	—	—
Supporting revenue	—	—	—	—	—	—	—	—	—	—	—
Diverted to other uses	—	—	—	—	—	—	—	—	1.389	—	1.389
Air											
Own-source revenue	—	—	—	18.307	—	—	—	18.307	—	—	—
Supporting revenue	—	—	—	2.186	—	—	—	2.186	—	—	—
Diverted to other uses	—	—	—	—	—	—	—	—	—	0.104	0.104
Water											
Own-source revenue	—	—	—	—	4.024	—	—	4.024	—	—	—
Supporting revenue	—	—	—	—	—	—	—	—	—	—	—
Diverted to other uses	—	—	—	—	—	—	—	—	—	—	—
Pipeline											
Own-source revenue	—	—	—	—	—	—	—	—	—	—	—
Supporting revenue	—	—	—	—	—	—	—	—	—	—	—
Diverted to other uses	—	—	—	—	—	—	—	—	—	—	—
General support											
Own-source revenue	—	—	—	—	—	—	—	—	—	—	—
Supporting revenue	—	—	—	—	—	—	—	—	—	—	—
Diverted to other uses	—	—	—	—	—	—	—	—	—	—	—
Total											
Own-source revenue	110.166	32.459	—	31.103	6.270	0.090	0.036	180.175	—	—	—
Supporting revenue	100.916	37.310	2.295	19.835	8.541	0.091	1.276	170.264	17.212	4.151	21.363
Diverted to other uses	—	—	—	—	—	—	—	—	—	—	—

Source: FHWA Government Transportation Financial Statistics, 2014.

Exhibit 2 Federal Support for OR and US Highway, Transit and Air Modes (2014–2015)

Program	Oregon ($million)	% by Program	United States ($million)	% by Program	OR as % of United States
Federal Highway Funding					
National highway performance	292.7	61	22,398.0	59	1.31
Surface transportation	134.6	28	10,302.4	27	1.31
Highway safety improvement	29.3	6	2241.3	6	1.31
Railway-highway crossings	2.9	1	220.0	1	1.31
Congestion mitigation and air quality improvement	19.4	4	2315.9	6	0.84
Metropolitan planning	3.5	1	320.5	1	1.09
Total highway	482.4	100	37,798.0	100	1.28
Federal Transit Funding					
Metropolitan planning	1.1	0.5	106.6	1.0	1.0
Statewide planning	0.2	0.1	22.9	0.2	1.0
Urbanized area formula	52.3	23.8	4833.4	45.1	1.1
Passenger ferry grants	–	0.0	30.0	0.3	–
Bus and bus facilities discretionary grants	1.7	0.8	100.0	0.9	1.7
Fixed guideway capital investment grants	124.4	56.6	2125.4	19.8	5.9
Enhanced mobility (senior/ disabilities)	3.3	1.5	257.5	2.4	1.3
Nonurbanized area formula	11.9	5.4	618.4	5.8	1.9
RTAP	0.2	0.1	10.6	0.1	1.7
Appalachian dev. public trans. assist. program	–	0.0	20.0	0.2	–
Indian reserv. formula	0.8	0.3	25.0	0.2	3.0
State of good repair	17.7	8.1	2150.1	20.0	0.8
Bus and bus facilities formula	5.9	2.7	427.8	4.0	1.4
Total transit	219.7	100.0	10,727.7	100.0	2.0
Federal Airport Funding					
Primary	30.5	72.4	2116.3	65.9	1.4
Commercial	0.6	1.3	58.7	1.8	1.0
Reliever	0.0	0.0	150.9	4.7	–
General aviation	10.8	25.6	604.3	18.8	1.8
State sponsored	0.3	0.7	26.3	0.8	1.1
State block grant	0.0	0.0	244.2	7.6	–
Other	0.0	0.0	11.0	0.3	–
Total AIP grants	42.1	100.0	3211.7	100.0	1.3

Source: FHWA, FTA, and FCC data sources.

Exhibit 3 **Trends in Transit Funding, by Level of Government (1991–2013)**

	1991 Funds Received ($million)	2013 Funds Received ($million)	Funding Growth Rate, 1991–2013 (%)	Change by Level of Govt (%) 1991–2013
	Federal Funds			
Oregon	$31.1	$266.4	756	10.7
All states	$3394.3	$10,608.1	213	2.5
	State Funds			
Oregon	$5.7	$103.7	1724	8.9
All states	$3811.5	$14,463.6	279	8.7
	Local Funds			
Oregon	$100.4	$427.3	326	−19.6
All states	$8220.2	$18,227.3	122	−11.2
	Total Funds			
Oregon	$137.18	$797.34	176	NA
All states	$15,426.00	$43,299.04	103	NA

Source: National Transit Database, TS1.1.

machinery to use federal influence to mine other states' financial resources to serve Oregon. Thus, Oregon is a textbook illustration of the corruption that can follow misallocation of power to the wrong level of government.

The differential exercise of political influence is illustrated in Exhibit 3 by comparing the rate of growth of federal and state funding of transit in Oregon, versus all states. Not only has Oregon enjoyed disproportionate growth relative to other states in the absolute level of federal and state funding, but also has been progressively more reliant on such nonlocal funding. Indeed, the local share of transit funding in Oregon has declined by more than 20 percentage points between 1991 and 2013—faster than the national average. Meanwhile, Oregon's relative reliance on Federal funding of transit has increased at over four times the average rate of all states.

Since its highway and airport allocation shares are also generally greater than its population shares, it cannot easily be argued that Oregon has sacrificed in other areas to enjoy the disproportionate share of funding it has received in the transit area. Thus, even from a high-level view, it is clear that the current involvement of higher levels of authority cannot possibly be efficient and likely results in serious misallocations of resources, delays in responding to local need and, ultimately, damage to the economy.

10.1.1 Implications for this study

It is relatively easy for an economist to recognize inherently inefficient institutional arrangements. This is because if an allocation process is insufficiently guided by consumer influence, it is inevitably subject to insufficient discipline to yield beneficial outcomes from the user's perspective. Economists thus focus on two main criteria when evaluating a resource allocation processes like the ones that drive the funding and spending allocations described above.

The first criterion is that there should be a close nexus between the costs imposed by the user of services like transportation services and funding responsibility. That is, the prices levied for the use of those services should be based—as intimately as possible—on the costs that usage imposes on the service provider. The second criterion concerns the locus of the authority to make allocative decisions. The closer to the consumer is the level of government (or the private provider) that offers the services, the more likely is the allocation process respectful of the part of the community it serves. Lobbying for inefficient or special-interest serving policies is more readily done when there is less local participation and process transparency.

From an economist's standpoint, therefore, the statistics presented earlier raise several important questions regarding the efficiency and responsiveness of the current pattern of public funding of transportation. First, are the allocations of decision-making responsibility among the federal, state, and local levels appropriate given the desire to have decision-making closest to the affected travelers and shippers? We will refer to this as the *Assignment of Authority* question. Second, is it appropriate for government funding of transportation to rely so heavily on broad-based taxation (supportive revenue) in lieu of user charges? We will refer to this as the *Pricing Question*. Third, is it necessary or desirable for governments, in the aggregate, to have a half-trillion-dollar footprint in the transportation sector? This represents about 17% of the entire transportation sector (private and public) share of US GDP. Even this number understates government involvement, because the regulatory footprint of government in this sector is also large but does not appear on GDP accounting. We will refer to this as the *Privatization Question*.

In the remainder of the chapter that follows, we will make the case for dramatic devolution from higher levels of government to lower, and from government in general to private interests in the provision of services. We will also make the case for pricing systems, in most of the major modes, that are more reflective of costs and that can be used to better guide decision making. Finally, we will address the issue of how to accomplish this devolution while still recognizing the need to coordinate activity in a network setting.

Again, to address state and local issues and distortions, this chapter addresses these issues in the empirical context of the State of Oregon and its localities, to the extent possible.

10.2   The role of governance in transportation

The term *governance* rather than *government* is used in this discussion because private entities exercise governance, too. When discussing the proper role of governance in transportation, however, it is important to distinguish between the early political and territorial motivations that were thought to justify government involvement from those that arise in a setting of technical advances, private property rights, and private enterprise for commercial purpose and public benefit.

10.2.1   Political and territorial motivations

The famous network of Roman roads is an ancient example of imperial motivation for transportation development on the part of governments. The 40,000 km network was developed over a 7-century period until about 475 AD to facilitate exploitation and unification of the empire's control of Roman and non-Roman places, peoples, and resources.[4]

Versions of the same political and territorial considerations also motivated government involvement in the American context. The early US postal road system was authorized by Article I, Section Eight, of the US Constitution to give Congress the power "to establish post offices and post roads" as a means of using communication to knit the disparate colonies into a single state. This clear and narrow power (not granted in the original Articles of Confederation) was, however, interpreted liberally and used to justify Congressional involvement in all roads and railroads. In practice, during America's expansion period, political and territorial motivations were admixed with private capital to develop the transportation facilities. The federal government owned or asserted ownership over the land used to develop rights of way for these facilities and often used this power to induce and regulate the development of these famous transportation innovations. The transcontinental railroad system is a primary example of the exercise of power through the land-grant form of subsidization.

10.2.2   National defense arguments

When war intervenes, national defense considerations are used to justify or reassert federal government involvement in what otherwise might be private enterprise, including the nation's nascent road network. This happened first in the context of the War of 1812, when privately developed roadways were deemed insufficient to respond to the needs of defense. This logic reached its apex in 1956 with President Eisenhower's call for a 41,000-mile system of the so-called "Federal-Aid Highways" that together formed the Interstate Highway System. The Federal Aid Highway Act provided for the federal government to pay 90% of the cost of the system via a doubling of the Federal tax on gasoline sales.

This massive expansion of federal authority over road building is most easily put in perspective by remembering the genesis of the program. Eisenhower and some in Congress had observed and envied Hitler's *reichsautobahn* system of "super highways" and interpreted the speed and mobility of this system as a national defense

---

[4] The nonmarket nature of Roman road development is reflected not only in its empire-building motivation, but also its enslavement of peoples encountered during its development to build the road system. Indeed, the very word "slave" from the Latin *slavicus* because the labor of Slavic peoples by the Romans was that most commonly exploited.

prerogative.[5] However, the notion that a *reichsautobahn*-like American road network was a natural military advantage was ironic since, in fact, the *reichsautobahn* was used to Hitler's *disadvantage* by Allied forces. Once allies pierced the peripheral defenses of Hitler's empire, the *reichsautobahn* facilitated ground invasion of Germany by the Allies. In addition, the real concerns America had about highways reveal that what was not a yearning for a national network, but rather, improvements to address local, urban congestion. As a Federal Highway Administration historical perspective concludes, congestion relief—not interstate mobility—was the nation's primary interest.

As a result, the Interstate System evolved very differently from Hitler's *reichsautobahn* network; rather than placing high-speed highways through rural areas as Hitler did, the interstate highway mainly provided urban congestion relief. To this day, local use is its primary use. It should also be noted that, from an authority scale perspective, the *reichsautobahn* served a country one-30th the size of the United States. It was a much weaker national assertion over local interests than was the interstate system in the United States.[6] Thus, the national, or federal, presence created by the Federal-Aid Highway Act was an unnecessary geographic overreach unjustified by either its purpose or the German example it was thought to emulate.

10.2.3 Economic arguments

As alluded to earlier, it is not obvious that roads and other transportation services cannot be provided privately—a subject to which we will return. Whether public or private, however, it must be determined to which organizational scale (level of government or private enterprise) the investment and operation of transportation services should be entrusted. In the absence of other considerations, decision-making power should be given to the smallest organizational entity. This will ensure a closer relationship between the decision-makers and the preferences of the public.

The appropriate organizational scale in transportation settings is determined by the consideration of four economic factors.

Spillover effects. The geographical scope and extent of the effects produced by the transport services may favor an organization whose scale matches the pattern of spillover effects. If a private activity has effects beyond that individual entity, a larger, rather than smaller, scale of an organization or government may be needed to internalize mutual spillover actions among individual entities. The larger scale entity, however, is only needed if a *significant portion* of the effects of individual actions spillover onto others or compensation for negative or positive spillover effects cannot be resolved in joint venture agreements.[7] The decision-making responsibility ideally should be allocated among individuals, localities, regions, or the state in proportion to

---

[5] In short, where Germany had intended to build the highways first and the vehicles second, America had the vehicles and no clear plan for building the highway network, in *The Man Who Changed America*, at http://www.fhwa.dot.gov/infrastructure/reichs.cfm.
[6] Prewar Germany was about the size of New Mexico in area.
[7] A homely analogy can be drawn from the "roaming" charge policies that were so common in the development of national cellular service to knit together smaller entities.

the magnitude of the effect (costs and benefits) the service has on each. This ensures that the interests of affected parties are weighted properly when decisions concerning transportation are made.

Network effects. Many transportation activities take place on interconnected networks. Placement and integration of infrastructure requires some coordinating force to arbitrate the several interests of developers and users of elements (links) of the network. Consideration of two simple types of networks can serve to make this clearer. The first is a parallel network effect. Say, for example, that expensive transportation infrastructure has to be built to connect point A and point B. If some other organization builds a parallel facility, the fiscal integrity of the first road may be adversely affected by diversion to that parallel facility. Some method is needed to avoid dissipating resources by building two roads from A to B only to have one, or both, fail financially. The second type of network effect is a serial effect. In this case, one organization wishes to connect its facility (going from point A to point B, say) with another organization's facility that goes from point B to point C. In general, serial effects are easier to manage bilaterally (between the two organizations) because there is likely a benefit to both from joining them at point B. Most real-world transportation networks involve a combination of parallel and serial effects. However, the potential for development of duplicative capacity, negative externalities, or other inefficient outcomes does not necessitate a commanding role for government, at any scale. The same potential exists, and is managed well, in the development of central business districts by negotiation among potentially conflicting parties. That this function is not crucial is most obvious in Houston, Texas, which has no zoning regulations in the heavy-handed, conventional sense. Rather, it relies instead on instruments like deed restrictions that are negotiated among landowners and buyers to address potentially adverse interactions among developments. In extreme cases, nuisance law or voter engagement provides further means to arbitrate such issues. Voters have turned down institution of government zoning regulations three times.

Economies of scale effects. If a transportation service requires a very large-scale operation in order to operate efficiently, decision-making responsibility may have to be given to a larger organizational body than otherwise desirable when spillover effects are addressed. In practice, this is a less important criterion than the spillover criterion because few transport services require extremely large scale in order to operate efficiently. Moreover, to the extent that large scale aggravates the arbitration efforts caused by network effects, large scale may bog down the speed and quality of decision-making.

Administrative constraints. The technology needed to administer and implement the finance and development of transportation investments and operations was a significant administrative constraint. The resulting pattern of sources and uses of funding presented in Exhibit 1 is, to a large degree, a legacy of challenges to pricing, communication, and raising capital that faced early efforts to develop transportation. For example, between 1792 and 1845, approximately 1500 private joint-stock companies were chartered for the purpose of building roads.[8] However, there was no easy way

---

[8] This section relies heavily on work by Klein (1990, 1994) and Klein and Fielding (1991).

to levy tolls without risk of evasion. Thus, many chartered transportation companies failed or never got off the ground, with the notable exception of private bridges where evasion was more difficult.[9] By 1825, much of the eastern United States was served by road and canal networks that had been privately initiated. However, gradually states or localities often took over or subsidized these developments with broad-based taxes that were easier to administer and usage was often "free" to the user.[10] In the modern context of electronic tolling, administration of usage-based finance is no longer haunted by these technological restrictions.

10.2.4   Evaluating the case for devolution

This chapter argues that the persistence of a governance structure that was defined by motivations and constraints that no longer exist needs to be redressed by radical reforms that satisfy the criteria outlined above. These criteria are kept in mind throughout this chapter to define and analyze the proper organizational role in transportation. It is this author's operating premise regarding devolution of authority that four practical facts emerge from study of spillover, network, economy of scale, and administrative considerations.

In this chapter, the length of the trips taken or distances shipped on a given mode of transport is used as the primary indicator of the appropriate organizational scale. Most real-world transportation networks involve a combination of parallel and serial effects on network users, and have the potential to require organization of the network elements to regulate and exploit network externalities. Although this would seem to justify government involvement at full network scale, this conclusion is not supported by real-world conditions. First, even when there is frank potential for the existence of positive network externalities and justification for large networks, private coordination is demonstrably capable of doing any necessary coordination of mutual interests. For example, there are approximately 80 cellular networks in the continental United States providing private cell phone services through interconnected cell-tower and microwave technologies. The fact that cell service providers have been able to interconnect without government involvement at continental (and larger) network scale suggests that private governance can work effectively to knit disparate elements into comprehensive networks. [11]

Second, unlike electronic networks, the individual elements (road segments) of transportation networks are typically organized in the most complex manner at a local

---

[9] The first private toll-bridge company developed the Charles-River Bridge in Massachusetts in 1786 and returned a 10.5% dividend annually to its private investors. It is estimated that 59 private bridge companies were chartered, principally in New England. At least two bridges were privately developed and operated in Oregon to span the Columbia River, one at Hood River, Oregon and another at North Bonneville, Oregon. Both were developed in the 1920s and successfully operated privately until their acquisition by public ports when the private owners chose to leave the business.

[10] Indeed, the early era of purely private toll roads ended in 1938 when, after 30 years, the private Long Island Motor Parkway succumbed to the "free" competition of parallel public roads funded by broad-based fuel and property tax levies.

[11] The Competitive Carriers Association provides a forum for assisting interconnectivity. See, CCAMobile.org.

scale. Thus, the concept that a network's value to consumers increases with the degree of connectivity to other consumers (measured as the ratio of links to nodes in the network) is not obvious when those links are congestible. If it is true that the most serious negative externalities (congestion, accidents, etc.) arise in high connectivity conditions, then transportation networks should be developed, managed, and priced at those points where connectivity is highest.

Third, empirically, few trips involve traversing multiple local or state facilities, because economic activity organizes itself spatially to limit costly and time-consumptive transportation costs. Thus, the economic interest that parties in State A have in the development of transportation facilities in State B, though potentially positive, is *de minimis* in practice. Moreover, it has long been known that the utilization of transport facilities that connect two localities or states typically falls away inversely with the square of distance between those economic centers.[12]

Finally, by definition, having shorter trips served primarily with smaller-scale, proximate entities improve responsiveness to consumer propensities and improve entity accountability and facility management. Of course, the propensity of trips to be longer is not per se a basis for higher-scale government or other organizational involvement. With the right pricing and incentives for coordination of smaller scale entities, facilities serving longer trips can and are provided by a network of smaller scale entities. In addition, for reasons given later, the spillover effects likely decline in significance at larger scale and what remains are mainly manageable serial network effects. Because most networks are combinations of serial and parallel network elements, there is theoretical support and evidence from other networks that the potentially destabilizing competitive redundancy of pure parallel network issues can be solved by pricing and management by organizations of relatively modest scale.[13,14] Thus, the degree of dominance of short-length travel makes a good *prima facie* case for devolution.

This chapter also argues that there should be a bias toward private provision of infrastructure and user-charge finance of the development and operation of that infrastructure. Doing so will yield outcomes that better satisfy user objectives. They also avoid intrusion of corrosive political motivations and behaviors, such as cross-subsidization, diversion of funds to nontransport uses, pork-barrel investment allocation, and the incentive dissipating influence of broad-based taxation. Residual public interests can be dealt with by government partnering with private financiers, developers, and operators.[15] The marginal cost basis of theory of congestion pricing supports pricing of the use of transportation capacity at the finest spatial and time-of-travel grain possible economically. By so doing, the differential performance and needs for improvement of elements of transportation networks can be paired specifically with the revenue created to resolve those deficits. The problem with today's systems of pricing public transportation infrastructure is that there is insufficient matching of revenue generated to capital and operating expenditure. Public transportation funds, however generated,

[12] Isard (1954).
[13] Zhang and Levinson (2005).
[14] Clayman et al. (2010).
[15] International Road Foundation Switzerland (2011). http://www.irfnet.ch/files-upload/pdf-files/irf_urbanppp_web.pdf.

are placed in large federal, state and local pools. The ultimate allocation to projects reflects more political bias than the spatial and diurnal distribution of need.

In the next section of this report, we examine empirically the indicators that can be used to guide devolution of transportation funding and decision-making to governments and private enterprises. If followed, the recommendations presented herein (and the studies that support it) will yield a more responsive, economical, and less politicized transportation system.

10.3   Transport propensities and devolution

The analysis in this section examines current passenger and freight travel propensities. To the extent possible, this discussion differentiates amongst the six major modes of transport (highway, transit, air, rail, water, and pipeline) and three scales of organizational involvement (national, regional, and local). Because so much government involvement already exists, our devolution discussion will also use the terms federal, state, and local government parlance interchangeably with more general, organizational scales.

10.3.1   Passenger transportation

We turn first to passenger transportation to examine information about trip lengths as an indicator of the scale of organization that might best address passenger transport issues. The most comprehensive source of this data is the Federal Highway Administration's National Household Travel Survey (NHTS). The most recent version of this survey for which survey data is fully available is the 2009 survey.[16] This survey provides information by mode of travel and purpose for about 1.1 million surveyed trips by households. Since those responding to the sample are selectively different from the population as a whole, weighting is applied to the various responses with the intention of making the information nationally representative.

Exhibit 4 summarizes the various reasons why persons travel. Home, shopping, and work purposes (all local in nature) comprise nearly 70% of household passenger travel. These are important, routine functions for which users deserve a fiscally viable and dynamic response from highway operations. Instead, they are commonly highly congested and fiscally incontinent. Since, as recalled above, the interstate highway system was supposed to address this issue, there is clearly something broken in the manner the major passenger uses of roads are served.

10.3.2   Passenger transport trip lengths and modes of travel

Households use a variety of modes to travel—some serving short and some serving longer trips. However, the overall trip distribution, as shown in the panels of

---

[16] The 2012 survey is not yet fully available at the time of this writing (2016).

Exhibit 4 **Passenger Trip Purpose Summary (HHTS, 2009)**

Trip Purpose	Percent	Cumulative Percent
Home	34.2	34.2
Shopping/errands	19.4	53.6
Work	16.2	69.8
Social/recreational	8.4	78.2
Transport someone	8.0	86.2
Meals	6.3	92.5
Family personal business/obligations	2.9	95.4
School/daycare/religious activity	2.8	98.2
Medical/dental services	1.6	99.8
Other reason	0.2	100.0

Source: NHTS database.

Exhibit 5a **Average Trip Length, by Selected Purpose, by Mode (NHTS, 2009)**

Mode	Home Trip Length (mi.)	Work Trip Length (mi.)	All Trips Length (mi.)	Share of Home Trips (%)	Share of Work Trips (%)	Share of All Trips (%)
Airplane	608.84	849.96	1131.35	0.0	0.1	0.1
Auto/other light vehicles	9.77	12.91	10.14	86.6	90.7	87.3
Bicycle/walk	0.85	0.94	0.83	10.2	4.7	9.4
Bus	6.06	10.27	6.93	2.1	1.0	1.8
Ferry	13.90	13.74	9.70	0.0	0.0	0.0
Intercity bus	33.09	57.36	45.47	0.0	0.0	0.1
Intercity rail	21.74	40.72	39.53	0.0	0.0	0.0
Unknown	8.92	13.35	8.45	0.1	0.1	0.1
RV	33.69	31.46	37.85	0.0	0.0	0.0
Special transit/ other	9.38	26.91	12.65	0.5	0.9	0.5
Street car/trolley	4.16	8.86	5.30	0.0	0.0	0.0
Taxicab	5.49	8.49	5.83	0.1	0.1	0.1
Truck	18.35	44.63	32.75	0.2	1.8	0.4
Urban rail	10.78	11.50	14.38	0.1	0.4	0.1
All modes	8.88	14.08	10.06	100.0	100.0	100.0

Source: 2009 National Household Travel Survey, weighted by survey response rates.

Exhibit 5a and 5b, reveals that short trips dominate travel. Over 98% of all trips average 10 miles in length or less and only 1% are longer than 12 miles. Thus, it is clear that the organizational scale needed to address the majority of vehicle trips is very local in nature. Everything else being equal, there is no case for dominant, national involvement in the provision of transportation services or infrastructure as it applies to

Exhibit 5b Mode, Trip Length, and Cumulative Shares, All Purposes (NHTS, 2009)

Mode	Average Trip Length (mi.)	Share of Reported Trips (%)	Cumulative Share of All Trips (%)
Bicycle or walk	0.83	9.383	9.38
Street car/trolley transit	5.30	0.013	9.40
Taxi	5.83	0.081	9.48
Transit bus	7.98	1.892	11.37
Unknown mode	8.45	0.139	11.51
Ferry	9.70	0.009	11.52
Autos and light trucks	10.14	87.327	98.84
Special transit and other	12.65	0.514	99.36
Rail transit	14.38	0.149	99.51
Intercity bus	19.21	0.004	99.51
Truck	32.75	0.374	99.89
RV	37.85	0.042	99.93
Intercity train	39.53	0.008	99.94
Airplane	1131.35	0.064	100.00
All modes	10.06	100.000	NA

Source: 2009 National Household Travel Survey, weighted by survey response rates.

passenger modes of travel, and a weak case for state level involvement. Local, county, or perhaps multicounty scale or private organizations can best represent and manage the highway component of vehicle travel.

Even as one disaggregates the trip data by the mode of travel, the picture emerges that the average trip length remains very short for all but recreational vehicle, passenger truck, intercity rail, and air travel on the basis of the NHTS data disaggregated by average trip length by mode.[17] Notably, the modes with longer than average trip lengths represent, in toto, a small share of the total trips reported in the NHTS, and, with the exception of the air travel mode, relatively short trips overall. Although there is a variation of trip length within any mode or purpose of travel, the relative lack of variability measured in the NHTS sample and across averages reported by trip purpose suggests that there is compelling evidence to support significant devolution.

Although it should be remembered that the NHTS is a national survey, it does report the mode and trip length for over 1.1 million trips. Therefore, from a statistical viewpoint, the reported shares are meaningful for the purposes of assessing the locus to which decision-making and funding should be devolved. Local and regional public and/or private entities can provide decision-making and financing responsibility. The longer trip propensity of air travel and the implicitly large-scale need for a uniform system of ATC system likely justifies the presence of a large-scale entity for

---

[17] Trip lengths are weighted averages by NHTS trip response rate by mode. Modes are consolidations of NHTS mode nomenclature for presentation purposes.

Exhibit 6 **Oregon Work Trip Share and Length, by Mode (ACS 2009)**

Mode	Estimated Work Trip Length (mi.)	Work Trip Share by Mode (%)
Car, truck, or van	10.93	82.70
Bus or trolley bus	21.20	2.83
Streetcar or trolley car	9.75	0.24
Subway or elevated	12.79	0.27
Railroad	37.35	0.16
Ferryboat	8.57	0.01
Taxicab	6.75	0.06
Motorcycle	9.33	0.38
Bicycle	1.52	2.19
Walk	0.48	3.80
Worked at home	0.00	6.70
Other method	13.70	0.66
All modes	9.94	100.00

Source: 2009 American Community Survey database.

this purpose, but a good case can be made for privatization of this system, and for eliminating subsidies to airports. (This will be discussed in a later section.)

It is unfortunate that the NHTS data from the state of Oregon are too sparse in number to usefully distinguish Oregonians' behavior from the national behavior as represented by the NHTS. The 2009 American Community Survey (ACS) of the US Census, used for comparability to the timing of the NHTS data, does permit some analysis of trips by mode. Exhibit 6 presents the Oregon trip length and mode share for the work trip purpose, illustrating the rough similarities in trip lengths and mode shares.[18]

The ACS only reports trip length for work trips, uses a different nomenclature of modes than the NHTS, and includes a work-at-home mode that is not specifically represented in the NHTS data. Nevertheless, the shares of passenger light vehicle modes are of similar orders of magnitude (in excess of 80%) as is the work trip length at 11–12 miles. Similarly, the various NHTS transit modes are likewise similar in average trip length and mode shares. Even the 5% share of bicycling and walking to work is roughly consistent with the NHTS data for the same trip purpose[19] and the range observed in the Census' American Community Survey data for the same year for other mild climate areas.[20]

---

[18] Another weakness of the ACS data is that travel time, not trip length, is surveyed. For the purpose of constructing Exhibit 5a,b, the author applied typical peak period travel speeds to the reported travel time estimates to infer trip distance. However, the absence of information on intercity train or bus, air, taxi, a specific truck-type categorization and focus on the work trip only makes the specific measures less useful than they otherwise might be, and less reliable than those from the national survey

[19] Computed from NHTS data detail not presented here.

[20] https://www.census.gov/prod/2011pubs/acs-15.pdf.

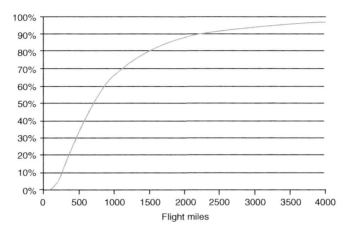

Exhibit 7 OR Passenger air trip miles (2014), cum. %.

Passenger air travel represents a small share of total trip making, but is an activity that more obviously requires a service infrastructure that handles long trips directly. Data are available for Oregon air travel from ticket analysis databases. Exhibit 7 displays the cumulative share of passenger trips on scheduled airlines, by flight length miles[21] for trips to or from Oregon airports in 2014.

As the figure reveals, 70% of passenger airline trips were less than 1000 miles in length and 90% were 2000 miles or less. Some collaborative system among states and other countries is necessary to manage the between-airport infrastructure of a national and international air transport systems. One has to assume that collaboration by private or other smaller scale entities would be inferior to FAA management of air travel to justify the level of federal government involvement. However, on the basis of the trip length analysis, the ATC system scale is a possible exception to the devolution logic that forms the basis of this chapter.[22] In sum, however, it is hard to make the case—for passenger travel overall—for funding passenger travel at a national level, with this one possible exception.

10.3.3 Freight transportation

We now turn our attention to freight transportation. As discussed in the introduction, the case for devolution of transport authority and financing to lower-level public or private entities is based partly, though not exclusively, on the distances that passengers

---

[21] The length examined here is the ticketed trip length which, of course, can be assembled from a series of shorter flights.

[22] The data in Figure 7 is derived by the author from a database of 160,000 in-bound and out-bound Oregon ticket itineraries obtained from the scheduled air travel origin-destination files at http://www.transtats. bts.gov. The graphic is a statistical representation of the individual ticket itinerary trip lengths ("track miles") found in that data, using an assumed log-normal distribution of trip lengths.

travel or commodities are shipped. In the context of passenger travel, the reported trip length is a natural measure of this propensity.

In the case of freight movement, we examine the propensity measures by using data that provide information on shipment lengths, that is, the distance traveled by a shipment from its origin to its destination. In both the passenger and freight contexts, multiple modes may be used in trip making, but in the case of freight, in particular, certain types of trips are strongly multimodal, and private carriage on privately operated modes is dominant. Public rights of way are employed by trucking and air and water modes, but as with passenger light vehicle travel, the ownership of the vehicles is almost exclusively private. The air freight mode, like the air passenger mode, operates on a system of publicly regulated virtual rights of way, but rail and pipeline modes use generally privately owned and maintained rights of way.

As was the case in the passenger mode, the data on trip (shipment) length propensity is obtained from surveys conducted at lengthy intervals by public or private entities. The primary source in the freight arena is the US Census Commodity Flow Survey (CFS). At this writing, detailed data (sufficient to support state level analysis) is available only from the 2007 CFS, with only summary preliminary statistics available from the 2012 CFS.

In contrast to the NHTS, more statistical measures of the distribution of trip lengths are available for the national perspective (and less robustly at the state perspective).

10.3.4   Freight transportation shipping distances and modes used

The freight shipment distance varies by mode, not surprisingly. What is surprising, and very relevant to the devolution case, is the dominant share of product that is shipped by truck and the short distances that such shipments involve. This is revealed in Exhibit 8 using the most recent Commodity Freight Survey data at a national level.

Several important aspects of freight movement are illustrated by Exhibit 8. First, freight shipments by truck represent over 70% of all shipments, whether measured by value or weight. The second and third largest shipment modes (by tonnage) are rail and pipeline, both of which are on rights of way that are mostly privately owned and operated—in contrast to trucking, which operates mostly on public roads. Second, fully 92% of truck shipments are less than 500 miles in length, by weight of shipment. Third, at the other end of the spectrum is air freight, whose shipments are primarily high value and shipped longer distances. By value, only 16% of air freight is shipped less than 500 miles. This is not surprising, given the higher cost per ton-mile to ship by air. Finally, and interestingly, 72% of pipeline tonnage travels less than 500 miles. These statistics are interesting examples of how major modes, using primarily privately developed facilities and largely private enterprise, are able to coordinate and manage short-distance shipments as well as long-distance shipments.

The categorical service ranges available from the CFS and used in Exhibit 8 make it difficult to compare the full distribution of trip lengths shipped by the various modes. To some degree, this categorization is necessitated by privacy and other considerations. However, the CFS also provides summary statistics for trip lengths. Specifically, it

Exhibit 8 Freight Service Range, by Mode, Value, and Tonnage (CFS, 2007)

Service Range (mi.)	Truck	Rail	Water	Air	Multiple Modes and Mail	Pipeline	Other/Unknown	Total
Shipment Value (in $ billions)								
Below 100	5492	77	84	2	244	396	239	6535
100–249	2247	50	32	9	182	93	58	2670
250–499	1696	81	24	35	242	86	55	2220
500–749	832	68	14	22	184	37	24	1180
750–999	565	66	9	28	209	39	22	938
1000–1499	603	101	20	38	290	78	32	1163
1500–2000	281	62	14	33	163	43	13	609
Over 2000	475	69	15	190	403	22	30	1204
Total	12,192	574	212	357	1917	794	472	16,518
Shipment Tonnage (in millions)								
Below 100	8004	273	228	0	98	747	189	9540
100–249	2982	206	88	0	64	191	57	3589
250–499	1336	370	84	0	91	172	30	2084
500–749	407	260	49	0	69	83	9	877
750–999	207	245	32	0	72	94	8	658
1000–1499	203	442	96	0	83	206	9	1039
1500–2000	86	176	46	0	33	118	3	463
Over 2000	110	53	32	2	58	60	12	326
Total	13,335	2024	655	5	568	1671	317	18,576

Source: USDOT, Freight Analysis Framework, 2012 analysis of 2007 data.

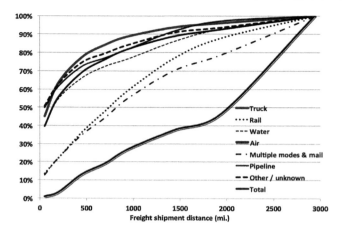

Exhibit 9 Freight cumulative modal shares, by distance (est. CFS 2007).

Exhibit 10 **Oregon Modal Shares, by Mode, Tonnage, and Value (CFS 2012)**

Mode	Value ($ million)	Mode (%)	Tons (in thousands)	Mode (%)
All trucks	101,093	68.8	149,917	81.2
For-hire truck	55,081	37.5	74,555	40.4
Private truck	46,012	31.3	75,363	40.8
Rail	3353	2.3	7204	3.9
Water	1859	1.3	8454	4.6
Air (incl truck and air)	5262	3.6	13	–
Multiple modes and mail	28,450	19.4	8312	4.5
Other	6441	4.4	10,671	5.8
All modes	146,458	100	183,986	100

Source: Author, from Commodity Flow Survey data.

provides the mean shipment distance and the coefficient of variation.[23] This permits construction of a graphical approximation of the full distribution of mode shares by distance, rather than by category. Exhibit 9 shows the mode shares by distance. Only air, multimodal shipments, and rail freight display a large cumulative share of tonnage shipped at longer distances. Thus, the issues of network management aside temporarily (we will return to this subject), the case for federal involvement is weak, with the *possible* exception of the air freight movements. (See discussion in the next section.)

As Exhibit 10 indicates, the national statistics on shares by mode are mirrored by Oregon-centric measures of trips originating in Oregon. As for the nation as a whole, the shares by the truck mode are dominant, whether measured by value or tonnage.

---

[23] The coefficient of variation (CV) is the ratio of the standard deviation of the observed trip lengths by mode to the mean distance.

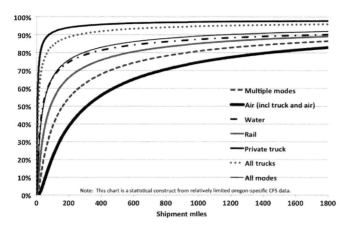

Exhibit 11 Cumulative Oregon freight modal shares, by distance (CFS 2012).

For-hire and private trucking have similar market shares, and other modal shares are similar to the national figures. Pipeline shipment quantity data are not available, most likely because identifying the flows would reveal private information or because of the low sampling rate at the state level. The "multiple modes and mail" mode usually represents shipments involving rail freight and truck freight combinations.

The available data at a state level is limited because of sample size and privacy limitations. However, the available Commodity Flow Survey data on shipping distances can be used to draw basic conclusions about Oregon freight mode distance distributions with some simple statistics and reasonable assumptions about determinants of interstate truck trip activity. The results yield measures of the cumulative share of shipments, by distance shipped, by mode.

The resulting computations employ the information included in the CFS of the variation (within the sample) of the measures obtained. By making reasonable assumptions about the particular distribution that characterizes the variability, it is possible to develop crude representations of the distribution of trip lengths, and compute cumulative share measures for each mode. The resulting computations are presented in Exhibit 11.[24]

For trucking, the dominant freight mode, it is not just the distance that *shipments* travel that is relatively short, but also the length of the truck *trips*, themselves. Using a study that relied upon GPS locations of a large number of trucks, the author has estimated the distribution of truck trip shares by length using Oregon as the out-bound shipping point.[25] The results of that simulation are depicted in Exhibit 12. The individual

---

[24] Specifically, using the CFS data on the mean and coefficient of variation, cumulative shipping distance distributions can be computed. It involves assuming that the shipment distances follow a log-normal distribution.

[25] The author did not have access to the raw GPS data. Rather, the state-pair volume data in the study relied upon was used to estimate a truck-trip distribution model by state. This was done econometrically, using a gravity-model mathematical formulation, with latitude/longitude information representing the centroid of each state to measure inter-state distances, and employment as a measure of the scale of each state economy.

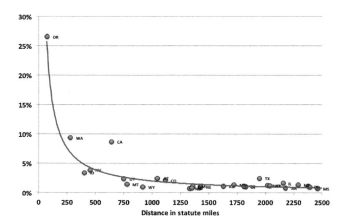

Exhibit 12 Estimated outbound OR truck trip shares by distance and state (2014).

data points are illustrative of the destinations of trips at the presented lengths. The results mirror the findings from the CFS data. Truly long truck trips are an extreme rarity compared to the number of trips that occur within a state or local region. Trips over 500 miles in length, for example, represent less than 5% of truck trips.

In the original study on trucks originating or ending trips in Florida, for example, of the 1.1 million truck trips started in that state, 84% ended in that state.[26] Very distant states show very small starting or endpoint activity. In particular, only about 30 of the 1.1 million trucks ended or began their trip in Oregon.

The Oregon measures reveal, in general, the expected pattern of (a) dominance of short-haul trucking and (b) confinement of longer-haul freight shipments to modes that are mostly privatized.

The two modes that display longer trip or shipment distance propensities are the air and water modes. In the air mode, the long distances require a coordinated system of ATC, certification, safety, and other regulation of the (mainly) private carriers who provide the users with service. The federal reach goes further, however, in providing funding to individual airports—primarily through the Airport Improvement Program.

The water mode involvement of the federal government involves dredging and maintenance of waterways. There is less high-level involvement in marine ports, with the ownership often being at the state and local levels, with funding from own-source revenue.[27] State involvement in the water ports is primarily regulatory and the use of loans and grants, through the port revolving loan fund (PRLF) that provides funding at below-corporate borrowing rates, and the port planning and marketing fund (PPMF) that provides grants funded by the interest earned on the PRLF loans.[28] Any port

---

[26] University of South Florida and American Transportation Research Institute (2014).

[27] Oregon has nine ports on the Columbia River that make up one-quarter of the 36-port Columbia-Snake system (there is one port in Idaho and 26 in Washington). The three ports on the lower Columbia (Astoria, St. Helens, and Portland) are deep-water ports—with largest being the Port of Portland's marine terminals. But Oregon also has 14 coastal ports, including the deep-water ports of Newport and the Oregon International Port of Coos Bay.

approved for incorporation and operation under ORS Chapter 777 or 778 may apply for funding. Since this funding can be sought by both air- and water-ports, and spent on industrial park and other indirect activities, this is a subtle cross-subsidy and other-use phenomenon in Oregon port activity.

Perhaps the greatest, recent imprint that government has had on ports in Oregon involves environmental opposition to Columbia River dredging to facilitate visitation by deep-draft vessels and opposition to establishment of liquefied natural gas (LNG) ports on the coast of Oregon.[29] The result is that the Port of Portland has been unable to attract the new, larger container vessels that are going instead to other Pacific coast ports. It recently lost its two largest container clients, Hanjin and Hapag Lloyd, after the Port's inability to control striking labor imposed large delay costs on these carriers and their customers.[30]

10.4   The implications for devolution

This chapter is focused on the issue of the appropriate role of governments in transportation. To do so, we have examined the current and historical patterns of finance and the patterns of travel amongst the major passenger and freight transport sectors. In this section, we discuss the implications of these observations for the potential of devolution to improve the efficiency and fairness of transport in the United States. We summarize the implications in the context of the three allocative questions raised in the introduction to this report.

10.4.1   The assignment of authority question

The key lessons of our review of the role and pattern of involvement government among the various modes are manifold. There is little evidence from the data on trip lengths and other measures of propensity to travel or ship to justify high level, large-scale involvement in either passenger or freight transport.

The lack of justification is most evident, among all the modes, in the transit sector. By definition, transit trips are extremely short and not important parts of larger networks. In addition, overwhelmingly, the primary beneficiaries of travel on these modes are the local population. The significant influence of federal and state governments

---

[28] http://www.orinfrastructure.org/Infrastructure-Programs/.

[29] http://www.oregonlive.com/politics/index.ssf/2015/05/lng_opponents_urge_gov_brown_t.html (27.05.2015).

[30] It is argued by some that the loss of container business, though significant for the Port of Portland, may be inevitable given the trend toward larger vessels. The Port is left with low-value, so-called break bulk (noncontainerized) business in wheat and rock products. The author, in 1993, showed that this business faces no-less vigorous competition in international export of product areas from ports as far away as the Gulf coast. As little as a one cent per bushel cost disadvantage to the Columbia River ports results in a half percentage point loss in market share to Gulf ports. Under the conditions that prevailed at the time, that translates into 2.3 million bushels of regional export activity annually.

in the direction of funding, provision of subsidies, and modal-cross subsidization is completely unnecessary, inappropriate, and distortionary. It violates all premises of public finance regarding nexus and locus of benefits. This is an area where, whatever the implications of the Pricing Question or the Privatization Question, government should not be using resources collected from other modes or "supportive resources". Federal and state governments should be out of the transit sector altogether, and rely on fare box revenue to ensure that the cost of the service is worthwhile to the user.[31]

Passenger and freight travel over roads constitutes, by far, the largest share of total transport services, but is also dominated overwhelmingly by short-distance travel. This usage pattern of the highway mode, second only to transit, does not justify the involvement of higher level government. Despite this, for imperial, historical, and administrative reasons, the intrusion of higher-level governmental entities has come to dominate the resource allocation process. Local areas have to beg counties or regional governments to respond to their needs, counties in turn have to beg to the states, and states have to lobby the federal government. Whether one believes we have major infrastructural shortfalls in the highway mode, or not, this upside pattern of authority assignment cannot possibly be allocated efficiently.[32]

The modes that operate primarily using privately owned rights of way and facilities—most notably rail and pipeline freight—to an important degree enjoy some autonomy from top–down authoritative meddling. Owners and operators of these rights of way provide both short-haul and long-haul service through inter-carrier agreements and other coordinating devices to a major degree without federal and government authoritative primacy (especially in rail). The heavy-handed and inefficient federal government regulation of the railways ended largely in 1980 with the passage of the Staggers Act. However, government (and states) does regulate the rates charged in the pipeline industry (probably to the detriment of efficiency). Both modes still suffer regulatory intrusions when new rights of way are desired, and when quasi-governmental services such as Amtrak operates on rights of way with government subsidy. Nonetheless, these two heavily networked modes stand as evidence that government involvement in operation and funding is not intrinsically necessary.[33]

In the air and water transport modes, government is involved in spending on the network that ties together the various ports (i.e. the ATC system and waterways, respectively). The airports, however also receive significant federally channeled funding, while seaports are primarily state and locally funded. Thus, the level of smaller-scale

---

[31] The argument in favor of subsidies is that the failure to price roads properly puts transit at a competitive disadvantage. This is likely true to some degree, although the cost of Oregon transit service is so high that correcting ills in pricing highways is unlikely to change transit's mode share. Transit cost containment should take precedence over heavy subsidization.

[32] The Motor Carrier Reform Act of 1980 largely deregulated the trucking industry itself (after observing the beneficial effects of deregulation of intrastate trucking in California—urged by among others, this author in 1976). See Pozdena and McElhiney (1976).

[33] Indeed, both of these modes are larger networks than the Interstate Highway System. Rail has 140,000 miles of road in the United States. There are 57,000 miles of crude oil pipelines alone. The Interstate Highway System is smaller than both at 42,000 centerline miles.

involvement is more localized in the seaport case and with greater reliance on "own-source" funding.

In sum, in terms of the *Assignment of Authority* question, the trip and travel propensity evidence does not support an *inherent* need for high-level government involvement in any of the major transportation modes. With the exception of the air mode, transcontinental-length travel constitutes a minuscule share of transit, passenger, and freight highway, and other federal and state-dominated modes. The counterargument, of course, is that because all of the modes operate as networks, some omniscient guiding public hand is needed to coordinate and administrate the integration of the network components, to protect "captive shippers" that have only one point of rail access, etc. Even if this were true, any such amorphous virtues would have to be balanced against the inefficiency and distortion introduced by bureaucratic attempts to second-guess diverse and complicated market forces.

Although this central-planning mentality is unlikely to die an easy death, it is empirically and theoretically erroneous. We will return to this topic in more detail in our discussion of the *Pricing question* and the *Privatization question* later in this chapter. Suffice to say here that the US rail system performance *after* deregulation belies this concern. As a nationally prominent Brookings Institution transportation economist concluded 25 years after deregulation:

> *The Staggers Rail Act of 1980 marked a dramatic change in the evolution of the U.S. railroad industry by eliminating or greatly reducing federal regulatory control over virtually every aspect of rail freight operations. … [After] 25 years of deregulation [the] evidence strongly indicates that rail deregulation has accomplished its primary goal of putting the U.S. rail freight industry on a more secure financial footing. … [Deregulation] has also turned out to be a great boon for shippers as rail carriers have passed on some of their cost savings to them in lower rates and significantly improved service times and reliability. I conclude that a fully deregulated environment, which would entail elimination of residual regulation by the Surface Transportation Board, will preserve this rare win-win outcome and yield even further benefits to railroads and shippers.[34]*

As of this writing, there are 560 Class I and Class II US railroads that provide freight common carriage on the approximately 140,000 US route miles, without rate regulation and without the prior, heavy-handed federal regulatory intervention.[35] Oregon is served by 2 Class I railroads and 15 Class II railroads.[36] It is a powerful example of the potential for devolution (to 560 private entities, in this case) of even a network that serves relatively long ship distances and requiring coordination of end-point attraction and distribution of shipments.

---

[34] Winston (2005).

[35] Source: railinc.com, Association of American Railroads, and http://en.wikipedia.org/wiki/List_of_common_carrier_freight_railroads_in_the_United_States.

[36] Class 1 and Class II railroads are distinguished by their annual revenue levels being above or below $250 m. per year, respectively.

10.4.2 The pricing question

The single most distinctive and distortionary feature of the dysfunctional parts of the US transportation system is the failure to price the use of transportation facilities properly. In this section, we (a) remind the reader of the degree to which pricing is dysfunctional for many US transportation modes and (b) characterize how devolution coupled with better pricing of dysfunctionally priced modes would yield more efficient, fairer, and less bureaucracy-dependent travel and investment decisions.[37]

The first lesson in economics is that goods and services cannot be allocated to their highest and best use unless there is a relationship between the prices users are charged and the cost that user imposes on the supplier of transportation services. Sadly, the most dysfunctionally priced transportation modes are also the most significant, quantitatively, in terms of the volumes of passengers carried or tons of freight moved.

10.4.3 Highway pricing: the current Oregon setting

Highways carry the vast majority of passengers and freight in the United States and in Oregon. Unfortunately, the pricing of Oregon's highways is not sufficient to reflect the costs imposed by users and there is a virtually nonexistent nexus between what projects are funded and who generated the revenue used for those projects.

In Oregon, pricing of roads used by passenger vehicles consists of a crude, fuel tax per gallon (for autos) that—on a per-vehicle-mile basis—does not vary by time of day or where the travel occurred. Thirty cents of the per-gallon tax remains with Oregon, and 18.7 cents is collected for and retained by the federal government.

Oregon trucks pay a diesel fuel tax in some states, but Oregon charges an in-state fee for heavy trucks that varies by weight-mile. It does not vary by time of day nor by the specific segment(s) of the highway network used, however, and the weigh in motion system does not have comprehensive coverage.

In contrast, the *load* on the capacity of the roadways varies systematically by time of day due to variations in the timing of trip making by autos, light trucks, and heavy trucks. This is because users in the peak period place a greater burden on existing capacity than do nonpeak users, but do not pay a commensurately higher price than off-peak users. This failure to reflect the scarcity of capacity at the peak causes overuse of the facility and wasteful congestion costs (the value of travel time delay). Not only is current usage distorted and traveler time dissipated, but also the apparent need for more capacity is exaggerated.

Implementing differential pricing *does not* necessarily mean that the highway users in the aggregate would face higher costs of travel. On the contrary, off-peak travel is over-priced, even if peak-travel is underpriced and, just as importantly, the resulting better utilization of the road network would reduce the travel time costs of users by reducing congestion and, in the long run, the cost of adding capacity that cannot pay for itself.

---

[37] This brief discussion of the dysfunction of in highway pricing is well elaborated on in ECONorthwest (2015), *2015 Oregon Highway Cost Allocation Study*, Supplementary Documents, Appendix B.1.

In addition to mispricing capacity, Oregon also misprices wear-and-tear costs. Heavy trucks (especially those with few axles), place a much greater *wear-and-tear* burden on roadways surfaces than do autos and light trucks. Oregon does levy an axel-adjusted weight-mile tax on trucks, which has the potential to compensate for the excess wear-and-tear they impose. However, though the actual wear and tear varies with the type of the road traveled, the weight-mile tax does not. Additionally, the weight-mile charge for heavy trucks does not vary with the time-of-day of travel and the effects of the trucks on capacity utilization.

Thus, it is fair to say that Oregon's pricing system for highways does not have the potential to properly ration the use of existing capacity, nor fairly and effectively accrue revenues to specific facilities on which the effects of pricing distortions (congestion and wear and tear) occur. Instead, the revenues collected from the major fee sources in Oregon are pooled at the state level, and allocated among the state, counties, and cities by crude and nonspecific formulae.

As one can imagine, clumsy and corruptible political judgments are used to allocate funding to the constituent parts of the roadway network in Oregon. Funding of individual projects and activities is accordingly unable to respect the travel proclivities of the local areas they primarily serve. A natural consequence of this is overused and worn-out roads and bridges in some cases, and over-building of roads in other cases. The lack of nexus between who pays and who benefits is so weak that Oregon voters routinely reject any increases in fuel taxes or other broad-based fees since they see their tax contributions diverted to others' benefit and to federal government and transit. Some local street and road development is funded by local voter-approved bond measures (and levy increments on property taxes) or system development charges levied on new development. Though enjoying somewhat closer nexus of payment and use, there is still no one-for-one connection between one's tax bill for roads and amount and specific use of the roads one actually makes.

10.4.4 Transit pricing: the current Oregon setting

The Oregon transit finance policy is also widely discordant with user-pay principles. Usage-based transit pricing is virtually nonexistent. In Oregon, only 16% of transit revenue comes from actual end-user charges (farebox charges). A zone-pricing system is employed that roughly corresponds to the distance traveled, but not the comparative costs of the vehicles and right-of-way that are used to provide the service, nor the time of day the user place demands on the systems. Instead of user-based charges, transit in Oregon relies heavily on federal funding (28%), state funding (11%), and subsidies paid for by broad-based taxes, such as a tax on all payrolls and other fees (45%). (See Exhibit 13.)

Ridership (measured as passenger-miles traveled (PMT) per employed person) has grown at an average rate of 2% per year between 1991 and 2013 as the region has grown and with the addition of more subsidized supply.[38] In metropolitan areas where

---

[38] Author, from National Transportation Database information from 1991 to 2013.

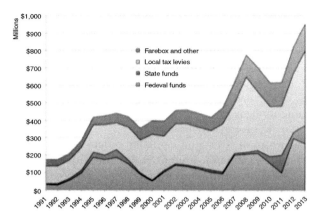

Exhibit 13 Funding of Oregon transit, by source, 1991–2013.

addition of capacity has been capital intensive (such as the Portland metro area where light rail service is strongly favored by planners), the average annual cost per PMT is particularly high, even though the cost of rights of way and vehicle capital amortization is not included in the reported, per passenger-mile cost data. (See Exhibit 14.)

As noted earlier, Oregon has been particularly aggressive and successful in obtaining federal funds to develop its transit service. This has permitted Oregon to invest in transit modes such as light rail and street car despite defeat of local funding measures by using its Congressional delegations political power in Washington, DC. Like other transit agencies that have built capital-intensive, rail transit systems, the ridership

Exhibit 14 Funding Source by OR Transit Operator, and Av. per PMT (2013)

Urban Area	Federal Funds	State Funds	Local Levies	Farebox and Other	Memo: Farebox and Local	Memo: Cost per Passenger Mile (PMT)
Albany, OR	$8.61	$1.89	$8.74	$1.37	$10.12	NA
Bend, OR	$27.71	$6.28	$15.53	$10.50	$26.03	$1.16
Corvallis, OR	$39.44	$1.98	$24.08	$4.13	$28.21	$0.90
Eugene, OR	$59.51	$15.36	$84.84	$34.56	$119.39	$1.01
Grants Pass, OR	$14.88	$3.19	$2.15	$2.93	$5.08	NA
Medford, OR	$39.16	$3.94	$12.92	$9.87	$22.79	$1.44
Portland, OR-WA	$118.81	$50.11	$211.72	$74.89	$286.61	$2.72
Salem, OR	$83.54	$23.71	$38.63	$14.17	$52.80	$1.97
Walla Walla, WA-OR	$1.53	$0.62	$1.10	$0.27	$1.37	NA

Source: Author, from National Transit Database, TS1.1.

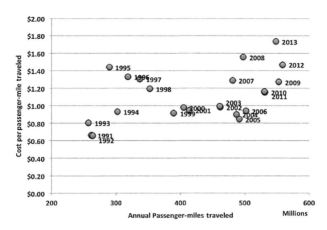

Exhibit 15 Average cost of Oregon transit ridership, 1991–2013.

appeal (and hence the operating costs per rider) has been distorted by the practice of cannibalizing prior local and freeway-flyer bus service.

Exhibit 15 shows that the average cost of servicing a passenger mile of transit travel in Oregon is approximately $1.70 in 2013, and has generally been rising over the past two decades. We know that the long-run *marginal* operating cost of attracting one *new* net PMT, therefore, is likely in excess of the average rate of $1.70. A regression of total transit operating costs against the PMT performed by the author, reveals that currently the marginal operating cost of attracting an additional passenger mile of transit system use in Oregon is approximately $2.60.

Oregon has lost control over its costs in part by the power of transit unions, and in having to accept federal transit employee work- and termination rules that bloat labor costs. As this is being written, the Portland area transit district is struggling with the scale of unfunded actuarial liabilities due to generous retirement schemes conceded to by the district. Just as importantly, the transit unions have managed to ban the servicing of its light rail stations by private or public service providers that do not pay union scale wages.

10.4.5 Other modes' pricing: the current Oregon setting

The nonhighway, nontransit modes operating in Oregon are dominated by rail and pipeline transportation. In the rail mode, freight transport pricing is largely unregulated, as it is in the United States as a whole.[39] Pricing practices in rail at the state and

---

[39] The federal Surface Transportation Board (STB) has the authority to intervene in rate making under certain conditions. However, two STB-commissioned studies of the postderegulation operation of the US rail system have concluded that STB rate reregulation is not necessary. To quote the most recent (2010) study, "… because the railroad industry has remained approximately revenue sufficient in recent years [unlike before deregulation], we reemphasize one of our original conclusions: providing significant rate relief to some shippers will likely result in rate increases for other shippers or threaten railroad financial viability" (Laurits and Christensen Associates Inc, 2010).

local levels are thus largely free of anything but nuisance intervention by government. However, passenger rail rates are subsidized at the national level. In 2008, however, federal subsidies for Amtrak passenger service were stopped on routes shorter than 750 miles. The northern route out of Oregon to the northwest and routes within the state thus lost federal subsidy at the time, as was true in other states. Thus, at the state level, Amtrak currently operates 21 state-supported routes in 15 states across the country, including Oregon.[40] According to press reports, Amtrak carried 117,000 passengers in Oregon in 2014—about half of which were wholly within Oregon. It is difficult to get useful measures of the subsidy rate, but Amtrak has stated that the subsidy rate is about 33% in Oregon. This likely excludes, however, the millions of dollars spent by Oregon to acquire rolling stock.[41]

In case of the pipeline mode, the Federal Energy Regulatory Commission (FERC) regulates the rates charged for interstate pipeline transportation of liquid petroleum, and some states also regulate intrastate prices. The amount charged is a function of the amount transported, the distance between receipt and delivery points, and competition to transport products in the market.[42] Natural gas pipeline rates are also regulated like a traditional monopoly utility. The reality, of course, is that petroleum and natural gas are competitive in many uses and both modes compete with rail and barge carriage of product. Current Oregon policy appears to be bowing to environmental pressure to block LNG ports and pipelines.[43] Although private capital is eager to take the financial risk to provide pipeline services in and through Oregon, develop port facilities, and accelerate coal-to-natural gas conversion, government involvement in pipelines is better viewed as a regulatory obstacle course than a subsidy policy.

Airports historically have charged airlines based primarily on aircraft weights, and under the US FAA rule were allowed only a flat amount to be charged regardless of the time of day and how busy the airport facilities are. President George W. Bush pressed for a rule change which allowed for peak pricing, but it was fought in the courts. In 2010, the appeals court ruled in favor of allowing the policy, and the airports are now allowed to vary pricing during peak times at congested airports.[44] This would spread passenger loads, reduce the need for more runway and apron capacity, etc. However, it does not appear from airport rate sheets that Oregon airports are doing so.[45]

---

[40] The states that contract with Amtrak are California, Illinois, Maine, Michigan, Missouri, New York, North Carolina, Pennsylvania, Oklahoma, Oregon, Texas, Vermont, Virginia, Washington and Wisconsin.

[41] Portland Tribune (2015).

[42] http://www.pipeline101.com/how-do-pipelines-work/what-is-the-cost-of-transportation.

[43] As recently as April 2015, for example, Oregon's Land Use Board of Appeals upheld Clatsop County's decision to deny a land use permit for a proposed pipeline by the Oregon LNG company. That pipeline would serve a proposed bidirectional LNG terminal at Warrenton, Oregon (near the Oregon coast). It would appear that, because it is an interstate facility, FERC has jurisdiction over the proposed pipeline. However, environmental lobbyists have pressed for levying a carbon tax on the fuel even though the LNG itself would not be used in Oregon.

[44] International Civil Aviation Organization (ICAO) policies were modified to permit some peak load pricing. See ICAO (2012).

[45] For example, the PDX July 2014 rate sheet itemizes the various landing fee, terminal rent, gate area fees, etc. The landing fee at PDX is a flat rate per 1000 pounds, despite diurnal and seasonal peaking patterns that might be better managed with peak-variant pricing.

Water ports in Oregon (like airports) are generally local public enterprises, surviving primarily on own-source revenues and occult subsidies in the form of tax exemptions. There are some loan and subsidy initiatives provided at the state levels, but the competition among ports is fairly sharp, and pricing—albeit set by public entities—is likely not particularly distortionary in an efficiency sense. The primary inefficiencies are introduced by subsidies, federal involvement in maintaining waterways, and countervailing environmental and other regulatory interventions.

In summary, Oregon pricing and subsidy policy distorts highway transportation and transit service most dramatically. The air, water, rail, and pipeline arenas are less affected by pricing distortions introduced by government at the state level in Oregon, but the regulatory footprint of all levels of government remains large, and noneconomic pricing is likely practiced in the airport element of the transportation system. Oregon's political/environmental stance has also interfered with the timely development of pipeline and LNG facilities, for example. This stance has been extended to limit the activities of the major North–South and East–West rail freight corridors. At the time of this writing, transport of coal and petroleum tank cars into and through Oregon to ocean ports is being subject to increased regulation. Oregon has allowed no motor fuel refining to occur in the state. Motor fuel is imported by pipeline or tanker truck from Washington and California.

In sum, the pricing and investment decision context in Oregon is affected not only by the failure to embrace tolling of highways, but also the distortions of regulatory intrusions and the willingness of the federal government to finance transit modes that the failure of local referenda suggest is not desired locally.

10.4.6   The privatization question

The distortions produced by inappropriate elevation of authority to higher levels of government and the associated broad-based tax system of "pricing" not only introduce their own distortions and inefficiencies, but also create a false pretext for excluding private supply of transportation infrastructure and services. This has affected efficiency and equity because public ownership and pricing practices of the associated transportation modes are not subject to the sharp, disciplinary forces of competition. In effect, the inherent allocative inefficiencies and retarded responsiveness to user needs is compounded by the lack of private alternatives in many of the transportation modes.

There are, of course, issues associated with privatization that are often offered to oppose private entry into public transport markets. This author believes that such arguments have little merit and are easily swept away by some very light touch public participation in the enterprises. To be specific, currently the private sector lacks the condemnation powers of the State which is the avenue by which necessary contiguous parcels of rights of way can be assembled. In addition, there may be certain operational safety and financial soundness conditions that other public policies compel. In instances of parallel network structures, as noted earlier, some coordination of supply may be necessary to avoid duplicative and/or financially unstable competition between alternative developers of transportation infrastructure. This author believes that these arguments point, at worst, to supportive public regulation and do not constitute fatal flaws to economical competitive and innovative private supply of transport services. Indeed, the fact that virtually every mode has historic or current examples of successful provision of private services belies the need for barriers to entry and operation that enemies of privatization tend to impose upon private initiatives. In any case, the virtues of competitive entry and efficient pricing dwarf the cost of addressing any of the aforementioned issues. This point will be illustrative quantitatively in the discussion that follows.

10.4.7   Privatization of Oregon highways

The privatization of highways is seen, in the context of its long history of public ownership, as an impossibility. In fact, however, as noted earlier, public ownership intervened historically mainly because of the difficulty of collecting tolls without evasion on private roads; private capital was eager to develop roads. Oregon had at least 12 private toll roads, according to ODOT historians.[46]

> *They were generally privately owned roads which may have been given, or sold, to the County or to ODOT for use as a highway. These private road[s] were supposedly cleared and maintained, thus worthy of the toll price. ...[However] Toll roads were a difficult business to operate profitably, make the toll to[o] high and travelers will simply find a way around your collection site.*

Indeed, the difficulty of enforcing toll collection was, in Oregon and elsewhere, the main motivation for ultimately giving or selling private facilities to government. The implementation of broad-based taxation with the power of government to collect the fees was, in the days of horse-based travel, perhaps a necessary evil at the time. However, this technological constraint is no longer operative, with the advent of cost-effective electronic tolling schemes.

The advent of inexpensive GPS-based pricing devices makes it possible—if archaic policy would relent—to price roads of all types differentially as a function of the load on a particular roadway, its resilience to heavy vehicles, time of use, and other important cost-drivers of highway services.[47]

Importantly for devolution strategy, such an approach would permit revenue generated to be traced back precisely—and dedicated to—the most troubled

---

[46] ODOT (2011).

[47] The Traffic Choices study done in the Puget Sound region was the first, well-designed demonstration in the United States that literally would allowed pricing from the garage to the destination (http://www.psrc. org/transportation/traffic). The private sector, where allowed, is making great strides in providing more affordable, fairer and responsive service. MetroMile, a car insurance company in Oregon, Washington, and California, for example, utilizes a small device that simply plugs into the cars existing ODB-II computer data port. This permits pricing insurance on the basis of the mileage traveled, while also providing the user the opportunity to view and replay (via the web) the trips they have taken, fuel used, and the travel times involved. The subscriber also receives eMails reporting any vehicle operational issues reported by the car's computer. It could easily be used to price road usage differentially—almost immediately—with no ground infrastructure costs (www.metromile.com).

segments of the road network. Specifically, those segments on which users suffer the greatest congestion delay and/or the consequences of excessive wear-and-tear by heavy vehicles would garner the most revenue. In so doing, private entities or localities could justifiably employ the generated road revenues to manage the maintenance and improvement in the segments of importance to their users. They would also have financial bargaining chips with which to coordinate their road maintenance and building activity with adjacent owners or jurisdictions. This is how the US railroad system, cellular systems, data networks, and others operate and grow to provide a nationwide service on a network from local and regional components.[48]

There are no important theoretical constraints to privatizing roads. For example, highways do not exhibit significant economies of scale, obviating the need to be regulated heavily to avoid monopoly pricing abuse. Nationally renowned transportation economist Kenneth Small concluded this after his own review of the potential and practice of privatization of highways:[49]

> *The public sector's apparent advantage in cost of capital is at least partly illusory due to differences in tax liability and to constraints on the supply of public capital. … Private firms are likely to promote more efficient pricing. … Effective private road provision depends on well- structured franchise agreements that allow pricing flexibility...*
>
> *Privately owned or operated roads, once common … are making a startling comeback … Spain, Portugal, Italy, and France have recently converted their high-speed intercity expressways to mostly private systems. The UK and Finland, among other countries, have taken steps in that direction; Australia and Canada have important private road projects; and in Latin America, privately built and operated toll roads are quite common … New roads have been privately financed in California, Virginia, and Texas, while existing public toll roads have been privatized in Illinois and Indiana.*

The most likely transitional path to fuller privatization will be the Public Private Partnership (P3) movement. This allows a state or locale to enjoy the infusion of private capital by selling or leasing an existing road to the private sector, and for the private sector to price roads with greater respect for the economics of congestion and wear and tear. This transitional step allows localities to rebalance their threadbare treasuries, while properly rating scarce and expensive capacity. Unfortunately, Oregon has, to date, been unfriendly to P3 innovation in the highway sector, refusing to entertain several P3 inquiries from private developers and investors. This author believes that this will gradually change, as the financial death-spiral that follows the failure to price properly, the lack of indigenous resources and voter recalcitrance to pay higher broad-based taxes takes its toll on the fiscal continence of the highway programs.

---

[48] Laurits and Christensen Associates, Inc. (2010)Laurits R. Christensen Associates (2009, 2010), *op cit.*, Vol. 1, Chapter 3.

[49] Small (2010).

10.4.8   *Privatization of Oregon transit*

As with roads, early urban transit systems were built by private companies in the 19th and early 20th centuries. Private companies also operated the first urban motor buses in the nation, and operated through the 1940s and 1950s and beyond in many places. Ultimately, the industry was taken over by regional public operators, partly with federal funding of the takeovers in 1965. However, the prospects of expanding urban transit service significantly with private supply are good if public policy were to change.

Partially as a failure to price roads properly, private mass transit finds itself unable to compete effectively with the underpriced use of roads during peak periods. This has led to gradual replacement of most private transit services with public local monopolies. If the implementation of proper road pricing were to occur (whether through public or private direction), this modal distortion would not exist and the necessity to have public monopolies and subsidies in mass passenger transport would evaporate.

There is now no technical or theoretical reason why private transit services cannot again be the dominant form of transit service supply. However, existing agencies that have accepted federal funding are now in a tight legal straight jacket that gives inordinate power to transit labor and reduces managerial flexibility.[50] In the Portland metro area, this power has been used to keep willing licensed cab drivers from serving light rail stations, for example.

As with highway transportation, technology is rapidly bulldozing the constraints to adding private supply of transit services, especially the rubber-tired type. Modern internet technology is being used to provide more reliable, responsive, and tailored services. In addition to the Uber and Lyft-type shared ride services, private urban bus competition is erupting in places like San Francisco, Singapore, and Brooklyn, New York.[51] By increasing the occupancy of vehicles that might otherwise be traveling anyway (with one driver) supporting paid shared ride services could very well reduce highway congestion, improve service, and improve vehicle utilization. Self-driving cars could, according to one study, reduce car ownership by 43%.[52]

If the difficulties Uber encountered in its attempt to enter the Portland market are any indication, Oregon policy makers seem more intent on protecting entrenched interests and using taxi policy to socially engineer the taxi workplace than seeing passengers be well served. But, as with Uber itself, ultimately the clamor of consumers to be allowed to use more responsive and flexible services will likely win out.

---

[50] Transit systems that have accepted federal funding assistance under the Federal Transit Act are hamstrung from privatizing their operations. Section 13(c) of that act requires "fair and equitable protective arrangements [that] must be made by the grantee to protect employees affected by such assistance." In effect, this not only burdens the transit operator with long-term employment costs if it lays of its workers, but also gives the transit unions sufficient power keep even new, private entrants from serving the grantee (http://onlinepubs.trb.org/onlinepubs/tcrp/tcrp_lrd_04.pdf). This power has been used in Oregon. Such control of transit operations by nonelected individuals makes privatization a difficult reform.

[51] See http://leaptransit.com, http://www.sharetransport.sg/bus/schedule and http://www.theatlantic.com/national/archive/2011/10/the-illegal-private-bus-system-that-works/246166/. The Brooklyn service, technically illegal, is reported to be the 20th largest transit system in the nation.

[52] Schoettle and Sivak (2015).

10.4.9   Privatization of Oregon air and water modes

As noted earlier, in the air mode, the development of airport facilities is funded through federal bureaucratic channels, and the ATC system, certification, and safety regulation are the purview of the federal government. Therefore, although the airlines themselves are largely deregulated and privatized,[53] the air traffic and airport infrastructure is not.

Privatization of the ATC, certification, safety oversight, and other national aspects of air system infrastructure are, demonstrably, able to be privatized. Indeed, Canada has a private, nonprofit entity that operates and develops its ATC system. It may not be possible to disaggregate the current ATC system into state-level elements, but Oregon can urge privatization to improve what is widely regarded as an out-of-date and dysfunctional ATC.

Oregon could privatize its airports. Over 100 airports around the world are privately owned and operated, including Heathrow, Frankfurt, London, Melbourne, Naples, Rome, Sydney, and Vienna.[54] According to an economics expert in this area, privatization would improve the operating model of airports by implementing peak period landing fee surcharges to reduce congestion, remove slot controls that limit price competition, and fight regulatory hurdles that can interfere with optimal capacity development, etc.[55]

Similar arguments can be made in favor of privatizing water ports. There are likely more modest benefits from doing so because of the strong competition that exists already among the various sea- and inland port operations run by local governments in Oregon. In addition, competition with other modes and ports in other states may limit the allocative inefficiencies that otherwise attend public operation.

10.5   Conclusions

This chapter has identified and quantified the extent to which transportation decision making and funding has been assigned to higher levels of government inappropriately. The analysis reveals that the current systems of pricing and funding are archaic, opaque and lacking in respect for user benefit—most especially in the highway and transit modes. In the passenger and freight aspects of the highway mode, there is an astonishing mismatch between the patterns of use and the complexity and centralization of public processes that serve those uses. Transit and the various distortions observed in that mode are significantly a side-effect of fundamental problems with highway finance, but the funding system encourages expensive and ineffective transit supply responses.

In both highway and transit, the elevation of authority to government, in general, and to the federal government in particular, bodes ill for the performance of the largest transportation sectors in our economy. The patterns of travel, the failure to enforce

[53] The airlines themselves were largely deregulated by the Airline Deregulation Act of 1978.
[54] Source: Poole and Edwards (2010).
[55] See Winston (2010).

close nexus between those paying for transportation and those who use the services, excessive cross-subsidization and fund pooling, all augur for the need to radically devolve authority to a more localized entity—whether private or public.

Unfortunately, pricing reform must disrupt a long history of transportation pricing and finance that is highly socialized and politically entrenched. The example of the disruption of the cab industry by ride-sharing platforms shows that both aggressive advocacy, end-runs of current practice, and technological force are necessary to introduce change. Oregon, with its dense thicket of land use, planning, and regulatory interventions is a particularly difficult setting into which to introduce market-based reforms. However, the fact of the depth of such interventions suggests that the opportunities for benefitting from reform are all the greater in a place like Oregon. Hopefully, disruptive innovations and the inevitable financial incontinence of existing practice will overcome the entrenched and bureaucratized processes that are prevalent in much of the transportation sector today.

References

Clayman, S., Clegg, R., Galis, A., Manzalini, A., 2010. Stability in Dynamic Networks. Department of Electronic Engineering, University College London, London, UK.
ECONorthwest, 2015. 2015 Oregon Highway Cost Allocation Study, Supplementary Documents, Appendix B1.
ICAO, 2012. Policies on Charges for Airports and Air Navigation Services, Doc. 9082, ninth ed.
International Road Foundation, Switzerland, 2011. Urban Road Networks: The Benefits of the Public Private Partnership Approach.
Isard, W., 1 May 1954. Location theory and trade theory: short-run analysis. The Quarterly Journal of Economics 68 (2), 305–320.
Klein, D., 1990. The Voluntary Provision of Public Goods? The Turnpike Companies of Early America. Department of Economics, University of California at Irvine, Reprint No. 18, Economic Inquiry, March 1990.
Klein, D., 1994. Private Highways in America, 1792–1916. The Freeman, February 1994.
Klein, D., Fielding, G., December 1991. Private Toll Roads: Learning from the Nineteenth Century. Department of Economics and Institute of Transportation Studies, University of California, Irvine, CA.
Laurits, R., Christensen Associates, Inc., 2010. An Update to the Study of Competition in the US Freight Railroad Industry, prepared for The Surface Transportation Board.
ODOT, 2011. History of State Highways in Oregon. Salem Headquarters Right of Way Engineering.
Poole, R., Edwards, C., 2010. Airports and Air Traffic Control. Cato Institute.
Portland Tribune, 2015. End of Line for Amtrak Subsidies? April 16, 2015.
Pozdena, R., 2014. Resurrecting User Fees in Public Finance. Cascade Policy Institute, Portland, OR.
Pozdena, R., McElhiney, P., 1976, 2013. Economic role of the state in transportation. California Transportation Plan Task Force, Issue Paper 13, 1976 (reprinted 2013).
Schoettle, B., Sivak, M., 2015. Potential Impact of Self-Driving Vehicles on Household Vehicle Demand and Usage. University of Michigan Transportation Research Institute, UM-TRI-2015-3.

Small, K., 2010. Private provision of highways: economic issues. Transport Reviews 30 (1).

University of South Florida and American Transportation Research Institute, 2014. Using truck fleet data in combination with other data sources for freight modeling and planning, report BDK84-977-20 for the Florida DOT, final report.

USDOT, Bureau of Transportation Statistics, 2014. Government Transportation Financial Statistics, Chapter 4.

Winston, C., 2005. The Success of the Staggers Rail Act of 1980. AEI-Brookings Joint Center for Regulatory Studies, Publication 05-24.

Winston, C., 2010. Last Exit: Privatization and Deregulation of the US Transportation System. Brookings Institution Press, Washington, DC.

Zhang, L., Levinson, D., 2005. The economics of transportation network growth. In: Milln, P.C., Inglada, V. (Eds.), Essays in Transportation Economics. Springer.

Further Reading

Airlines for America, 2014. Government-imposed taxes on air transportation (accessed 25.06.14).

Akarca, A.T., Long, T.V., 1980. On the relationship between energy and GNP: a re-examination. Journal of Energy and Development 5, 326–331.

Almon, S., 1965. The distributed lag between capital appropriations and expenditures. Econometrica 33, 178–196.

Atkinson, R.D., Castro, DD., Andes, S.M., Correa, D.K., Daily, G., Gifford, J.L., Hedlund, J.A., 2008. Digital quality of life: understanding the personal & social benefits of the information technology revolution. The information technology and innovation foundation report.

Barker, R., Puckett, J., 2007. Design of Highway Bridges: An LRFD Approach, Second ed. John Wiley & Sons, New York, NY.

Basmann, R., 1957. A generalised classical method of linear estimation of coefficients in a structural equation. Econometrica 25, 77–83.

Bel, G., Fageda, X., 2010. Privatization, regulation, and airport pricing: an empirical analysis for Europe. Journal of Regulatory Economics 37 (2), 142–161.

Bentley Associates, 2008. World airport privatization 2008 and beyond. Manchester, UK.

Bilotkach, V., Clougherty, J.A., Mueller, J., Zhang, A., 2012. Regulation, privatization, and airport charges: panel data evidence from European airports. Journal of Regulatory Economics 42 (1), 73–94.

Boarnet, M.G., Crane, R., 2001. The influence of land use on travel behavior: specification and estimation strategies. Transportation Research Part A 35, 823–845.

Boarnet, M.G., Greenwald, M.J., 2001. The Built Environment as a Determinant of Walking Behavior: Analyzing Non-Work Pedestrian Travel in Portland, Oregon. University of California, Irvine, CA.

Boarnet, M.G., Sarmiento, S., 1996. Can Land Use Policy Really Affect Travel Behavior? A Study of the Link Between Non-Work Travel and Land Use Characteristics. Department of Urban and Regional Planning and School of Social Ecology, University of California, Irvine, CA.

Boarnet, M.G., Nesamani, K.S., et al., 2003. Comparing the Influence of Land Use on Nonwork Trip Generation and Vehicle Distance Traveled: An Analysis using Travel Diary Data. Center for Activity Systems Analysis.

Brady, F., Nguyen, N., Young, 2006. Turning Points in the Transportation Service Index (TSI) and the Economy. DOT/RITA, Bureau of Transportation Statistics.

Cervero, R., 2002. Induced Demand: An Urban and Metropolitan Perspective, Working To-gether to Address Induced Demand. ENO Transport Foundation, Washington, DC.

Cervero, R., Hansen, M., 2002. Induced travel demand and induced road investment. Journal of Transport Economics and Policy 36 (3), 469–490.

Cheng, B.S., 1995. An investigation of cointegration and causality between energy consump-tion and economic growth. Journal of Energy and Development 21, 73–84.

Choo, S., Mokhtarian, P.L., 2007. Telecommunications and travel demand and supply: ag-gregate structural equation models for the US. Transportation Research Part A-Policy and Practice 41 (1), 4–18.

Crane, R., 2000. The influence of urban form on travel: an interpretive review. Journal of Plan-ning Literature 15, 3.

Design. Final report, Transportation Research Board, miscellaneous report, undated.

Dezember, R., Glazer, E., 2013. Drop in traffic takes toll on investors in private roads. The Wall Street Journal, 20 November, <http://online.wsj.com/news/articles/ SB10001424052702303482 504579177890461812588>.

Downs, A., 1962. The law of peak-hour expressway congestion. Traffic Quarterly 16 (3), 393–409.

Duranton, G., Turner, M.A., 2012. Urban growth and transportation. The Review of Economic Studies 79 (4), 1407–1440.

Eaves, J., Eaves, S., Fall 2007. Neither renewable nor reliable. Regulation 30 (3).

Erol, U., Yu, E.S.H., 1987. On the relationship between electricity and income for industrial-ized countries. Journal of Electricity and Employment 13, 113–122.

Ewing, R., 1997. Is Los Angeles-style sprawl desirable? Journal of the American Planning Association 63 (1), 107–126.

Ewing, R., Cervero, R., 2001. Travel and the built environment—synthesis. Transportation Research Record (1780), 87–114.

Ewing, R., Deanna, M.B., et al., 1996. Land use impacts on trip generation rates. Transportation Research Record (1518), 1–6.

Ewing, R., Bartholomew, K., et al., 2007. Growing Cooler: The Evidence on Urban Develop-ment and Climate Change. Urban Land Institute, Washington, DC.

FAA, 2012. The business case for the next generation air transportation system, report, August.

Fagnant, D.J., Kockelman, K.M., 2013. Preparing a nation for autonomous vehicles: opportuni-ties, barriers and policy recommendations. Eno Center for Transportation, William P Eno Research Paper.

FHWA, 2013. Reducing non-recurring congestion. http://ops.fhwa.dot.gov/program_areas/ reduce-non-cong.htm (accessed 25.06.14).

Forsyth, P., 2008. Airport policy in Australia and New Zealand: privatization, light-handed regulation, and performance. In: Winston, C., de Rus, G. (Eds.), Aviation Infrastructure Performance: A Study in Comparative Political Economy. Brookings Institution Press, Washington, DC, pp. 65–99.

Fröhlich, P., 2003. Induced traffic: review of the explanatory models. Conference paper STRC 2003.

Fu, G., Feng, J., Dekelbab, W., Moses, F., Cohen, H., Mertz, D., Thompson, P., 2003. Effect of truck weight on bridge network costs. NCHRP (National Cooperative Highway Research Program) report 495.

Fulton, L., Meszler, D., Noland, R., Thomas, J., 2000. A statistical analysis of induced travel effects in the U.S. Mid-Atlantic region. Journal of Transportation and Statistics 3 (1), 1–14.

Garrison, D., Mannering, F., 1990. Assessing the traffic impacts of freeway incidents and driver information. ITE Journal 60 (8), 19–23.

Ghali, K.H., El-Sakka, M.I.T., 2004. Energy use and output growth in Canada: a multivariate cointegration analysis. Energy Economics 26, 225–238.

Glaister, S., 2006. Britain: competition undermined by politics. In: Gómez-Ibáñez, J.A., de Rus, G. (Eds.), Competition in the Railway Industry: An International Comparative Analysis. Edward Elgar Publishing Limited, Cheltenham, UK, pp. 49–80.

Gómez-Ibáñez, J.A., 2006. An overview of the options. In: Gómez-Ibáñez, J.A., de Rus, G. (Eds.), Competition in the Railway Industry: An International Comparative Analysis. Edward Elgar Publishing Limited, Cheltenham, UK, pp. 1–22.

Gómez-Ibáñez, J.A., Meyer, J.R., 1993. Going Private: The International Experience with Transport Privatization. Brookings Institution Press, Washington, DC.

Graham, A., 2008. Airport planning and regulation in the United Kingdom. In: Winston, C., de Rus, G. (Eds.), Aviation Infrastructure Performance: A Study in Comparative Political Economy. Brookings Institution Press, Washington, DC, pp. 100–135.

Granger, C., 1969. Investigating causal relations by econometric models and cross-spectral methods. Econometrica, 424–438.

Greene, W., 2000. Econometric Analysis, Fourth ed. Macmillan, New York, NY.

Gujarati, D., 1995. Basic Econometrics, Third ed. McGraw-Hill, New York, NY.

Halsey, A., Craighill, P.M., 2013. Drivers see less congestion on area roads. The Washington Post, 30 June. http://www.washingtonpost.com/local/trafficandcommuting/drivers-see-less-congestion-on-area-roads/2013/06/29/085b1b50-dea0-11e2-b94a-452948b95ca8_story.html.

Handy, S., Cao, X., Mokhtarian, P., 2005. Correlation or causality between the built environment and travel behavior? Evidence from Northern California. Transportation Research Part D 10, 427–444.

Hansen, M., Huang, Y., 1997. Road supply and traffic in California urban areas. Transportation Research A 31 (3), 205–218.

Hansen, M., Gillen, D., Dobbins, A., Huang, Y., Puvathingal, M., 1993. The Air Quality Impacts of Urban Highway Capacity Expansion: Traffic Generation and Land Use Change. University of California, Institute of Transportation Studies, Berkeley, CA.

Holden, E., Norla, I.T., 2005. Three challenges for the compact city as a sustainable urban form: household consumption of energy and transport in eight residential areas in the greater Oslo region. Urban Studies 42, 2145.

Jacob, B., 2010. Weigh-in-motion for road safety, enforcement and infrastructures. Unpublished manuscript, Laboratoire Central des Pontset Chaussées.

Karp, G., 2014. Winglets go a long way to give airlines fuel savings. Chicago Tribune, 4 March. http://articles.chicagotribune.com/2014-03-04/business/ct-airline-winglets-0302-biz-20140304_1_fuel-savings-jet-fuel-southwest-airlines.

Keane, T.F., 1996. The Economic Importance of the National Highway System. Public Roads, On-line, U. S. DOT, Federal Highway Administration, Washington, DC.

Klein, D.B., Fielding, G.J., 1992. Private toll roads: learning from the 19th century. Transportation Quarterly 46 (3), 321–341.

Lajnef, N., Rhimi, M., Chatti, K., Mhamdi, L., Faridazar, F., 2011. Toward an integrated smart sensing system and data interpretation techniques for pavement fatigue monitoring. Computer-Aided Civil and Infrastructure Engineering 26 (7), 513–523.

Langer, A., Winston, C., 2008. Toward a comprehensive assessment of road pricing accounting for land use. Brookings-Wharton Papers on Urban Affairs 2008, 127–175.

Lave, C., Lave, L., 1999. Fuel economy and auto safety regulation: is the cure worse than the disease? In: Gómez-Ibáñez, J.A., Tye, W.B., Winston, C. (Eds.), Essays in Transportation Economics and Policy: A Handbook in Honor of John R. Meyer. Brookings Institution Press, Washington, DC, pp. 257–289.

Lee, C.C., 2006. The causality relationship between energy consumption and GDP in G-11 countries revisited. Energy Policy 34, 1086–1093.

Lee, D., Klein, L., Camus, G., 1999. Induced traffic and induced demand. Transportation Research Record 1659, 68–75.

Levine, M.E., 2007. Congestion Pricing at New York Airports: right idea, but can we really start here and now? Reason Foundation Policy Brief No 66.

Lindsey, R., 2012. Road pricing and investment. Economics of Transportation 1 (1), 49–63.

Little, D.N., Memmott, J., McFarland, F., Goff, Z., Smith, R., Wootan, C.V., Zollinger, D., Tang, T., Epps, J., 1997.

Mannering, F.L., Washburn, S.S., 2013. Principles of Highway Engineering and Traffic Analysis, fifth ed. John Wiley and Sons, New Jersey.

McCartney, S., 2014. The case for heated runways: researchers seek ways to warm snowy airport surfaces. The Wall Street Journal, 19 February, <http://online.wsj.com/news/articles/SB10001424052 7023049142045793928833809689994>.

McDougall, G., Roberts, A., 2008. Commercializing air traffic control: have the reforms worked? Canadian Public Administration 51 (1), 45–69.

McKinnon, A.C., 2005. The economic and environmental benefits of increasing maximum truck weight: the British experience. Transportation Research Record Part D: Transport and Environment 10 (1), 77–95.

McNally, M.G., Kulkarni, A., 1996. An Assessment of the Interaction of the Land use-Transportation System and Travel Behavior. University of California, Irvine, CA, UCI-ITS-AS-WP-96.4.

Meyer, J.R., Tye, W.B., 1988. Toward achieving workable competition in industries undergoing a transition to deregulation: a contractual equilibrium approach. Yale Journal on Regulation 5 (2), 273–297.

Miller, T.C., 2014. Improving the efficiency and equity of highway funding and management: the role of VMT charges. Mercatus Center Working Paper No 14-04.

Morrison, S.A., Winston, C., 1989. Enhancing the Performance of the Deregulated Air Transportation System. Brookings Papers on Economic Activity: Microeconomics, 1989, pp. 61–112.

Narayan, P.K., Smyth, R., 2008. Energy consumption and real GDP in G7 countries: new evidence from panel cointegration new evidence from panel cointegration with structural breaks. Energy Economics 30, 2331–2341.

Nash, C., 2006. Europe: alternative models for restructuring. In: Gómez-Ibáñez, J.A., de Rus, G. (Eds.), Competition in the Railway Industry: An International Comparative Analysis. Edward Elgar Publishing Limited, Cheltenham, UK, pp. 49–80.

National Transportation Operations Coalition, 2007. National traffic signal report card – executive summary.

Ng, C.F., Small, K.A., 2012. Tradeoffs among free-flow speed, capacity, cost, and environmental footprint in highway design. Transportation 39 (6), 1259–1280.

Noland, R., 2001. Relationships between highway capacity and induced vehicle travel. Transportation Research A 35 (1), 47–72.

Noland, R., Cowart, W., 2000. Analysis of metropolitan highway capacity and the growth in vehicle miles of travel. Presented at the 79th Annual Meeting of the Transportation Research Board. Washington, DC.

Noland, R., Lem, L., 2002. A review of the evidence for induced travel and changes in transportation and environmental policy in the US and the UK. Transportation Research D 7 (1), 1–26.

Oster, C.V., Jr., 2006. Reforming the federal aviation administration: lessons from Canada and the United Kingdom, report, IBM Center for the Business of Government, Washington DC.

Oum, T.H., Yan, J., Yu, C., 2008. Ownership forms matter for airport efficiency: a stochastic frontier investigation of worldwide airports. Journal of Urban Economics 64 (2), 422–435.

Palmer, K., Oates, W.E., Portney, P.R., 1995. Tightening environmental standards: the benefit-cost or the no-cost paradigm? Journal of Economic Perspectives 9 (4), 119–132.

Papageorgiou, M., Kosmatopoulos, E., Papamichail, I., 2008. Effects of variable speed limits on motorway traffic flow. Transportation Research Record: Journal of the Transportation Research Board 2047, 37–48.

Pasztor, A., 2013. FAA authorizes the use of commercial-drone testing: six operators selected to conduct research, setting stage for eventual widespread use. The Wall Street Journal.

PB Americas, Inc, 2007. Active Traffic Management Feasibility Study. Submission for Puget Sound Regional Council to Washington State Department of Transportation, November.

Pickrell, D., 2002. Induced demand: definition, measurement, and significance, working together to address induced demand, ENO Transport Foundation, Washington, DC.

Pindyck, R., Rubinfeld, D., 1998. Econometric Models and Economic Forecasts, fourth ed. McGraw-Hill, New York, NY.

Poole, R.W. Jr., 2009. Will We Get Serious about Aviation Security?, Reason.com, 29 December.

Poole, Jr, R.W., 2013. Organization and Innovation in Air Traffic Control. Hudson Institute Initiative on Future.

Pozdena, R., 1979. Making transit work. FRBSF Economic Letter, Federal Reserve Bank of San Francisco.

Pozdena, R., 1984. Airline Deregulation. FRBSF Weekly Letter, Federal Reserve Bank of San Francisco.

Pozdena, R., 2009. Vehicle Miles Traveled and the Economy: The Challenge for Climate Policy. QuantEcon, Incorporated, Manzanita, Oregon.

Pozdena, R., Schmidt, R., Martin, D., 1990. Market-based solutions to the transportation crisis: the concept. Bay Area Economic Forum, A two-part report. pp. 560–569.

Robyn, D., 2007. Reforming the air traffic control system to promote efficiency and reduce delays. Paper prepared for the Council of Economic Advisors by The Brattle Group, Inc in association with GRA, Incorporated, 29 October.

Roland, G., 2008. Private and public ownership in economic theory. In: Roland, G. (Ed.), Privatization: Successes and Failures, Initiative for Policy Dialogue. Columbia University Press, New York, NY, pp. 9–31.

Schimek, P., 1996. Household motor vehicle ownership and use: how much does residential density matter? Transportation Research Board 1552.

Schrank, D., Eisele, B., Lomax, T., 2012. 2012 Urban mobility report. Annual report from Texas A&M Transportation Institute in partnership with INRIX.

Schweikart, Jr., L., Folsom, Jr., B.W., 2013. Obama's false history of public investment: entrepreneurs built our roads, rails and canals far better than government did. The Wall Street Journal.

Sherk, J., 2011. Repealing the Davis–Bacon Act Would Save Taxpayers US$10.9 Billion. The Heritage Foundation WebMemo No 3145.

Shin, K., Washington, S.P., van Schalkwyk, I., 2009. Evaluation of the Scottsdale Loop 101 automated speed enforcement demonstration program. Accident Analysis & Prevention 41 (3), 393–403.

Small, K., Verhoef, E.T., 2007. The Economics of Urban Transportation. Routledge, Abingdon, UK.

Small, K., Winston, C., 1988. Optimal highway durability. The American Economic Review 78 (3.).

Small, K., Winston, C., Evans, C., 1989. Road Work: A New Highway Pricing and Investment Policy. Brookings Institution Press, Washington, DC.

Small, K.A., Winston, C., Yan, J., 2005. Uncovering the distribution of motorists preferences for travel time and reliability. Econometrica 73 (4), 1367–1382.

Soytas, U., Sari, R., 2003. Energy consumption and GDP: causality relationship in G7 countries and emerging markets. Energy Economics 25, 33–37.

Soytas, U., Sari, R., 2006. Energy consumption and income in G7 countries. Journal of Policy Modeling 28, 739–750.

Spieser, K., Treleaven, K., Zhang, R., Frazzoli, E., Morton, D., Pavone, M., 2014. Toward a systematic approach to the design and evaluation of automated mobility-on-demand systems: a case study in Singapore. In: Meyer, G., Beiker, S. (Eds.), Road Vehicle Automation, Lecture Notes in Mobility. Springer, Cham, Switzerland, pp. 229–246.

Starkie, D., 2008. The airport industry in a competitive environment: a United Kingdom perspective. Organisation for Economic Co-operation and Development and International Transport Forum Joint Transport Research Centre Discussion Paper 2008-15.

Starkie, D., 2013. Transport infrastructure: adding value. Institute of Economic Affairs Discussion Paper No 50.

Stern, D.I., 1993. Energy and economic growth in the USA. Energy Economics 15, 137–150.

Stern, D.I., 2000. Multivariate cointegration analysis of the role of energy in the US macroeconomy. Energy Economics 22, 267–283.

Stiglitz, J., 1998. Distinguished lecture on economics in government: the private uses of public interests: incentives and institutions. Journal of Economic Perspectives 12 (2), 3–22.

The Road Information Program, 2010. Key facts about America's surface transportation system and federal funding. Fact Sheet.

Todd, K., Fall 2004. Traffic control: an exercise in self-defeat. Regulation, 10–12.

TRB Superpave Committee, 2005. Superior Performing Asphalt Pavement: SUPERPAVE Performance by.

Vickers, J., Yarrow, G., 1991. Economic perspectives on privatization. The Journal of Economic Perspectives 5 (2), 111–132.

Winston, C., 2013. How to avoid another FAA Fiasco: the U.S. should consider following the lead of Canada and England by privatizing transportation services. The Wall Street Journal.

Wright, R.E., Murphy, B.P., 2009. The Private Provision of Transportation Infrastructure in Antebellum America: Lessons and Warnings. unpublished manuscript, Augustana College.

Yan, J., Winston, C., 2014. Can private airport competition improve runway pricing? The case of San Francisco Bay Area airports. Journal of Public Economics 115, 146–157.

Yu, E.S.H., Choi, J.Y., 1985. The causal relationship between energy and GDP: an international comparison. Journal of Energy Development 10, 249–272.

Yu, E.S.H., Hwang, B.K., 1984. The relationship between energy and GDP: further results. Energy Economics 6, 186–190.

The elusive effects of CAFE standards

Kenneth A. Small
University of California at Irvine, CA, USA

Chapter Outline

Dedication

I started graduate work in economics enthused about the emerging field of environmental economics. I soon found that another newcomer to Berkeley—Ted Keeler, a new assistant professor from MIT—specialized in a closely related subject, namely Transportation Economics. I leaped at his offer to give me a reading course in Transportation Economics, then again at the opportunity to be a research assistant on his collaborative project comparing costs of urban transportation modes. I knew this was in part a response to the pervasive influence of Meyer, Kain, and Wohl's *The Urban Transportation Problem*, and to Ted's desire to test some of its findings in another setting. I liked his approach of letting the data tell the story without a goal of confirming or contradicting that earlier work.

Over the years, I learned that Ted's approach was uncompromisingly practical in seeking answers to questions that have important policy implications. He insisted on using the best possible

Transportation Policy and Economic Regulation. http://dx.doi.org/10.1016/B978-0-12-812620-2.00011-0

empirical techniques, as well as sound theory to set up the problem but not so much theory as to prejudge the conclusion. I was also fortunate that Ted was open to my incorporating work that was then novel and innovative, namely Daniel McFadden's urban travel demand forecasting project. I continue to follow Ted in looking for varied but rigorous approaches to policy issues and hope the paper here contributes to that mission.

11.1 Introduction

Fuel efficiency standards for motor vehicles remain a controversy, despite four decades of experience in the United States with its Corporate Average Fuel Economy (CAFE) standards. Economists disagree on the magnitudes of some of the most relevant market responses,[1] including some—especially the so-called "energy paradox"—that could make standards more efficient than fuel taxes.

This ambiguity is partly due to the complexity of markets for the purchase and use of motor vehicles. While research has led to increasingly sophisticated understanding of consumers' demand for vehicles and of automakers' responses to regulations, it has proved impossible to develop a single framework that fully captures all the relevant aspects such as consumers' perceptions of vehicle attributes, their expectations about fuel prices, manufacturers' decisions about new technologies, consumers' decisions how much to use and when to retire vehicles, and used-vehicle market adjustments.

This paper makes a first step toward a more general model, using a modified version of the US Energy Information Administration's National Energy Modeling System (NEMS). While any large-scale model may omit or over-simplify key economic responses, NEMS is more complete and flexible than single-purpose models and so has the potential to explore the many factors that may be relevant to policy evaluation. One advantage, in particular, is that it represents in a very detailed way the technologies available to automobile manufacturers for improving fuel efficiency. Furthermore, being a simulation model, it is not restricted by the particular economic specifications and functional forms that may be required by a purely econometric model or by one that seeks to create a comprehensive welfare framework.

For these reasons, I set out to adapt NEMS to estimate the quantitative effects of some of the more important features of an ideal model if it were available. In doing so, I am applying a key lesson from Theodore Keeler, to whom this paper is dedicated: use practical methods, guided insofar as possibly by sound theory, to search for answers to significant economic questions.

In what follows, I discuss key modeling issues and behavioral parameters in assessing CAFE and then describe how I specify or modify NEMS to address them. I then construct a baseline scenario and use it to simulate the effects of variations representing different combinations of behavioral and environmental parameters, market responses, and types of standards. I consider how those variations affect the simulated impact of higher CAFE standards—in particular the tightening of CAFE standards to the levels promulgated under the Obama Administration for new vehicles of model

[1] See, for example, Jacobsen (2013), Anderson et al. (2011), and Knittel (2012, 2013).

years 2017–2025. Although I have chosen these standards mainly to test the models, the counterfactual in which they are not imposed (and thus standards remain at the levels previously adopted for 2016) is still policy-relevant as their continuation is subject to a legislatively mandated review, being carried out by an administration with a declared hostility to the standards.

11.2 Modeling issues

Motor vehicle use involves several interconnected markets. Consumers purchase new and used vehicles, decide how much to drive them, and eventually sell or scrap them. Domestic and foreign automakers design, build, and price vehicles with certain features, including fuel economy. Both vehicles and the investments required to manufacture them are long-lasting, yet consumer preferences and vehicle designs are constantly changing—some year by year, some over few years in advance, and some over many years in advance through research, development, and investment in new technologies. Fuel efficiency standards and other policies affect all of these markets, making it extremely difficult to capture all their effects.

In this section, I discuss several key elements of these markets and how they might be incorporated into models used to evaluate policies.

11.2.1 Consumer behavior and vehicle demand

When consumers choose among the vehicle models offered, they take into account their valuation of fuel economy and expectations of future fuel prices as well as the value they place on other vehicle attributes. Following purchase, they may also change the amount they drive and how long they keep the vehicle in response to changes in the cost of driving and in the prices of new and used vehicles.

11.2.1.1 Consumer valuation of fuel economy

Much recent work has considered whether consumers fully value the savings in fuel economy generated by CAFE (or any other action). The term "energy paradox" is often applied to the possibility that they do not fully value those savings.[2] However, the concept "fully value" conflates two interrelated questions of interest for policy evaluation. One is whether consumers respond rationally to the environment they themselves face, whereas the other is whether that environment involves externalities that could cause even rational consumers to deviate from socially optimal behavior.

Consider first consumer rationality. While economists like to start with full rationality as a hypothesis, there is ample evidence of irrationality in consumers' behavior toward long-lived investments involving uncertain payoffs, including specifically their

---

[2] For reviews see Helfand and Wolverton (2011), Allcott and Greenstone (2012), Gillingham and Palmer (2014), and Gerarden et al. (forthcoming).

understanding of energy use by automobiles.[3] The extent of rationality is sometimes characterized by the valuation ratio, defined as the fraction of discounted fuel cost savings that consumers consider when trading off higher vehicle prices against greater fuel efficiency.[4] The variation of empirical estimates of this ratio is very wide, most falling in the range 33%–100%. Some authors have suggested that the ratio is 100%, but this usually means that they *cannot reject* the null hypothesis of 100%, which is not necessarily the most theoretically likely value.[5] At the other end of the plausible range, the default parameters for NEMS used in the EIA's forecasts imply that the valuation ratio is only 30%. Our assessment is that the weight of evidence is around 80%, close to the value of 76% found in Allcott and Wozny (2014). Thus, I perform simulations for valuation ratios ranging from 30% to 100%, with 80% serving as the baseline value.

Now consider social efficiency. This depends in part on whether the markets for car loans and for used cars are socially efficient. Car loans, like other credit markets, are subject to problems of asymmetric information as lenders attempt to accurately gauge the riskiness of potential borrowers. To the extent that future fuel costs affect buyers' ability to repay loans, choice of fuel efficiency could be distorted; however, I know of no empirical evidence relating to this.

As for used car markets, asymmetric information is well established as a source dragging down the resale value of used cars (Akerlof, 1970), but whether this differentially affects cars of high and low fuel efficiency is unknown. Most evidence suggests at least that used car prices respond quickly and significantly to changes in fuel prices.[6]

Now consider model-building in light of possible market failures, including consumer irrationality. I take several key lessons from the literature, especially the review by Gerarden et al. (forthcoming). First, there are many ways a model can produce

---

[3] For example, consumers are subject to "MPG illusion" (Larrick and Soll, 2008; Allcott, 2013), by which they falsely believe that a given differential in fuel efficiency (miles per gallon or MPG) will lead to a given annual fuel saving, whatever the initial level of MPG. See Turrentine and Kurani (2007) for an overall assessment of consumer rationality in motor vehicle markets.

[4] This definition presumes that a known market interest rate is used for discounting. An alternative approach, more common especially in older literature, is to define the discount rate that would produce a valuation ratio of 1. In this chapter, I use the market interest rate for car loans, discussed later, to define valuation ratios.

[5] For example, Busse et al. (2013) compute the real implicit discount rates implied by prices and fuel efficiencies in both new and used car markets (their Table 9). Accounting for varying assumptions about how vehicle usage is calculated, the price elasticity of fuel usage, and the particular quartiles of fuel efficiency being compared, they compute implied discount rates ranging from -6.6% to $+20.9\%$, whereas they estimate the real interest rates for car loans faced by their sample at -0.9% to $+16.9\%$ (p. 246). While they are thus correct to conclude that their results cannot definitively refute the hypothesis of consumer rationality, a more accurate characterization of the results is that they cannot determine whether or not there is an energy paradox. In fact, Allcott and Wozny (2014, p. 782) state that: "When using assumptions that correspond most closely to ours, they [Busse et al.] find an implied discount rate for used vehicles of 13%"—a rate that is well above the average rate for car loans.

[6] Li et al. (2009), Busse et al. (2013), Sallee et al. (2016), and Bento et al. (2018). However, the opposite conclusion appears in Allcott and Wozny (2014, p. 781).

apparently nonoptimal behavior, some by modeling behavior realistically but others by failing to capture all aspects of a decision. Second, the empirical evidence is strong that there are some behavioral nonoptimalities, especially information asymmetry, salience, and principal/agent problems with commercial transactions; but their size and even direction are quite uncertain. Third, there is great heterogeneity of consumers' responses and valuations, but it is unclear how this affects results of models that ignore it. All these possibilities motivate the need to understand quantitatively how much difference various modeling choices make to predicted outcomes.

11.2.1.2 Expectations of future fuel prices

Consumers purchase vehicles based on implicit or explicit beliefs about future fuel prices. Their behavioral response to CAFE is directly related to how they form those expectations. Most research assumes either that consumers assume current fuel prices will last throughout the life of their vehicle or that they correctly forecast the future. Recently, a few studies have investigated this question directly, by asking consumers what prices they expect in the future. The answer, at least during the period 1992–2010, seems to be that usually they take the current price as the best predictor of future prices, but that occasionally they apply mean reversion (Anderson et al., 2013). The main example of mean reversion is that immediately after the sharp downturn in prices in late 2008, consumers expected prices to return to a level observed 2 years prior. A third possibility is that consumers extrapolate from values observed in the recent past to forecast fuel prices, which is what is assumed in NEMS. In this analysis, I simulate the results of these three alternative ways that consumers could form expectations of future fuel prices.

11.2.1.3 Rebound effect: sensitivity of vehicle-miles traveled to fuel economy

By reducing vehicle-operating costs, CAFE could induce more driving and thereby offset some energy savings from improving fuel efficiency. This so-called "rebound effect" could also increase other external costs of driving, including congestion, air pollution, and traffic accidents. Because this effect is largely independent of the others, and its consequences are thoroughly explored elsewhere, I do not further consider it here.

11.2.1.4 Scrappage rates

Most analyses of CAFE ignore the used car market, but some recent studies have begun to remedy this. Bento et al. (2018) and Jacobsen and van Benthem (2015) demonstrate that some motorists respond to higher new-vehicle prices resulting from tighter standards by purchasing used vehicles. This raises their prices, resulting in declining scrappage rates as people repair and continue to drive older vehicles longer than they otherwise would. Both studies also incorporate model-specific changes in scrappage rates caused by relative shifts in the prices of different vehicles.

Jacobsen and van Benthem measure an overall supply elasticity for scrappage of –0.7, meaning that on average, an equilibrium price increase of 1% for a vehicle of any given type and age results in a 0.7% decrease in the fraction of such vehicles that are retired. The authors interpret this as a change in the probability that such a vehicle will face present discounted repair costs (including from accidents) greater than its price. They go on to estimate equilibrium effects on vehicle markets, including the average fuel efficiency of the total fleet of light duty vehicles (LDVs), with and without a particular change in CAFE standards.

Because NEMS lacks an explicit model of used car price determination or consumer choice between new and used cars, there is no transparent way to incorporate these findings into alternative modeling scenarios within NEMS. I therefore do not attempt to model alternative assumptions about used car markets.

11.2.1.5 Manufacturer behavior

Many models that analyze CAFE assume that automobile manufacturers must comply with the CAFE standards. As noted, however, the strategies they use may include adjusting vehicle prices to change the sales mix of their fleet (presumably raising the relative prices of less fuel-efficient vehicles) and investing in new technologies to improve their vehicles' fuel economy. Few papers incorporate the pricing response, and fewer still do so while also allowing for technological changes.[7] I do so here by modifying NEMS to allow for pricing responses.

Theory and common sense suggest that manufacturers will adjust the prices of various models to help them meet CAFE requirements in the most profitable way possible. Specifically, one expects them to raise the price of low-efficiency models (whose sales make it harder to meet the standard) and/or to lower the price of other models, so as to encourage consumers to help them meet the standard through their vehicle choices. I show in Appendix A what such profit-maximizing prices look like: basically, manufacturers incorporate into their cost tradeoff a component reflecting the cost the manufacturer must incur at the margin in order to improve fuel efficiency through technology. This component can be described technically as the "shadow cost" of meeting the standard. The shadow cost is capped by the fine, if manufacturers have the option of paying a fine instead of complying *and* if they choose to take that option.[8]

However, it is also important to consider nonmonetary motivations for compliance. Jacobsen (2013) develops a model where manufacturers perceive a political or public-relations cost of being out of compliance. Depending on the shadow cost of meeting

---

[7] Empirical industrial organization studies, such as Berry et al. (1995) and Goldberg (1995), have analyzed competition in the automobile industry, but they have not accounted for both pricing and technological responses to changes in CAFE standards.

[8] In contrast, Anderson and Sallee (2011, Table 8) estimate much smaller shadow costs, on the order of \$9–\$28 for all three American manufacturers, as revealed by the takeup of special provisions related to flexibly fueled vehicles. Those estimates cover years 1996–2006, but in some cases only a lower bound is estimated because, unlike Jacobsen, Anderson and Sallee assume that each firm will opt to pay the legally permitted fine if it is lower than the shadow cost.

the standard, this may cause some firms to comply even if it would be cheaper to pay fines. Jacobsen estimates a revealed value for this political or public-relations cost. He finds it quite large for some American manufacturers in 1997–2001, a time when fuel prices were low: expressed as the cost per unit change in efficiency (mi/gal) per vehicle, for General Motors it is \$438 for cars and \$264 for light trucks. I investigate the quantitative implications of such a high perceived penalty for American firms.

In addition, I consider the possibility of policies that impose much greater penalties for noncompliance for all manufacturers. In particular, the Obama administration developed a coordinated enforcement mechanism for fuel efficiency regulations, administered by the National Highway Traffic Safety Administration (NHTSA), and for greenhouse-gas regulations, administered by the Environmental Protection Agency (EPA). Most CAFE studies have assumed that penalties for noncompliance are those set by law and administered by of NHTSA. But EPA—whose legal mandate is specifically to protect the public health—has great discretionary power and could use it to effectively increase fines. Therefore, I also consider a scenario in which penalties are five times as high as in the base scenario. This is potentially important because, as we will see, there is substantial noncompliance in the later years of the upgraded standards in some of the scenarios.

11.3   The modified NEMS model

11.3.1   Description of NEMS

NEMS[9] is a general-equilibrium model of the US economy with emphasis on its energy sectors, developed by the EIA. I make use only of its module covering transportation by light-duty passenger vehicles, more fully described in EIA (2012).[10] This means that I do not incorporate any general equilibrium effects via induced changes in fuel prices—an advantage in our case because such effects are uncertain and could hide the direct effects through the transportation sector.

In NEMS, LDVs are divided into two classes, cars and light trucks; each of these in turn is divided into six size classes, each intended to represent a relatively homogeneous product in terms of measurable characteristics valued by consumers.[11] Each size class also encompass up to 16 fuel types, the most important of which are conventional gasoline, conventional diesel, E85 (a blend of 85% ethanol and 15% gasoline), and gasoline–electric hybrid. Finally, LDVs are produced by seven manufacturer groups, each treated by the model as a single manufacturer for determining CAFE

[9] This description is adapted from that in Small (2012).

[10] I use the 2011 version of the NEMS model for the baseline forecasts, as well as the 2011 Annual Energy Outlook oil and fuel price assumptions, except as modified as explained in the text. I maintain, as appropriate, these same assumptions when I analyze alternative scenarios. NEMS has developed more recent versions of its model, but the baseline forecasts of important transportation variables do not differ much from the forecasts based on the 2011 model.

[11] The classes for cars are mini-compact, subcompact, compact, midsize, large, and two-seaters (sports cars); those for light trucks are small and large pickups, small and large vans, and small and large SUVs.

compliance.[12] Three of these groups represent foreign producers, whose reactions are fully integrated into the model.

Responses to energy markets occur in the model at several points. First, each manufacturer group chooses which technologies to adopt in a given year, taking into account consumers' valuation of attributes including fuel savings as well as CAFE regulations.[13] The available technologies improve exogenously over time and their costs also exhibit the effects of pronounced industry-wide learning by doing; but no explicit process of research and development is modeled, and the technologies are basically those known today, giving the model a somewhat conservative bias in analyzing very strong policies. Manufacturers' decisions about technologies are of course shaped by their understanding of consumer response and by the regulatory regime being simulated. Those decisions produce a set of market shares for the technologies, which in turn determine the range of vehicle characteristics that are offered within each fuel type and size class.

Next, consumers as a group make several choices, modeled as aggregate demand functions.[14] First, they choose the shares of cars and light trucks according to a logit-like formula that predicts the change in market share from the previous year as a function of changes in variables including income, fuel price, and new-vehicle fuel efficiency.[15] Second, they choose among the six size classes available for each of the cars and light trucks according to an aggregate model that again predicts change in market share from the previous year. Third, consumers choose market shares of various fuel types through a three-level aggregate nested logit model whose variables describe vehicle price, fuel cost, range, acceleration, and other factors. EIA has calibrated the coefficients of these aggregate choice models to match known market shares in recent years and has added some projected variation in them over time representing judgments about the likely evolution of tastes and marketing practices.

Finally, NEMS tabulates various properties of the resulting market outcomes: for example, the market shares of various types of vehicles, their fuel efficiencies (including differences between testing efficiency and on-the-road efficiency), and manufac-

---

[12] The groups are: domestic car manufacturers, imported car manufacturers, three domestic light truck manufacturers, and two imported light truck manufacturers.

[13] Thus, manufacturers are assumed to consider any applicable fines for CAFE violations, currently $50 per vehicle per unit mpg deficit, as part of production costs. I have increased the fine used in the model to $100, reflecting anticipated tougher enforcement. A more sophisticated approach is taken by Jacobsen (2013), who includes the CAFE standard as a constraint that can be violated at some fixed shadow cost (representing political considerations) plus the cost of fines; he finds that the constraint is binding on the largest US manufacturers, with shadow cost for passenger cars varying from $52 per vehicle for Ford (approximately equal to the actual fine) to $438 for GM. This result accords with the conventional industry view that US manufacturers comply with CAFE even though it would be cheaper for them to pay fines.

[14] An additional, simpler, module replaces consumer choices in the case of fleet vehicles, such as those of government agencies or rental companies. Fleets account for 10%–20% of vehicle sales.

[15] This formula seems not well documented in the NEMS model descriptions, but was provided to me by OnLocation, Inc./Energy Systems Consulting, the private firm that adapted NEMS as discussed here and ran it for this study.

turing costs. The stock of LDVs on the road is determined by combining new-vehicle sales, as described above, with exogenous vehicle survival rates. Total vehicle-miles traveled (VMT) are modeled as a consumer choice determined by a lagged adjustment process following a log-linear regression with just two variables: income and fuel cost per mile. These VMTs are apportioned exogenously by vintage, a key part of determining total energy consumption.

Despite its advantages in comprehensiveness and realism, NEMS contains several limitations for our purposes. First, choices cannot respond to various factors that might be influenced indirectly by policy, such as marketing or perceived reliability of new technologies.[16] Second, manufacturers are assumed to set the price of each vehicle type equal to its average production cost, including any fines, fees, or rebates; this assumption does not allow them to use price differentials to influence sales mix as part of a strategy to meet regulations.[17] Third, there is no used-vehicle market, but rather scrappage of old cars is exogenous; this precludes some possibly important effects such as delayed scrappage (due to more expensive new vehicles) or differential scrappage of efficient and inefficient vehicles.

11.3.2   Modifications of NEMS

To fully assess CAFE's economic effects, I modify NEMS in several ways to better account for previously noted behavioral adjustments by consumers and automakers.

11.3.2.1   Valuation of fuel economy

As discussed in Section 11.2, I choose three scenarios for analysis: 100% ("Market"), 80%, and 30% valuations, with 80% valuation serving as the base scenario. These valuation ratios are calculated assuming the market interest rate r is 5.16%—which is the projected real interest rate for car loans in NHTSA's regulatory impact analysis (NHTSA, 2012, p. 991)—and that the true lifetime T is 15 years, very close to the current average car lifetime.[18] In the simulations, alternative valuation ratios are

---

[16] I account for changing perceptions in a very limited way by adjusting a constant in the model of vehicle-type choice that expresses a preference against gasoline-electric hybrid technology, other things equal. Specifically, I assume (both in the base and policy cases) that this constant diminishes gradually to zero, meaning that consumers fully accept hybrid technology by the end of the analysis period. The same change was made for an earlier version of the model, used by Small (2010, 2012).

[17] The literature contains considerable variation in its findings about how important changes in sales mix are in response to policies aimed at fuel efficiency. Whitefoot et al. (2013), using an engineering model to simulate manufacturers' design responses, find that redesign, as opposed to sales mix, accounts for nearly two-thirds of the response to a tighter CAFE standard over even a short time horizon 2011–2014.

[18] The NHTSA regulatory impact analysis uses 14 years for cars and 16 for light trucks (NHTSA, 2012, p. 989). Bento et al. (2018) find an average life of 15.6 years. I have calculated the valuation ratios implied by any given r and T as the ratio of present discounted fuel cost for the market values ($r = 0.0516$, $T = 15$) to that for the values under consideration. The calculation uses discrete-year discounting and incorporates an expected change in fuel price of 1.35% per year, which is the average annual growth rate of the real price of motor gasoline over years 2010–2035 in the AEO 2011 reference scenario. It also uses the same age-specific declines in annual mileage with vehicle age assumed in NEMS (Lu, 2006, Tables 5 and 6).

implemented by choosing alternative values for discount rate r and time horizon T as shown in Table 11.1.[19]

To implement these alternative valuations, I alter NEMS parameters from their default values in two places for the "market" and "moderate undervaluation" scenarios. First is the module governing manufacturers' choice of vehicle technologies, where the interest rate and time horizon are explicit parameters and so the assumptions in Table 11.1 can be inserted directly into the NEMS equations.[20] Second is the logit model governing consumers' choice of fuel type (e.g. conventional gasoline, hybrid, diesel, or all-electric). This model contains a utility component linear in vehicle price and expected fuel cost, whose ratio implies a particular valuation ratio; I alter the ratio of those two coefficients to be consistent with the scenario I am considering. This is described in Section A.2.1.

This second change requires a recalibration of two other constants in the equation governing choice of vehicle type, in order to again produce correct market shares for diesels, gas–electric hybrids, and flexible-fuel vehicles. Apparently, the EIA calibrated those constants to reproduce observed behavior in recent years (as well as to reflect its beliefs about the development of future technology), but the change in valuation

Table 11.1 **Scenarios representing alternative consumer valuation of fuel cost savings**

Scenario	Interest Rate (r)	Time Horizon (T)	Capital Recovery Factor (CRF)	Implied Valuation Fraction for Fuel Savings[a]
Market	0.0516	15	0.134	1.0
Partial under-valuation	0.0936	15	0.168	0.8
Severe under-valuation	0.1500	3	0.456	0.3

[a] Calculated assuming a market interest rate of 5.16% and true lifetime of 15 years.

[19] Of course, many combinations of r and T could yield a given valuation ratio. For the "Market" scenario, I have chosen what I think are the true values. For the "Severe undervaluation" scenario, I use the default NEMS values of those parameters ($r = 0.15$ and $T = 3$). For the "Moderate undervaluation" scenario (80% valuation), I choose to adjust r rather than T from its "market" value, that is, I set $T = 15$ and determine the discount rate r for which the ratio of first-year fuel cost savings to present discounted value is $(0.1342/0.80) = 0.1678$. (I call that ratio the "capital recovery factor" in Table 11.1 and Appendix A.)

[20] In the simulations described in the 2011 American Energy Outlook, these parameters were specified to change unintuitively over the time of evaluation: they begin at $r = 0.10$ and $T = 0$, then shift to $r = 0.15$ and $T = 15$ for years 2017–2025, then shift to $r = 0.50$ and $T = 1$ by the end of the projection period. I have eliminated these changing parameters and used the middle set throughout.

ratio just described causes this calibration to break down.[21] Those calculations are explained further in Section A.2.2.[22]

11.3.2.2   Manufacturers' pricing and technology strategies

In·Appendix A.1, I show that a profit-maximizing manufacturer constrained to achieve a CAFE standard will add a price component to each vehicle which plays exactly the same role as the marginal fee or rebate in a "feebate" policy. The latter is a policy in which the manufacturer must pay the government for missing the standard or receive a rebate for exceeding the standard, the payment or rebate being proportional to how far from the standard that model car is. This differential is basically a shadow cost of fuel efficiency multiplied by the difference between the fuel efficiency of that model and the standard that applies.

Because the actual shadow cost is not known until the model is computed, actual calculation involves iterating to find the shadow cost that, when applied to all models in a given manufacturer's fleet, causes that manufacturer to meet the standard. In the calculation, any fine paid is added to this shadow cost.

I have implemented the pricing strategy in all scenarios, with the following exception. In order to explore its effect on model outcomes, I also compute a few scenarios in which such pricing is not allowed by the model. That is in fact the case in NEMS itself, so this comparison enables me to see how much it matters whether pricing responses are incorporated. I discuss those results in Section 11.4.2.

11.3.2.3   Noncompliance

NEMS allow firms to pay fines instead of meeting the standards if that would be less costly. As discussed earlier, the status of such fines in the future is unclear but they are likely to effectively rise. Therefore, in the base scenarios, I assume the fine will be about twice the recent legal value, or $100 per vehicle per unit deficit (in miles/gal) when a manufacturer's fleet average fuel efficiency falls short of the standard as applied to that manufacturer. The fine is assumed to be incorporated by the manufacturer into the price paid by the consumer.

As noted in Section 11.2, some researchers have found that American manufacturers perceive political or public-relations penalties for not meeting the standards. If

---

[21] Specifically, when I alter the two coefficients just mentioned, the model no longer predicts the observed 2010 sales shares. Rather, under the market scenario, the model drastically over-predicts the market shares of diesel engines, strongly over-predicts gas–electric hybrids, and slightly over-predicts flexible-fuel vehicles. Although diesels and hybrids do not currently have large market shares, they are potentially an important part of automakers' responses to CAFE because such vehicles get high mileage; thus, errors in policy evaluation can arise if I over- or under-predict their market shares.

[22] Starting with the default NEMS values, I first make the adjustment to reproduce the correct 2010 shares in the Market scenario. I then adjust them for the partial undervaluation scenario in proportion to the change in valuation ratio, that is, I change them as in the market scenario but with the changes reduced by the fraction $(0.8–0.3)/(1–0.3)$.

those penalties are small, as found by Anderson and Sallee (2011), the fine itself is an adequate representation. But if the implicit penalties are large, as found by Jacobsen (2013), they would be perceived like higher fine levels. As noted earlier, higher fines also may be imposed via the greenhouse gas regulations. I therefore run one scenario with higher values for fines, namely $500/mpg.[23] I run this scenario as a variation of the "severe undervaluation" scenario, because that is the only scenario with large amounts of noncompliance.

I also modified NEMS to more accurately depict the manufacturer's cost tradeoff when considering new technologies in the presence of an option to pay fines for noncompliance. The NEMS model computes an effective shadow price for adopting more fuel-efficient technologies, in terms of dollars per improvement in fuel *efficiency* (mi/gal). But actually the CAFE law computes the degree of noncompliance by taking a harmonic average of the efficiencies of a manufacturer's various models, that is, it is based on the average fuel *intensity* (gal/mi). Thus, a manufacturer minimizing the cost of meeting the CAFE standard would equalize the shadow price of reducing fuel *intensity* (gal/mi) across different vehicles. In the modified NEMS, therefore, I based the calculation on fuel intensity. Thus, for example, a technology cost or fine of $100 per unit efficiency (mi/gal) is placed into the model as a cost or fine of $100·$E^2$ per unit of fuel intensity (gal/mi), where E is the CAFE standard expressed in mi/gal. This is because the deviation ΔE in fuel efficiency is approximately equivalent to a deviation in fuel intensity $\Delta F = -E^2 \cdot \Delta E$. Further details are in Appendix A.3.

11.3.2.4 Consumers' expectations of fuel prices

Price expectations enter NEMS explicitly only in the vehicle manufacturers' technology choice model, where they interact with the varying assumptions about evaluation of future fuel savings. But price expectations are implicitly part of the vehicle type choice model as well, which depicts the tradeoff between vehicle price and first-year fuel cost savings. Therefore, I adapt the coefficients of both of these component models consistently.

I consider three alternative assumptions about formation of price expectations. The first is the default assumptions in NEMS: expectations in year t are based on the 5-year average of past prices, lagged 3 years (i.e. the average of prices from $t-8$ to $t-4$), but modified by extrapolating the change in this 5-year average between $t-4$ and $t-3$ if that change was positive. The rationale is that decisions on such technological features of a vehicle must be made 3 years in advance.[24]

---

[23] This compares to an unweighted average shadow cost for General Motors, Ford, and Chrysler's car and truck fleets, measured by Jacobsen over the period 1997–2001, of $256 per mpg.

[24] Note this means that manufacturers are forming expectations about consumers' future expectations: specifically, manufacturers form expectations, three years in advance, concerning what fuel prices consumers will anticipate over their time horizon at time of purchase.

In the second scenario, "random walk," consumers simply use the current (real) price as the best predictor. This is in practice not much different from the consumer expectations found by Anderson et al. (2013), which differed from random walk only following the sharp downturn in 2008—a downturn that does not occur in any of the AEO projections for future years.

In the final scenario, "rational expectations," consumers use the AEO 2011 forecast (extrapolating beyond its horizon of 2035 by using a constant growth rate of real prices based on years 2025–2035). Effectively, the "rational expectations" scenario is like "random walk" plus an expectation of a secular rise in price of motor fuel.

11.3.2.5   Oil prices

Simulations depend strongly on the course of actual fuel prices that are modeled, given that these prices have major effects on consumers' willingness to pay for more fuel-efficient vehicles. I present two scenarios on either side of the base scenario, using the AEO 2011 "low oil price" and "high oil price" scenarios. In these scenarios, crude oil prices rise from 2010 to 2035 at average annual rates of −3.5% and +3.9%, respectively, bracketing the rate of 1.7% in the central ("reference") scenario.

Gasoline prices vary by less than oil prices across these scenarios, ranging across annual growth rates of −0.8% to +2.9% (reference scenario: 1.4%). Table 11.17 in Appendix B shows the projected prices of motor gasoline in these three scenarios for selected years, all in constant 2009 dollars.

In order to hold as much as possible constant across oil-price scenarios, I first ran the fully integrated NEMS system with oil prices following a given scenario, otherwise using the base assumptions. This provided an internally consistent path of prices for all the fuels used in motor vehicles, including electricity. I then carried out the simulations with those latter price paths held fixed, that is, as with the other simulations, macroeconomic feedbacks that might affect fuel prices endogenously are not accounted for. This makes these experiments consistent with the other experiments.

11.3.3   Remaining uncertainties

Even with these modifications, extensive experimentation revealed some features of the model system that imply either nonoptimizing behavior or implicit externalities. For example, both the original and modified versions of NEMS contain coefficients that govern consumers' willingness to consider alternative vehicle types, such as diesel or gasoline–electric hybrids, which have only a small market share currently. These coefficients were chosen to facilitate calibration of predictions with observed results in and shortly after 2010, but I know of no attempt to compare them with other evidence on how such willingness evolves over time as market shares change. Similarly, consumers' choices between cars and trucks have economic dimensions not explicitly optimized in the model, so the model system may or may not embody consumer rationality. As yet another example, the assumptions behind manufacturers' technology choices in NEMS involve strong industry-wide scale economies as well as externalities of industry-wide learning-by-doing.[25]

The question of whether such features accurately depict behavior in these markets, and if so whether they represent externalities, would greatly affect an overall welfare evaluation of CAFE. To the best of my knowledge, no consensus on such questions exists in the research literature. Given the importance of potential externalities to CAFE evaluation, it would be valuable to take a comprehensive look at how they are incorporated in NEMS and what is known about them.

11.4 Results

In order to assess the impact of CAFE, in each experiment (scenario) I run at least two cases. One is a "base case," which assumes all current policies through 2016, including CAFE increases; it then holds CAFE standards constant from 2016 on. The CAFE policies through 2016 require an approximately 26% increase in the average standard for LDVs between 2010 and 2016, from 25.3 mi/gal to 33.3, given the assumptions about the mix of vehicle footprints made by NHTSA and EPA in their regulatory documents.

The other is a "CAFE case": it adds the increase in standards most recently adopted during the Obama administration, which applies to new vehicles in years 2017–2025. This regulation is intended to raise the average standard for LDVs by another 44%, to 47.9 mi/gal, by year 2025. This case assumes that the standards as originally written continue to apply following the legislatively mandated interim evaluation in 2018. It does not include the special credits for zero-emission vehicles, in order to permit examination of a pure increase in standards unobscured by this complexity.

I simulate these two cases in a variety of scenarios, each differing in one or more of the dimensions already discussed. I begin by describing a "base scenario," which embodies the default assumptions from which I depart one at a time, or occasionally two at a time, in order to test the importance of those assumptions. Typically, I focus on how the policy impact of the higher CAFE case depends on the assumption being tested.

---

[25] For example, NEMS assumes that consumers value hybrids more highly the larger the hybrid market, on the rationale that people value the service options and technical expertise of vehicle repair workers that develop only with a large market. This is reflected by including variable MMAVAIL, defined as "vehicle make and model diversity availability relative to gasoline," in the equation explain market share of gasoline-electric hybrid vehicles (EIA, 2012, pp. 61–63). As another example, NEMS assumes that certain optional energy-saving technologies for conventional vehicles become cheaper as the cumulative industry-wide production of those vehicles increases (EIA, 2012, pp. 19, 31). Both of these assumptions are consistent with economic theory, but it is difficult to assess whether or not the quantitative magnitudes incorporated into NEMS are realistic.

11.4.1   Policy impacts of CAFE in the base scenario

Table 11.2 shows some results for the base scenario (partial valuation with price adjustments), with and without the higher CAFE standards phased in between 2017 and 2025 per current law. The first two rows show the projected gasoline prices (from AEO 2011) and the CAFE standards,[26] while the remaining rows show modeled results. Note that the "base case" of this "base scenario" is essentially a forecast of what would happen if no further policy were implemented starting in 2016 (except that, as already noted, it does not include special provisions favoring electric vehicles).

The base (no-policy) case suggests that when consumers value fuel savings at 80% of their objective value, manufacturers go part way toward achieving the higher CAFE standards even when they are not imposed. I use year 2025 as a convenient milepost, since that is when the new standards, if imposed, would fully take effect. That standard, calculated at the expected mix of vehicle sizes endogenously chosen in 2025, is 48.2 mi/gal, resulting in a 56% increase in average new-vehicle fuel efficiency over the previous 10 years; but even when the standard is not imposed, fuel efficiency rises by 25%.[27] As a result, the policy impact of the higher standard on fuel efficiency (a gain of about 25%) is much less than the change in the standard itself (which increases by 43%). The policy impact in 2035 is even smaller, as manufacturers would continue to increase efficiency even in the base scenario; this is due to a combination of continuing fuel-price increases, declines in technology costs over time, and the model's assumption about technological inertia—namely, that once a new technology is adopted, it is not abandoned.

This finding that fuel economy is moderately high even without an increase in CAFE is driven by the robust consumer demand for fuel-efficient cars in this scenario, coupled with the gradual increase in gasoline price. As we shall see, it is strongly dependent on the assumed valuation of cost savings by consumers.

As part of the market adjustment with or without higher CAFE standards, there are significant shifts in the market shares of unconventional engines. Conventional diesel remain a small share, but hybrids (both gasoline–electric and diesel–electric) rise significantly by 2025, to a 18% share even without the CAFE policy and 28% with it. Interestingly, with the policy in place (but no increase in stringency after 2025), the market share of hybrids falls back by several percentage points after 2025, as other technologies come on line to achieve the fuel standards without requiring the more

---

[26] Recall that the legal requirement is not actually a specific number but rather a schedule of mandated fuel efficiencies by vehicle footprint. Thus the "standard" shown here, as well as in most descriptions of CAFE policies, results from a combination of stringency of regulations and vehicle-mix decisions by manufacturers and consumers. This is why it changes modestly after 2025 even though there is no change in the legal requirement.

[27] Even in the base case, CAFE standards rise slightly through 2016 due to earlier regulations. Furthermore, slight changes in the anticipated mix of footprint sizes cause the effective standard as calculated here to rise to 33.7 by 2025 in the base case, as shown in Table 2.

Table 11.2 **Policy results: base scenario**

	Base Case			CAFE Case			Policy Impact	
	2015	2025	2035	2015	2025	2035	2025	2035
Inputs							(% diff.)	
Gasoline price (2010$/ gal)	3.16	3.58	3.79	3.16	3.58	3.79	0.0%	0.0%
CAFE standard, avg. (mi/gal)	31.9	33.7	34.1	31.9	48.2	48.8	42.9%	43.2%
Outcomes								
Market shares							(%-point diff.)	
Conventional gasoline	67%	55%	52%	67%	41%	47%	−13.8%	−5.2%
Diesels	5%	3%	3%	5%	3%	3%	−0.3%	0.0%
Hybrids (excl. plug-ins)	5%	18%	19%	5%	28%	22%	10.2%	3.0%
Plugs-ins and dedicated elec.	1%	7%	11%	1%	16%	14%	8.4%	2.9%
Fuel efficiency (newveh's-mi/gal)							(% diff.)	
Cars	35.7	41.7	45.5	35.7	57.1	56.7	36.9%	24.7%
Trucks	27.3	35.6	39.6	27.3	41.3	41.4	16.0%	4.5%
All LDVs	31.2	38.9	43.0	31.2	48.8	49.3	25.4%	14.6%
Fuel efficiency-veh stock (mi/gal):								
All LDVs	22.2	26.8	31.5	22.2	28.7	36.2	7.1%	14.9%

(Continued)

Table 11.2 Policy results: base scenario (*Cont.*)

	Base Case			CAFE Case			Policy Impact	
	2015	2025	2035	2015	2025	2035	2025	2035
VMT (billions)	2966	3518	4145	2966	3542	4206	0.7%	1.5%
Fuel use (billions gal)	134	131	132	134	123	116	−6.0%	−11.7%

expensive hybrid technology.[28] Thus, it appears that hybrid technologies are key to achieving those last increments of fuel efficiency demanded by the 2025 standards.

Vehicles using external electric power—plug-in hybrids and dedicated electrics—also gain market share, to about 7% in 2025 without the higher standards and 16% with them. (They decline in share after 2035 in the CAFE case, for the same reason as hybrids.) In practice, vehicles with batteries will probably grow in market share more than projected here due to recent faster-than-expected advances in battery technology. This is especially true for all-electric vehicles if current provisions giving double credits for zero-emission vehicles (such credits being included in neither the base case nor CAFE case as modeled here) are retained.

The vehicle fleet, of course, does not change nearly as quickly as the cohort of new vehicles. As a result, fleet fuel efficiency is impacted less dramatically by the standards, namely by 7.1% in 2025 and 14.9% in 2035. Actual fuel use falls by even less, due to the rebound effect causing VMT to be somewhat higher in the policy case.

11.4.2 Effects of price adjustments

Table 11.3 shows selected results with and without the price adjustments that I incorporate into most of the scenarios. Results are shown for year 2025. As before, the CAFE standards are footprint-based, that is, they are more lenient the larger the surface area covered by the wheels of the vehicle.

There are several striking differences in how markets are predicted to respond to stricter CAFE standards if manufacturers' pricing responses are not accounted for. First, the average fuel efficiency of new vehicles with the higher CAFE standard in place would be about 4% lower without pricing: the 2025 standard of 48.2 mi/gal would not be met, whereas it is met and even slightly exceeded with pricing responses allowed.

Second, without pricing, more effort would be put into technologies on conventional gasoline cars, and less into increasing the market share of unconventional engines. Indeed, as seen in the second and third rows of numbers, with higher CAFE regulations the efficiency of conventional gasoline vehicles rises by several percent-

---

[28] This can occur in the model partly because the market share of hybrids is chosen by consumers through an explicit choice model, whereas the adoption of technologies on conventional vehicles is chosen by manufacturers based on assumed paths of technology costs.

Table 11.3 Effects of Price Adjustments, 2025

	Base (80%)			Base (80%) w/o Price adj.		
	Base	**CAFE**	**CAFE Impact**	**Base**	**CAFE**	**CAFE Impact**
Average new-vehicle fuel economy (mi/gal)			(% diff.)			(% diff.)
All light-duty vehicles	38.9	48.8	25.4%	39.2	46.8	19.4%
Conventional gasoline car	37.0	43.9	18.7%	37.3	47.9	28.3%
Conventional gasoline truck	31.2	34.9	11.7%	31.4	36.5	16.4%
Sales share by vehicle type			(diff in % pts)			(diff in % pts)
Conventional gasoline	55.3%	41.5%	−13.8%	55.1%	56.3%	1.2%
Diesel	3.0%	2.6%	−0.3%	2.9%	2.6%	−0.4%
Hybrids (excl. plug-ins)	17.5%	27.7%	10.2%	17.5%	16.5%	−1.0%
Plugin hybrids + dedicated electric	7.3%	15.7%	8.4%	7.3%	7.0%	−0.3%
Sales share by technology used						
Micro hybrid (engine off at idle)	19.1%	48.9%	29.7%	21.1%	61.8%	40.7%
Material subst'n (most advanced)	1.4%	31.6%	30.3%	1.4%	56.9%	55.5%

age points more when pricing flexibility is absent. But this is more than compensated by the much smaller penetration of hybrids and other unconventional vehicles when pricing response is unavailable.

The manner in which conventional gasoline engines are improved is exemplified by two technologies, shown in the last two rows of the table: automatic powering off (so-called "micro-hybrid" technology), and advanced material substitution to reduce vehicle weight.[29] Essentially, manufacturers unable to influence consumer purchases by pricing must instead invest in expensive technologies for each given type of vehicle in order to raise average fuel efficiency.

Just how expensive this is can be seen in Table 11.4. In the nonprice-responsive scenario, the manufacturer's costs of making various types of new vehicles rise by significantly more than in the price-adjustment scenario. Table 11.4 also shows some examples of the price adjustments themselves, when they are allowed by the model: they range between roughly $750 and $1750 per vehicle in magnitude, which is about 3%–6% of the manufacturer's cost.[30]

In the "severe undervalue" scenario (30% valuation), presented in the next subsection, the importance of price adjustment is even greater. Results like those in Tables 11.3 and 11.4 are shown in Tables 11.18 and 11.22, for 30% valuation. (They also differ by assuming a higher fine, which is needed to achieve results approaching the CAFE standard with such low valuation by consumers.) In those scenarios, the CAFE policy would again cause micro-hybrids to gain well over half the conventional-car market without price adjustments, but far less with price adjustments. With pricing response allowed, price markups and markdowns are much larger with severe undervaluation of fuel efficiency, as manufacturers struggle to shift consumers from conventional to unconventional engines.

11.4.3   Effects of consumer valuation of fuel price savings

Tables 11.5 and 11.6 show results comparable to Tables 11.3 and , this time comparing the base scenario (80% valuation) to the "severe undervalue" scenario (30% valuation). We see that with severe undervaluation, manufacturers and consumers do not respond strongly to rising gasoline prices in the absence of stricter regulation, causing the policy impacts of CAFE—as measured by the differences in fuel economy, sales shares, and technology application—to be much greater. When CAFE is applied in this scenario, manufacturers shift to hybrids even more strongly, but make little use of expensive technologies for conventional vehicles, such as micro-hybrids and advanced materials (Table 11.5). In addition, with severe undervaluation manufacturers rely more on price incentives: for example, by applying a price markup to a conventional midsize car equal to 15% of its base cost, more than twice the markup applied in the base scenario (Table 11.6).

As expected, the "full valuation" scenario differs in the opposite direction; I show it in Tables 11.23 and 11.24. In that scenario, average fuel efficiency in 2025 under the base case (no increase in CAFE) is 40.8 mi/gal, a little higher than under "Partial undervaluation," whereas hybrid penetration is 20.6%, also somewhat

---

[29] The EIA defines micro hybrid vehicles as "vehicles with gasoline engines, larger batteries, and electrically powered auxiliary systems that allow the engine to be turned off when the vehicle is coasting or idling and then quickly restarted. Regenerative braking recharges the batteries…" (EIA, 2012, p. 30). However, I use the slightly broader definition used in the EIA's detailed charts, namely "Engine off at idle".

[30] This cost includes return to capital and a normal profit.

Table 11.4 **Effects of price adjustments on selected vehicle costs, 2025**

	With Price Adjustments			Without Price Adjustments		
	Base	**CAFE**	**CAFE Impact**	**Base**	**CAFE**	**CAFE Impact**
Vehicle cost (2010$)			(% diff.)			(% diff.)
Midsize car (conv gasoline)	28,235	29,874	5.8%	28,349	30,665	8.2%
Small SUV (conv gasoline)	25,941	27,096	4.5%	25,988	27,573	6.1%
Midsize car (gas–elec hybrid)	34,255	35,013	2.2%	34,302	35,967	4.9%
Small SUV (gas–elec hybrid)	31,449	32,014	1.8%	31,466	32,362	2.8%
Vehicle price markup (2010$)			(% of cost in base case)			(% of cost in base case)
Midsize car (conv gasoline)	0	1742	6.2%	0	0	0.0%
Small SUV (conv gasoline)	0	752	2.9%	0	0	0.0%
Midsize car (gas–elec hybrid)	0	−951	−2.8%	0	0	0.0%
Small SUV (gas–elec hybrid)	0	−1089	−3.5%	0	0	0.0%

Table 11.5 **Effects of valuation, 2025**

	Partial Valuation (80%)			Severe Undervalue (30%)		
	Base	**CAFE**	**CAFÉ Impact**	**Base**	**CAFE**	**CAFÉ Impact**
Average new-vehicle fuel economy (mi/gal)			(% diff.)			(% diff.)
All light-duty vehicles	38.9	48.8	25.4%	34.9	48.7	39.6%
Conventional gasoline car	37.0	43.9	18.7%	35.5	39.1	10.3%
Conventional gasoline truck	31.2	34.9	11.7%	27.4	32.0	16.8%
Sales share by vehicle type			(diff in % pts)			(diff in % pts)
Conventional gasoline	55.3%	41.5%	−13.8%	60.7%	34.0%	−26.8%
Diesel	3.0%	2.6%	−0.3%	4.2%	4.8%	0.6%
Hybrids (excl. plug-ins)	17.5%	27.7%	10.2%	11.9%	31.2%	19.3%
Plugin hybrids + dedicated electric	7.3%	15.7%	8.4%	5.4%	21.4%	16.0%
Sales share by technology used						
Micro hybrid (engine off at idle)	19.1%	48.9%	29.7%	5.9%	16.8%	10.9%
Material subst'n (most advanced)	1.4%	31.6%	30.3%	0.5%	6.3%	5.7%

Table 11.6 Effects of valuation on selected vehicle costs, 2025

	Partial Valuation (80%)			Severe Undervalue (30%)		
	Base	**CAFE**	**CAFE Impact**	**Base**	**CAFE**	**CAFE Impact**
Vehicle cost (2010$)			(% diff.)			(% diff.)
Midsize car (conv gasoline)	28,235	29,889	5.9%	27,880	28,562	2.4%
Small SUV (conv gasoline)	25,941	27,103	4.5%	25,076	26,107	4.1%
Midsize car (gas–elec hybrid)	34,255	35,005	2.2%	34,148	34,426	0.8%
Small SUV (gas–elec hybrid)	31,449	32,005	1.8%	31,490	31,885	1.3%
Vehicle price mark-up (2010$)			(% of cost in base case)			(% of cost in base case)
Midsize car (conv gasoline)	0	1726	6.1%	0	4199	15.1%
Small SUV (conv gasoline)	0	746	2.9%	0	2696	10.7%
Midsize car (gas–elec hybrid)	0	−943	−2.8%	0	−762	−2.2%
Small SUV (gas–elec hybrid)	0	−1080	−3.4%	0	−2007	−6.4%

higher. Because efficiency is somewhat higher even without the boost in CAFE standards, that boost has less impact in this scenario: the policy impact on efficiency of new LDVs in 2025 is 19.4%, aided by an 8.2 percentage-point increase in hybrid share.

I also explored two intermediate scenarios, with 60% and 45% valuation, one of which is shown in the same tables (in Appendix B). As expected, results mostly vary smoothly with the degree of valuation.[31]

11.4.4   Effects of magnitudes of fines for noncompliance

In this section, I report the result of raising the fine by a factor of five, to $500 (in 1990$) per vehicle per unit deviation from the standard as stated in miles per gallon. I test this within the "severe undervaluation" scenario, because that is the only scenario with large amounts of noncompliance. Note that the model assumes that manufacturers pass these fines on to their customers.

Even with severe undervaluation, so long as price adjustments are allowed (there is almost full compliance with CAFE even with the lower fine). As a result, raising the fine makes practically no difference to the outcome except for the amounts paid in fines in the high CAFE cases, which is still not very large.[32] (These fines are paid entirely by the manufacturing group representing sports cars,[33] whose market share is small.) For this reason, the results shown in this subsection are for a scenario in which price adjustments are not allowed - calling further attention to the importance of such price responses by manufacturers.

With price adjustments are not allowed, high fines are predicted to have discernable impacts on achieved fuel efficiency, on manufacturing costs, and on the sales shares of unconventional cars. Tables 11.7 and 11.8 compare the predicted impacts of low and high fines in this situation. They show that without price adjustments, the year-2025 impacts of high CAFE would be predicted to be about 3 percentage points greater on achieved fuel economy with high fines compared to low fines (although still not quite meeting the standards); 6 percentage points greater in the use of microhybrids; and 10 percentage points greater in use of the most advanced materials. The costs of individual vehicle types and classes would be predicted to rise about two percentage points more with high fines than with low fines (Table 11.8). Fines paid would rise to more than $1900 per vehicle on average for cars (much less for light trucks). More detailed figures, not shown in the tables, reveal that the fines are also more widespread in this scenario, ranging across manufacturing groups from approximately $1300–$9400 per vehicle for cars, and from zero to $250 per vehicle for light trucks.

11.4.5   Effects of fuel price expectations

Alternative fuel price expectations turn out to have little effect on the simulations. Some results are shown in appendix Table 11.19, comparing the NEMS default

---

[31] There is an apparent small lack of monotonicity in CAFE impacts on vehicle prices. This is probably due to minor quirks in the model involving when particular discrete technologies are introduced. The vehicle prices themselves are monotonic; but the prices in the reference case vary with valuation at slightly different rates from those in the CAFE case, so their differences are not monotonic.

[32] The fine paid in the Severe Undervaluation scenario with price adjustments allowed is an average of $81 per vehicle in year 2025, compared to $16 in the low-fine scenario.

[33] These fines amount to $14,200 per vehicle for sports cars in the high-fine scenario.

Table 11.7 Effects of fines, 2025 (severe undervalue scenarios, without price adjustments)

	Standard Fines			High Fines		
	Base	CAFE	CAFE Impact	Base	CAFE	CAFE Impact
Average new-vehicle fuel economy (mi/ gal)			(% diff.)			(% diff.)
All light-duty vehicles	35.8	46.4	29.5%	35.8	47.4	32.4%
Conventional gasoline car	36.3	47.8	31.8%	36.3	49.0	35.2%
Conventional gasoline truck	28.0	36.8	31.7%	28.0	37.6	34.5%
Sales share by vehicle type			(%-pt diff)			(%-pt diff)
Conventional gasoline	60.3%	59.1%	−1.2%	60.3%	59.6%	−0.6%
Diesel	3.6%	3.8%	0.2%	3.6%	3.8%	0.3%
Hybrids (excl. plug-ins)	12.4%	13.5%	1.1%	12.4%	13.2%	0.7%
Plugin hy-brids + dedi-cated electric	5.7%	6.3%	0.6%	5.7%	5.9%	0.2%
Sales share by technology used						
Micro hybrid (engine off at idle)	9.2%	55.9%	46.7%	9.2%	61.4%	52.3%
Material subst'n (most advanced)	0.4%	53.6%	53.2%	0.4%	64.0%	63.6%

expectations with random walk expectations (i.e. expected price is the same as the current price except for a constant trend growth). The CAFE impact on new-vehicle fuel efficiency is just 1.0 percentage point greater with random walk. This is mainly because the current price is almost always equal to or slightly less than NEMS-default expectations, leading consumers to choose slightly less fuel efficiency in the base case. Rational expectations are very similar to random-walk expectations.

Table 11.8 **Effects of fines on selected vehicle costs, 2025 (severe undervalue scenarios, without price adjustments)**

	Standard Fines			High Fines		
	Base	CAFE	CAFE Impact	Base	CAFE	CAFE Impact
Vehicle cost (2010$)			(% diff.)			(% diff.)
Midsize car (conv gasoline)	28,097	30,267	7.7%	28,097	30,803	9.6%
Small SUV (conv gasoline)	25,207	27,130	7.6%	25,207	27,708	9.9%
Midsize car (gas-elec hybrid))	34,246	35,414	3.4%	34,246	36,194	5.7%
Small SUV (gas-elec hybrid))	31,536	32,128	1.9%	31,536	32,803	4.0%
Fines paid in lieu of compliance ($/vehicle)			(% of base-case price)			(% of base-case price)
Cars	4	587	2.1%	4	1918	6.9%
Trucks	0	86	0.3%	0	55	0.2%

These results are due mainly to the very slow growth in fuel prices in the AEO projections and also to their lack of volatility. For this reason, I thought there might be a greater difference if I used the AEO "high oil price" scenario as a starting point, but that proved not to be the case. Even that scenario has very modest growth in oil prices (see the next section) over the periods of interest here, namely after 2017; most of the difference in growth rates between scenarios occurs in the years 2010–2015. That comparison is shown Table 11.20. (In this case, I show rational expectations; once again, random walk is very similar.)

If the AEO projections included randomly generated volatility, comparable to past volatility, there would be more differences because the NEMS default expectations would reflect the occasional large upward trend that consumers would project from a particular one-year increase in fuel price. This would cause the NEMS default to produce higher fuel economy without CAFE, hence a smaller impact of CAFE. But such results would be suspect on several grounds. First, there is only scant evidence that consumers have such one-sided expectations, coming from a single episode of a price drop in 2008 which, according to surveys, consumers expected (correctly) to be reversed (Anderson et al., 2013). Second, the trend extrapolation assumed in NEMS on the part of consumers is very specific and arbitrary, whereas the evidence just cited suggests that consumers are more nuanced in their projections. Third, any quantitative forecasts of future volatility in fuel prices would be highly uncertain themselves, compounding the uncertainty in forecasts of price levels.

Finally, it seems likely that consumers react to volatility itself, as opposed to simply using it to change their forecasts of future prices. However, it is not clear in which direction price volatility would tilt their decisions. If they view a new car as a significant investment, they may defer purchase, hoping that some of the uncertainty in future prices is resolved; this could be represented in NEMS as a volatility-dependent lengthening of the average age of vehicle scrappage. On the other hand, risk aversion could cause consumers to invest in extra fuel efficiency as a hedge against the risk of finding themselves trapped with a car too expensive to operate. To model this properly would require new research into consumer reactions.

I also explored whether the extent of under-valuation of fuel efficiency affects the impacts of alternative price expectations, but found that any such effects are small. The relevant impacts for the case of severe undervaluation are shown in Table 11.21. Roughly speaking, changing fuel price expectations has similar effects to making small changes in valuation: they affect CAFE impact by changing the base case.

11.4.6   Effects of fuel prices

One can expect the course of fuel prices to have large effects on the base case (without high CAFE), especially in those scenarios when consumers value a high fraction of the cost savings from fuel efficiency. The higher the fuel price, the more consumers will adopt high efficiency voluntarily and therefore the impact of standards will be smaller.

Table 11.9 shows that this is indeed the case. I use the base assumptions (which include price expectations informed by recent price movements) in all respects except for replacing EIA's standard scenario with its "low oil price" or "high oil price" scenario. The low and high oil price projections for year 2025 portray manufacturers voluntarily achieving 34.8 and 43.1 mi/gal, respectively (vs. 38.9 mi/gal under the Reference Case forecast), even without the imposition of new CAFE standards. The higher figure is 87% of the efficiency (49.6 mi/gal) achieved in the same scenario with the higher CAFE in place.

With CAFE in place, manufacturers over-comply on average when oil prices are high, leading to a 5% higher average fuel efficiency than with low oil prices. It is interesting to see how this is accomplished. With high prices, conventional gasoline vehicles, mainly cars, have their efficiencies boosted even further, through technologies exemplified by the projected high penetration of microhybrids and a big increase in the use of advanced materials. Comparing the two oil-price scenarios, advanced material use spans the range from just 0.5% in the base case with low oil prices to

Table 11.9 **Effects of oil prices, 2025**

	Low Oil Price			High Oil Price		
	Base	**CAFE**	**CAFE Impact**	**Base**	**CAFE**	**CAFE Impact**
Average new-vehicle fuel economy (mi/gal)			(% diff)			(% diff.)
All light-duty vehicles	34.8	47.3	35.9%	43.1	49.6	15.1%
Conventional gasoline car	36.1	41.7	15.5%	39.7	45.1	13.6%
Conventional gasoline truck	28.9	33.7	16.3%	34.7	36.9	6.4%
Sales share by vehicle type			(diff in % pts)			(diff in % pts)
Conventional gasoline	61.1%	37.2%	−23.9%	40.9%	37.6%	−3.4%
Diesel	2.0%	1.9%	−0.1%	3.8%	3.7%	−0.1%
Hybrids (excl. plug-ins)	11.4%	31.6%	20.1%	20.6%	24.7%	4.1%
Plugin hybrids + dedicated electric	4.3%	17.2%	12.9%	9.8%	14.5%	4.7%
Sales share by technology used						
Micro hybrid (engine off at idle)	15.7%	37.4%	21.7%	36.9%	57.3%	20.5%
Material subst'n (most advanced)	0.5%	17.5%	17.0%	5.2%	35.5%	30.4%

over 35% in the CAFE scenario with high oil prices. Use of gas–electric hybrids also increases when CAFE is adopted, but in the high oil price scenario this effect is small: apparently, given the technology assumptions modeled here, when consumers are willing to spend money on fuel efficiency, manufacturers prefer to put a lot of technology into conventional gasoline cars rather than to market hybrids and electric cars extensively.

This strategy for meeting CAFE can be seen in Table 11.10, which shows manufacturing costs (upper panel) and price markups adopted as incentives (lower panel), for selected vehicles. The price markups are quite large in the low oil price scenario, which is a major reason for the increase in hybrid and electric market shares. In the high oil price scenario, markups are more modest, indicating that the constraint imposed by CAFE is less tightly binding.[34]

11.4.7   Non-footprint-based standards

As noted earlier, the current form of CAFE standards makes them more lenient for larger vehicles, as measured by the surface area covered by its wheels (its "footprint"). This feature is intended to prevent the standards from creating incentives to make vehicles smaller. This raises the question: would the regulations be more effective, or less costly, if they were not based on the vehicle's footprint?

I consider a scenario in which the connection between the standard and the vehicle size is partially relaxed, by means of what I call a dual standard: one standard for all cars, another for all light trucks. This is in fact the approach that prevailed for most of the US CAFE regulations' history, being supplanted by a gradual transition to footprint-based standards starting in 2008. The dual standard still forgoes one incentive, which may be important: to shift from light trucks to cars. However, for technical reasons it would be difficult to modify NEMS to simulate such a uniform standard.

Tables 11.11 and 11.12 show the results, using the base scenario for all other aspects. Table 11.11 shows that the type of standards makes only a small improvement in achieved fuel efficiency. The dual standard results in slightly more use of unconventional vehicles, and little change in use of advanced technologies for conventional vehicles. Table 11.12 shows that there is little effect on the vehicle size mix, with the dual standard inducing a small increase in the market share of compact cars but also (inexplicably) in that of large pickup trucks. All these differences are within the probable margins of modeling error.

The effects on size mix are slightly larger if we start with the "severe undervaluation" case, but still not very large. These are shown in appendix Table 11.25. This insensitivity occurs despite the fact that in that scenario, price responses with any CAFE standard in place are enormous, amounting to charging a premium in year 2025 of over $4600 for a conventional midsize car and a discount of over $1700 on a hybrid small

---

[34] The differences are not due to different degrees of compliance: in both scenarios all manufacturers comply except the group that makes sports cars; the latter does not even fully comply in the base case, indicating their cars are not quite meeting the 2016 standard even by 2025.

Table 11.10 **Effects of Oil Prices on Selected Vehicle Costs, 2025**

	Low Oil Price			High Oil Price		
	Base	**CAFE**	**CAFE Impact**	**Base**	**CAFE**	**CAFE Impact**
Vehicle manuf cost (2010$)			(% diff.)			(% diff.)
Midsize car (conv gasoline)	28,174	29,329	4.1%	28,899	30,154	4.3%
Small SUV (conv gasoline)	25,485	26,682	4.7%	26,796	27,393	2.2%
Midsize car (gas–elec hybrid)	34,231	34,641	1.2%	34,457	35,323	2.5%
Small SUV (gas–elec hybrid)	31,282	31,782	1.6%	31,812	32,201	1.2%
Vehicle price mark-up (2010$)			(% of cost in base case)			(% of cost in base case)
Midsize car (conv gasoline)	0	3658	13.0%	0	892	3.1%
Small SUV (conv gaso-line)	0	2037	8.0%	0	118	0.4%
Midsize car (gas–elec hybrid)	0	−1195	−3.5%	0	−609	−1.8%
Small SUV (gas–elec hybrid)	0	−2023	−6.5%	0	−224	−0.7%

SUV (Table 11.13). The model predicts that such price incentives affect fuel type much more than size mix, mainly causing a large migration to hybrids and electric vehicles.

This lack of significant size response is consistent with several other studies, although at odds with the predictions of empirical models from industrial organization.

Table 11.11 Effects of dual CAFE standard, 2025 (partial undervaluation scenario)

	Footprint Standards			Dual (Car/Truck) Standards		
	Base	CAFE	CAFÉ Impact	Base	CAFE	CAFÉ Impact
Average new-vehicle fuel economy (mi/gal)			(% diff)			(% diff.)
All light-duty vehicles	38.9	48.8	25.4%	38.9	48.9	25.8%
Convention-al gasoline car	37.0	43.9	18.7%	37.0	44.1	19.1%
Convention-al gasoline truck	31.2	34.9	11.7%	31.2	34.5	10.6%
Sales share by vehicle type			(diff in % pts)			(diff in % pts)
Convention-al gasoline	55.3%	41.5%	−13.8%	55.3%	40.5%	−14.8%
Diesel	3.0%	2.6%	−0.3%	3.0%	2.7%	−0.2%
Hybrids (excl. plug-ins)	17.5%	27.7%	10.2%	17.5%	30.4%	12.8%
Plugin hy-brids + dedi-cated electric	7.3%	15.7%	8.4%	7.3%	15.0%	7.7%
Sales share by technol-ogy used						
Micro hybrid (engine off at idle)	19.1%	48.9%	29.7%	19.1%	46.7%	27.6%
Mate-rial subst'n (most advanced)	1.4%	31.6%	30.3%	1.4%	32.5%	31.1%

Table 11.12 **Effects of dual CAFE standard on vehicle mix, 2025 (partial undervaluation scenario)**

	Footprint Standards			Dual (Car/Truck) Standards		
	Base	**CAFE**	**CAFÉ Impact**	**Base**	**CAFE**	**CAFÉ Impact**
Sales share by size class (non-fleet vehicles):			(%-pt. diff.)			(%-pt. diff.)
Car						
Mini-compact	1.3%	1.3%	0.0%	1.3%	1.4%	0.0%
Subcom-pact	22.8%	22.9%	0.0%	22.8%	22.9%	0.0%
Compact	19.5%	19.4%	0.0%	19.5%	19.9%	0.4%
Midsize	33.2%	33.2%	0.0%	33.2%	33.0%	−0.2%
Large	20.0%	20.0%	0.0%	20.0%	19.7%	−0.3%
Two seater	3.1%	3.1%	0.0%	3.1%	3.2%	0.0%
Truck						
Small pickup	4.5%	4.3%	−0.2%	4.5%	4.1%	−0.4%
Large pickup	21.3%	21.1%	−0.2%	21.3%	22.3%	1.0%
Small van	1.8%	1.8%	0.0%	1.8%	1.7%	−0.1%
Large van	9.5%	9.4%	−0.1%	9.5%	9.1%	−0.5%
Small utility	34.2%	34.6%	0.3%	34.2%	34.1%	−0.1%
Large utility	28.6%	28.8%	0.2%	28.6%	28.7%	0.1%

Table 11.13 Effects of dual CAFE standard on price markups, 2025 (severe undervaluation scenario)

	Footprint Standards			Dual (Car/Truck) Standards		
	Base	CAFE	CAFE Impact	Base	CAFE	CAFE Impact
Vehicle price markup (2009$)			(% of base-case cost)			(% of base-case cost)
Midsize car (conv gasoline)	0	4199	15.2%	0	4621	16.7%
Small SUV (conv gasoline)	0	2695	10.8%	0	895	3.6%
Midsize car (gas–elec hybrid)	0	−762	−2.3%	0	−507	−1.5%
Small SUV (gas–elec hybrid)	0	−2007	−6.4%	0	−1714	−5.5%

At this point I am unable to definitively state whether such a small effect on vehicle size mix is indeed a feature of automobile markets, or is due to something lacking in the way NEMS models them.

11.4.8 Impacts on manufacturing and fuel costs

This section assesses the effects of CAFE policies on two metrics that are part of a social welfare calculation, under the various scenarios considered in previous sections. The metrics are the change in the average manufacturing cost of a new car, and the change in fuel cost per 1000 miles traveled. The Regulatory Impact Analysis of these same standards (NHTSA, 2012) suggests that these two (offsetting) factors play the dominant role in calculations of total costs and benefits of the policies.

I do not attempt to compute total welfare impacts, however, because there are too many unknown factors in the path between these metrics and a social welfare calculation. This fact would cause large potential error, considering that net welfare involves large and partially offsetting effects. In addition, total costs and benefits would require discounting, introducing yet another source of uncertainty: namely, the appropriate discount factor.[35] Nevertheless, the comparisons across scenarios presented here should give a good indication of the relative importance of those uncertainties that I have quantified.[36]

11.4.8.1 Change in the average manufacturing cost of a new car

NEMS tracks the technologies used for each vehicle type and size, along with a calculation of their costs and consequences for fuel efficiency. In addition, consumers change their purchases of alternative-fueled vehicles in response to the CAFE policy, for example, by purchasing more gasoline–electric hybrids, more purely electric cars, and more diesel cars. All these changes result in higher vehicle manufacturing costs. Our first metric is the aggregate of such extra costs over the 16-year period during which the simulated policy change is primarily active (2020–2035), divided by the total number of vehicles produced during that period under the CAFE policy.[37]

11.4.8.2 Change in fuel cost per 1000 miles traveled

Our second metric is the cost savings due to higher fuel efficiency[38] divided by total postpolicy VMT by *all* vehicles (not just those purchased under the new standards). Thus, the metric is an indicator of policy impact on *all* travelers through reducing their average cost of travel. The cost savings are calculated at pretax fuel prices, and thus represent a saving in social cost (but not including externalities related to carbon emissions or petroleum usage). To account for cars purchased near the end of the evaluation period (2035), the fuel savings for each car are projected over its expected

---

[35] Note that discounting affects the cost savings from greater fuel efficiency much more than the extra cost of new vehicles, because the savings are realized gradually over a longer time period. Thus, the higher the discount rate, the more will the extra cost of vehicles tend to overshadow the fuel-cost savings.

[36] I do not estimate the environmental or petroleum-related benefits of the policy, which of course are its primary purpose. This is both because I am interested in the net policy costs of achieving the goals of the policy (and those goals vary among proponents), and because the environmental benefits as estimated by NHTSA (2012) were in fact considerably smaller than either of the two components I am focusing on here.

[37] Approximations are used to estimate the size mix for each vehicle type, using information about which size classes are offered in the market for a given type. Specifically, the 16 vehicle types distinguished by NEMS are grouped into eight: conventional gasoline, gas–electric hybrid, diesel, diesel–electric hybrid, 100-mile electric, ethanol flex–fuel, plug-in hybrid, and all other. For each alternative-fueled vehicle type (i.e. all those other than conventional gasoline), and each broad size category (car or truck), I assume that the distribution across those size classes that are produced for that type is the same as the distribution of all light-duty vehicles across those same size classes. Thus, the sales of type t in size category s is approximated as $q(t, s) = D(t, s)Q(t)\dfrac{Q_A(s)}{\Sigma_{s'} D(t, s')Q_A(s')}$, where D is a dummy variable for whether vehicles were produced of type t and size s, $Q(t)$ is total sales of type t vehicles, $Q_A(s')$ is total sales of size s' vehicles, and the summation is over sizes within the same broad size category (car or truck).

[38] The cost savings are those actually realized over the lifetimes of vehicles subject to each standard, which are not necessarily equal to the savings accounted for by consumers when they purchased the vehicles.

lifetime of 15 years; VMT is projected similarly.[39] The figures shown are aggregate total savings divided by aggregate VMT, with no discounting.

11.4.8.3 Comparisons among scenarios

To focus on the sensitivities revealed in earlier subsections, I highlight here two sources of variation in CAFE policy evaluation: namely, consumer valuation of fuel price savings and future oil prices.

Table 11.14 shows the two metrics for three valuation ratios, spanning the rather large range of uncertainty identified earlier. The table shows that both metrics vary by a factor of about 2.5 between the full valuation and the severe undervaluation scenarios. Since these two metrics act in opposite directions, the net policy cost—whether positive or negative—is thus likely to be larger in magnitude when consumers are assumed to undervalue fuel savings.

Table 11.15 shows similar results for the three alternative oil-price scenarios, all assuming 80% valuation. (The middle column thus repeats the "partial valuation" scenario appearing in Table 11.14).

The fuel cost savings are only modestly different across the oil-price scenarios, and in fact not monotonic: they are highest at the intermediate ("reference") price, not at either extreme. This is because the low oil price scenario produces a greater difference in fuel consumption, but fuel savings are worth less per gallon; conversely for the high oil price scenario.

Table 11.14 Evaluation metrics of increased CAFE standards: alternative valuations of fuel savings

	Full Valuation	Partial Valuation	Severe Under-value
	(100%)	(80%)	(30%)
Change in cost of average new vehicle (2010$)			
(total 2020–2035, undiscounted)	1082	1492	2584
Change in fuel cost per 1000 miles by all vehicles (2010$)			
(total 2020–2050, undiscounted)	−7.86	−11.55	−20.25

---

[39] Both projections simply assume that the relevant aggregate quantity (fuel savings or VMT) declines linearly over this 15-year period to a value of zero.

Table 11.15 **Evaluation metrics of increased CAFE standards: alternative oil price scenarios**

	Low Oil Price	Reference Oil Price	High Oil Price
Change in cost of average new vehicle (2010$) (total 2020–2035, undiscounted)	2995	1492	785
Change in fuel cost per 1000 miles by all vehicles (2010$) (total 2020–2050, undiscounted)	−10.23	−11.55	−7.88

By contrast, the extra cost of producing cars varies greatly across oil-price scenarios. By this measure, the CAFE policy is nearly four times as costly at low oil prices as at high oil prices. This is because at low prices, the policy is more tightly binding, meaning that much more is spent on new vehicles in order to achieve changes in efficiencies which, at higher oil prices, occur voluntarily. Note that this does not mean cars are more costly to produce at low than at high oil prices; but rather, more of the cost is attributable to CAFE.

As a result of these patterns, the higher CAFE policy will tend to have a much higher net cost (increased manufacturing costs less fuel price savings) if oil prices are lower than expected, because the more expensive cars it requires will have only a modest payoff in fuel cost savings. Of course, the environmental benefits, in terms of reduced CO_2 emissions, will also be highest in that scenario, so one cannot say from these observations which oil prices would most favor a tight CAFE policy in a full welfare assessment.

11.5   Conclusion

Of the factors I have evaluated, the two with greatest impacts on CAFE evaluation are consumers' fuel-cost valuations as reflected in manufacturers' decisions (i.e. the extent of an "energy paradox"), and the course of oil prices. A great deal of research has already gone into both topics, so I suspect they reflect irreducible uncertainties rather than uncertainties that can be significantly narrowed through more research. If this is correct, policy evaluation must simply accept the resulting uncertainty in policy impacts. The sensitivity with respect to future oil prices is especially daunting because those prices greatly affect the manufacturing costs incurred in meeting a CAFE standard, but have a much smaller effect on the offsetting savings in fuel expenditures realized by consumers. Thus, the net cost of the policy is quite uncertain, as is the size of its desired impacts on carbon emissions and fossil-fuel consumption. On the other hand, a CAFE policy does reduce the uncertainties manufacturers face as to what levels of fuel efficiency they should plan for.

Some other factors that might seem important are less so, according to the modeling reported here: price expectations, how the standard varies by vehicle size, and the magnitude of fines. This finding could be subject to revision if better ways are found to model these three factors.

It is very important to properly incorporate manufacturers' pricing responses to CAFE policies in order to accurately predict those policies' impacts. If manufacturers are unrealistically assumed to always price at production cost plus normal profit, policy evaluation will miss the significant changes in market shares that manufacturers will induce through various price markups and discounts. It is urgent for modelers to incorporate such responses where they currently do not. It would also be beneficial to develop more sophisticated models in which the oligopolistic rivalry among manufacturers, their medium- and long-term planning requirements, and their marketing strategies are more fully recognized.

Given the results of this study, it is entirely possible that a simpler model than NEMS would be adequate to capture the most important effects of CAFE policies. Thus, there is still room for limited purpose models that focus on one aspect, such as vehicle size mix or used-vehicle markets. Yet there is room as well for continued large-scale modeling of the type exemplified by NEMS, if only to identify which factors are important to understand various other energy policies that are also under consideration.

Appendix A: Modifications of NEMS

A.1   Adding price responsiveness for manufacturers

A.1.1   Profit maximizing with elastic demand

Suppose a firm faces a demand curve for a product with elasticity $\eta < 0$ and production cost $C(q)$ as a function of output q. It is choosing a price p at which to sell its output.

To maximize profits, it chooses q to maximize:

$$\Pi = pq - C(q).$$

First-order maximization condition:

$$0 = p + q\frac{dp}{dq} - C'$$

Denote marginal cost C' by mc, and note that $(p/q)dq/dp = \eta$. Then

$$\frac{p-C'}{p} = \frac{1}{|\eta|}$$

or equivalently,

$$p = C' \cdot \mu, \quad \text{where} \quad \mu = \left(\frac{1}{1 - \frac{1}{|\eta|}}\right) = \frac{|\eta|}{|\eta|-1}. \tag{A.1}$$

The term μ is the fractional markup. Note that this solution (in either form) is valid only if $|\eta| > 1$ (assuming $mc > 0$).

The equation is modified if the firm produces several products with interacting demands; then, the cross-elasticities of demand also enter the equation determining the markup. Here for simplicity I assume those cross-elasticities are zero.

A.1.2 Profit maximization to meet a CAFE constraint (single standard)

Suppose for simplicity that the firm produces just two products, with no cross-elasticity. Now impose an average efficiency constraint for the two products, so the firm has to maximize

$$\Pi = p_1 q_1 + p_2 q_2 - C(q_1, q_2)$$

subject to a constraint on the average fuel intensities f_1 and f_2 (gal/mi) of the two products:

$$f_1 q_1 + f_2 q_2 \leq \bar{f} \cdot (q_1 + q_2) \tag{A.2}$$

where $\bar{f}$ is the inverse of the CAFE standard. The solution is found by maximizing the Lagrangian function:

$$\Pi = p_1 q_1 + p_2 q_2 - C(q_1, q_2) + \lambda \cdot \left[\left(\bar{f} - f_1\right) q_1 + \left(\bar{f} - f_2\right) q_2 \right] \tag{A.3}$$

The first-order condition for each product is

$$0 = p_i + q_i \frac{dp_i}{dq_i} - C_i + \lambda \cdot \left(\bar{f} - f_i\right)$$

where $C_i \equiv \partial C / \partial q_i$ is the marginal cost of product i. This can be written as

$$\frac{p_i - C_i'}{p_i} = \frac{1}{|\eta_i|} + \lambda \frac{\left(f_i - \bar{f}\right)}{p_i}$$

or, to solve explicitly for p_i:

$$p_i = \left[C_i' + \lambda \cdot \left(f_i - \bar{f}\right) \right] \cdot \mu_i \qquad \qquad \text{(A.4)}$$

where μ_i is defined analogously to (A.1).

The term μ_i is a product-specific markup factor related to demand elasticity. The Lagrangian multiplier λ is the shadow price of fuel efficiency, indicating that an additional price $\lambda \cdot \left(f_i - \bar{f}\right)$ is added to a vehicle with fuel intensity f_i, *before* applying the markup.

One can argue that the initially observed prices already account for the product-specific markup, μ_i. Marginal costs embedded in NEMS also account for μ_i insofar as the overhead added to the engineering cost is meant to cover this, although it may be an average markup $\bar{\mu}$ rather than an individual markup μ_i. Therefore, the shadow price that we measure is really not λ but $\lambda\mu_i$ (at least approximately), and the observed marginal costs in the model can be interpreted as $mc_i \equiv c_i' \cdot \mu_i$. Then (A.4) becomes

$$p_i = mc_i + \lambda\mu_i \cdot \left(f_i - \bar{f}\right). \qquad \qquad \text{(A.4')}$$

We can determine $\lambda\mu_i$ iteratively by simulating a feebate policy (in which the last term of (A.4') is the fee or rebate) that is just stringent enough to cause the stated CAFE standard to be met.

A.1.3 Footprint-based standards

Now suppose there is a different standard for each product, but the firm is allowed to trade across products—which is now the case for footprint-based standards. The constraint is that the firm's fleet average has to be at least as efficient as the sales-weighted average of the product-specific intensity standards, $\bar{f}_i$:

$$f_1 q_1 + f_2 q_2 \le \bar{f}_1 q_1 + \bar{f}_2 q_2 \qquad \qquad \text{(A.5)}$$

The first-order condition is modified to

$$0 = p_i + q_i \frac{dp_i}{dq_i} - C_i + \lambda \cdot \left(\bar{f}_i - f_i\right)$$

which yields

$$\frac{p_i - mc_i}{p_i} = \frac{1}{|\eta_i|} + \lambda \frac{\left(f_i - \overline{f_i}\right)}{p_i}$$

or equivalently,

$$p_i = \left[mc_i + \lambda \cdot \left(f_i - \overline{f_i}\right) \right] \cdot \mu_i. \tag{A.6}$$

So the shadow prices of the different vehicles are now much closer to each other because they depend on deviations of f_i from $\overline{f_i}$ instead of from a single value $\overline{f}$. In fact, if the solution were for each product to just meet its standard, the shadow price applied to the vehicle, $\lambda \cdot (f_i - \overline{f_i})$, would be zero and we would be back to the single-product solution (A.1) for each product. But this is unlikely to happen because it will usually be cheaper to improve fuel efficiency in some vehicles than in others. For example, if manufacturers find it cheaper to improve fuel efficiency in product 1 than in product 2, they will choose to make $f_1 < \overline{f_1}$ (more than meet the standard for product 1) and $f_2 > \overline{f_2}$; in that case, they will also lower the price of vehicle 1 and raise the price of vehicle 2, by amounts that include the markup. This of course is to help them meet the standard by changing the mix of vehicles toward those that are easier to make efficient. The price differential between them will then be changed by an amount that depends on both markup factors:

$$\Delta p \equiv p_2 - p_1 = \Delta mc + \lambda \cdot \left[\left(f_2 - \overline{f_2}\right)\mu_2 - \left(f_1 - \overline{f_1}\right)\mu_1 \right] \tag{A.7}$$

A.1.4 Choice of fuel intensity (i.e. technology)

Suppose unit costs are functions of fuel intensities f_i, and so are the prices at which consumers would choose a given quantity. We can represent this as demand functions

$$q_i = d_i \left[p_i + \varphi_i \left(f_i\right) \right]$$

where $d_i[\cdot]$ is a demand function for product i, *with the second term in the square brackets acting as a penalty which the consumer places on extra fuel intensity.* For simplicity I assume the cost function is linear in quantities, with coefficients c_i that fall with fuel intensity:

$$C\left(q_1, f_1, q_2, f_2\right) = q_1 c_1(f_1) + q_2 c_2(f_2).$$

Note that we expect $\varphi_i' > 0$ and $c_i' < 0$. Invert the demand function to get each price as a function of quantity and fuel intensity:

$$p_i = d_i^{-1}(q_i) - \varphi_i(f_i)$$

Note that $\varphi_i(f_i)$ is represented in NEMS as a calculation in the manufacturers' vehicle choice submodule, in which the manufacturer assumes certain parameters for how consumers value future fuel savings. We now examine the how the quality decision, i.e. the provision of fuel efficiency, is affected by policy.

A.1.4.1   Without CAFE:
The profit-maximizing condition for choosing fuel intensity with no CAFE is then to maximize:

$$\Pi = q_1 \cdot \left[d_1^{-1}(q_1) - \varphi_1(f_1) \right] + q_2 \cdot \left[d_2^{-1}(q_2) - \varphi_2(f_2) \right] - q_1 c_1(f_1) - q_2 c_2(f_2)$$

The first-order condition for choosing f_i is

$$0 = -q_i \varphi_i' - q_i c_i'$$

or

$$-c_i' = \varphi_i'$$

This is approximately how NEMS represents the decision in the manufacturers' technology choice submodule: manufacturers add technology to reduce fuel intensity by one unit so long as the cost per vehicle of doing so $(-c_i')$ is no greater than its value per vehicle to consumers (φ_i'). (NEMS differs in one important detail, however, as described in Section A.3.)

A.1.4.2   With CAFE (single standard):
Now add constraint (A.2). The first-order condition now includes the effects of the Lagrangian, as follows:

$$0 = -q_i \varphi_i' - q_i c_i' - \lambda q_i$$

or

$$c_i' = \varphi_i' + \lambda. \tag{A.8}$$

So, consumers' valuation of fuel economy is augmented by the same "shadow price of fuel intensity" as we observed in the pricing equations, λ. This is identical to how I modified NEMS in earlier work (Small, 2012) to handle feebates; hence λ can be extracted from that calculation, already programmed.

A.1.4.3   With CAFE (footprint-based standard):
Now the constraint is (A.5), but the first-order condition is the same, leading again to condition (A.8).

A.1.4.4   Fines in lieu of compliance:
If a manufacturer has the option of paying a fine $\bar{\lambda}$ per unit of fuel intensity by which it exceeds the standard $\bar{f}$, then the solution remains the same provided $\lambda \leq \bar{\lambda}$. When λ would otherwise exceed $\bar{\lambda}$, the objection function becomes (A.3) with λ replaced by $c_i' = \varphi_i' + \lambda$. The first-order conditions for setting price and technology are again (A.4) and (A.8) but with λ replaced by $\bar{\lambda}$. In other words, the overall solution is (A.4) and (A.8) with λ capped at $\bar{\lambda}$.

The manufacturer may choose to comply even when its unit shadow cost of compliance exceeds $\bar{\lambda}$ if it perceives additional benefits, such as political or public-relations benefits, of compliance. This may lead to solutions (A.4) and (A.8) even when λ exceeds $\bar{\lambda}$. When λ is high enough, the benefits of compliance will no longer exceed the costs and the solution will revert to one with an implicit fine. Whether that fine will be the legal fine $\bar{\lambda}$ or some higher value depends on how the perceived benefits of compliance vary with the magnitude of noncompliance. I will assume it depends linearly on the deviation from mandated fuel intensity, in which case such a situation can be approximated by assuming a level of fine larger than the legal level.

A.1.4.5   Summary:
Note that in every case considered here, the quality decision is governed by the standard response to consumer preferences (undistorted by market power) plus a shadow price or fine arising from an energy-efficiency policy mandate. As so often happens in economics, even when a lack of pure competition distorts pricing, it does not distort choice of quality.

A.1.5   Overall summary of vehicle pricing and quality under CAFE

When CAFE is introduced, technology choice proceeds just as it does with a feebate: manufacturers set the marginal cost of reducing fuel intensity equal to consumers' valuation ϕ_i plus a shadow price λ whose size reflects how tight the CAFE standard is.

Vehicle pricing with CAFE also takes λ into account. If there is a single standard, price differentials are introduced between different products with fuel-intensity differences Δf. If demands were infinitely elastic, the price differential between two vehicles would be the difference in production cost plus *either* $\lambda \Delta f$ (for a single standard) or $\lambda \cdot \left(\Delta f - \overline{\Delta f} \right)$ (for separate standards). Accounting for demand elasticities, the price differential is instead given by (A.7).

A.2   Adjusting coefficients in type choice model

A.2.1   Vehicle cost and fuel cost coefficients

Our three scenarios involving different valuations by consumers of fuel savings are defined by the assumed consumer tradeoffs between vehicle price and fuel costs, as embodied in the interest rate and time horizon used in the NEMS module determining whether vehicle manufacturers will add particular technologies to their vehicle models. But consumers also trade off capital and operating costs in their choice of vehicle type, that is, their choice among various engine and fuel types such as conventional gasoline, diesel, gas–electric hybrid, and all-electric vehicles. This choice is governed in NEMS by a logit model, which implicitly involves maximizing a random utility function whose systematic components include various vehicle characteristics.

Utility in this vehicle type-choice model includes the following component involving total ownership cost:

$$U = \beta_{pm} p_m + \beta_{pv} p_v \equiv x + y \tag{A.9}$$

where $p_m \equiv p_f/E$ is fuel cost per mile, p_f and p_v are fuel price and vehicle price, respectively, and E is the efficiency of the car being considered for purchase. Define the effective capital recovery factor, CRF^e, as the multiplier on capital cost that equates the marginal utility of first-year operating cost to that of annualized capital cost:

$$\frac{\partial U}{\partial (p_m M_1)} = \frac{\partial U}{\partial (p_v \cdot CRF)} \Rightarrow \frac{x}{y} = \frac{p_m M_1}{p_v \cdot CRF} \Rightarrow \frac{\beta_{pm}}{\beta_{pv}} = \frac{M_1}{CRF^e} \tag{A.10}$$

where M_1 is the first-year mileage. If annual mileage and expected fuel prices were constant, CRF^e would equal the conventionally defined capital recovery factor at interest rate r and expected asset life T:

$$CRF(r,T) = \frac{1}{\sum_{t=1}^{T} (1+r)^{-t}} = \frac{r}{1 - (1+r)^{-T}}. \tag{A.11}$$

Accounting for changes in fuel price and annual vehicle mileage, it is instead the ratio of first-year fuel cost to present discounted value of all future fuel costs.[40]

Let superscript 0 represent the default parameters in NEMS, so that Eq. (A.10) implies:

$$\frac{x^0}{y^0} = \frac{p_m M_1}{p_v \cdot CRF^{e0}}.$$ (A.12)

I henceforth omit the superscript e on CRF.

Suppose we change r and T from their default values, r^0 and T^0, to some other values r and T, thus changing the CRF from $CRF(r^0,T^0)$ to $CRF(r,T)$. We want to know how to change parameters β_{pm} and β_{pv} to be consistent. To do so, I impose two conditions. First is the continued validity of their ratio as embodied in (A.10):

$$\frac{x/y}{x^0/y^0} = \frac{1}{R}$$ (A.13)

where $R \equiv CRF/CRF^0$ is assumed to follow (A.11):

$$R = \frac{r}{r^0} \cdot \frac{1-(1+r^0)^{-T^0}}{1-(1+r)^{-T}}$$

Second is that the utility component (A.9) remains unchanged, so that its relative importance compared to that of other attributes (represented in the parts of utility other than (A.9)) is unchanged. This implies

$$x + y = x^0 + y^0$$ (A.14)

The solution to (A.13) and (A.14) is

$$\frac{\beta_{pm}}{\beta_{pm}^0} \equiv \frac{x}{x^0} = \frac{x^0 + y^0}{x^0 + Ry^0}; \frac{\beta_{pv}}{\beta_{pv}^0} \equiv \frac{y}{y^0} = R \cdot \frac{x^0 + y^0}{x^0 + Ry^0}$$ (A.15)

To calculate (A.15), we need to know all the components of x^0 and y^0, namely the initial values of the coefficients and the values of the variables they apply to (p_m and p_v). These vary by size class and year; for simplicity I choose average values for each size class over the years 2017–2025 (which are the years over which the CAFE standards are ramped up in the high CAFE policy simulated here). I calculate it for the values of the ratio R corresponding to our five valuation scenarios; in each case, R is simply the ratio of the valuation fraction for the "severe undervaluation" scenario (0.2946) to that in the scenario in question (viz. 0.2946, 0.45, 0.60, 0.80, or 1.00). The values are as follows:

Reference scenario (accurate valuation): $R = 0.2946$

Mild undervaluation: $R = 0.3683$

60% valuation: $R = 0.6547$

45% valuation: $R = 0.4910$

---

[40] If fuel cost grew at constant rate g_{Pf} and mileage declined at constant rate g_M with age, (A.10) would apply approximately with r replaced by $r - g_{Pf} + g_M$.

Severe undervaluation: $R = 1.0000$ (by definition)

A.2.2   Other coefficients

In order to calibrate correctly to observed 2010 sales shares of diesels, hybrids, and flex-fuel vehicles, I adjust two other coefficients of the model—the alternative specific constant for diesel vehicle and a coefficient indicating preference for vehicles already having a substantial market share. I describe here the adjustment for the full valuation scenario (our market scenario); the adjustment for the partial undervaluation scenario is done proportionally.[41]

Table 11.16 shows the sales shares for 2010 calculated by the model with its default parameters (i.e. those used in AEO 2011) and, in the 100% valuation ("market") scenario, with adjustment of β_{pm} and β_{pv} as described in Section A.1. The three most prominent differences are that the uncalibrated market scenario, compared to actual, understates the market share for conventional gasoline vehicles and overstates those for gasoline–electric hybrids and, especially, for diesels. It also slightly overstates the market share for flexible-fuel vehicles (i.e. those that can operate on either gasoline or ethanol).

Table 11.16 Market shares (%) predicted by modified NEMS for 2010, with adjustments only to β_{pm} and β_{pv}

	Severe Undervaluation Scenario[a]	Market Scenario Uncalibrated	Market Scenario Recalibrated
Conventional gasoline	84.1	76.8	82.4
Diesel	2.0	7.1	2.2
Hybrid	2.5	3.9	2.4
Flex-fuel	11.3	12.1	12.9
Other	0.07	0.11	0.02
Total	100.0	100.0	100.0

[a] These 2010 shares are nearly identical to those in the AEO 2011 projection tables.

[41] For example, the full valuation scenario changes the valuation ratio by 0.7 (from 0.3 in the NEMS default to 1.0), whereas the partial undervaluation scenario changes the valuation ratio by 0.5 (from 0.3 to 0.8). Therefore, in the partial undervaluation scenario I adjust the NEMS default parameters by 0.5/0.7 of the amount that I adjust them for the market scenario; and similarly for 60% and 45% valuations.

We know that EIA has set various other parameters in the model to calibrate sales shares under its default parameters (my "Severe Undervaluation Scenario") to the actual shares shown in the first column of numbers in Table 11.16. If in fact people value fuel savings fully, some of these parameters must actually be different from those assumed by EIA. I choose two as the mostly likely to be important: the coefficient of "make and model availability," and the alternative-specific constant for diesel engines.

The first of these parameters governs the importance of the availability of a wide selection of makes and models of a given vehicle type. Thus, it penalizes vehicle types that are less available than are conventional gasoline vehicles, on the grounds that consumers lack sufficient choice or that they fear lack of wide availability of fuels, parts, or competent service. I adjust this coefficient upward by 66.7%, except for flex-fuel vehicles. The reason for the adjustments is that if people are indeed fully rational in their fuel valuation, then the low market share of diesels and hybrids likely indicates that people find low availability a bigger barrier than assumed by NEMS. However, I do not let this adjustment apply to flex-fuel vehicles, for three reasons: their engines are virtually identical to gasoline engines, they are mostly used with gasoline rather than ethanol, and their sales share is heavily influenced by special CAFE credits under current law. Therefore, for flex-fuel vehicles consumers have little reason to worry about either fuel availability or service.

The second parameter I adjust is an alternative specific constant for diesel vehicles, which reflects any undesirable features relative to gasoline vehicles, such as the reputation for reliability, anticipated odor from fumes, or availability of extensive dealer service. In the NEMS default values, this constant is set in 2010 to a positive value (0.5) for cars and to a very small negative value (−0.05) for trucks; the value then decreases over time for cars and increases over time for trucks. I found that a simple downward adjustment of 0.4 gives a good calibration, in particular, bringing diesel share in 2010 somewhat below hybrid share, as seen in the actual sales figures.

The results of these two adjustments are shown in the last column of Table 11.16. This calibration slightly understates conventional gasoline and overstates flex-fuel sales shares in 2010, but it is really the sum of these that is important to policy outcomes because flex-fuel vehicles are so similar to gasoline.

A.3   Optimization in the manufacturers' technology choice component (MTCC)

The manufacturers' technology choice component (MTCC) of NEMS depicts how manufacturers decide on whether to implement each of a long list of technologies on each of the size classes of cars and trucks it produces. The calculation compares the per-car cost of implementing the technology with the fuel-savings benefit realized by consumers (aggregated over the assumed time horizon and discounted at the assumed rate, all figured at the consumer's assumed fuel-price expectation). If the cost is less than the benefit, the technology is adopted.

I have modified NEMS with respect to the details of this calculation. In standard NEMS, the cost of technology is given as a parameter which is constant *per unit of increase in fuel efficiency* (miles per gallon, or mpg). This parameter is compared with the calculated benefit to consumers per unit increase in mpg. Suppose E is the efficiency of a size class, ΔE is the change in fuel efficiency per vehicle caused by a particular technology, and ΔC is the per-vehicle cost of this technology. Then the per-vehicle cost for this size class is ΔC, while the per-car annual benefit is $M \cdot P_F \cdot \Delta E$, where M is the mileage driven in that year and P_F is the consumer's expected fuel price. Expressed per unit of fuel efficiency, then, the comparison is between $\Delta C / \Delta E$ and $M \cdot P_F$, with the latter added and discounted over the number of years specified as the time horizon. Note that $M \cdot P_F$ and its aggregate over years are constant across all technologies within a given size class.

In NEMS, each technology cost is specified by a parameter giving the value of $\Delta C / \Delta E$, which I refer to here as the "unit technology cost".

When CAFE regulations apply, this setup conveniently allows the regulations to be taken into account by adding a shadow price of the regulation (called "regulatory cost" in NEMS) to the unit technology cost. This is what is depicted in Eq. (A.8).

However, note that although NEMS calculates the shadow price in terms of *fuel efficiency*, Eq. (A.8) involves *fuel intensity*, because c' is defined as the marginal cost per vehicle of reducing fuel intensity (holding performance constant). This is necessary because, although CAFE standards are described legally in terms of fuel efficiency (mpg), they are actually implemented in terms of fuel intensity (gallons per mile, or gpm): that is, it is the fuel intensities of different model cars or trucks that are averaged across manufacturers in calculating whether their average efficiency meets the standard.

Specifically, in the CAFE law, each manufacturer's compliance with CAFE is determined by the (sales-weighted) *harmonic* average of the fuel efficiency (mpg) of all the vehicles it produces. This ensures that the computed average efficiency is in fact equal to total mileage divided by total fuel use. Taking the harmonic average of mpg involves taking the average gpm, then inverting it. Thus, if the manufacturer is trying to meet the CAFE standard, it is per-unit cost of reducing gpm that must be equated across technologies. A manufacturer wanting to achieve that standard at lowest cost will need to consider the incremental cost of any changes to gpm in its various models and equalize them.

I have therefore modified the MTCC module to use fuel intensity rather than fuel efficiency to compute the regulatory cost which is added to the consumer's benefit to determine whether or not it is worth installing a given technology on a given size class. The effect of this change is to increase the value to a manufacturer of adding a given incremental fuel savings to a low-efficiency car, and decrease it for a high-efficiency car, compared to the standard version of NEMS.

What if the manufacturer instead plans to pay fines for noncompliance? The law describes the fines in terms of mpg (although they are not exactly linear in mpg). But that fine is applied to the deviation of the *harmonic average* of mpg from the specified fuel efficiency standard. Thus, just as in the case of meeting the standard, a manufacturer seeking to minimize its cost including fines paid must compare the cost of reducing fuel intensity (gpm) to the fine expressed in terms of $/gpm. Therefore, in our modified NEMS, the regulatory fine is converted into one proportional to fuel intensity, using the CAFE standard itself as it applies to that manufacturer.

For both the technology cost and the regulatory cost, the conversion to proportionality with fuel intensity uses a first-order approximation in the deviation ΔF in fuel intensity between the achieved fuel intensity and the standard. Let E be the standard in terms of fuel efficiency (mpg) and F be the standard in terms of fuel intensity (gpm). Let ΔE and ΔF be deviations from the standard. The first-order approximation is $\Delta E = \Delta(1/F) \approx -(1/F)^2 \Delta F = E^2 \cdot (-\Delta F)$. For example, the default level of fine in 2011 was taken to be $50 per unit of mpg. So, the payment for the fine, P, is

$$P = 50\Delta E.$$

But it can be expressed equivalently as

$$P = -50 \cdot F^2 \cdot (-\Delta F),$$

where $F = 1/E$. Note the fine was initially expressed in units of $/(mi/gal), whereas it is now expressed in units of $/(gal/mi). But the calculations are equivalent (to first order in deviations $\Delta F/F$), because they result in the same payment P.

Without this change, the manufacturer is modeled as inefficiently putting too much technology into improving high-mpg cars and not enough into improving low-mpg cars (from the manufacturer's own perspective). In other words, it treats the manufacturers as having the same "miles-per gallon (MPG) illusion" that consumers have been found to have, as noted in the text. But actually it is inconceivable that manufacturers would have this illusion about such a basic fact of their business.

Appendix B: Other simulations

Tables 11.17–11.25

Table 11.17 Price of motor gasoline, selected years (2010 $/gal)

Scenario	2015	2020	2025	2030	2035
Low oil price	2.19	2.33	2.14	2.26	2.16
Reference	3.16	3.40	3.58	3.67	3.79
High oil price	4.27	4.84	5.06	5.26	5.38

Table 11.18 Effects of price adjustments, 2025 (30% valuation, high fines)

	With Price Adjustments			Without Price Adjustments		
	Base	CAFE	CAFE Impact	Base	CAFE	CAFE Impact
Average new-vehicle fuel economy (mi/gal)			(% diff.)			(% diff.)
All light-duty vehicles	34.9	48.6	39.1%	35.8	47.4	32.4%
Conventional gasoline car	35.5	39.0	10.0%	36.3	49.0	35.2%
Conventional gasoline truck	27.4	31.9	16.4%	28.0	37.6	34.5%
Sales share by vehicle type			(%-pt diff)			(%-pt diff)
Conventional gasoline	60.7%	33.9%	−26.8%	60.3%	59.6%	−0.6%
Diesel	4.2%	4.8%	0.6%	3.6%	3.8%	0.3%
Hybrids (excl plug-ins)	11.9%	31.3%	19.4%	12.4%	13.2%	0.7%
Plugin hybrids + dedicated electric	5.4%	21.3%	15.9%	5.7%	5.9%	0.2%

(Continued)

Table 11.18 Effects of price adjustments, 2025 (30% valuation, high fines) (*Cont.*)

	With Price Adjustments			Without Price Adjustments		
	Base	CAFE	CAFE Impact	Base	CAFE	CAFE Impact
Sales share by technology used						
Micro hybrid (engine off at idle)	5.9%	16.4%	10.5%	9.2%	61.4%	52.3%
Material subst'n (most advanced)	0.5%	6.0%	5.5%	0.4%	64.0%	63.6%

Table 11.19 Effects of fuel price expectations, 2025 (80% valuation)

	Default Expectations			Random Walk		
	Base	CAFE	CAFE Impact	Base	CAFE	CAFE Impact
Average new-vehicle fuel economy (mi/gal)			(% diff.)			(% diff.)
All light-duty vehicles	38.9	48.8	25.4%	38.6	48.8	26.4%
Conventional gasoline car	37.0	43.9	18.7%	36.9	43.3	17.3%
Conventional gasoline truck	31.2	34.9	11.7%	31.0	34.9	12.4%
Sales share by vehicle type			(diff in % pts)			(diff in % pts)
Conventional gasoline	55.3%	41.5%	−13.8%	56.4%	41.0%	−15.3%
Diesel	3.0%	2.6%	−0.3%	3.0%	2.5%	−0.4%

(*Continued*)

Table 11.19 Effects of fuel price expectations, 2025 (80% valuation) (*Cont.*)

	Default Expectations			Random Walk		
	Base	CAFE	CAFE Impact	Base	CAFE	CAFE Impact
Hybrids (excl. plug-ins)	17.5%	27.7%	10.2%	16.8%	27.7%	10.9%
Plugin hybrids + dedicated electric	7.3%	15.7%	8.4%	7.0%	16.3%	9.3%
Sales share by technology used						
Micro hybrid (engine off at idle)	19.1%	48.9%	29.7%	19.8%	48.5%	28.8%
Material subst'n (most advanced)	1.4%	31.6%	30.3%	1.3%	30.7%	29.4%

Table 11.20 Effects of fuel price expectations, 2025 (high oil price scenario)

	Default Expectations			Rational Expectations		
	Base	CAFE	CAFE Impact	Base	CAFE	CAFE Impact
Average new-vehicle fuel economy (mi/gal)			(% diff.)			(% diff.)
All light-duty vehicles	43.1	49.6	15.1%	42.7	49.7	16.4%
Conventional gasoline car	39.7	45.1	13.6%	39.0	44.5	14.1%
Conventional gasoline truck	34.7	36.9	6.4%	34.4	36.9	7.3%
Sales share by vehicle type			(diff in % pts)			(diff in % pts)

(Continued)

Table 11.20 Effects of fuel price expectations, 2025 (8high oil price scenario) (*Cont.*)

	Default Expectations			Rational Expectations		
	Base	CAFE	CAFE Impact	Base	CAFE	CAFE Impact
Conventional gasoline	40.9%	37.6%	−3.4%	40.5%	36.8%	−3.7%
Diesel	3.8%	3.7%	−0.1%	3.9%	3.7%	−0.2%
Hybrids (excl. plug-ins)	20.6%	24.7%	4.1%	20.6%	25.0%	4.4%
Plugin hybrids + dedicated electric	9.8%	14.5%	4.7%	9.8%	15.2%	5.3%
Sales share by technology used						
Micro hybrid (engine off at idle)	36.9%	57.3%	20.5%	35.0%	57.3%	22.2%
Material subst'n (most advanced)	5.2%	35.5%	30.4%	4.7%	35.7%	30.9%

11.21 Effects of fuel price expectations, 2025 (30% valuation)

	Default Expectations			Random Walk		
	Base	CAFE	CAFE impact	Base	CAFE	CAFE impact
Average new-vehicle fuel economy (mi/gal)			(% diff.)			(% diff.)
All light-duty vehicles	34.9	48.7	39.6%	34.9	49.0	40.4%
Conventional gasoline car	35.5	39.1	10.3%	35.6	39.6	11.4%
Conventional gasoline truck	27.4	32.0	16.8%	27.4	32.0	16.7%
Sales share by vehicle type			(%-pt diff)			(%-pt diff)

(Continued)

Table 11.21 Effects of fuel price expectations, 2025 (30% valuation) (*Cont*).

	Default Expectations			Random Walk		
	Base	**CAFE**	**CAFE impact**	**Base**	**CAFE**	**CAFE impact**
Conventional gasoline	60.7%	34.0%	−26.8%	60.2%	33.9%	−26.3%
Diesel	4.2%	4.8%	0.6%	4.1%	4.6%	0.5%
Hybrids (excl. plug-ins)	11.9%	31.2%	19.3%	11.9%	31.1%	19.2%
Plugin hybrids + dedicated electric	5.4%	21.4%	16.0%	5.4%	21.6%	16.3%
Sales share by technology used						
Micro hybrid (engine off at idle)	5.9%	16.8%	10.9%	6.6%	18.1%	11.4%
Material subst'n (most advanced)	0.5%	6.3%	5.7%	0.5%	7.5%	7.0%

Table 11.22 Effects of Price Adjustments on Vehicle Costs, 2025 (30% Valuation, High Fines)

	With Price Adjustments			Without Price Adjustments		
	Base	**CAFE**	**CAFE Impact**	**Base**	**CAFE**	**CAFE Impact**
Vehicle cost (2010$)			(% diff.)			(% diff.)
Midsize car (conv gasoline)	27,880	28,513	2.3%	28,097	30,803	9.6%

(*Continued*)

**Table 11.22 Effects of Price Adjustments on Vehicle Costs, 2025 (30%
Valuation, High Fines)**(*Cont.*)

	With Price Adjustments			Without Price Adjustments		
	Base	**CAFE**	**CAFE Impact**	**Base**	**CAFE**	**CAFE Impact**
Small SUV (conv gasoline)	25,076	26,070	4.0%	25,207	27,708	9.9%
Midsize car (gas-elec hybrid)	34,148	30,178	−11.6%	34,246	36,194	5.7%
Small SUV (gas-elec hybrid)	31,490	29,143	−7.5%	31,536	32,803	4.0%
Vehicle price markup (2010$)			(% of base-case cost)			(% of base-case cost)
Midsize car (conv gasoline)	0	4248	15.2%	0	0	0.0%
Small SUV (conv gasoline)	0	2753	11.0%	0	0	0.0%
Midsize car (gas-elec hybrid)	0	−757	−2.2%	0	0	0.0%
Small SUV (gas-elec hybrid)	0	−2006	−6.4%	0	0	0.0%
Fines paid in lieu of compliance ($/vehicle)			(% of base-case price)			(% of base-case price)
Cars	22	81	0.3%	18	1918	6.9%
Truks	0	0	0.0%	0	55	0.2%

Table 11.23 Effects of full range of valuations, 2025

	Full valuation (100%)			Partial valuation (80%)			60% valuation			Severe undervalue (30%)		
	Base	CAFE	CAFE impact	Base	CAFE	CAFE impact	Base	CAFE	CAFE impact	Base	CAFE	CAFE impact
Average new-vehicle			(% diff.)			(% diff.)			(% diff.)			(% diff.)
All light-duty vehicles	40.8	48.8	19.4 %	38.9	48.8	25.4%	37.0	48.9	32.1%	34.9	48.7	39.6%
Conventional gasoline car	38.2	44.9	17.4%	37.0	43.9	18.7%	36.0	42.6	18.3%	35.5	39.1	10.3%
Conventional gasoline truck	32.8	34.8	6.0%	31.2	34.9	11.7%	29.6	34.3	15.8%	27.4	32.0	16.8%
Sales share by vehicle			(diff in % pts)			(diff in % pts)			(diff in % pts)			(diff in % pts)
Conventional gasoline	52.5%	41.9%	−10.6%	55.3%	41.5%	−13.8%	58.6%	38.9%	−19.7%	60.7%	34.0%	−26.8%
Diesel	2.4%	2.1%	−0.3%	3.0%	2.6%	−0.3%	3.6%	3.4%	−0.3%	4.2%	4.8%	0.6%
Hybrids (excl. plug-ins)	20.6%	28.8%	8.2%	17.5%	27.7%	10.2%	14.5%	30.6%	16.1%	11.9%	31.2%	19.3%

	Full valuation (100%)			Partial valuation (80%)			60% valuation			Severe undervalue (30 %)		
	Base	CAFE	CAFE impact	Base	CAFE	CAFE impact	Base	CAFE	CAFE impact	Base	CAFE	CAFE impact
Plugin hybrids + dedicated electric	7.9%	14.3%	6.5%	7.3%	15.7%	8.4%	6.2%	16.4%	10.2%	5.4%	21.4%	16.0%
Sales share by technology used												
Micro hybrid (engine off at idle)	29.7%	52.6%	22.9%	19.1%	48.9%	29.7%	10.9%	35.5%	24.6%	5.9%	16.8%	10.9%
Material subst'n (most advanced)	2.7%	37.7%	35.0%	1.4%	31.6%	30.3%	0.8%	23.5%	22.7%	0.5%	6.3%	5.7%

Table 11.24 Effects of full range of valuations on selected vehicle costs, 2025

	Full Valuation (100%)			Partial Valuation (80%)			60% Valuation			Severe Undervalue (30%)		
	Base	CAFE	CAFE Impact	Base	CAFE	CAFE Impact	Base	CAFE	CAFE Impact	Base	CAFE	CAFE Impact
Vehicle cost (2010$)			(% diff.)			(% diff.)			(% diff.)			(% diff.)
Midsize car (conv gasoline)	28,573	30,143	5.5%	28,235	29,889	5.9%	28,024	29,426	5.0%	27,880	28,562	2.4%
Small SUV (conv gasoline)	26,443	27,135	2.6%	25,941	27,103	4.5%	25,473	26,445	3.8%	25,076	26,107	4.1%
Mid-size car (gas–elec hybrid)	34,351	35,270	2.7%	34,255	35,005	2.2%	34,197	34,728	1.6%	34,148	34,426	0.8%
Small SUV (gas–elec hybrid)	31,470	31,885	1.3%	31,449	32,005	1.8%	31,479	31,889	1.3%	31,490	31,885	1.3%
Vehicle price markup (2010$)			(% of cost in base case)			(% of cost in base case)			(% of cost in base case)			(% of cost in base case)

	Full Valuation (100%)			Partial Valuation (80%)			60% Valuation			Severe Undervalue (30%)		
	Base	CAFE	CAFE Impact	Base	CAFE	CAFE Impact	Base	CAFE	CAFE Impact	Base	CAFE	CAFE Impact
Midsize car (conv gasoline)	0	1,323	4.6%	0	1726	6.1%	0	2719	9.7%	0	4199	15.1%
Small SUV (conv gasoline)	0	608	2.3%	0	746	2.9%	0	288	1.1%	0	2696	10.7%
Mid-size car (gas–elec hybrid)	0	−907	−2.6%	0	−943	−2.8%	0	−838	−2.4%	0	−762	−2.2%
Small SUV (gas–elec hybrid)	0	−868	−2.8%	0	−1080	−3.4%	0	−898	−2.9%	0	−2007	−6.4%

Table 11.25 Effects of dual CAFE standard on vehicle size mix, 2025 (severe undervalue scenario)

	Footprint Standards			Dual (Car/Truck) Standards		
	Base	CAFE	CAFÉ impact	Base	CAFE	CAFÉ impact
Sales Shares by Size Class (Nonfleet vehicles):			(%-pt. diff.)			(%-pt. diff.)
Car						
Minicompact	1.3%	1.3%	0.0%	1.3%	1.4%	0.1%
Subcompact	22.8%	23.0%	0.2%	22.8%	23.0%	0.1%
Compact	19.5%	19.3%	−0.1%	19.5%	20.1%	0.7%
Midsize	33.2%	33.2%	0.0%	33.2%	32.9%	−0.3%
Large	20.0%	20.0%	0.0%	20.0%	19.4%	−0.7%
Two seater	3.2%	3.1%	0.0%	3.2%	3.2%	0.0%
Truck						
Small pickup	4.5%	4.3%	−0.3%	4.5%	4.0%	−0.6%
Large pickup	21.4%	20.9%	−0.4%	21.4%	23.0%	1.6%
Small van	1.8%	1.7%	−0.1%	1.8%	1.6%	−0.2%
Large van	9.6%	9.2%	−0.3%	9.6%	8.7%	−0.9%
Small SUV	34.2%	34.8%	0.6%	34.2%	34.0%	−0.1%
Large SUV	28.5%	29.0%	0.5%	28.5%	28.8%	0.3%

References

Akerlof, G.A., 1970. The market for 'lemons': quality uncertainty and the market mechanism. Quarterly Journal of Economics 84 (3), 488–500.

Allcott, H., 2013. The welfare effects of misperceived product costs: data and calibrations from the automobile market. American Economic Journal: Economic Policy 5 (3), 30–66.

Allcott, H., Greenstone, M., 2012. Is there an energy efficiency gap? Journal of Economic Perspectives 26 (1), 3–28.

Allcott, H., Wozny, N., 2014. Gasoline prices, fuel economy, and the energy paradox. Review of Economics and Statistics 96 (5), 779–795.

Anderson, S.T., Sallee, J.M., 2011. Using loopholes to reveal the marginal cost of regulation: the case of fuel-economy standards. American Economic Review 101 (4), 1375–1409.

Anderson, S.T., Parry, I.W.H., Sallee, J.M., Fischer, C., 2011. Automobile fuel efficiency standards: impacts, efficiency, and alternatives. Review of Environmental Economics and Policy 5 (1), 89–108.

Anderson, S.T., Kellogg, R., Sallee, J.M., 2013. What do consumers believe about future gasoline prices? Journal of Environmental Economics and Management 66 (3), 383–403.

Bento, A., Roth, K., Zuo, Y., 2018. Vehicle lifetime trends and scrappage behavior in the U.S. used car market. Energy Journal 39 (1), doi:10.5547/01956574.39.1.aben.

Berry, S., Levinsohn, J., Pakes, A., 1995. Automobile prices in market equilibrium. Econometrica 63 (4), 841–890.

Busse, M.R., Knittel, C.R., Zettelmeyer, F., 2013. Are consumers myopic? Evidence from new and used car purchases. American Economic Review 103 (1), 220–256.

EIA, 2012. Transportation sector module of the National Energy Modeling System: model documentation. http://www.eia.gov/forecasts/nemsdoc/transportation/pdf/m070(2012).pdf.

Gerarden, T.D., Newell, R.G., Stavins, R.N., forthcoming. Assessing the energy-efficiency gap. Journal of Economic Literature.

Gillingham, K., Palmer, K., 2014. Bridging the energy efficiency gap: policy insights from economic theory and empirical evidence. Review of Environmental Economics and Policy 8 (1), 18–38.

Goldberg, P.K., 1995. Product differentiation and oligopoly in international markets: the case of the U.S. automobile industry. Econometrica 63 (4), 891–951.

Helfand, M.R., Wolverton, A., 2011. Evaluating the consumer response to fuel economy: A review of the literature. International Review of Environmental and Resource Economics 5 (2), 103–146.

Jacobsen, M.R., 2013. Evaluating US fuel economy standards in a model with producer and household heterogeneity. American Economic Journal: Economic Policy 5 (2), 148–187.

Jacobsen, M.R., van Benthem, A.A., 2015. Vehicle scrappage and gasoline policy. American Economic Review 105 (3), 1312–1338.

Knittel, C.R., 2012. Reducing petroleum consumption from transportation. Journal of Economic Perspectives 26 (1), 93–118.

Knittel, C.R., 2013. Transportation fuels policy since the OPEC embargo: paved with good intentions. American Economic Review Papers and Proceedings 103 (3), 344–349.

Larrick, R., Soll, J., 2008. The MPG illusion. Science 320 (5883), 1593–1594.

Li, S., Timmins, C., von Haefen, R.H., 2009. How do gasoline prices affect fleet fuel economy? American Economic Journal: Economic Policy 1 (2), 113–137.

Lu S., Vehicle Survivability and Travel Mileage Schedules, Technical Report DOT HS 809 952, National Highway Traffic Safety Administration, Jan. 2006.

NHTSA, 2012. Corporate average fuel economy for MY 2017-MY 2025 passenger cars and light trucks: final regulatory impact analysis, August. www.nhtsa.gov/staticfiles/rulemaking/pdf/cafe/FRIA_2017-2025.pdf.

Sallee, J.M., West, S.E., Fan, W., 2016. Do consumers recognize the value of fuel economy? Evidence from used car prices and gasoline price fluctuations. Journal of Public Economics 135, 61–73.

Small, K.A., Energy policies for automobile transportation: a comparison using the National Energy Modeling System. Background report for Toward a New National Energy Policy:

Assessing the Options, Resources for the Future and National Energy Policy Institute, June 2010. http://www.rff.org/Documents/Features/NEPI/RFF-BCK-Small-AutoPolicies.pdf.

Small, K.A., 2012. Energy policies for passenger motor vehicles. Transportation Research Part A: Policy and Practice 46 (6), 874–889.

Turrentine, T.S., Kurani, K.S., 2007. Car buyers and fuel economy? Energy Policy 35, 1213–1223.

Whitefoot, K.S., Fowlie, M., Skerlos, S.J., 2013. Compliance by design: industry response to energy efficiency standards. Working paper, Carnegie Mellon University. https://scholar.google.com/citations?view_op=view_citation&hl=en&user=3W2VK5sAAAAJ&citation_for_view=3W2VK5sAAAAJ:UeHWp8X0CEIC.

Further Reading

EIA, 2011. Annual energy outlook 2011 with projections to 2035, U.S. Energy Information Administration, U.S. Department of Energy, April. http://www.eia.gov/forecasts/archive/aeo11/pdf/0383(2011).pdf.

EIA, 2013. Transportation demand. Assumptions to AEO2013pp. 73–98, http://www.eia.gov/forecasts/aeo/assumptions/index.cfm.

Broker/third party logistics provider and shipper responsibility in motor carrier selection: considering carrier safety performance

12

Thomas M. Corsi
University of Maryland, College Park, MD, United States

Chapter Outline

Dedication

My father, who was the Public Relations director for the United Transportation (Rail Union), was instrumental in my decision to pursue a career in the field of transportation. With my initial interest in the railroad industry as a result of my father's influence, I was introduced by my academic advisor to the seminal works of Ted Keller in the area of railroad economics and public policy. His early works inspired me to earn more about railroad industry operations and the impact of public policies on the industry. In fact, with his work as my model, I have pursued an entire career looking at the interface of surface transportation modes and the role of government, with a special emphasis on the safety programs and policies of the federal government.

Transportation Policy and Economic Regulation. http://dx.doi.org/10.1016/B978-0-12-812620-2.00012-2

12.1   Introduction

Congress[1] established the Federal Motor Carrier Safety Administration (FMCSA) as a separate administration within the US Department of Transportation in the Motor Carrier Safety Improvement Act of 1999 (Public Law 106-159) and established its primary mission "to reduce crashes, injuries, and fatalities involving large trucks and buses."[2] This paper is designed to provide a context for assessing the progress that has been made by the FMCSA in achieving the goal of reducing truck crashes, injuries, and fatalities. It will examine the statistical data on the changes that have occurred in the large truck injury and fatal crash rates over the period between 1975 and 2015 (for fatal crashes) and between 1995 and 2015 (for injury crashes). From its establishment, the FMCSA has undertaken a series of programs and initiatives designed to assist in accomplishing its mission of reducing truck crashes. This paper will review those programs and initiatives.

With the background of the statistical evidence of truck crash rates over time and the initiatives taken by the FMCSA to reduce those crashes, this paper will turn to its major focus by addressing the responsibilities that both brokers/third party logistics providers and shippers bear in the process of selecting motor carriers to physically transport freight from one location to another. As the issues differ between brokers/third party logistics providers and shippers, the paper will include a separate discussion of the respective responsibilities of both groups.

The paper concludes that brokers/third party logistics providers and shippers do, indeed, share in the responsibility to select competent and safe motor carriers. Their selection and use decisions are enhanced by the FMCSA safety performance measurement systems (including the SMS). The SMS measures carrier performance in a wide range of categories and disseminates this information on a monthly basis through its publically available website. There have been recent efforts to restrict some of these data from the public website. The paper concludes with the argument that the FMCSA SMS data are a vital component of the carrier selection and use process and any efforts to restrict the information from the public websites should be vigorously opposed. The overall effort to reduce truck crash rates is linked to having brokers/third party logistics providers and shippers make informed selection and use decisions by relying on individual carrier safety performance data from FMCSA.

12.2   The dynamics of large truck fatal and injury crash rates

The National Highway Traffic Safety Administration began a compilation of fatal large[3] truck crash rates in 1975 and injury large truck crash rates in 1995. Between 1975 and 2009, there was a steady decline in the fatal crash rate (large trucks involved

---

[1] https://www.fmcsa.dot.gov/mission
[2] https://www.fmcsa.dot.gov/mission
[3] A large truck is defined as a truck with a gross vehicle weight greater than 10,000 lbs.

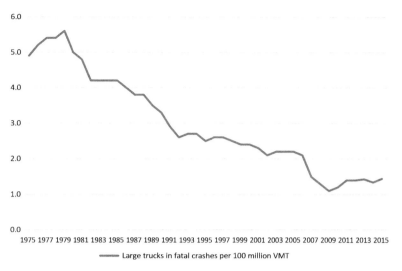

Figure 12.1 Large truck fatal crash rate: 1975–2015.

in fatal crashes per 100 million vehicle-miles traveled (VMT)). During this time, the fatal crash rate declined from 5.6 large trucks involved in fatal crashes per 100 million VMT to a rate of 1.1 large trucks involved in fatal crashes per 100 million VMT—a decline of 80%. In contrast, between 2009 and 2015, the fatal crash rate increased by 27% from 1.1 large trucks involved in fatal crashes per 100 million VMT to 1.4 large trucks involved in fatal crashes per 100 million VMT. This recent increase should not diminish the fact that in 2015 the large truck fatal crash rate was 75% below its peak level reached in 1979. Fig. 12.1 provides a graph of the large trucks involved in fatal crashes per 100 million VMT from 1975 through 2015 (Federal Motor Carrier Safety Administration, 2016, Figure 2).

The large truck injury rate declined during the 1995–2015 time period. It reached a peak level of 51.3 large trucks involved in injury crashes per 100 million VMT in 1996. Between 1996 and 2009, the injury crash rate fell by 64% to a level of 18.5 large trucks involved in injury crashes per 100 million VMT in 2009. However, between 2009 and 2015, the injury crash rate increased by 39% to a level of 31.2 large trucks involved in injury crashes per 100 million VMT in 2015. Fig. 12.2 provides a graph of the large trucks involved in injury crashes per 100 million VMT from 1995 through 2015 (Federal Motor Carrier Safety Administration, 2016, Figure 4).

Despite significant progress in reducing the large truck fatal and injury crash rates, especially through 2009, the trend for these rates between 2009 and 2015 is moving upward, especially for the large truck injury crash rate. In 2015 there were 3598 fatal crashes involving a large truck. The FMCSA estimates that each of these crashes has an economic cost of $7.2 million.[4] This represents a total economic cost from fatal truck crashes of approximately $26 billion. In 2015 there were approximately

[4] https://www.fmcsa.dot.gov/sites/fmcsa.dot.gov/files/docs/FMCSACrashCostCalculationsDec08.pdf

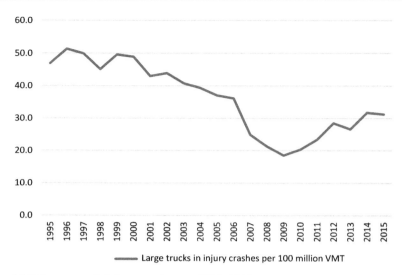

Figure 12.2 Large truck injury crash rate: 1995–2015.

83,000 injury crashes involving large trucks. The FMCSA estimates that each injury crash involving a large truck carries an economic cost of $331,108.[5] This represents a total economic cost from injury truck crashes of approximately 27.5 billion. Thus, in 2015, the total economic cost of large truck injury and fatal crashes is estimated at $53.5 billion. Clearly, the nation continues to face a huge economic and social cost from large truck fatal and injury crashes. This paper has as its focus on assessment of the responsibility of brokers/third party logistics providers and shippers in selecting motor carriers in ways that will contribute to reducing the rate of large truck injury and fatal crashes.

12.3   FMCSA's programs to reduce the large truck fatal and injury crash rates

12.3.1   Safety fitness rating

The Motor Carrier Safety Act of 1984 (Section 215, Public Law 98-554, October 30, 1984) commissioned the Secretary of Transportation to determine the safety fitness of motor carriers in interstate commerce. The Office of Motor Carrier Safety within the Federal Highway Administration used data from compliance reviews (CRs) (onsite inspections to review carrier compliance with the safety regulations) to assign one of three safety fitness ratings to motor carriers (satisfactory, conditional, or unsatisfactory).[6] The safety fitness determination emerged from an evaluation of a carrier's

---

[5] https://www.fmcsa.dot.gov/sites/fmcsa.dot.gov/files/docs/FMCSACrashCostCalculationsDec08.pdf
[6] https://www.ecfr.gov/cgi-bin/retrieveECFR?gp=1&ty=HTML&h=L&mc=true&=PART&n=pt49.5.385

crash frequency as well as its answers to a detailed questionnaire concerning implementation of various safety policies and programs. A proposed safety rating of "unsatisfactory" is a notice to the motor carrier that the FMCSA has made a preliminary determination that the motor carrier is "unfit to continue operating in interstate commerce, and that the prohibitions in CFR 385.13 will be imposed after 45 or 60 days if necessary safety improvements are not made. According to CFR 385.13, a motor carrier rated "unsatisfactory" is prohibited from operating a commercial motor vehicle (CMV) in motor carrier operations in commerce. A motor carrier may request a change to a proposed or final safety rating based on its acting on and implementing a corrective action plan. Unless a carrier with an "unsatisfactory" safety rating has its rating changed because of a positive review of changes initiated by its corrective action plan, a carrier's assigned safety rating remains in place until it receives a subsequent CR. Thus the safety fitness determination constituted a static evaluation of a carrier's safety performance on a given date rather than a real-time or near real-time assessment of its ongoing safety performance. In addition, as there were only a limited number of CRs conducted on an annual basis, there was no expectation that the Office of Motor Carriers could assign a safety fitness rating to the dynamic set of the nation's interstate carriers. Thus a carrier's safety fitness rating became a static, incomplete assessment of its safety performance and, in no way, did it reflect its ongoing, real-time safety performance record.

12.3.2 SafeStat

The Intermodal Surface Transportation Efficiency Act of 1991 (Public Law 102-240, December 18, 1991 authorized the Federal/State Performance and Registration Information Systems Management program. Under the auspices of this program, the Office of Motor Carrier Safety contracted with the Volpe National Transportation Systems Center to develop a Motor Carrier Safety Status Measurement System (SafeStat) to evaluate and rank the safety performance of motor carriers based on their ongoing record of safety performance as opposed to a single, static assessment of their safety profile (Volpe National Transportation Systems Center, 2004). The SafeStat system included an evaluation of carrier performance in the following safety evaluation areas (SEAs): Driver SEA, Vehicle SEA, Safety Management Evaluation Area, and Accident SEA. SafeStat compiled a time-weighted, size adjusted score in each of these SEAs for each carrier with ongoing data from roadside inspections, CRs, enforcement actions, and crashes. Carriers were then sorted into groups based on their size (measured by power units in their fleets). Within each size group and for each SEA, carriers were arrayed by their SEA score from lowest (best safety record) to highest score (worst safety record). These scores were then converted into percentile scores from 0 (best safety performance) to 100 (worst safety performance). With four SEAs, a carrier's maximum possible overall score was 400. Carriers were placed into groups to prioritize them based on their total score. Carriers with higher scores were targeted for additional interventions and inspections. In each SEA, a carrier's score of 75 or greater was "above the threshold" level and provided a justification for a greater number of inspections and reviews. Carrier performance was time-weighted with more recent events being of greater importance in determining a carrier's score than more distant events. The SafeStat methodology covered a carrier's overall performance over a 2-year period. Carrier scores in the SafeStat methodology became updated monthly, with the 2-year period constantly updated to reflect the most recent 24 months of performance. From December 1999 through November 2010 (when the safety measurement system came online), SafeStat results were made available to the public via the Internet on the Analysis & Information (A&I) website at www.ai.volpe. dot.gov/. SafeStat reflected a near-real time, comprehensive assessment of a carrier's safety performance in reviews and roadside inspections. The Office of Motor Carrier Safety used the SafeStat percentile scores as a basis for targeting carriers with high scores for CRs and a higher frequency of roadside inspections.

It should also be noted that the implementation of the SafeStat system did not replace the safety fitness determination associated with a CR. The SafeStat data supplemented the safety fitness determination with ongoing safety performance results of individual carriers. Thus individual motor carriers continued to report their safety fitness through the outcome of CRs as "satisfactory," "conditional," or "unsatisfactory." Thus, the safety fitness determination continued to be based on static incomplete performance assessment, while the SafeStat online system provided more complete, dynamic assessment of a carrier's safety performance record.

The FMCSA increasingly relied on the SafeStat methodology and assessment system to rank carrier performance and to identify candidates for targeted CRs and/or roadside safety inspections. FMCSA developed an algorithm, labeled the Inspection Selection System, which provided roadside inspectors with information that enabled the ranking of individual carriers for inspection priority. Carriers with higher SafeStat scores received a higher priority for roadside inspections than did carriers with significantly lower scores.

The FMCSA significantly increased its roadside inspection activity during this time. Indeed in 2000 there were 2.45 million roadside inspections. However, by 2010, this number had increased to 3.57 million roadside inspections on an annual basis (Office of Freight Management and OperationsOffice of Freight Management and Operations, Federal Highway Administration, US Department of Transportation, 2012). Indeed the SafeStat system moved safety performance evaluation from an incomplete, static assessment to a more complete, dynamic one, useful as a tool to monitor, evaluate, and regulate safety performance.

3.3   Compliance, safety, and accountability (CSA) 2010: safety measurement system (SMS)

Recognizing some limits associated with SafeStat, the FMCSA launched the Comprehensive Safety Analysis 2010 Initiative (Volpe National Transportation Systems Center, 2008). Compliance, safety, and accountability (CSA) 2010 developed a new methodology building upon SafeStat to provide a more detailed, finer grained assessment of the ongoing safety performance of individual carriers. There are several very important differences between the safety measurement system (SMS) associated with CSA 2010 and the SafeStat approach.

First, as noted SafeStat divided carrier safety performance into four categories: driver, vehicle, safety management, and accident. In contrast, the SMS associated with CSA 2010 defines safety performance in six Behavior Analysis and Safety Improvement Categories (BASICs) as well as a crash involvement measure (crash indicator). The seven BASICs are: unsafe driving, fatigued driving, driver fitness, controlled substances and alcohol, vehicle maintenance, crash indicator, and hazardous materials compliance. These BASICs differ in several ways from SafeStat's SEAs. First, the BASICs are finer grained than are the SEAs. The Driver SEA is broken into four BASICs. Second, with SafeStat all violations, defined as "out-of-service" violations, had the same weight in the scoring system. Within the SMS, individual violations are assigned severity weights, based on crash probability/likely impact factors, and carriers are penalized more if they violate regulations with a higher severity weight (Volpe National Transportation Systems Center, 2007). Carriers are scored on each of the BASICs as well as the crash indicator. Just as in SafeStat, the BASICs time-weight violations and size-adjust carrier performance so that carriers are compared to their peers in the ranking system.

The SMS compiles a record of carrier violations (there are approximately 900 types of violations considered) during roadside inspections, CRs, enforcement actions, and moving violations. Carriers are grouped into size categories (or total number of safety events or VMT estimates) and compared with carriers in their own groups. The grouping of carriers also differentiates between carriers relying on combination vehicles (over 70%) and those who have less than 70% combination vehicles in their fleet. Initially, carriers are assigned a measure score based on the frequency and severity of their violations, given either their size (unsafe driving BASIC and crash indicator BASIC) of the total number of their safety events (driver fitness BASIC, drug and alcohol BASIC, vehicle maintenance BASIC, and hazardous materials BASIC). Carriers within each group are arrayed based on their measure score from lowest to highest and assigned a within group percentile score. However, for a carrier to have its measure score converted to a percentile, it must meet the data sufficiency standards set by the FMCSA. For the unsafe driving BASIC, the data sufficiency standard is at least three inspections with at least one violation; for the hours-of-service BASIC, the data sufficiency standard is at least three inspections with at least one violation; and for the vehicle maintenance BASIC, the data sufficiency standard is at least five inspections with at least one violation.

The FMCSA has set threshold percentile scores for each BASIC. Carriers exceeding the threshold score for a BASIC are identified as candidates for additional monitoring or interventions by the FMCSA. The FMCSA assigned threshold levels on each BASIC because of the documented association between high BASIC percentile scores and greater future crash likelihood for carriers exceeding the threshold percentile score. The threshold score for the hours-of-service compliance BASIC and the unsafe driving BASIC are set at 65 for combination carriers, while the vehicle maintenance, controlled substances/alcohol abuse, driver fitness, and hazardous materials BASICs were all set at 80.

Volpe National Transportation Systems Center conducted evaluations of the effectiveness of the BASICs to identify future crash risks of carriers with above threshold scores in individual BASICs (Volpe National Transportation Systems Center, 2014). The fundamental methodology used by Volpe involved establishing a carrier's BASIC scores with the established methodology at a fixed point in time (covering a carrier's safety events over the previous 24 months with events time and severity weighted) and then assessing the record of the carrier's crashes over a subsequent 18-month period. The determination of the effectiveness of the BASICs involved a comparison of crash rates during the 18-month period between carriers who did not have a BASIC percentile score above the threshold versus the crash rate of carriers with BASIC percentile scores above the threshold. The comparison was conducted for each individual BASIC. The Volpe assessment also looked at the crash record of carriers with multiple BASICs above their respective thresholds again versus carriers with no BASICs above the respective thresholds set for each BASIC.

The results demonstrated that carriers with above threshold percentile scores had significantly higher crash rates in the 18-month subsequent period than did carriers without above threshold percentile scores. Table 4 of the Volpe report indicates that the crash rate (crashes per power unit) for carriers with above threshold unsafe driving BASIC percentile scores was 93% higher than the national average crash rate for all carriers during the 18-month period. The carriers with above threshold percentile scores in the crash indicator BASIC had crash rates that were 85% higher than the overall national average crash rate for all carriers. Regarding hours-of-service compliance, the comparable percentage increase in crash rates for above threshold carriers was 83%. For carriers with above threshold percentile scores in vehicle maintenance the percentage increase in crash rates above the national average was 65%. The comparable percentages in above the national average crash rate for carriers with above threshold percentile scores in the controlled substance/alcohol abuse BASIC and the hazardous materials compliance BASIC were 34% and 31%, respectively. While overall the carriers with above threshold percentile scores in the driver fitness BASIC have a lower crash rate in the 18-month period in comparison to the national average crash rate, if the sample is restricted to only combination areas the combination carriers with percentile scores in the driver fitness BASIC above the threshold have crash rates that are 40% higher than the national average crash rate for all carriers (National Academy of Sciences/Transportation Research Board, 2017). Furthermore, carriers with multiple BASIC percentile scores above the established threshold levels had significantly higher crash rates in comparison to carriers with no BASIC percentile scores above the threshold. In fact, the Volpe Study showed that carriers with two BASIC scores above the threshold had crash rates during the 18-month period that were more than twice as high as the crash rate for carriers with no BASIC scores above the threshold (Volpe National Transportation Systems Center, 2014, p. 10).

[7] Public Law 114–94.

12.3.4   FAST Act and NAS/TRB Panel on Motor Carrier Safety Measurement

In December 2015, Congress passed the Fixing America's Surface Transportation (FAST) Act.[7] This legislation recommended that FMCSA fund a study by the National Academy of Sciences in collaboration with the Transportation Research Board to analyze the SMS methodology and its ability to discriminate between low and high risk carriers, to assess the public usage of SMS data, and to provide advice on safety assessment methodologies. The FAST Act mandated that FMCSA remove the BASIC percentile scores from the Analysis and Information public website as of 1 January 2016. The FMCSA continues to provide individual carrier measure scores on its Analysis and Information public website.

The National Academy of Sciences/Transportation Research Board issued its report in July 2017 (National Academy of Sciences/Transportation Research Board, 2017, 133 p.). It examined issues that various parties had raised regarding the SMS methodology, developed by Volpe National Transportation Systems Center and implemented by FMCSA. According to the report, the areas of criticism of the SMS involved the following issues: (1) predictive ability of BASICs, (2) data sufficiency standards set by SMS, (3) use of absolute versus relative metric, (4) data from nonpreventable crashes, (5) state differences in rates of inspections and violations, (6) stratification of SMS in addition to safety event groups, (7) better measures of exposure, (8) quality of Motor Carrier Management Information System (MCMIS) data, (9) appropriateness of severity weights and violation coding, (10) uncollected variables that might substantially improve SMS, (11) sparsity of some violations, (12) selection effects, (13) transparency of the SMS algorithm, and (14) making percentile ranks public. It is not the purpose of this paper to review each of these points and the conclusions reached by the Panel on each item. Instead, it is relevant to review some of the overall observations and findings issued by the Panel in its report and to relate them to this paper's central focus: that is, the responsibility of brokers/third party logistics providers in their carrier selection process.

The Panel reached the following overall conclusion regarding the SMS. They stated (National Academy of Sciences/Transportation Research Board, 2017, Sum-2): "We believe that the general approach taken by SMS is sound, and shares much with similar programs in other areas of transportation safety. Further, we have examined, to the extent possible, the various issues that have been raised in criticism of SMS. We have found, for the most part, that the current SMS implementation is defensible as being fair and not overtly biased against various types of carriers, to the extent that data on MCMIS can be used for this purpose." At another point in the study, the Panel made the following observations: "Conceptually, SMS is structured reasonably. Using the number of violations found during inspections, and the number of crashes, with violations bundled into groups that represent related areas of safe operations, weighting these frequencies by severity and time weights, properly standardizing these counts, stratifying carriers into similarly sized peer groups, and then seeing which carriers are doing worse than the others, is a reasonable approach to the identification of unsafe carriers (National Academy of Sciences/Transportation Research Board, 2017, pp. 2–29). The Panel did not, however, reach a recommendation on whether the FMCSA should make all the SMS percentile ranks public (National Academy of Sciences/ Transportation Research Board, 2017, Sum-6).

The Panel did conclude the following about the association between carriers with above threshold BASIC percentile scores and higher than average crash rates. The Panel said: "The consensus of our Panel is that the evaluations carried out by FMCSA supports the judgement that six of the seven BASICs are positively (sometimes very strongly) associated with future crash risk, and that the unconditional correlation of Driver Fitness's percentile ranks with future crash frequency is insufficient to remove it from SMS" (National Academy of Sciences/Transportation Research Board, 2017, pp. 2–18).

The Panel did suggest an alternative approach/methodology for scoring and evaluation of carrier safety performance. However, what is important for the purposes of this investigation is the fact that Panel viewed in a positive way the examination of carrier safety performance through the analysis of available safety event data in a comprehensive and ongoing manner. Indeed, as illustrated in the above discussion, the FMCSA has provided comprehensive and ongoing safety performance data on individual carriers to industry stakeholders (insurance companies, brokers, third party logistics providers, shippers, and the carriers themselves) through its Analysis and Information online website. The following sections focus on the responsibility of brokers/third party logistics providers and shippers in selecting motor carriers to handle the physical movement of freight in interstate commerce.

12.4   Brokers/third party logistics providers

CFR 371.2 defines a broker as a "person who, for compensation, arranges, or offers to arrange the transportation of property by an authorized motor carrier." Throughout this discussion, brokers and third party logistics providers are equated because they both arrange freight transportation by authorized motor carriers. While CFR 371.2 suggests a transactional role for brokers/third party logistics providers, these entities currently engage as active participants in the total end-to-end process of freight deliveries. The following sections will argue that the relationship by broker/third party logistic provider can better be portrayed as a joint venture/partnership or a relationship in which the broker/third party logistic provider exercises significant control over the actions of the carrier. In both cases, the broker/third party logistic provider shares the same obligation as the carrier to insure the delivery of safe and efficient transportation services. Regardless of the characterization of the broker/third party logistic provider relationship, these entities have the duty, established through various court rulings and industry practices, to use reasonable care in the selection of motor carriers. This section is divided into the following three subsections: discussion of broker/third party logistic provider relationship as a joint venture/partnership; discussion of the significant control commonly exercised by brokers/third party logistics providers over the carriers engaged to provide transportation services; and a discussion of the standard of reasonable care to be exercised by brokers/third party logistics providers in carrier selection.

12.4.1 Joint venture/partnership

Joint ventures are defined as business arrangements in which two or more parties pool their resources for accomplishing a specific task.[8] In the partnership, the parties share returns and risks. Agreements between brokers/third-party logistics providers and carriers reflect joint ventures/partnerships in contrast to situations wherein the carriers operate as "independent contractors" simply providing physical transportation services.

Brokers/third-party logistics providers and carriers are engaged in a "joint venture" for the mutual benefit of both parties as they in concert provide transportation services to shippers. It is the standard practice for a broker/third party logistics provider and a shipper customer to agree on a price for the transportation services required to move freight from an origin to a destination. After the agreement between the shipper and the broker/third party logistics provider, the broker/third party logistics provider searches for a carrier to provide the transportation services at a fixed price, hopefully below the price agreed to by the shipper and the broker/third-party logistics provider. The higher the spread between what the broker/third party logistics provider has negotiated with the carrier and the amount that the broker/third party logistics provider pays the carrier, the greater the profit margin to the broker. Thus the carrier's payment to the broker/third party logistics provider for the shipment is "shared" between broker/third party logistics provider and the carrier it selects to provide the transportation services. However, it is conceivable that a broker/third party logistics provider would be unable to find a carrier to handle a shipment at a price below or equal to the amount that the broker/third party logistics provider has negotiated with the shipper. Indeed, in such cases, the broker/third party logistics provider would break even or suffer a loss. Furthermore, it is conceivable that the carrier will accept a price from a broker/third party logistics provider that will require the carrier to suffer a loss as the amount received from the broker/third party logistics provider is below its actual direct costs for providing the stipulated transportation services. Clearly, there is an element of risk involved in the process that is shared between the broker/third party logistics provider and the carrier.

Clearly, in a system where the profit margin for the broker/third party logistics provider consists of the difference between what the broker/third party logistics provider receives from the shipper and the amount that they pay to the carrier, the broker/third party logistics provider has an incentive to assign loads to carriers offering to handle the shipment at a lower price. Indeed, the lower the payment that the broker/third party logistics provider makes to the carrier, the larger will its profit be on that shipment. This system of carrier selection has a significant safety risk as carriers who consistently offer their services for lower prices are likely to have lower profits. Furthermore, prior research has statistically demonstrated a relationship between lower carrier profitability and poorer safety outcomes (Britto et al., 2010; Miller and Saldanha, 2016).

---

[8] http://www.investopedia.com/terms/j/jointventure.asp?lgl=rira-baseline-vertical

12.4.2   Control

Brokers/third party logistics providers exercise a great deal of control over the actions of the carriers they select such that their relationship with the carriers is more accurately described as a "principal/agent" as opposed to a characterization of carriers as "independent contractors." The following discussion substantiates the various ways in which brokers/third party logistics providers control carriers as they take responsibility for the management and delivery of freight shipments for their shipper clients.

It is not uncommon for brokers/third party logistics providers to advertise their services to shippers in a comprehensive way by assuring shippers that the brokers/third party logistics providers will manage/control the shipment from origin to destination. For example, a major broker recently had a web page entitled "benefits of nonasset based brokerage service" on its website as recently as 2016.[9] It read: "While on the road, we maintain control of the shipment throughout our detailed dispatch and check call policy. Before receiving pickup information, each logistics account executive communicates important details and runs through a detailed checklist with carriers. Then, Logistics Account Executives (LAE) monitor the load's progress by speaking with the carrier company at least twice a day by phone. This policy enables our LAEs' to provide our customers with frequent status updates.... Our nonasset based brokerage model allows us to provide our customers with greater capacity and flexibility while meeting their expectations for quality and control." Another significant example of the control and direction exercised by brokers/third party logistics providers is evidenced by C.H. Robinson's Transportation Guide (Robinson, 2006) It states: "We may arrange appointments for drivers, dispatch, monitor the freight progress from start to finish, bill the shipper, and pay the carrier.... CH Robinson assumes the direct responsibility for loss or damage to freight in transit, and works with carriers to resolve cargo claims when necessary. We provide global logistics expertise and transportation services from origin to destination." The Transportation Guide for C.H. Robinson also describes its transportation management services: "Carrier Management services include taking over some or all of the day-to-day work with carriers (dispatching, monitoring pickup and delivery, monitoring their progress in transit) for the customer." These statements are consistent with the view that the actions of brokers/third party logistics providers involve a significant control over the actions of their carrier partners as they manage the delivery of the freight on behalf of their shipper clients.

Broker-Carrier agreements give further specific evidence of the control exercised by brokers/third party logistics providers through a series of specific provisions. In many of these agreements, the carrier waives its rights to any lien on any freight or other property of the shippers. These rights are considered standard for motor carriers who have any disputes with shippers over the transportation and delivery of goods. These agreements also frequently include a clause stating that the carrier shall not contact or communicate with the shipper clients of the broker/third party logistics

---

[9] This specific web-page was present on the web-page of a major broker/third party logistics provider as of 2016. The specific name of the broker is withheld due to nondisclosure agreements in legal proceedings.

provider. These agreements frequently state that, if the agreement is terminated, the carrier shall not solicit freight or provide transportation services to any of the shipper clients of the broker/third party logistics provider. Furthermore, the agreements specify that the payments for transportation services flow directly from the shipper to the broker/third party logistics provider, not the carrier.

Typically, brokers/third party logistics providers issue Rate Confirmation Sheets to their carriers providing specific information about the payment the carrier will receive as well as an outline of specific requirements that the carrier is obligated to fulfill. These requirements vary according to the individual shipments but the following are typical of the requirements included: specification of the type, size, and condition of equipment to be provided (e.g., air-ride trailer); specific requirements for temperature inside the trailer (at loading and during the entire trip); specific routing instructions to follow for pick-up and delivery; requirements for carrier to contact broker/third party logistics provider on a daily basis, with penalties for failure to comply; and requirements to notify broker/third party logistics provider if any delays in shipment deliveries, with penalties for late arrivals.

12.4.3   Reasonable care in selection of carriers

In a joint venture partnership or when exercising significant control over the actions of its carrier partners, brokers/third party logistics providers assume the same responsibility as assigned by the FMCSA to carriers to provide safe and efficient transportation. As such, they are directly responsible for the actions of the carriers they select and assume the same liability as the direct carrier partner. In this environment, it is incumbent upon the broker/third party logistics provider to use reasonable care in the selection of a carrier. The specifics of exercising this duty will be outlined in the following discussion.

Previous court decisions in cases involving a major broker (C.H. Robinson) have recognized that the broker/third party logistics provider's examination of the safety performance record of a motor carrier is part of the duty to use reasonable care in the carrier selection process and not to be considered as onerous, but a critical and necessary requirement. In Schramm v. Foster, the court stated:

> *This duty to use reasonable care in the selection of carriers includes, at least, the subsidiary duties (1) to check the safety statistics and evaluations of the carriers with whom it contracts available on the SafeStat database maintained by FMSCA, and (2) to maintain internal records of the persons with whom it contracts to assure that they are not manipulating their business practices to avoid unsatisfactory SafeStat ratings. Cf. L.B. Foster Co., Inc. v. Hurnblad, 418 F.2d 727 (9th Cir. 1969). These obligations are not onerous, and I do not find that imposition of such a common-law duty would be incompatible with the regulations promulgated by the FMCSR. …To the contrary, imposing a common-law duty upon third party logistics companies to use reasonable care in selecting carriers furthers the critical federal interest in protecting drivers and passengers on the nation's highways (Schramm v. Foster, 2004).*

Furthermore, in the Jones v. C.H. Robinson case, the Court ruled that a major broker's (again, C.H. Robinson) failure to examine safety performance data about its selected motor carrier "through a variety of public sources of information at the time and hiring of the carrier to haul the subject load" constituted a "proximate cause of the accident which resulted in plaintiff's injuries" (Jones v. C.H. Robinson Worldwide, Inc., 2008)

In view of these significant court rulings, it is important to review some of the practices that brokers/third party logistics providers currently employ in exercising reasonable care in the selection of motor carriers. In 2013, the Transportation Intermediaries Association (TIA) issued Carrier Selection Guidelines (Parker, 2013). These guidelines provide specific direction to a broker who is considering dispatching a motor carrier with no safety fitness rating.

If a carrier is "UNRATED" or "NONE": If the carrier has no safety rating, you must conduct your own investigation into the carrier's record of accidents, FMCSA inspection reports, driver compliance with hours of service regulations, its compliance with record-keeping regulations, medical exams, accident reports, etc. The Schramm court ruled that "it seems entirely reasonable to require firms, including third party logistics companies, who assist newcomers with market entry, to evaluate their safety control measures in the absence of a DOT rating."

It is instructive to review several examples of the types of investigations that brokers/third party logistics providers undertake before engaging the services of carriers without a safety fitness rating. As noted in Schneider Logistics' carrier qualification website: "Carriers who have not been rated by the DOT may qualify to haul freight for Schneider, but will be subject to additional carrier qualification procedures prior to activation."[10] Stevens Transport requires carriers without a safety rating to complete a carrier profile questionnaire. This questionnaire requires the carriers to answer the following set of questions[11]:

- Please provide a description of the training programs you have in place for your drivers.
- Please provide a description of the programs and procedures you have in place to supervise your drivers.
- Please provide a description of your safety program, including a description of the programs and procedures in place to confirm that your drivers are operating in compliance with FMC-SRs (attach any supporting documentation that you have).

It is also relevant to note that many prominent brokers/third-party logistics providers continue a policy of hiring only carriers with a satisfactory safety rating. Included in this group are the following: NFI Logistics; USA Truck Brokers; Werner Enterprises; Epes Logistics Services, Inc.; AmeriLux Logistics; Express Transport America Logistics; Taylor Made Express, Inc.; Elite Logistics; US Freight Brokers; and Central Logistics.

Other brokers/third-party logistics examine the safety records of their selected carriers on an ongoing basis. Brokers/carriers with brokerage operations who continuously monitor the safety performance of the carriers they select, include the following:

---

[10] https://schneidercarrier.rmissecure.com/_s/reg/generalrequirements.aspx
[11] http://www.stevenstransport.com/wp-content/uploads/2011/05/2012.2013-New-Carrier-Packet-1.pdf

Ryder Logistics; Cardinal Transportation; Swift Transportation, Inc.; D.B. Schenker; Universal Truckload; and Yusen Logistics. These brokers are conducting real-time ongoing investigations into the carrier's safety records, including crashes, compliance, and violations of safety regulations.

Another group of prominent brokers/carriers with brokerage operations subject their carriers to initial and ongoing, real-time evaluation of each carrier's BASIC scores. Some of these brokers refuse to engage carriers with one or more BASIC score above a threshold value, while others continually monitor a carrier's BASIC scores, prior to each use of the carrier and will not dispatch a load to a carrier with one or more BASIC scores above the threshold. Brokers/carriers with brokerage operations who rely on the BASIC scores for initial qualification and continuous monitoring include the following: Ryder Logistics; Cardinal Transportation; Swift Transportation, Inc.; D.B. Schenker; Universal Truckload; and Yusen Logistics. Swift Transportation, Inc. has the following provision of its carrier selection criteria that states: "At any time a carrier has one (1) score of 90% or higher in any of the 5 BASIC FMCSA scores (unsafe driving, hours of service, driver fitness, controlled substance, and vehicle maintenance), the carrier is automatically disqualified.[12]

Other brokers have devised similar means of ensuring that loads are not entrusted to unreliable carriers. DB Schenker USA, a freight forwarder based in Freeport, N.Y., put in place a program of intensive scrutiny of motor carrier performance 4 years ago. The company worked with a software developer, Veroot LLC, to create a program that delivers alerts when a motor carrier falls below the company's threshold for safety compliance. "They (Veroot LLC) give us a list of carriers every day, identifying those that fall above the threshold and considering CSA scores and other measures of performance," Gifford (DB Schenker spokesperson) said. "It's a proactive approach" (Bearth, 2013, p. A10) DB Schenker USA is owned by Deutsche Bahn AG in Germany and, with estimated net revenue of $1.2 billion in 2011, ranks No. 7 on the Transport Topics Top 50 list of the largest logistics companies in the United States, Canada, and Mexico.

Obviously, these policies were all established prior to the FAST Act provision removing the BASIC percentile scores from the FMCSA public website. Yet, the FMCSA continues to calculate the BASIC percentile scores and make them available to the carriers, who are free to release this information to brokers/third party logistics providers. Furthermore, third party data providers have re-engineered the FMCSA SMS methodology and continue to make available for sale data on the BASIC percentile scores of individual carriers.

12.5   Shippers

Shippers, like brokers/third party logistics providers, have significant needs for transportation services to deliver their freight to manufacturing, wholesale, or retail sites. As noted above, the transportation of freight in large trucks involves inherent risks

[12] https://swiftcarriers.rmissecure.com/_s/reg/generalrequirements.aspx

of fatal or injury crashes with significant economic costs. As a result of this inherent risk, 49 US Code, Section 14101 specifies that "motor carriers shall provide safe and adequate service, equipment, and facilities."

Shippers have the option of either relying on the services of brokers/third party logistics providers to select motor carriers or to perform the selection task themselves. If shippers directly select motor carriers, they have the responsibility to select safe and efficient carriers. The following pages will support this opinion with examples of industry practices.

In a similar fashion to brokers/third party logistics providers, shippers directly selecting their motor carriers frequently initiate formal agreements with their selected carriers, often labeled as shipper-carrier agreements. Like similar agreements that brokers/third party logistics providers initiate with motor carriers, the shipper-carrier agreement declares that the carrier selected is an independent contractor over which the shipper has no control. However, the actual relationship between shippers and carriers is representative of a principal-agent relationship as the shipper exercises significant control over the actions of carriers. The following paragraphs will illustrate the various aspects of the shipper's control over the carrier.

12.5.1 Control

While there is variety in the specifics of shipper-carrier agreements, these agreements have many similarities to the broker-carrier agreements discussed above with respect to the extent of control exercised over the actions of the carriers. These agreements have provisions stipulating that the carrier submit its equipment to inspection prior to dispatching the truck to handle an individual shipment on behalf of the shipper. Other provisions may stipulate that the carrier have all of its drivers certified for safety purposes. Additional specific requirements included in these agreements include the following requirements: (1) carrier equipment must be no older than a specified number of years; (2) carrier equipment must have electronic logbook technology; (3) carrier equipment must have speed governing technology; (4) carriers must implement training programs for its drivers on new technology; and (5) carriers must provide daily progress reports and notification of deliveries.

12.5.2 Reasonable care in the selection of carriers

There is strong evidence that shippers, acting on their own to select and retain motor carriers, do take their responsibility to select safe carriers in a very serious manner. In fact, shippers do regard the examination of a carrier's BASIC scores as an integral component in the carrier selection and retention process. Micah Lueck and Rebecca Brewster's (2012) of the American Transportation Research Institute, the research arm of the American Trucking Associations, published a report in December 2012 in which they collected data from dozens of shippers representing tens of billions of dollars of freight movement. They report that 96.8% of the shipper respondents indicated that they monitor the CSA scores of carriers they currently contract with. Importantly, the study indicated that shippers often require carriers with undesirable BASIC scores to develop a Corrective Action Plan for improving those scores and resolving safety and/or compliance problems. The study also reported that 100% of the respondents either check or plan to check BASIC scores before contracting a new carrier for the first time and 50% report that poor BASIC scores alone were sufficient reason to avoid contracting with a prospective carrier (Lueck and Brewster, 2012).

It is also instructive to refer to the American Chemistry Council's Responsible Care initiative, adopted in 1988.[13] Under the Responsible Care Management System shippers are required to assess the health, security, and environmental management capability and performance of the for-hire carriers they select for their shipments. Specifically, member companies are required to evaluate their transportation companies prior to hiring them. Member companies use the Motor Carrier Assessment Protocol to evaluate their transportation companies. The Protocol is an 18-page questionnaire covering numerous aspects of a company's safety performance and policies. The Protocol asks for companies' safety performance experience—a Safer snapshot; driving training and management; regulatory compliance; operating procedures; risk management; and vehicle inspection and maintenance. The Responsible Care guidelines are mandatory for the 175 member companies of the American Chemistry Council.

12.6 Conclusions

The nation continues to experience significant economic and social cost from large truck fatal and injury crashes. After an extended period of steady decline in these crashes, the recent trends have disturbingly been in the opposite direction. The FMCSA has as its primary mission the objective to reduce fatal and injury large truck crashes. As such, it has initiated a number of programs to monitor and evaluate the safety performance of motor carriers on an ongoing and comprehensive basis and to target those carriers falling below established safety performance thresholds. Specifically, FMCSA developed and initiated the Safety Measurement System (SMS) and made its results available on its public website. The SMS provides comprehensive and ongoing safety performance data on the nation's carriers in seven categories of safety performance.

As part of the FAST Act, the FMCSA initiated a National Academy of Sciences and Transportation Research Board study to assess the SMS with a specific emphasis on addressing criticisms that had been leveled against the system. The National Academy of Sciences/Transportation Research Board (NAS/TRB) Panel concluded that SMS was a reasonable and sound approach to use in identifying carriers to prioritize for safety interventions. They did provide an alternative safety measurement system, viewed as superior to the SMS, but involving a significantly more comprehensive data inputs.

---

[13] https://www.qualitydistribution.com/QualityDistribution/media/QualityDistribution/PDFs/Motor-Carrier-Assessment-Protocol.pdf

The focus of this paper has been on the responsibility of both brokers/third-party logistics providers and shippers in motor carrier selection with a special emphasis on their use of comprehensive and ongoing FMCSA publically available data. For both entities, the notion that their relationship with motor carriers is defined by the carriers being identified as "independent contractors" does not reflect reality. Instead, the relationship is more appropriately viewed as either a joint venture/partnership or a principal-agent relationship with the broker/third-party logistics provider and the shipper exercising significant control over the activities of the carrier.

In this environment, the broker/third party logistics provider and the shipper have a responsibility, articulated in court decisions and confirmed by industry practices, to evaluate in a careful and systematic manner the safety management practices and records of the carriers they select. The best hope for improvement in the large truck fatal and injury crash rate is for the brokers/third-party logistics providers and the shippers to be vigilant in their efforts to insure that the motor carriers they select operate in a safe and efficient manner.

The recent efforts to restrict the safety performance data from the SMS made available on the FMCSA's publically available website should be vigorously resisted. This paper has argued that shippers, brokers, and third party logistics providers have a joint responsibility to select and use safe and efficient motor carriers. The use of SMS data on carrier safety performance is a vital component of informed decision making by these parties. Reversing the upward tick in truck crash injury and fatality rates requires that shippers, brokers, and third party logistics providers make informed decisions relying on individual carrier safety performance data. The FMCSA's efforts to collect and disseminate this information in its SMS must be protected from any efforts to restrict either the collection or dissemination of this information. In fact, FMCSA should be provided additional resources to strengthen and improve the SMS by incorporating some of the specific recommendations of the TRB/NAS Panel.

References

Bearth, D., 2013. Shippers, brokers use data services to closely monitor carriers' performance. Transport Topics, A10, February 18.

Britto, R., Corsi, T.M., Grimm, C.M., 2010. Impact of motor carrier firms' financial performance on safety performance. Transp. J. 49 (4), 42–51.

Federal Motor Carrier Safety Administration, 2016. Large Truck and Bus Crash Facts 2015. Washington, DC.

Jones v. C.H. Robinson Worldwide Inc., 2008. United States District Court for the Western District of Virginia (Roanoke Division), Civil Action No. 7:06CV00547.

Lueck, Brewster, 2012. Compliance, safety, accountability: evaluating a new safety measurement system and its implications. American Transportation Research Institute.

Miller, J., Saldanha, J.P., 2016. A new look at the longitudinal relationship between motor carrier financial performance and safety. J. Bus. Logist. 37 (3), 284–306.

National Academy of Sciences/Transportation Research Board, 2017. Improving Motor Carrier Safety Measurement. The National Academies Press, Washington, DC.

Office of Freight Management and Operations, Federal Highway Administration, US Department of Transportation, 2012. Freight Facts and Figures 2011. Washington, DC.

Parker, B.E., 2013. Carrier Selection Guidelines: 2013. Transportation Intermediaries Association.

C.H. Robinson, Transportation Guide, Version 3, July 2006.

Schramm v. Foster, 341 F. Supp.2d 536, 2004.

Volpe National Transportation Systems Center, 2004. SafeStat: Motor Carrier Safety Status Measurement System, Methodology: Version 8.6. Prepared for the Federal Motor Carrier Safety Administration, Cambridge, MA.

Volpe National Transportation Systems Center, 2007. Violations Severity Assessment Study: Final Report. U.S. Department of Transportation (prepared for the Federal Motor Carrier Safety Administration), Cambridge, MA.

Volpe National Transportation Systems Center, 2008. Comprehensive Safety Analysis (CSA 2010): Safety Measurement System (SMS) Methodology, Version 1.0. Prepared for the Federal Motor Carrier Safety Administration, U.S. Department of Transportation, Cambridge, MA.

Volpe National Transportation Systems Center, 2014. The Carrier Safety Measurement System (CSMS) Effectiveness Test by Behavior Analysis and Safety Improvement Categories (BASICs). Prepared for Federal Motor Carrier Safety Administration, Washington, DC.

Further Reading

Federal Motor Carrier Safety Administration (FMCSA), U.S. Department of Transportation, 2005. Report to Congress on the Large Truck Crash Causation Study, Washington, DC.

Sturdy inference and the amelioration potential for driverless cars: The reduction of motor vehicle fatalities due to technology*

13

Richard Fowles*, Peter D. Loeb**
*University of Utah, Salt Lake City, UT, USA; **Rutgers University, Newark, NJ, USA

Chapter Outline

13.1   Introduction

In the last decade, motor vehicle-related fatalities continued to range between 42,196 in 2001 and 32,999 deaths in 2010. This is a considerable reduction since 1972 when these deaths amounted to 54,589. Still, these number of fatalities are significant from a public health and economic perspective. A major reduction in these fatalities occurred between 2007 and 2010 when fatalities fell by 20%.[1] This precipitous drop in deaths may be due to things other than or in addition to what contributed to the prior trend. For example, some of this decline may be due to economic events, that is, the Great Recession as well as a change in taste among the public. That is, there seems to be a preference, especially among the youth, to move from the suburbs to the cities where there is a greater reliance on public transportation and walking. Furthermore, while the baby boomers

---

* An earlier version of this paper was presented at the Meetings of the Transportation and Public Utilities Group of the American Economic Association in Chicago on January 6, 2017.
[1] See NHTSA (2016) for data on crash fatalities.

Transportation Policy and Economic Regulation. http://dx.doi.org/10.1016/B978-0-12-812620-2.00013-4

had a strong desire to obtain powerful cars while in their teens, the current population of youths may be more inclined to desire powerful cell phones and electronic equipment. Regardless of these changes in preferences, there remains a significant number of crash-related fatalities in the United States which scientists attempt to explain.

Most troubling has been the recent increase in traffic-related fatalities. More specifically, there has been a 9% increase in traffic fatalities during the first half of 2012 compared to the same period in 2011.[2] To make matters even more concerning, the National Highway Traffic Safety Administration comparing the first-half of 2015 and 2016 notes a 10.4% increase in motor vehicle fatalities.[3] The causes of these fatalities, as mentioned above, are still a matter of concern to economists, public health scientists, and policy makers. Determining the significance of the contributing factors of these crashes resulting in fatalities can lead to policy and technical developments that may mitigate these losses. The advent of "driverless cars" may assist in reducing the losses on roadways should the factors leading to crashes be amenable to their use.

Driverless or autonomous vehicles may be particularly useful in reducing motor vehicle highway fatalities given that 94% of crashes have been attributed to drivers.[4] It has been argued that driverless cars will reduce these crashes due to their safety attributes. Should the technology be as expected, they should be able to avoid crashes, stop automatically in unexpected crash conditions, park themselves, and provide human drivers a reasonable alternative to driving by safely navigating the roadways during daytime and nighttime as well as in inclement weather.

To some extent, the technology needed for driverless vehicles is currently available and is expected to improve so as to allow for a large presence of fully functional autonomous vehicles in the very near future. Delphi currently is operating a fleet of six driverless taxis in Singapore and plans a fleet of 50 taxis by 2019.[5] Nutonomy also plans to provide taxi service in Singapore by 2018. In addition, most car manufactures plan to have autonomous vehicles available shortly. For example, Ford plans to have such vehicles available by 2020/2021; General Motors by 2020; BMW in 2021; Tesla by 2021–2023; Audi (A8) in 2017; Nissan by 2020; and Google by 2018.[6]

The question remains as to whether autonomous vehicles will indeed provide the safety that might be expected from them. Some evidence has been suggested regarding this issue by Schoettle and Sivak (2015). They compared the safety record of self-driving vehicles for three companies (Google, Delphi, and Audi) with conventional vehicles for the year 2013. They found that the crash and injury rates for the driverless vehicles were higher than for traditional vehicles. However, they could not determine if there was a significant difference. They also found that the crashes involving driverless vehicles were not due to the driverless vehicle. Finally, they noted that the injuries associated with driverless vehicles were of less severity than those associated with conventional vehicles. This latter point is tainted by new data forthcoming in 2016 due to a crash between a Tesla and a tractor-trailer which resulted in a fatality.[7] The results

[2] See NHTSA (2012).
[3] By the end of 2015, 35,092 fatalities were reported. See NHTSA (2016).
[4] See NHTSA (2015).
[5] See Kirk (2016).
[6] See Hars (2016).

are suspect as well due to the small sample size used to investigate the relative safety of driverless vehicles versus conventional ones. The data associated with the driverless cars were based on low mileage tests in California and Texas (Google data associated with 1.2 million miles of driving), a single trip from San Francisco to New York (Delphi data, associated with 3400 miles of driving) and a single trip from San Francisco to Las Vegas (Audi data associated with 550 miles of driving). In addition, these self-driving vehicle results are associated with driving in the South during periods where bad weather was not experienced. These results are then compared with conventional vehicle data covering about 3 trillion miles.[8]

To date, there are insufficient data available to address directly the safety record of driverless cars vis-à-vis conventional vehicles. To get a handle on this issue, the current paper considers the determinants of motor vehicle fatality rates using classical econometric methods and then, a new Bayesian technique developed by Leamer referred to as Sturdy-values. This Bayesian method addresses the ambiguity and uncertainty associated with models which are not addressed using classical methods.

Many factors thought to contribute to motor vehicle crashes and crash fatalities have been examined over the last two decades. However, their relationship to driverless vehicles has not been investigated. In general, we can classify these factors into three categories: those associated with vehicles, those associated with drivers (and pedestrians), and those associated with roadways. The potential contributing variables that have been investigated in the past include: motor vehicle speed, speed variance, alcohol consumption, speed limits, vehicle miles traveled, measures of income and wealth, unemployment rates, the age of the motor vehicle fleet, seat belt usage and seat belt legislation, and the deregulatory climate of the 1980s, among others.[9] Many of these effects have been investigated using econometric methods and models similar to those posed early on by Peltzman (1975). More recently, there has been an interest in the effect of cell phones, the age of the motor vehicle fleet, and the trend in suicides on these fatalities.[10] This paper considers these three factors along with many of the above-mentioned variables as to their contributing influence on crash fatalities. Again, we focus on these determinants of motor vehicle fatalities using both a traditional modeling approach, that is, classical econometrics, as well as from a Bayesian perspective developed by Leamer (2016) referred to as Sturdy-values or S-values.

Considering these last three mentioned factors, cell phone usage has been shown to have a significant impact on motor vehicle rates in some studies, but not all. The age of the fleet, or perhaps better phrased, the newness of the fleet, should address the issue of technology improvements over time. (One can speculate that forthcoming "newness" attributes may very likely be impacted by driverless cars.) A more recent consideration has been with regard to suicidal propensities. Suicides have been related in previous work with railroad accidents.[11] Blattenberger et al. (2013) have included it

---

[7] See Dreamer (2016).

[8] See Schoettle and Sivak (2015).

[9] See Loeb et al. (1994) for a more complete list and discussion of these contributing influences.

[10] See Blattenberger et al. (2013).

[11] See, for example, Savage (2007, 2010).

in earlier work to address changes in risk-taking propensities over time, or companion effects, when examining motor vehicle fatality rates. Their results suggest that this determinant is worthy of additional investigation. All three of these factors, should they prove to be of significance, might lead to policy measures and the incorporation of new technologies which could result in reductions in the fatalities in question.

Clearly, not all of the above factors mentioned can be influenced by driverless vehicles. However, once the causes of crashes are identified, one can determine which ones may be affected by driverless vehicles and rank them according to their impact. Then reasonable inferences can be made as to the benefits forthcoming from driverless vehicles in reducing fatality rates.

One has to recognize that driverless vehicles have costs as well as benefits. For example, there may be litigation effects, environmental factors (both positive and negative) as well as others. In addition, it is not reasonable to think that driverless vehicles, should they prove to be capable of reducing crashes, will reduce motor vehicle-related fatalities to zero.

We provide a background for our research in Section 13.2. Our data described in Sections 13.3 and 13.4 provide some classical econometric results which form the basis for the "prior" utilized in the Bayesian analysis which follows. Section 13.5 lays out the general Bayesian framework underlying the procedures we use in this type of analysis and then introduces Sturdy-values, that is, S-values. Analysis by S-values is then applied to models of motor vehicle fatality rates. Section 13.6 provides a comparison of the relative importance of the explanatory variables using normalized data and classical econometrics with special regard to autonomous vehicles. Section 13.7 provides some caveats pertaining to the advent of driverless cars into the motor vehicle fleet. Finally, some concluding comments and policy recommendations are provided in Section 13.8.

13.2   Background

Most of the factors considered to be important determinants of crash fatalities have been investigated using econometric models based on classical methods. These models have attempted to examine whether various potential crash determinants had significant statistical effects on fatalities and to provide a measure of their marginal effects. Many of these determinants are reviewed in Loeb et al. (1994, 2009). The models have often followed the classic approach suggested by Peltzman (1975). His model is of particular interest given that he was concerned with the potential offsetting behavior of drivers as they adjusted their driving behavior in the face of various imposed regulations by the state. For example, one can recognize that drivers (as well as other members of society) have a given risk tolerance. If seat belts were required by law, risk imposed on the driver might be reduced, all else equal. However, drivers might then increase other risk behaviors, such as driving faster, which might not only affect their vehicle, but impose additional risks on, for example, pedestrians. (A related alternative question might enquire as to whether drivers compensate for factors which may increase risk, e.g. using a cell phone or texting while driving.) In any case, many factors have been evaluated by econometric models and not all of them have provided consistent results which might be expected from economic theory, public heath experiences and various previous statistical studies viewing the same determinants. Differences between studies may be due to, for example, the use of different models, different estimation techniques, data differences, and changes which occur over time. As suggested above, the examined factors affecting safety are numerous. Some of the more significant ones (although not all of them) are reviewed below.

Motor vehicle inspection has been imposed in different degrees by many states over the last several decades. The catalyst for these regulations stems from the Highway Safety Act of 1966 which set standards for inspection and used the threat of withholding federal highway funds for noncompliance. In 1976, Congress relaxed its position regarding the imposition of state inspections. Numerous studies were conducted over time on the effectiveness of inspection on safety resulting in varying conclusions. Crain (1980), for example, did not find strong statistical results suggesting the effectiveness of inspection. Garbacz and Kelly (1987) also did not find reason to support vehicle inspection. These results were countered by other investigators including, Loeb (1985, 1988, 1990) and Loeb and Gilad (1984), among others.[12] The reason for such different results may be due to model uncertainty and different time regimes under investigation. To address some of this, Loeb often made use of specification error analysis to minimize the likelihood of model misspecification. In more recent work using Bayesian methods, Blattenberger et al. (2012) found the effects of inspection to be fragile. However, the efficacy of inspection may also have changed over time as the age of the fleet, and hence the technologies available, changed. Keeler (1994) finds some evidence for this where inspection is found efficacious using data for the period 1970 but not so using data for 1980.

Speed and later speed variance were considered major factors contributing to crash-related injuries and deaths. Speed adds to utility by diminishing travel time and, at least for some, provides thrills. Yet, it is argued that speed comes at a price of increasing the probability of crashes and deaths. This has been found to be the case in papers, for example, by Peltzman (1975), Forester et al. (1984), Zlatoper (1984), Sommers (1985), and Loeb (1987, 1988), among others. However, Lave (1985) has argued that it is primarily speed variance as opposed to vehicle speed itself which is the speed-related factor contributing to fatalities. Levy and Asch (1989) and Snyder (1989) found some evidence for this as well. In addition, Fowles and Loeb (1989) using Bayesian methods found support for both speed and speed variance.

Speed limits have also been investigated as contributors to crashes especially after the Arab Oil Embargo in 1973. Statistical results varied among studies depending on model specifications and data used. Contributing effects have been found by Forester et al. (1984) and Loeb (1991), among others. However, speed limits have been found also to reduce measures of crash fatalities by Garbacz and Kelly (1987) and Loeb (1990). More variable results are found, for example, in Keeler (1994), Blattenberger et al. (2012), and Fowles et al. (2010).

---

[12] See Loeb et al. (1994) for a more complete review of the literature.

The effect of alcohol use has almost uniformly been found to have significant effects on motor vehicle crashes in recent research. This result is found both using classical as well as Bayesian methods as seen in Loeb et al. (2009), Fowles et al. (2010), and Blattenberger et al. (2012), among others.[13] The effect of the minimum legal drinking age has also been investigated with varying results. For example, Sommers (1985) found a negative relationship between the minimum legal drinking age and fatality rates, while more recently, Blattenberger et al. (2012) and Fowles et al. (2010) find fragile results regarding the effect of the minimum legal drinking age on crash-related fatalities.[14]

Related to alcohol consumption itself has been an analysis of the use of varying blood alcohol thresholds to determine if a driver is operating a vehicle under the influence. Recently, some evidence has been found by Loeb et al. (2009) indicating more severe limits on blood alcohol concentration (BAC) to designate driving while impaired reduced vehicle fatalities. Some additional evidence of this can be found from a Bayesian perspective in Blattenberger et al. (2013) using extreme bounds analysis (EBA).

An interesting observation was found by Fowles and Loeb (1992) when examining the effects of alcohol on motor vehicle-related crashes. They found evidence that altitude intensifies the adverse effect of alcohol on highway safety. This may be due to the fact that at higher altitudes, oxygen intake is less than at lower altitudes and may adversely impact reaction time.[15]

Seat belts (and airbags) have been shown to have life-saving and injury reducing attributes. Researchers have estimated that seat belts have the potential to reduce fatalities by 40% or more.[16] Seat belt laws, both primary and secondary, have been imposed so as to induce the driving public to wear belts. New York was the first state to impose a seat belt law and currently 34 states and the District of Columbia have primary seat belt laws and 15 states have secondary laws.[17] The laws vary further from state to state with respect to who must wear a belt (front seat versus all seats) and the fine structures imposed for violating the law. Numerous studies have been conducted regarding the efficacy of these laws. Most early studies found seat belt laws reduced various measures of fatalities and injuries. These include studies by Campbell and Campbell (1986), Campbell et al. 1986 ,1987), Hatfield and Hinshaw (1987), Hoxie and Skinner (1987), Lund et al. (1987), Reinfurt et al. (1988), Skinner and Hoxie (1988), Streff et al. (1989), and Loeb (1991). Womble (1989), however, did not find necessarily a uniform reduction in injury rates due to seat belt laws depending on the types of injuries investigated. More recently, Cohen and Einav (2003) found additional evidence of the efficaciousness of mandatory seat belt laws and, in particular, the benefits of primary laws. Additional evidence on the effectiveness of seat belt laws

[13] See Loeb et al. (1994) for a review of earlier work including those resulting in opposite or insignificant results.

[14] See Loeb et al. (1994) for additional reviews.

[15] See Newman (1949) and Mazess et al. (1968).

[16] See Partyka (1988) and Evans (1991).

[17] See Governors Highway Safety Association (2015).

is provided from a classical probability perspective by Fowles et al. (2010) where a statistically significant effect is found. However, from a Bayesian perspective, both Blattenberger et al. (2012, 2013) and Fowles et al. (2010) found fragile results.

Measures of income have been of particular interest to economists and public policy makers. Assuming that driving intensity and safety are both normal goods, then the demand for each should increase with income. Peltzman (1975) argued that income would have an ambiguous impact on crashes given their offsetting effects.[18] The net effect of income would then depend on the relative strengths of these offsetting effects. In addition, Peltzman argued that different types of income would have different effects on crashes, for example, transitory income should have a lesser life-saving effect than an equal amount of permanent income. Furthermore, one might expect different results from models based on time-series data (possibly portraying short-run effects) as opposed to models based on cross-section data (possibly portraying long-run effects).[19] The bottom line is then an empirical matter. Recently, Blattenberger et al. (2012) found a positive and significant effect of real income per household on fatality rates with additional support from several Bayesian methods.

Time trends have also been incorporated in many models to adjust for changes in technology and to proxy permanent income.

Additional normalizing variables included in past studies have been: population characteristics, measures of poverty and unemployment, and measures of education. Regarding population, researchers are concerned not only with the size of the population, which may be highly correlated with other factors such as income and a time trend, but the age distribution of the population as well. One might speculate that youthful drivers are more likely to be involved in crashes due to a lack of experience. Asch and Levy (1987), Garbacz (1990), Loeb (1990), and Saffer and Grossman (1987a, b) are examples of studies finding a relationship between youthful drivers and measures of fatalities. However, McCarthy (1992) and Loeb (1985) find a significant negative relationship between youthful driving and fatality or injury measures. From a Bayesian Extreme Bounds perspective, Blattenberger et al. (2013) found fragile results with respect to the percent of young males in the population on motor vehicle fatality rates.

Education levels, crime rates, and suicide rates were also examined with regard to an association with crash fatalities. One might argue that higher levels of education are associated with greater stocks of human capital which would be expected to be inversely related to crash fatalities. This has been investigated by various researchers, for example, Blattenberger et al. (2012), indicating a negative association between college education rates and crash fatalities.

Miles driven and types of roadways have also been examined by various researchers. Loeb et al. (1994) review many of the early statistical studies where evidence suggests safety associated with urban interstate mileage. However, some more recent studies, for example, by Loeb et al. (2009), do not find a statistically significant effect on total vehicle fatalities due to interstate highway mileage.

---

[18] See Peltzman (1975) and Loeb et al. (1994) for a discussion.

[19] See Loeb et al. (1994) for a review of this literature.

Weather and daylight conditions have been examined as well. Most notably, Coate and Markowitz (2004) found that moving to daylight savings time is associated with a reduction in both pedestrian and occupant fatalities.

Hospital access, the price of an accident, insurance attributes, and geographical locations have also been examined.[20] More notably, numerous studies have been conducted regarding the deregulatory effect of the 1980s on safety. Even airline deregulation has been shown to have an impact on motor vehicle fatalities. Bylow and Savage (1991), for example, have shown that deregulation of the airlines led to a reduction in motor vehicle deaths between 1978 and 1988. Perhaps of more interest was the impact of the deregulation of the trucking industry by the Motor Carrier Act of 1980. Concern arose regarding the potential increase in crashes associated with this act. Statistical models, such as those reported by Loeb and Clarke (2007) found no significant impact of deregulation on truck safety. In addition, there was concern that the deregulation of the railroad industry by the Staggers Act of 1980 might have resulted in more fatalities, including those at grade crossings involving motor vehicles. Clarke and Loeb (2005) did not find statistical evidence supporting this using their econometric models.[21]

More recently, safety researchers have been addressing the impact of cell phone use and availability on motor vehicle crashes. In addition, the age of the fleet and the relationship of suicidal propensities have gained increased interest in transportation safety. It is these three factors which we focus on next.

It is argued that cell phone usage leads to crashes for several reasons. Cell phones are considered to have a distracting effect on drivers and to diminish attention spans and increase reaction time. Furthermore, the number of cell phone subscribers, and hence usage rate, has increased exponentially over the last two decades. More specifically, the number of cell phone subscribers has increased from about 340 thousand in 1985 to more than 310 million in 2010.[22] Not only has the number of cell phones increased dramatically over time, but the propensity of drivers to use them has also increased. Glassbrenner (2005) has estimated that 10% of all drivers are using a cell phone while operating their vehicles during daylight hours. As such, 14 states plus the District of Columbia have banned the use of hand-held phones by drivers (California, Connecticut, Delaware, Hawaii, Illinois, Maryland, Nevada, New Hampshire, New Jersey, New York, Oregon, Vermont, Washington, and West Virginia).[23]

Statistical evaluations of the effects of cell phones on crashes have not always provided consistent results. The study by Redelmeier and Tibshirani (1997) is perhaps the most well-known early study of the effect of cell phones on motor vehicle crashes. They attribute a fourfold increase in property-only crashes to the use of cell phones. Violanti (1998) attributes a ninefold increase in fatalities to the use of cell phones and McEvoy et al. (2005) also find an increase in risk from cell phones. Neyens and Boyle (2007) found that cell phones increased the likelihood of rear-end collisions relative

---

[20] See Loeb et al. (1994) for a review of some part of this literature.

[21] See Loeb et al. (1994) for reviews of other studies on truck, air, and railroad deregulation.

[22] See CTIA—The Wireless Association (2011). By December 2015, the number of wireless subscriber connections rose to 377.9 million as per CTIA–The Wireless Association (2016).

[23] Strangely, the bans do not include hands-free devices even though research indicates that such devices have a similar adverse effect. See, for example, Consiglio et al. (2003).

to fixed-object collisions amongst teenage drivers. In addition, Consiglio et al. (2003) using a laboratory environment found that brake reaction time was increased when cell phones were in use, regardless of whether they were hand-held or -free devices. Similarly, Beede and Kass (2006), using a laboratory environment, also found that hands-free devices adversely affected driving performance. These results are what one would expect a priori. However, not all empirical results are consistent with the above.

Laberge-Nadeau et al. (2003) using logistic regression and Canadian data initially found a relationship between cell phone use and crashes. However, this risk diminished as their basic models were extended. The life-taking effect of cell phones were countered as well by Chapman and Schoefield (1998) who argued that cell phones should be credited with saving lives instead of taking them. They found that, "Over one in eight current mobile phone users have used their phones to report a road accident."[24] They attribute this beneficial effect of cell phones to the "golden hour," the time period crucial for survivorship from various medical emergencies and crashes which cell phones could affect. Hence, given a crash, the probability of survivorship is influenced by the speed with which help can be obtained. Sufficient cell phones in the hands of the public increases the likelihood of medical help arriving at the scene of the crash promptly. Sullman and Baas (2004) added to these investigations using survey data pertaining to crashes of all levels of severity. They did not find a significant correlation between cell phone use and crash involvement after normalizing for demographics and other factors. Similarly, Poysti et al. (2005) claim that, "phone-related accidents have not increased in line with the growth of the mobile phone industry."[25]

These convoluting results led to studies by Loeb et al. (2009) and Loeb and Clarke (2009) using classical econometrics where cell phones were found to have a nonlinear effect on crash-related fatalities: initially associated with an increase in such fatalities with low volumes of cell phone subscribers, a decrease in fatalities as cell phone subscribers rose over time, and then an increase of fatalities as cell phone subscriptions rose substantially again later on. Blattenberger et al. (2012) and Fowles et al. (2010), using Bayesian methods, demonstrated a relationship between cell phones and crash fatalities as well.[26]

The age of the fleet has also been of interest to investigators. One would anticipate that an aging fleet would be associated with more crashes as vehicle parts wear out, all else equal. Further, older fleets do not avail themselves to newer technologies which may mitigate accidents (provided they are not offset by additional risks taken by drivers). The age of the fleet has been investigated to some extent with mixed results previously.[27] However, the age of the fleet may prove to be of greater importance as autonomous/driverless cars become relevant as a percent of the fleet in the future.

Suicide rates have rarely been used as a potential determinant of crash fatalities. Recently, however, Blattenberger et al. (2012) examined the effect of suicide rates on crash fatalities as a way of controlling for factors not already addressed in their

[24] See Chapman and Schoefield (1998, p. 817).

[25] See Poysti et al. (2005, p. 50).

[26] See also Fowles et al. (2013).

[27] See Loeb et al. (1994) and Blattenberger et al. (2013).

models and to potentially account for unexplained societal characteristics over time. They found that suicide rates had a statistically significant effect on fatalities from both a classical and a Bayesian perspective. This possibly unexpected result, from some researchers' perspective, is not completely without prior statistical evidence. For example, Phillips (1979) examined the importance of imitation and suggestion and found that there was a 31% increase in automobile fatalities three days following a publicized suicide.[28] Pokorny et al. (1972) also claim a relationship between suicide and fatal automobile crashes. Porterfield (1960) also found a strong correlation between suicides and motor vehicle fatalities. He summarized that, "Whatever factors play a part in the positive correlation of suicide, …, and accident death rates, there is no reason to doubt that aggressive, hazardous driving is likely to be a characteristic of persons similar to those who have suicidal … tendencies …."[29] Along these lines, Conner et al. (2001) utilizing a case–control method observe violent behaviors to be consistent for persons exhibiting suicidal tendencies. More recently, Murray and DeLeo (2007) used Australian data from the Gold Coast Suicide Prevention Community Survey to examine suicide attempts by drivers. In a sample of 1196 respondents with a history of suicidal ideation or behavior, they found 412 individuals (14.8%) who planned or made arrangements to commit suicide using a motor vehicle. The authors conclude "that the percentage of individuals who have planned or attempted suicide through a motor vehicle collision is high, …"[30] However, the association between suicides and automobile crashes is not consistent among studies. Some studies have not found a uniformly strong relationship, for example, Connolly et al. (1995), Huffine (1971), and Souetre (1988). Others, for example, Etzerdorfer (1995), indicate the difficulty which arises in determining whether a crash victim was indeed a suicide.

The effect of suicides on other modes of transportation has also been investigated to some extent. Some association has been found regarding suicides and aircraft use, but the numbers appear small.[31] Meanwhile, the relationship between suicides and railroad-related fatalities with respect to trespassers has been investigated recently by Savage (2007, 2010). Although there is difficulty in determining the exact number of suicides, the author suggests a rather large proportion of trespasser deaths are associated with suicide. Clearly the suicide–automobile crash link is controversial with mixed empirical findings. Yet, we consider it of interest not only in serving as a measure of societal risk-taking propensities, but also in taking cognizance that it may minimize the stigma associated with attempting suicide since it may appear that such deaths were due to traditional traffic crashes. In addition, suicides committed by motor vehicles may have potential economic effects for the families of the deceased due to insurance benefits.

[28] Phillips (1977) had earlier found a 9.12% average increase in motor vehicle fatalities following front-page newspaper suicide stories in California.

[29] In Porterfield (1960, p. 900).

[30] Murray and DeLeo (2007, p. 246).

[31] See, for example, Bills et al. (2005), Cullen (1998), and Lewis et al. (2007).

Along with suicide rates, there are extraordinarily large numbers of potential contributors to crash fatalities. Many have been suggested by economic theory, some based on conventional wisdom along with statistical studies, as noted above. Some of the contributing factors, such as alcohol, have been consistently found to be major determining factors. Others, such as motor vehicle inspection, have been found to have fragile effects. These may be due to the types of models investigated, the data sets, and changes over time. Hence, over time, various factors have been added to and others deleted from models of crash fatalities. Importantly, there is no one model. As such, there is reason to believe that classical estimation lends itself to purposeful data mining and, more importantly, parameter and model uncertainty. How one selects a model, or a group of models, as true, is often ambiguous at best. For these reasons, explorations are made in this paper over many models with the goal to provide statistically reliable and inferentially meaningful results. Such a statistical procedure must account for both model ambiguity and the uncertainty associated with parameter estimation. This is the focus of the current paper which is conducted making use of a new Bayesian econometric method developed by Leamer (2016) which is ideally suited to deal with the problem of model ambiguity and parameter uncertainly. Model uncertainty/ambiguity is an inferential problem difficult to address via conventional methods which require a single posited model being true that forms the basis of the observed data generating process.

13.3 Data

We utilize a newly compiled set of data collected on 50 states and Washington, DC over the period from 1980 to 2010.[32] The number of fatalities per 100 million vehicle miles traveled is our dependent variable. Our choice of explanatory variables is based on a rich literature (reviewed in Section 13.2) highlighting the importance of policy, safety, demographic, and economic determinants of fatality rates. Issues related to the choice of these variables, as well as the general form of the models, are well described in Blattenberger et al. (2009, 2012, 2013), Fowles et al. (2010), and Loeb et al. (2009). These form the basis for the "prior" used in the Bayesian analysis in this paper.

Our data cover years during which there were significant changes in several important variables that are a priori plausible predictors of fatalities. A new series includes the median age of cars in states to account for the fact that some fleet ages are older (e.g. in Montana) and some ages are newer (e.g. in Connecticut). Over the span of our data, this series is designed to quantify improvements in automobile safety. The data also capture the explosive growth in cell phone subscriptions from effectively zero to over 300 million. Annual subscription data at the state level were only available beginning in year 2000. For the earlier years, we used national-level data and

---

[32] We are grateful to Christopher Fowles for his assistance in collecting the data.

imputed state-level subscriptions to be proportional to state population proportions for the prior years.[33] Another major change observed in the data relates to changes in Federal law that allowed individual states to modify the 55-mile per hour speed limit on their interstate highways. Our data record the highest posted urban interstate speed limit that was in effect during the year for each state. Within the data, per se BAC laws vary widely, even though by 2005 all states and the District of Columbia had mandated a 0.08 BAC illegal per se law.[34] Seat belt legislation varies widely across states. Our data records the years in which a state mandatory primary or secondary seat belt law came into effect. Additionally, the data allow us to examine the effects of education and poverty on motor vehicle fatality rates. These are of particular interest given the review of the literature in Section 13.2. However, we concentrate, in particular, on four variables: cell phones, age of the fleet as measured by the median car model year, and suicidal propensities, along with alcohol consumption. The data are organized by geographical coding of states into 11 regions. The variables are defined and described in Table 13.1 along with their expected effects (priors) on fatality rates.[35]

13.4 Classical econometric results

Various specifications of the form

$$Y = X\beta + \mu \tag{13.1}$$

are estimated using ordinary least-squares (OLS) method. The full ideal conditions[36] are expected to be upheld where $b = (X^TX)^{-1}X^TY$ and

$$\mu \sim N(0, \sigma^2 I) \tag{13.2}$$

with Y as the vector of fatality rates and X as the matrix of explanatory variables whose composition conceivably varies across specified models.

   Table 13.2 presents regression results starting from a very simplistic model using only four core variables (with constant and regional dummies) and extending to a more fully inclusive model with all of the variables in Table 13.1 included.[37] The

---

[33] Our method of imputing cell phone subscriptions correlates with the actual data with a correlation coefficient of 0.9943.

[34] The per se law refers to legislation that makes it illegal to drive a vehicle at a blood alcohol level at or above the specified BAC level. BAC is measured in grams per deciliter.

[35] See Blattenberger et al. (2009).

[36] See Ramsey (1974) and Ramsey and Zarembka (1971).

[37] Subsets of these models have been investigated in prior research for specification errors of omission of variables, misspecification of the structural form of the regressors, simultaneous equation bias, serial correlation, and nonnormality of the error term and found to be in compliance with the Full Ideal Conditions. See, for example, Loeb et al. (2009).

results are generally in compliance with our a priori expectations. Most notably, with regard to our core variables, all four (beer, cell phones, suicides, and the median car model year) are stable in terms of the sign of their respective coefficients and all are statistically significant at a 1% significance level. As such, these specifications, which are based on economic theory and previous statistical results and have been verified using a new panel data set, provide a basis for the Bayesian analysis which follows.

Table 13.1 Explanatory Variables[a] Cross-Sectional—Time Series Analysis of Traffic Fatality Rates For 50 States and DC from 1980 to 2010

Name	Description	Expected sign
MCMY	Median car model year divided by 1000	−
PERSE	Dummy variable indicating the existence of a law defining intoxication of a driver in terms of blood alcohol concentration (BAC). PERSE = 1 indicates the existence of such a law and PERSE = 0 indicates the absence of such a law. (More precisely, PERSE = 1 when the BAC indicating driving under the influence is 0.1 or lower.)	−
SPEEDHI	Maximum posted speed limit, urban interstate highways	+
BELT	Indicator for presence of a legislated seat belt law	−
BEER	Per capita beer consumption (in gal) per year	+
MLDA	Minimum legal drinking age	−
YOUNG	Percentage of males (16–24) relative to population of age 16 and over	+
CELLPOP	Number of cell phone subscribers per capita	+
POVERTY	Poverty rate (percentage)	+
UNEMPLOY	Unemployment rate (percentage)	−
REALINC	Real per household income in 2000 dollars	?
EDHS	Percent of persons with a high school diploma	−
EDCOLL	Percent of persons with a college degree	−
SUICIDE	Suicide rate (suicides per 100,000 population)	?

[a]For data sources, see Appendix A.

Table 13.2 **Subsets of OLS Estimates[a] Cross-Sectional—Time Series Analysis of Traffic Fatality Rates For 50 States and DC from 1980 to 2010**

Variable	Model 1		Model 2		Model 3	
	Estimate	t-Stat	Estimate	t-Stat	Estimate	t-Stat
MCMY	−0.0111	−36.04	−0.0975	−19.39	−0.080	−14.57
PERSE			−0.198	−5.62	−0.160	−4.92
SPEEDHI			0.006	2.58	0.001	0.458
BELT			−0.084	−2.26	−0.018	−0.548
BEER	0.290	5.77	0.307	6.17	0.443	9.474
MLDA			−0.012	−0.76	−0.003	−0.228
YOUNG					2.510	5.802
CELLPOP	0.010	14.56	0.085	9.34	0.007	6.865
POVERTY					0.028	8.128
UN-EMPLOY					−0.039	−7.485
REALINC					0.00001	1.794
EDHS					−0.008	−2.958
EDCOLL					−0.023	−7.265
SUICIDE	0.040	8.55	0.039	8.47	0.023	4.686

[a]A constant and regional variable dummies included but not reported.

13.5 Bayesian S-values and the determinants of motor vehicle fatality rates

Although it is common to indicate regression results for a variety of model specifications, reported statistics are valid on the presumption of a given model's truth. In practice, alternative tests are made on competing models, each sequentially assumed to be true. Inferences based on sequential search procedures are fraught with problems regarding the statistical validity of models' reported summary statistics. Bayesian theory, however, can directly address both estimation uncertainty and model ambiguity. In this paper, we utilize advances in Bayesian research regarding model choice as discussed, for example, in Key et al. (1999) and Clyde (1999). An early investigator in model uncertainty was Leamer (1978, 1982, 1983, 1985, 1997) who, in a book and series of articles, dealt with specification searches.

One Bayesian approach that addresses model uncertainty is EBA developed by Leamer (1978). It is a methodology of global sensitivity analysis that computes the possible maximum and minimum values for Bayesian posterior means in the context of linear regression models.[38] One might think of this as an examination of the stability or lack of fragility of coefficients associated with the variables we are focusing on across a multitude of linear models which differ in terms of the different combinations of regressors included which would provide up to 2^k different models, where k is the number of regressors including the constant, but possibly omitting the variables we are focusing on. This set of models using our data can easily exceed several million.[39] The global bounds are illustrated in Fig. 13.1 for a two-variable regression model. A typical likelihood ellipse is centered at the OLS estimate. The other ellipse is the same shape and passes through the origin (the prior mean) and the OLS estimate. It contains the set of possible posterior means that could be obtained for all prior variance matrices that are positive-definite. This larger ellipse is called the feasible ellipse and highlights a main drawback of EBA: that bounds are very wide. In this example, only the second quadrant (negative Beta 1 and positive Beta 2) is excluded as a joint region that could contain the posterior mean. Marginally, both Beta 1 and Beta 2 are fragile in the sense that there exist prior variance matrices that could result in negative or positive posterior estimates for either variable.

That the coefficients for all variables in a regression are necessarily fragile from a global EBA perspective highlights the importance of the prior variance. We incorporate a new perspective on the prior variance developed by Leamer (2014, 2016). S-values (sturdiness statistics) reveal aspects of parameter fragility for minimally specified prior variance matrices that "tame" the global bounds from EBA. Fig. 13.2 illustrates how S-values are obtained for a two-variable regression problem. As in Fig. 13.1, we plot typical likelihood ellipses that are centered at the OLS estimate. There are also two circles centered at the origin that represent two iso-prior probability contours that would result from a prior that is centered at zero with spherically symmetric prior variances. The points of tangencies trace the posterior mean from zero to the OLS point. From a non-Bayesian perspective, this is exactly the ridge regression trace (Hoerl and Kennard, 1970). If the prior variance increases, the posterior mean will fall closer to the OLS point and if the prior variance decreases, the mean falls closer to the origin.

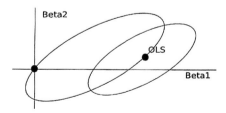

Figure 13.1 Bayesian EBA Example.

[38] Mathematical developments are found in Leamer (1982).

[39] See, for example, Leamer (1978, 1982, 1983) and Blattenberger et al. (2012, 2013).

Two middle points are associated with two values of the prior variance. These values translate to prior R^2 (variance).[40] The larger prior R^2 gives more weight to the explanatory variables in the model, and thus the trace is closer to the OLS point. In Fig. 13.2, there is also a shaded ellipse that contains the possible posterior means associated with all linear combination of the two explanatory variables. Here, notice that the limits for Beta 2 are fragile, but that the limits for Beta 1 are unambiguously positive. The extreme values for means within such an ellipse form the basis for S-values which are computed as the midpoint of the extremes divided by half their length.

As suggested by Leamer (2014, 2016), useful prior R^2 are associated with values of 0.1–1 (wide), 0.1–0.5 (pessimistic), and 0.5–1 (optimistic). A pessimistic belief is that the explanatory variables would not account for much of the variation in the dependent variable whereas an optimistic belief is that they do and thus the prior defers to the data.[41]

Table 13.3 summarizes the findings for our variables of interest based on standardized data.[42] The column "Simple" (column 11) regresses the fatality rate on only the one specified explanatory variable and measures the pairwise correlation between the two variables. Leamer argues that these simple correlations "are a feature of the data, while the "partial" regression coefficients are cooked up by the analyst when he or she selects the control variables."[43] A different sign in the simple correlation and the partial correlation (column 12) then, "requires scrutiny."[44] It is here that S-values are particularly useful.

Columns 2–7 provide lower and upper extreme values for the three specified prior variances. Columns 2 and 3 provide the extreme values for the wide prior (prior R^2

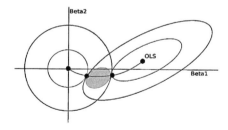

Figure 13.2 Bayesian S-value Example.

Table 13.3 **Coefficients, Bounds, and S-values for US Fatality Rates**[a]

	R^2 0.1 to 1 (wide)		R^2 0.1 to 0.5 (pessimistic)		R^2 0.5 to 1 (optimistic)		Wide S-value	Pessimistic S-value	Optimistic S-value	OLS simple	OLS All	t-Stat All
	Lower	Upper	Lower	Upper	Lower	Upper						
MCMY	**−0.7757**	**−0.3993**	**−0.7185**	**−0.4073**	**−0.7246**	**−0.6600**	**−3.122**	**−3.618**	**−21.436**	−0.709	−0.777	**−14.554**
PERSE	**−0.0834**	**−0.0504**	**−0.0812**	**−0.0527**	**−0.0683**	**−0.0638**	**−4.048**	**−4.696**	**−29.384**	−0.413	−0.066	**−4.916**
SPEEDHI	−0.0353	0.0276	−0.0325	0.0215	−0.0019	0.0071	−0.122	−0.204	0.581	−0.210	0.008	0.458
BELT	−0.0815	0.0014	**−0.0789**	**−0.0086**	**−0.0303**	**−0.0177**	−0.965	**−1.246**	**−3.786**	−0.581	−0.011	−0.548
BEER	**0.1154**	**0.1547**	**0.1186**	**0.1524**	**0.1307**	**0.1361**	**6.873**	**8.015**	**48.716**	0.325	0.132	**9.440**
MLDA	−0.0430	0.0040	**−0.0415**	**−0.0016**	**−0.0139**	**−0.0069**	−0.832	**−1.082**	**−2.948**	−0.472	−0.003	−0.227
YOUNG	**0.0762**	**0.1358**	**0.0831**	**0.1335**	**0.0930**	**0.1023**	**3.555**	**4.303**	**20.986**	0.318	0.090	**5.793**
CELLPOP	**0.0173**	**0.3093**	**0.0252**	**0.2669**	**0.2077**	**0.2576**	**1.118**	**1.208**	**9.335**	−0.568	0.293	**6.862**
POVERTY	**0.1013**	**0.1679**	**0.1044**	**0.1615**	**0.1380**	**0.1475**	**4.046**	**4.659**	**30.231**	0.452	0.148	**8.125**
UN-EMPLOY	**−0.1153**	**−0.0709**	**−0.1101**	**−0.0723**	**−0.1054**	**−0.0989**	**−4.200**	**−4.829**	**−31.211**	0.320	−0.108	**−7.472**
REALINC	−0.0335	0.1420	−0.0196	0.1289	**0.0475**	**0.0746**	0.618	0.736	**4.505**	−0.687	0.058	1.792
EDHS	**−0.2148**	**−0.0503**	**−0.2076**	**−0.0689**	**−0.1238**	**−0.0981**	**−1.612**	**−1.994**	**−8.624**	−0.688	−0.091	**−2.957**
EDCOLL	**−0.2517**	**−0.1132**	**−0.2394**	**−0.1218**	**−0.2039**	**−0.1830**	**−2.635**	**−3.071**	**−18.503**	−0.686	−0.199	**−7.250**
SUICIDE	**0.0590**	**0.1511**	**0.0663**	**0.1450**	**0.0961**	**0.1095**	**2.283**	**2.687**	**15.355**	0.345	0.101	**4.657**

[a]S-values are obtained by simply taking the ratio of sum of the lower and upper bounds to the difference between them. Bold values indicate nonfragile bounds, S-values greater than 1 in absolute value, and t-statistics greater than 2 in absolute value.

from 0.1 to 1); columns 4 and 5—the pessimistic prior (prior R^2 from 0.1 to 0.5); and columns 6 and 7—the optimistic prior (prior R^2 from 0.5 to 1). S-values are provided in columns 8–10. Column 8 provides S-values associated with the wide prior; column 9 the values associated with the pessimistic prior; and column 10 with the optimistic prior. Column 11 provides the "simple" regression result while columns 12 and 13 provide the OLS coefficients and associated t-values.

The bold values in Table 13.3 highlight aspects of model and parameter uncertainty/ambiguity. There are eight variables, that is, MCMY, PERSE, BEER, YOUNG, POVERTY, EDHS, EDCOLL, and SUICIDE for which all values are in bold. For these variables, the signs of parameters are always the same, the absolute value of the S-values are always greater than one (in absolute value) and the absolute values of the t-statistics are greater than 2. These eight variables exhibit the highest level of sturdiness. CELLPOP shows sturdiness on the basis of S-values, on conformity of S-values with t-statistics, as well as nonfragility of all bounds. However, there is sign switching when viewing the SIMPLE correlation and the coefficient in the full model. This result is due to an aspect of falling fatality rates when cell phones became popular. Again, when other control variables are introduced, CELLPOP is regarded as a sturdy variable. Also, UNEMPLOY may be considered sturdy in spite of the sign switch when comparing the "SIMPLE" correlation and the coefficient in the full model given the stability of all bounds, the S-values being greater than 1 in absolute value, the sign associated with its coefficient in the full model, and its large t-value (in absolute value). Hence there are up to 10 variables which may be considered sturdy.

For non-Bayesians, Table 13.3 also demonstrates that there is agreement between calculated S-values and t-statistics.[45] Notice that the variable REALINC has a large S-value (column 10) and a small t-statistic, that is, less than 2 (column 13). This is due to the fact that the bounds for the optimistic prior are not fragile. If one is dubious that REALINC is an important explanatory variable, then its bounds are fragile (when considering the wide prior and pessimistic prior) and the corresponding S-values are shown to be less than 1. An important feature of this reporting style is that each reader can come to the table with his or her own attitude towards the importance of the variable shown.

These relationships from Table 13.3 are illustrated in Fig. 13.3 with horizontal lines at ±2 (significant) and vertical lines at ±1 (sturdy). Variables in the northeast and southwest quadrants are associated with more certain and sturdy estimates.

13.6 Some additional insights on the relative importance of explanatory variables

By using standardized data and our OLS regression results, we can assess the relative importance of each explanatory variable from a classical perspective as shown in Fig. 13.4.[46] It is important to note that the most important variables selected, that is,

---

[45] For the prior R^2 at 1, the correlation is 0.8877.

[46] See Table 12.2, Model 3 for the basis for this specification using raw data. All variables are standardized to mean 0 and variance 1 so as to allow unit-free comparisons.

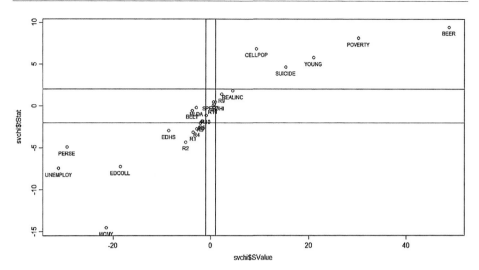

Figure 13.3 *t*-Statistics and S-values.

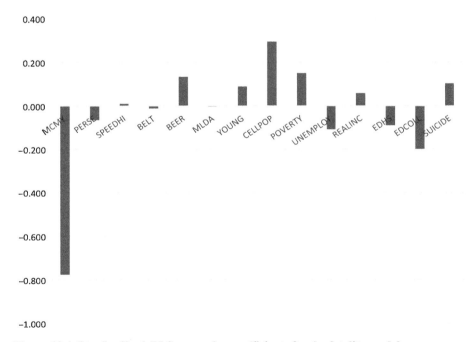

Figure 13.4 Standardized OLS regression coefficients for the fatality model specification.

those with the greatest impact, include those which we have considered as our focus variables. Once again, they entail measures of: the age of the fleet (the newness of the fleet), cell phone usage, suicidal propensities, and alcohol use. Furthermore, we find these factors are selected from a Bayesian S-value perspective as well.

The foremost variable in terms of classical regression using standardized data is MCMY which highlights how improvements in automobile safety have had a pronounced effect on lowering fatality rates. The statistical results using standardized data show the unambiguous effect of vehicle modernization on reducing fatality rates. Clearly, autonomous vehicles will make up larger and larger proportions of the motor vehicle fleet and, as such, more and more drivers and passengers will be able to avail themselves to the anticipated safety associated with technologically advanced cars and trucks.

The next most important variable in terms of magnitudinal effects on fatality rates is cell phone use as measured by CELLPOP. One clearly expects the distraction effect of cell phone use to result in additional fatalities as demonstrated by Loeb et al. (2009) and Fowles et al. (2010). However, the relative size of this effect, as demonstrated in Fig. 13.4, might have been unexpected. Autonomous cars, once again, may prove quite effective in reducing motor vehicle fatality rates by allowing drivers to forgo the piloting of their vehicles while using phones or other distracting devices. This, of course assumes that drivers make use of the technology autonomous cars promise to bring to the driver's seat.

The model using normalized data then ranks the percent of the population with a college education, EDCOLL, followed by the poverty rate, POVERTY, in importance regarding effects on motor vehicle fatality rates. Obviously, driverless cars will not directly interact with these factors. However, there is an indirect association which will be explored in Section 8.

Alcohol consumption as measured by BEER is the next ranked factor affecting motor vehicle fatality rates. The importance of this factor on motor vehicle fatality rates has long been demonstrated.[47] Here, autonomous vehicles may truly result in major life saving should drivers who have consumed alcohol make use of the technology such vehicles could afford them.

Suicide and suicidal propensities have been shown to have an effect on motor vehicle fatality rates. Suicide statistics rank next in importance with respect to motor vehicle fatality rates. Fatality rates might be diminished by autonomous vehicles should they provide individuals with such propensities with time to consider their alternative behaviors and provide those with violent/aggressive tendencies an opportunity to forgo dangerous driving.

As such, our discussion regarding the relative importance of our four focus variables, using a single classically estimated equation and normalized data, suggests that these factors are relevant with regard to their effects on motor vehicle fatalities as measured by beta coefficients. Further, it is easy to recognize that these variables will be even more relevant with the coming driverless/autonomous car revolution. As noted in Section 13.1, Google and many car manufacturers and technology-related companies

---

[47] See, for example, Loeb et al. (2009), Fowles et al. (2010), and Fowles and Loeb (1992).

are heavily invested in this new technology and some autonomous vehicles are already in limited use, such as in Singapore. It is expected that many car manufacturers will have the technology as well as some vehicles in place within the US market by 2020 or 2021, if not earlier.

One can anticipate that the successful introduction of autonomous vehicles will contribute to the reduction of vehicle fatalities by removing the task of driving from those who might otherwise drive while under the influence of alcohol and other drugs, as well as those who might otherwise be distracted by the use of cell phones or other such distracting devices. Autonomous cars may also diminish the risk of crashes due to driving inexperience and alcohol use inexperience associated with youthful drivers or those with diminished reflex actions. We may also notice a decline in crashes and fatalities due to suicidal propensities should these proclivities serve as a proxy for greater risk taking on the part of individuals or society. The technology in driverless vehicles may even prevent aggressive and suicidal drivers from using their vehicles in a reckless manner.

The newness of the vehicle fleet, as portrayed in MCMY, has been shown, from the above classical analysis to have the major impact on vehicle-related fatality rates. As the fleet is modernized, one can anticipate that the proportion of autonomous vehicles on the roads will increase substantially. Assuming this technology proves to be as successful as anticipated and that would-be drivers make use of it without compensating with other risky behavior, a reduction in fatality rates and crashes should be observed.

The above discussed results, of course, are based on a single model using normalized data. Questions of model ambiguity and parameter uncertainty still need to be addressed. The Bayesian approach using Sturdy-values adds significantly to this discussion.

13.7 Some caveats

Autonomous/driverless cars promise to have many beneficial contributions. For more than a decade, various technologies have been introduced which benefit the public. They include cruise control, technologies to warn of lane swerving, automatic braking features to diminish the likelihood or rear-end collisions, assistance in parking, and others. More advances are clearly being tested and are on the way by the major auto manufacturers, companies such as Google and Uber, as well as by research teams at universities.

In addition, driverless vehicles allegedly will reduce environmental pollution, stress on drivers, allow for better use of drivers' time, and ameliorate parking difficulties in congested areas.

However, there are still many technicalities that need to be addressed so as to bring autonomous cars onto the roadway in a significant manner. The sheer technical advancements that need to be made are quite substantial.

Driverless vehicles require a combination of factors to operate efficiently and safely. Accurate global positioning system (GPS) needs to be put in place and continuously updated. That alone is a significant requirement for a country the size of the United

States. Laser rangefinders have to be improved so as not to be misguided by the environment, for example, by dust and the absorbency of the signal as it is directed at the horizon or asphalt. These vehicles may use cameras and they too can be affected by the brightness of light. Millimeter wave radar can discount overhead information and inertial measurement units can be affected by magnetic fields. Further, wheel odometry can be impacted by slippery roadways. In addition, other sensors may be incorporated in the guidance of these vehicles and they all need to interact properly with one another. There needs to be a ranking system whereby the machines can properly decide which system or systems to adhere to when there is not unanimity amongst them. This might be no small task.[48] Further, even if these technical difficulties can be addressed, there is the issue of how driverless cars are programmed so that they not only can interact with one another, but interact with driver-controlled vehicles and how drivers may interact with driverless ones. This problem may be an evolving one as the ratio of autonomous vehicles to driver operated vehicles changes over time.[49]

In addition to these technical challenges, there are legal, ethical, and moral issues to address. The technology will need to consider issues in which there are no sure winners, for example, when a decision needs to be made as to whether to run into another vehicle and perhaps put the occupants of the vehicle(s) in great danger or to strike a pedestrian. The moral and legal issues are compounded by the fact that traditional insurance for driving may change since, without a driver controlling the vehicle, will it be the car manufacturers, the technology providers, the government, or some combination who will be held liable. The liability issue is not a small one to address.[50]

13.8   Concluding comments

One of the most important statistical problems today is the task of variable selection in regression model choice.[51] Dealing with both parameter uncertainty and model ambiguity is a challenging endeavor due to the sheer magnitude of the number of models that need to be considered. In this paper, we have looked at a newly developed Bayesian method which addresses these issues with reference to variables thought to be related to motor vehicle fatalities in the United States. With our data, there are millions of potential model specifications. Sturdy-values are nicely suited to explore this high-dimensional model space to discover plausible model specifications. It allows for different opinions regarding the strength of belief one has on the importance of factors affecting, in our case, motor vehicle fatality rates. The procedure is based on solid probability and statistical theory and provides researchers with inferential tools that

---

[48] See Zoz Cannytrophic Design for the basis of this discussion with emphasis on hacking.

[49] Our discussion does not take into account the possibility that autonomous vehicles may increase the propensity of drivers to drink and/or use cell phones and other distracting devices. In the event that these vehicles have a systems failure, there may then be more vehicles being piloted by distracted drivers or those driving under the influence of alcohol.

[50] See Villasenor (2014) for a discussion on liability and the driverless car.

[51] See Breiman (2001).

are not a part of the non-Bayesian toolkit. As such, this technique adds considerable confidence to the results presented and to the policy measures suggested.

The S-values note the importance of MCMY as a fundamental determinant of crash-related fatalities. This result is consistent with both the Bayesian results (Table 13.3) and classical results (Figs. 13.3 and 13.4). Our estimates suggest that there would be a 64% decline in fatality rates if a state could modernize their cars by 7 years, which is about a 1 standard deviation change of MCMY in our sample.[52] We note in passing that Wyoming did exhibit a 55% decline in fatality rates coinciding with a fleet modernization of 7 years. Upgrading the fleet of motor vehicles is almost automatic through time as vehicles wear out and are replaced. The force of modernization is a potentially important policy recommendation. More specifically, the efficaciousness of government funded rebates and/or the reduction of taxes on newly purchased vehicles could be evaluated with respect to life-saving, injury-prevention, and property damage avoidance. The advent of autonomous vehicles, as outlined above, should be observed with the modernization of the fleet and should this technology prove efficacious, one should anticipate a life-saving effect and a reduction in crashes, especially as they reduce crashes due to distracted and inexperienced drivers and those who forgo driving due to alcohol use, etc.

Cell phone usage, as measured with CELLPOP, is also found to be nonfragile using Sturdy-values. As mentioned above, we would anticipate that autonomous vehicles would reduce crash-related fatalities when they replace drivers who may be disposed to using cell phones or other distracting devices. In addition, policies reducing the use of cell phones by drivers are advisable and are already enacted in 14 States and the District of Columbia with regard to hand-held phones. The extension of cell phone bans to include hands-free devices and a complete ban on text-messaging by all drivers across states is worthy of study. Also evaluating the effect of stricter police enforcement combined with different fine structures and educational announcements so as to limit cell phone use by drivers are potentially important areas of investigation.

Alcohol consumption remains unambiguously a major contributor to crash fatalities as seen by S-values. The issue of imposing stricter sanctions against drinking and driving via fines and stricter policing and the use of substance abuse treatment centers are worthy of additional investigation.[53] Once again, we would anticipate that autonomous vehicles may prove to be advantageous in reducing alcohol-related vehicle fatalities if they replace drivers who have been drinking, assuming alternative risk behaviors are not encouraged as drivers attempt to reach a given risk tolerance.

Of particular interest are our Bayesian results associated with suicides, especially considering that motor vehicle fatalities and suicides are among the leading causes of death among young persons in the United States.[54] Suicides have been found to be an issue in other areas of transportation safety, such as with respect to railroad-related

---

[52] See Blattenberger et al. (2013).

[53] See Chaloupka et al. (1993) and Freeborn and McManus (2007).

[54] See Centers for Disease Control and Prevention, National Center for Injury Prevention and Control (2012).

fatalities.[55] Our findings replicate earlier studies showing that the high suicide states are also the high motor vehicle fatality states.[56] As noted earlier, the association between these two variables is strong and is not generally well understood. It may well be the case that suicide rates represent changes in the risk-taking behavior by individuals and act in a manner similar to a companion variable to account for unobservable factors. A potential avenue of future research may be investigating the effectiveness of posting phone numbers/help lines for those in need of emotional/psychiatric assistance and/or investing public monies for additional psychiatric health care, or policies designed to reduce recklessness and violent behaviors.[57] Regardless, if suicidal propensities and risky driving are associated with one another, then driverless vehicles may also reduce crashes with drivers so motivated by preventing, at least some of, these risky behaviors.

S-values also indicate the importance of lowering BAC which indicates driving while impaired due to alcohol consumption. The results found are very stable and unambiguous. Autonomous vehicles may assist in taking alcohol affected drivers out of the driver's seat should the would-be driver allow the technology to drive on their behalf.

Similarly, the percentage of young males in the population is found to have a non-fragile effect of increasing motor vehicle fatality rates. Autonomous cars may prove to be very useful in reducing deaths due to inexperienced drivers.

The strength of the poverty link is most likely associated with fundamental infrastructural differences between high and low poverty states. Such differences can be manifest in improved highways, traffic enforcement, newer fleet age, and faster emergency response to vehicle crashes.[58]

Finally, the education variables are found to have significant and nonfragile effects on reducing crash-related fatality rates. This may be due to the association between education and income. Individuals with higher investments in education often earn higher incomes than their less educated counterparts. Such individuals may also be more likely to afford high tech autonomous vehicles as they enter the market which could then reduce fatalities, all else equal.

The results, in any case, found using S-values are supported by traditional classical methods on raw data as well as models using standardized data. However, the Bayesian S-values afford the reader of statistical evaluations, such as presented here, with a way of dealing with various degrees of ambiguity and uncertainty they are willing to entertain as priors to the investigation. Our results over various widely different degrees of uncertainty have found strong evidence on the effects of our focus variables as well as others. Autonomous vehicles hold the possibility of reducing motor vehicle-related fatalities based on this evidence provided technology and legal/moral issues can rise to the occasion.

[55] See, for example, Savage (2007).

[56] These are Region 9 states in our model.

[57] See Savage (2007) and Conner et al. (2001).

[58] These factors are well described in Cubbin and Smith (2002).

Dedication

We have never met Professor Keeler. But like most in the transportation fellowship, we know him quite well through his research, his membership in the Transportation and Public Utilities Group, and, of course, through his PhD students.

Our first interaction with Ted was via a phone call initiated by one of his former students, James Peoples. At the time we were involved in building econometric models dealing with transportation fatalities using specification error analysis. This was well within the purview of Ted's research and he invited us to present a seminar at the Institute of Transportation Studies at Berkley. This was in 1988. The paper was well received, but Ted was called out of town at the last minute.

Richard's and my work continued over the years merging classical econometrics with Bayesian techniques to address issues of risk and uncertainty in transportation safety models. We often investigated similar questions as those of interest to Ted. Our work addressed issues such as the efficacy of vehicle inspection and other factors on safety.

Over the years, we were not only influenced by Ted's careful academic research but by interacting with his many PhD students, often at meetings of the Transportation and Public Utilities Group and at the AEA meetings. It is clear that Professor Keeler expanded the horizon of our understanding of transportation safety not only through his own work, but by mentoring a continuous flow of transportation economists to carry on the tradition of expanding our portfolio of knowledge.

It was indeed a pleasure to nominate Professor Keeler for the Distinguished Member Award of the Transportation and Public Utilities Group in 2012. We look forward to finally meeting him in person at one of the many professional meetings we all attend.

Appendix A: Data sources

Name	Data source
FATAL	Highway Statistics (various years), Federal Highway Administration, Traffic Safety Facts (various years), National Highway Traffic Safety Administration
MCMY	National Automobile Dealers Association (various years) and the National Household Travel Survey, US Department of Transportation
PERSE	Digest of State Alcohol-Highway Safety Related Legislation (various years), Traffic Laws Annotated 1979, Alcohol and Highway Safety Laws: A National Overview 1980, National Highway Traffic Safety Administration
SPEEDHI	Highway Statistics (various years), Federal Highway Administration

Name	Data source
BELT	Traffic Safety Facts (various years), National Highway and Traffic Safety Administration
BEER	US Census Bureau, National Institute on Alcohol Abuse and Alcoholism
MLDA	A Digest of State Alcohol-Highway Safety Related Legislation (various years), Traffic Laws Annotated 1979, Alcohol and Highway Safety Laws: A National Overview of 1980, National Highway Traffic Safety Administration, US Census Bureau
YOUNG	State Population Estimates (various years), US Census Bureau http://www.census.gov/population/www/estimates/statepop.html
CELLPOP	Cellular Telecommunication and Internet Association Wireless Industry Survey, International Association for the Wireless Telecommunications Industry
POVERTY	Statistical Abstract of the United States (various years), US Census Bureau website http://www.census.gov/hhes/poverty/histpov19.html
UNEMPLOY	Statistical Abstract of the United States (various years), US Census Bureau
REALINC	State Personal Income (various years), Bureau of Economic Analysis website http://www.bea.doc.gov/bea/regional/spi/dpcpi.htm
EDHS	Digest of Education Statistics (various years), National Center for Education Statistics, Educational Attainment in the United States (various years), US Census Bureau
EDCOLL	Digest of Education Statistics (various years), National Center for Education Statistics, Educational Attainment in the United States (various years), US Census Bureau
SUICIDE	Statistical Abstract of the United States (various years), US Census Bureau
REGION	US States 1: ME, NH, VT; 2: MA, RI, CT; 3: NY, NJ, PA; 4: OH, IN, IL, MI, WI, MN, IA, MO; 5: ND, SD, NE, KS; 6: DE, MD, DC, VA, WV; 7: NC, SC, GA, FL; 8: KY, TN, AL, MS, AR, LA, OK, TX; 9: MT, ID, WY, CO, NM, AZ, UT, NV; 10: WA, OR, CA; 11: AK, HI

References

Asch, P., Levy, D.T., 1987. Does the minimum drinking age affect traffic fatalities? Journal of Policy Analysis and Management 6, 180–192.

Beede, K.E., Kass, S.J., 2006. Engrossed in conversation: the impact of cell phones on simulated driving performance. Accident Analysis and Prevention 38, 415–421.

Bills, C.B., Grabowski, J., Li, G., 2005. Suicide by aircraft: a comparative analysis. Aviation, Space, and Environmental Medicine 76 (8), 715–719.

Blattenberger, G., Fowles, R., Loeb, P.D., Clarke, W.A., January 2009. Understanding the cell phone effect on motor vehicle fatalities using classical & Bayesian methods. Presented at the Allied Social Sciences Associations Meeting (TPUG). San Francisco, USA.

Blattenberger, G., Fowles, R., Loeb, P.D., Clarke, W.A., 2012. Understanding the cell phone effect on vehicle fatalities: a Bayesian view. Applied Economics 44, 1823–1835.

Blattenberger, G., Fowles, R., Loeb, P.D., 2013. Determinants of motor vehicle crash fatalities using Bayesian model selection methods. Research in Transportation Economics 43, 212–222, (Special Issue on: The Economics of Transportation Safety).

Breiman, L., 2001. Statistical modeling: the two cultures. Statistical Science 16 (3), 199–231.

Bylow, L.F., Savage, I., 1991. The effect of airline deregulation on automobile fatalities. Accident Analysis and Prevention 23, 443–452.

Campbell, B.J., Campbell, F.A., 1986. Seat Belt Law Experience in Four Foreign Countries Compared to the United States. AAA Foundation for Traffic Safety, Falls Church, VA, 1–73.

Campbell, B.J., Stewart, J.R., Campbell, F.A., 1986. Early Results of Seat Belt Legislation in the United States of America. University of North Carolina Highway Safety Research Center, Chapel Hill, NC.

Campbell, B.J., Stewart, J.R., Campbell, F.A., 1987. 1985–1986 Experience with Belt Laws in the United States. University of North Carolina Highway Safety Research Center, Chapel Hill, NC.

Centers for Disease Control and Prevention, National Center for Injury Prevention and Control, 2012. Web-based injury statistics query and reporting system (WISQARS): http://www.cdc.gov/injury/wisqars/ (accessed 7.7.12).

Chaloupka, F.J., Saffer, H., Grossman, M., 1993. Alcohol-control policies and motor vehicle fatalities. Journal of Legal Studies 22, 161–218.

Chapman, S., Schoefield, W.N., 1998. Lifesavers and samaritans: emergency use of cellular (mobile) phones in Australia. Accident Analysis and Prevention 30, 815–819.

Clarke, W.A., Loeb, P.D., 2005. The determinants of train fatalities: keeping the model on track. Transportation Research Part E 41, 145–158.

Clyde, M.A., 1999. Bayesian model averaging and model search strategies. Bayesian Statistics 6, 157–185.

Coate, D., Markowitz, S., 2004. The effects of daylight and daylight savings time on US pedestrian fatalities and motor vehicle occupant fatalities. Accident Analysis and Prevention 36 (3), 351–357.

Cohen, A., Einav, L., 2003. The effects of mandatory seat belt laws on driving behavior and traffic fatalities. Review of Economics and Statistics 85 (4), 828–843.

Conner, K.R., Cox, C., Duberstein, P.R., Tian, L., Nisbet, P.A., Conwell, Y., 2001. Violence, alcohol, and completed suicide: a case–control study. The American Journal of Psychiatry 158, 1701–1705.

Connolly, J.F., Cullen, A., McTigue, O., 1995. Single road traffic deaths: accident or sui-
cide? Crisis: The Journal of Crisis Intervention and Suicide Prevention 16 (2), 85–89.
Consiglio, W., Driscoll, P., Witte, M., Berg, W.P., 2003. Effect of cellular telephone conver-
sations and other potential interference on reaction time in braking responses. Accident
Analysis and Prevention 35, 495–500.
Crain, W.M., 1980. Vehicle Safety Inspection Systems. American Enterprise Institute for Public
Policy Research, Washington, DC.
CTIA–The Wireless Association, 2011. http://www.ctia.org (accessed 10.2.11).
CTIA–The Wireless Association, 2016. http://www.ctia.org/industry-data/ctia-annual-wireless-
industry-survey (accessed 07.11.16).
Cubbin, C., Smith, G.S., 2002. Socioeconomic inequalities in injury: critical issues in design
and analysis. Annual Review of Public Health 23, 349–375.
Cullen, S., 1998. Aviation suicide: a review of general aviation accidents in the U.K., 1970–96,
aviation. Space and Environmental Medicine 69 (7), 696–698.
Dreamer, K., 2016. What the first driverless car fatality means for self-driving tech, live science.
http://www.livescience.com/55273-first-self-driving-car-fatality.html (accessed 06.02.17).
Etzerdorfer, E., 1995. Single road traffic deaths: accidents or suicide? Comment. Crisis: The
Journal of Crisis Intervention and Suicide Prevention 16 (4), 188–189.
Evans, L.E., 1991. Traffic Safety and the Driver. Van Norstrand Reinhold, New York.
Forester, T., McNown, R.F., Singell, L.D., 1984. A cost benefit analysis of the 55 mph speed
limit. Southern Economic Journal 50, 631–641.
Fowles, R., 1988. Micro EBA. American Statistician 4, 274.
Fowles, R., Loeb, P.D., 1989. Speeding, coordination, and the 55-mph limit: comment. American
Economic Review 79, 916–921.
Fowles, R., Loeb, P.D., 1992. The interactive effect of alcohol and altitude on traffic fatalities.
Southern Economic Journal 59, 108–112.
Fowles, R., Loeb, P.D., Clarke, W.A., 2010. The cell phone effect on motor vehicle fatality
rates: a Bayesian and classical econometric evaluation. Transportation Research Part E 46,
1140–1147.
Fowles, R., Loeb, P.D., Clarke, W.A., 2013. The cell phone effect on truck accidents: a speci-
fication error approach. Transportation Research Part E, http.//dx.doi.org/10.1016/j.
tre.2012.10.002.
Freeborn, B.A., McManus, B., 2007. Substance abuse treatment and motor vehicle fatalities.
College of William and Mary, Department of Economics, Working Paper Number 66.
Garbacz, C., 1990. How effective is automobile safety regulation? Applied Economics 22,
1705–1714.
Garbacz, C., Kelly, J.G., 1987. Automobile safety inspection: new econometric and benefit/cost
estimates. Applied Economics 19, 763–771.
Glassbrenner, D., 2005. Driver cell phone use in 2005—overall results, traffic safety facts: re-
search note, NHTSA, DOT HS 809967. http://www-nrd.nhtsa.dot.gov/Pubs/809967.PDF
(accessed 11.02.11).
Governors Highway Safety Association, 2015. Laws, November 2016. www.ghsa.org/html/
stateinfo/laws/seatbelt_laws.html (accessed 07.11.16).
Hars, A., 2016. Self-driving vehicles as instruments for the coordination of mobility, driverless
car market watch. http://www.driverless-future.com/?page_id=384 (accessed 06.02.17).
Hatfield, N.J., Hinshaw, W.M., 1987. Evaluation of the Fatality Reduction Effectiveness of the
Texas Mandatory Safety Belt Law. The Texas A&M University System, Texas Transportation Institute, College Station, Texas.

Hoerl, A.E., Kennard, R.W., 1970. Ridge regression: biased estimation for nonorthogonal problems. Technometrics 12 (1), 55–67.

Hoxie, P., Skinner, D., 1987. Effects of Mandatory Seatbelt Use Laws on Highway Fatalities in 1985. US Department of Transportation, Research and Special Programs Administration, Transportation Systems Center, Cambridge, MA.

Huffine, C.L., 1971. Equivocal single-auto traffic fatalities. Life-Threatening Behavior 1 (2), 83–95.

Keeler, T.E., 1994. Highway safety, economic behavior, and driving environment. American Economic Review 84 (3), 684–693.

Key, J.T., Pericchi, L., Smith, A.F.M., 1999. Bayesian model choice: what and why? Bayesian Statistics 6, 343–370.

Kirk, M., 2016. Why Singapore will get self-driving cars first, the Atlantic Citilab. https://www.citylab.com/transportation/2016/08/why-singapore-leads-in-self-driving-cars/494222/ (accessed 20.03.17).

Laberge-Nadeau, C., Maag, U., Bellavance, F., Lapiere, S.D., Desjardins, D., Messier, S., Saidi, A., 2003. Wireless telephones and risk of road crashes. Accident Analysis and Prevention 35, 649–660.

Lave, C.A., 1985. Speeding, coordination, and the 55 mph limit. American Economic Review 75, 1159–1164.

Leamer, E.E., 1978. Specification Searches: Ad Hoc Inference with Non-Experimental Data. Wiley & Sons, New York.

Leamer, E.E., 1982. Sets of posterior means with bounded variance priors. Econometrica 50 (3), 725–736.

Leamer, E.E., 1983. Let's take the con out of econometrics. American Economic Review 73 (1), 31–43.

Leamer, E.E., 1985. Sensitivity analyses would help. American Economic Review 75 (3), 308–313.

Leamer, E.E., 1997. Revisiting Tobin's 1950 study of food expenditure. Journal of Applied Econometrics 12 (5), 533–553.

Leamer, E.E., 2014. S-values and all subsets regressions. University of California at Los Angeles. Working Paper.

Leamer, E.E., 2016. S-values and Bayesian weighted all-subsets regressions. European Economic Review 81, 15–31.

Levy, D.T., Asch, P., 1989. Speeding, coordination, and the 55-mph limit: comment. American Economic Review 79, 913–915.

Lewis, R.J., Johnson, R.D., Whinnery, J.E., Forster, E.M., 2007. Aircraft-assisted pilot suicides in the United States, 1993–2002. Archives of Suicide Research 11 (2), 149–161.

Loeb, P.D., 1985. The efficacy and cost-effectiveness of motor vehicle inspection using cross-sectional data—an econometric analysis. Southern Economic Journal 52, 500–509.

Loeb, P.D., 1987. The determinants of motor vehicle accidents with special consideration to policy variables. Journal of Transport Economics and Policy 21, 279–287.

Loeb, P.D., 1988. The determinants of motor vehicle accidents—a specification error analysis. Logistics and Transportation Review 24, 33–48.

Loeb, P.D., 1990. Automobile safety inspection: further econometric evidence. Applied Economics 22, 1697–1704.

Loeb, P.D., 1991. The effectiveness of seat belt legislation in reducing driver involved injury and fatality rates in Texas, Maryland, and California. Final Report, U.S.D.O.T./NHTSA.

Loeb, P.D., Clarke, W.A., 2007. The determinants of truck accidents. Transportation Research Part E 43, 442–452.

Loeb, P.D., Clarke, W., 2009. The cell phone effect on pedestrian fatalities. Transportation Research Part E 45, 284–290.

Loeb, P.D., Gilad, B., 1984. The efficacy and cost-effectiveness of vehicle inspection—a state specific analysis using time series data. Journal of Transport Economics and Policy 18, 145–164.

Loeb, P.D., Talley, W.K., Zlatoper, T., 1994. Causes and Deterrents of Transportation Accidents: An Analysis by Mode. Quorum Books, Westport, CT.

Loeb, P.D., Clarke, W.A., Anderson, R., 2009. The impact of cell phones on motor vehicle fatalities. Applied Economics 41, 2905–2914.

Lund, A.K., Pollner, J., Williams, A.F., 1987. Preliminary estimates of the effects of mandatory seat belt use laws. Accident Analysis and Prevention 17, 219–223.

Mazess, R.B., Picon-Reategui, E., Thomas, R.B., Little, M.A., 1968. Effects of alcohol and altitude on man during rest and work. Aerospace Medicine 39, 403–406.

McCarthy, P., 1992. Highway safety implications of expanded use of longer combination vehicles (LCVs). Paper presented at the 6th World Conference on Transport Research. Lyon, France.

McEvoy, S.P., Stevenson, M.R., McCartt, A.T., Woodward, M., Haworth, C., Palamara, P., Cercarelli, R., 2005. Role of mobile phones in motor vehicle crashes resulting in hospital attendance: a case-crossover study. British Medical Journal 33, 428–435.

Murray, D., DeLeo, D., 2007. Suicidal behavior by motor vehicle collision. Traffic Injury Prevention 8, 244–247.

Newman, H.W., 1949. The effect of altitude on alcohol tolerance. Quarterly Journal on Studies of Alcohol 10, 398–403.

Neyens, D.M., Boyle, L.N., 2007. The effect of distractions on the crash types of teenage drivers. Accident Analysis and Prevention 39, 206–212.

NHTSA, 2012. Early estimate of motor vehicle traffic fatalities for the first half (January–June) of 2012, traffic safety facts: crash stats, DOT HS 811 680. http://www.-nrd.nhtsa.dot.gov/Pubs//811680.pdf (accessed 17.11.12).

NHTSA, 2015. Critical reasons for crashes investigated in the national motor vehicle crash causation survey, traffic safety facts: crash stats, DOT HS 812 115. https://crashstats.nhtsa.dot.gov/Api/Public/ViewPublication/812115 (accessed 20.03.17).

NHTSA, 2016. Early estimate of motor vehicle traffic fatalities for the first half (January–June) of 2016, traffic safety facts: crash stats, DOT HS 812 332. https://crashstats.nhtsa.dot.gov/Api/Public/ViewPublication/812332 (accessed 05.11.16).

Partyka, S.C., 1988. Lives saved by seat belts from 1983 through 1987. NHTSA Technical Report, Washington, DC.

Peltzman, S., 1975. The effect of automobile regulation. Journal of Political Economy 93, 677–725.

Phillips, D.P., 1977. Motor vehicle fatalities increase just after publicized suicide stories. Science 196, 1464–1466.

Phillips, D.P., 1979. Suicide, motor vehicle fatalities, and the mass media: evidence toward a theory of suggestion. American Journal of Sociology 84 (5), 1150–1174.

Pokorny, A.D., Smith, J.P., Finch, J.R., 1972. Vehicular suicides. Life-Threatening Behavior 2 (2), 105–119.

Porterfield, A.L., 1960. Traffic fatalities, suicide, and homicide. American Sociological Review 25 (6), 897–901.

Poysti, L., Rajalin, S., Summala, H., 2005. Factors influencing the use of cellular (mobile) phones during driving and hazards while using it. Accident Analysis and Prevention 37, 47–51.

R Development Core, 2016. R: a language and environment for statistical computing. http://www.R-project.org (accessed 10.01.16).

Ramsey, J.B., 1974. Classical model selection through specification error tests. In: Zarembka, P. (Ed.), Frontiers in Econometrics. Academic Press, New York, pp. 13–47.

Ramsey, J.B., Zarembka, P., 1971. Specification error tests and the alternative functional form of the aggregate production function. Journal of the American Statistical Association, Applications Section 57, 471–477.

Redelmeier, D.A., Tibshirani, R.J., 1997. Association between cellular-telephone calls and motor vehicle collisions. New England Journal of Medicine 336, 453–458.

Reinfurt, D.W., Campbell, B.J., Stewart, J.R., Stutts, J.C., 1988. North Carolina's Occupant Restraint Law: A Three Year Evaluation. University of North Carolina Highway Safety Research Center, Chapel Hill, NC.

Saffer, H., Grossman, M., 1987a. Beer Taxes, the legal drinking age, and youth motor vehicle fatalities. Journal of Legal Studies 16, 351–374.

Saffer, H., Grossman, M., 1987b. Drinking age laws and highway mortality rates: cause and effect. Economic Inquiry 25, 403–417.

Savage, I., 2007. Trespassing on the railroad. In: Dennis, S.M., Talley, W.K. (Eds.), Research in Transportation Economics: Railroad Economics. Elsevier Science, Amsterdam.

Savage, I., 2010. Analysis of data on pedestrian/rail safety in Illinois 2005–2009. Pedestrian Rail Safety Symposium, June 22, 2010 and Proceedings of the DuPage Rail Safety Council Conference, September 29, 2010.

Schoettle, B., Sivak, M., 2015. A preliminary analysis of real-world crashes involving self-driving vehicles. University of Michigan Transportation Research Institute, UMTRi-201-34, October 2015.

Skinner, D., Hoxie, P., 1988. Effects of Seatbelt Laws on Highway Fatalities: Update—April 1988. U.S. Department of Transportation, Research and Special Programs Administration, Transportation Systems Center, Cambridge, MA.

Snyder, D., 1989. Speeding, coordination, and the 55-mph limit: comment. American Economic Review 79 (4), 922–925.

Sommers, P.M., 1985. Drinking age and the 55 mph speed limit. Atlantic Economic Journal 13, 43–48.

Souetre, E., 1988. Completed suicides and traffic accidents: longitudinal analysis in France. Acta Psychiatrica Scandiavica 77 (5), 530–534.

Streff, F.M., Schultz, R.H., Wagenaar, A.C., 1989. Changes in Police Reported Injuries Associated with Michigan's Safety Belt Law: 1988 Update. The University of Michigan, Transportation Research Institute, Ann Arbor, MI.

Sullman, M.J., Baas, P.H., 2004. Mobile phone use amongst New Zealand drivers. Transportation Research Part F: Traffic Psychology and Behavior 7, 95–105.

Villasenor, J., 2014. Products liability and driverless cars: issues and guiding principles for legislation. http://www.brookings.edu/research/papers/2014/04/products-liability-driverless-cars-issues-and-guiding-principles-for-legislation/ (accessed 05.05.16).

Violanti, J.M., 1998. Cellular phones and fatal traffic collisions. Accident Analysis and Prevention 30, 519–524.

Womble, K.B., 1989. The estimated effect of safety belt use laws on injury reduction. U.S. Department of Transportation, NHTSA, Washington, DC.

Zlatoper, T.J., 1984. Regression analysis of time series data on motor vehicle deaths in the United States. Journal of Transport Economics and Policy 18, 263–274.

Further Reading

Zoz Cannytrophic Design, 2016. Hacking driverless cars. https://www.youtube.com/watch?v=k5E28fp4oc0 (accessed 21.11.16).

Index

9780128126202